AMERICAN CIPHER

AMERICAN CIPHER

BOWE BERGDAHL AND THE U.S. TRAGEDY IN AFGHANISTAN

MATT FARWELL *and*
MICHAEL AMES

PENGUIN PRESS | NEW YORK | 2019

PENGUIN PRESS
An imprint of Penguin Random House LLC
penguinrandomhouse.com

Image credits appear on page 345.

LIBRARY OF CONGRESS CATALOGING-IN-PUBLICATION DATA

Names: Farwell, Matt, author. | Ames, Michael, author.
Title: American cipher : Bowe Bergdahl and the U.S. tragedy in Afghanistan / Matt Farwell and Michael Ames.
Description: New York : Penguin Press, 2019. | Includes bibliographical references and index.
Identifiers: LCCN 2018046632 (print) | LCCN 2018058587 (ebook) | ISBN 9780735221055 (ebook) | ISBN 9780735221048 (hardcover)
Subjects: LCSH: Bergdahl, Bowe, 1986- | Soldiers—United States—Biography. | Afghan War, 2001- | Bergdahl, Bowe, 1986—Trials, litigation, etc. | Trials (Military offenses)—United States.
Classification: LCC DS371.43. B47 (ebook) | LCC DS371.43. B47 F37 2019 (print) | DDC 958.104/78 [B] —dc23
LC record available at https://lccn.loc.gov/2018046632

Printed in the United States of America
1 3 5 7 9 10 8 6 4 2

Designed by Amanda Dewey

To Dr. Hannah Tyson and Michael Hastings

—MATT FARWELL

For my mom, my friend:
Elyse Ames (1941–2017)

—MICHAEL AMES

CONTENTS

ACT III. **TRAPPED**

ACT IV. **BRING BOWE HOME**

ACT V. **CODES OF CONDUCT**

OPERATION ENDURING FREEDOM
THEATERS OF OPERATION
2009–2014
HINDU KUSH
KASHMIR
AFGHANISTAN
SWAT VALLEY
Indus River
Bamyan
Kabul
Helmand River
Jalalabad
North
Abbottabad
TORA BORA
Peshawar
Khyber Pass
Islamabad
Waziristan
Batai Pass
Rawalpindi
AREA of DETAIL
on facing page
Ghazni
Gardez
Khost
Sharana
Miran Shah
Federally Administered Tribal Areas (FATA)
PAKTIKA
South
Waziristan
PUNJAB
Indus River
N
BALOCHISTAN
Border–Federally Administered Tribal Areas (FATA)
Province Boundary
Quetta
0 25 50 75 100 miles
PAKISTAN

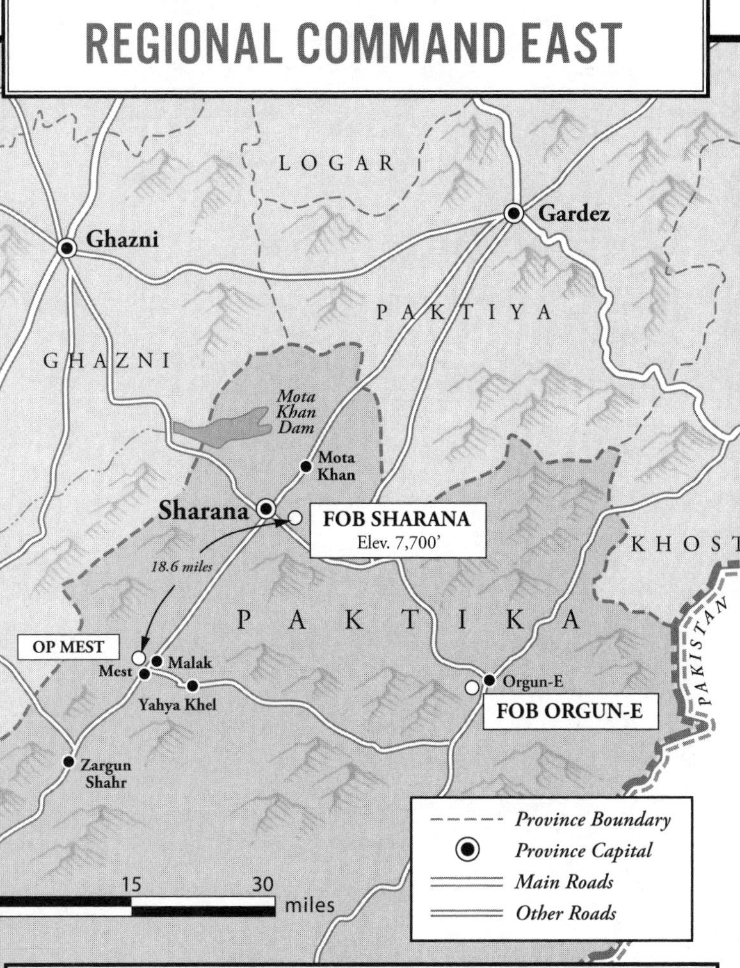

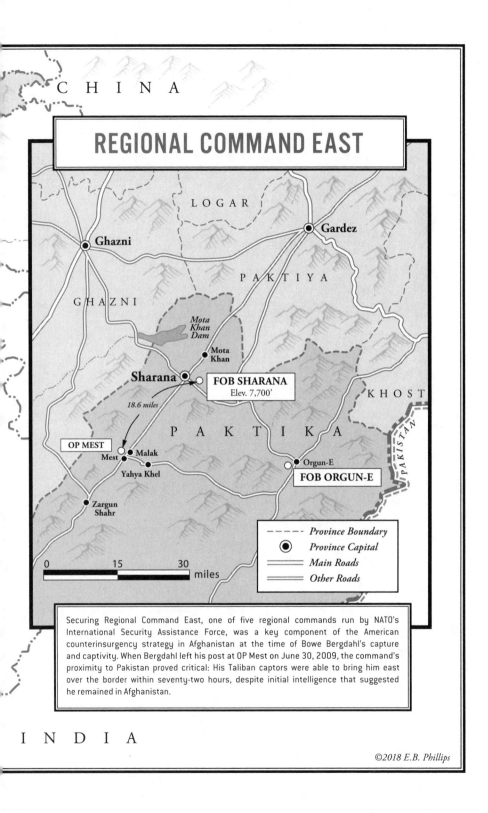

Securing Regional Command East, one of five regional commands run by NATO's International Security Assistance Force, was a key component of the American counterinsurgency strategy in Afghanistan at the time of Bowe Bergdahl's capture and captivity. When Bergdahl left his post at OP Mest on June 30, 2009, the command's proximity to Pakistan proved critical: His Taliban captors were able to bring him east over the border within seventy-two hours, despite initial intelligence that suggested he remained in Afghanistan.

PROLOGUE

Five years and five weeks after he walked alone and unarmed into the Afghanistan night, Sergeant Bowe Bergdahl was scheduled for an interview with the U.S. Army general investigating his crime. They met at eight in the morning in Building 268 on Fort Sam Houston in San Antonio, Texas. Bergdahl's civilian attorney, Eugene Fidell, a Yale Law School professor and military justice historian, accompanied him. Major General Kenneth Dahl sat across from them. In an adjoining room, the Army stenographer began the recording.

"Sergeant Bergdahl, obviously I'm reading you your rights warning certificate because I am the investigating officer conducting an Army Regulation 15-6 investigation. You are the subject of that investigation. Your suspected offenses are absent without leave and desertion."

Bergdahl listened, motionless.

"Before I ask you any questions, you must understand your rights. Number one, you do not have to answer my questions or say anything. Do you understand that?"

"Yes," Bergdahl said.

"If you would just initial number one," said Dahl, pointing to the form. Bowe Robert Bergdahl wrote his initials—BRB.

"Number two, anything you say or do can be used as evidence against you in a criminal trial. Now do you understand that?"

"Yes."

"I don't mean to insult your intelligence, but it's better to be thorough up front," the general explained.

"Understood, sir."

With the paperwork complete, Dahl continued, "It's great that you're home, welcome home. Everybody is glad you're home. And now there is an opportunity to hear your story."

Bergdahl sat up straight. His square frame filled the shoulders of his drab green civilian shirt. Even in street clothes, he looked every bit the soldier. "Let me just start by leaving it open-ended and ask you to relax, get comfortable," Dahl tried. "You have to be eager and anxious to tell your story. . . . So here's an opportunity for you, and I will turn it over to you."

The twenty-eight-year-old sergeant did not move.

"Relax," said Fidell.

"Yes, absolutely," Dahl said.

"You look tense," Fidell said.

"Take as much time as you want," Dahl offered. "You can lean back and relax."

"If I lean back, it hurts my back," Bergdahl said, but did not explain why.

The country seemed to have already made up its mind. Bergdahl was a national disgrace, the loudest voices said—a coward and a deserter at the very least, a traitor to many, and probably a de facto member of the Taliban. ("Tali-Bowe" was a popular moniker on social media.) The prisoner swap that freed Bergdahl in exchange for five high-value Taliban detainees at Guantanamo Bay, Cuba, was a rotten deal; according to one poll, 43 percent of Americans felt it was "the wrong thing to do." The night of Bergdahl's release, Donald Trump, whose political aspirations were only hypothetical at the time, tweeted: "At some point Sgt. Bergdahl will have to explain his capture. In 2009 he simply wandered off his base without a weapon. Many questions!" Bergdahl's hometown of Hailey, Idaho (population: 8,000), announced a celebration party. When the city hall and several businesses were deluged by hundreds of threats by phone and email, and after the local police chief was warned of an imminent invasion from two thousand protesting patriotic bikers, the party was canceled. Bowe wasn't the only target—his family was placed under FBI protection as rumors swirled that his father, Bob Bergdahl, was a closet Muslim. *Time* magazine asked, "Was He Worth It?"

To the Pentagon, Sergeant Bergdahl was a public relations disaster. After fourteen years of war, the last thing the Army needed was for all the soldiers who thought the war was dumb to walk off. Dahl was a fifty-two-year-old career officer and a two-star major general expecting a third star. The Army was his life—his West Point sweetheart and wife of thirty-one years, Lieutenant Colonel Celia FlorCruz, was a decorated helicopter pilot—and this investigation, a once-in-a-generation event for the Army, had the potential to ruin his career. His report would be scrutinized at the highest levels of the Pentagon and amplified by the loudest megaphones in the media. But "the 15-16" was also a formal, legal process codified by Army regulations. In short, it was his job, and Dahl intended to do it right.

For the prior fifty-two days, since the chief of staff of the Army had assigned him this task, Dahl had been trying to get inside the head of the enigmatic twenty-three-year-old Army private who was now a traumatized twenty-eight-year-old former prisoner. Dahl talked to dozens of government and military officials who had worked the case; he conferred with teams at the Pentagon and at Central Command (CENTCOM) in Tampa and with Army personnel in Germany, Afghanistan, and San Antonio. He read Bergdahl's psychological evaluations and met with his doctors and the experts who debriefed him. He studied classified FBI analyses. He watched the proof-of-life videos filmed by the Haqqani Network in Pakistani safe houses and videos recorded by U.S. intelligence officers in Afghanistan and Germany after Bergdahl's recovery. He spoke with officers at the United States Coast Guard, with whom Bergdahl had briefly attended basic training in 2006. He met with Bergdahl's older sister, Sky, and her husband, Lieutenant Commander

Michael Albrecht, an Annapolis graduate and naval aviator. He spoke by phone with Bergdahl's parents in Idaho and also met Kim Dellacorva, the soldier's surrogate godmother. He chatted for hours with Bergdahl's friends, twentysomethings working at coffee shops in Oregon and Idaho. He questioned the soldiers who went to Army basic training with him at Fort Benning, and he spoke with his company and battalion commanders from Afghanistan.

Why had he just walked off? Who was he? There were no clear answers. Bergdahl was a code no one had cracked. When Dahl interviewed each of the twenty-three soldiers in 2nd Platoon, Blackfoot Company, who were on OP Mest when Bergdahl vanished, he heard twenty-three theories:

He was going to walk to China, or to India, where he would be "a shadow in the mountains and kill bad people and help children." Or he wanted to walk to Russia, so he could join the mob. One soldier couldn't recall the details, but knew that Bergdahl "was going on an incredible adventure."

As General Dahl neared the deadline to submit his report to his superiors at the Pentagon, he confronted the same impasse as the officers assigned to the case five years earlier: Motive was the mystery.

"If you want to stand, you can stand. If you want to get up and stretch, you can stretch," the general said to Bergdahl. "This is not intended to be a miserable experience. It's not an interrogation. . . . This is an informal investigation; it's a fact-finding mission."

Bergdahl had cooperated up to this point. At Bagram Airfield north of Kabul, at Landstuhl Regional Medical Center in Germany, and at the Brooke Army Medical Center in South Texas, he gave answers that satisfied, and in most cases impressed, the survival experts, intelligence analysts, and FBI agents who questioned him.

"Don't feel like this is about catching you," Dahl said. "I don't expect you to have a perfect memory."

"I understand," Bergdahl finally replied. "Just a question: Is there a specific point where you want to start, because if you want the story, it doesn't just start that day."

"Sure," Dahl said. "Does it start before you joined the Army, or does it start when you joined the Army?"

"I'd say it probably started before I joined the Army."

ACT I.

A FANTASTIC PLAN

ONE

LITTLE AMERICA

After a couple of semesters at the University of California, Santa Barbara, Bob Bergdahl knew that college wasn't for him. His parents had taught him to read widely and stay informed, and though he had plans to major in anthropology, he was also a nationally ranked cyclist with his eyes on the Olympics and didn't see much sense in spending more time in classrooms listening to professors explain what he could learn on his own. The Bergdahls of 1960s Santa Monica were a family of brainy athletes—all-American California Republicans. Bob's mother volunteered for presidential candidate Barry Goldwater, and in their liberal, Jewish Santa Monica neighborhood, Bob's father was the only guy on the block wearing a Nixon button. Robert Bergdahl Sr. had been an all-star blocking back for the UCLA Bruins, played in two Rose Bowls, and returned to coach eight seasons after he graduated. Bob's sister was a nationally ranked swimmer and an alternate for the 1972 Summer Olympics in Munich when she was just sixteen years old.

Bob was on a similar path. By his senior year in high school his family had moved to Santa Barbara, and he had become one of the fastest road and track cyclists in the country. After qualifying for the U.S. Junior World team in 1978, he trained alongside future three-time Tour de France champion Greg LeMond and Chris Carmichael, who would go on to a career as Lance Armstrong's personal coach.

As much as he liked road racing, Bob was better on the track, where the velodrome and the track bike's fixed gears demanded intense focus. At seventy miles per hour, one uneven pedal stroke could send him careening into the walls; just slowing down required a coordinated resistance against the inertia of the machine. After winning several Olympic development races in California, the U.S. Cycling Federation invited him to Colorado Springs, Colorado, to train with the development team ahead of the 1980 Summer Olympics in Moscow. He was more focused than at any time in his life, and it looked as if he might qualify, until Friday night, January 4, 1980, when current events collided with his Olympic dream.

Networks cut away from prime-time programming for President Jimmy Carter's live national address from the Oval Office. On Christmas Day, fifty thousand troops of the Soviet 40th Army had invaded "the small, nonaligned, sovereign nation of Afghanistan." Moscow, Carter said, was "attempting to conquer the fiercely independent Muslim people of that country."

Protests, many organized and encouraged by American and Western intelligence agencies, erupted in capitals across Europe and the Muslim world. In Bangladesh, a mob stormed the gated campus of the Soviet Cultural Center. Muslim demonstrators marched with dirty sandals tied to placards threatening Soviet Prime Minister Leonid Brezhnev's life. In London, the crowds carried signs that read:

RUSSIANS ARE INVADERS

LET AFGHANS CHOOSE THEIR OWN GOVERNMENT

NO EAST NO WEST—ISLAM IS THE BEST

Publicly, the White House shared in the outrage. From the Oval Office, Carter warned the Soviets about the dangers of empire building: "History teaches, perhaps, very few clear lessons. But surely one such lesson learned by the world at great cost is that aggression, unopposed, becomes a contagious disease." Claiming that Soviet militarism endangered the lives of athletes and spectators in Moscow, Carter threatened an Olympic boycott. The White House was already preoccupied with Afghanistan's neighbor to the west; at Christmastime, more than fifty Americans remained hostage inside the U.S. Embassy in Tehran, and Carter didn't have many good options in either country.

Four years after the fall of Saigon, another American war in Asia was unthinkable. Looking for any political leverage they could find, the White House and CIA saw potential in Islamic fundamentalism, and framed the anti-Soviet sentiments spreading across the Muslim world as inherently pro-democracy. By summertime, Carter's Olympic boycott had swelled to sixty countries.

But privately, in the corridors of the Pentagon, the CIA, and Capitol Hill, the Soviet invasion was a welcome development, and had come as no surprise. Six months earlier, on July 3, 1979, Carter's national security adviser, Zbigniew Brzezinski, had encouraged the president to begin arming a network of loosely affiliated Pashtun tribal militias already fighting the Soviets from their homeland along the Afghan-Pakistani border. In notes Brzezinski handed Carter that day, he predicted that the Muslim rebels could lure the Soviets into an "Afghan trap."

Brzezinski saw cycles of history at work. Afghanistan was a storied battleground, the "graveyard of empires" where the great powers of nineteenth-century Europe played their Great Game. If the Russians were foolish enough to drift into an Afghan quagmire, Washington was happy to pull them in deeper. Weeks after the Christmas invasion, Brzezinski flew to Pakistan to recruit and coordinate a wider international effort. Afghanistan's eastern neighbor had a vital self-interest in the American plan, and its spy agency, the Inter-Services Intelligence (ISI), was the only government entity in the world with influence over the Pashtun tribes in its western provinces. The U.S.- and Pakistani-led coalition recruited support from Egypt, the U.K., China, and Saudi Arabia. The Saudis agreed to match American investment dollar for dollar.

The CIA had its assignment. Working with Britain's MI6, Pakistan's ISI, and the Saudi General Intelligence Directorate (GID), Langley initiated what would become an unprecedented covert war. Operation Cyclone, as the agency named it, was a hit with the incoming Reagan administration, which began funding the secret program at $700 million per year, or roughly 80 percent of the entire annual budget for the agency's paramilitary operations. The money was spent on everything from arms and training to propaganda and bundles of cash for the tribal warlords the CIA and ISI identified as their most effective proxies. The CIA sourced weapons for the mujahideen—Arabic for "holy warrior"—from a variety of black markets, eventually including the Soviet Army itself, which, as Brzezinski later noted, became so corrupt that Moscow could not keep track of its own profligate war machine.

Decades earlier, Afghanistan had also been a laboratory for gentler experiments of American Cold War influence. The primary example could be found in Lashkar Gah, the capital of Helmand Province and, from the mid-1940s to the late 1970s, the site of an economic, agricultural, and social engineering project known as "Little America." On the bleak southern desert flatlands, a Levittown-esque housing development blossomed by the confluence of the Helmand and Arghandab Rivers. A vast irrigation plan, built around two earthen dams, would bring water to farms and villages across more than five hundred square miles of desert. The American initiative with the New Deal–inspired name—the Helmand and Arghandab Valley Authority—included more than a thousand miles of new roads, three hundred miles of canals, and a town that featured a Bollywood movie theater and the country's only coed high school. For the heavy construction and dam building, USAID contracted with the Boise, Idaho–based engineering firm Morrison-Knudsen. Southern Idaho, like Afghanistan, is a land of high-mountain rivers flowing into desert plains, and before the state was settled, it, too, had required hundreds of square miles of irrigation—the federal government had hired Morrison-Knudsen for those as well.

If Lashkar Gah and the flowing waters of Helmand's irrigation canals stood as goodwill monuments of American influence, Operation Cyclone brought more complex dividends. Before the Soviet withdrawal in 1989, Washington would funnel somewhere between $4 billion and $5 billion into the effort. The majority poured into the tribal territories along the Afghan-Pakistani border, where, along with rifles and bullets, it also funded religious propaganda and the construction of Islamic schools (or madrassas) to help spread the strains of a violent, and at the time, fringe Islamic ideology.

Before its end, the Russian occupation would trigger one of the largest refugee crises in recorded history. About six million Afghans (roughly one-third of the country's total population) fled in the exodus, most of them to refugee camps in Iran and Pakistan. In southeastern Paktika Province, at least 77,000 refugees crossed the border to camps in Miran Shah and Peshawar. The Soviets attempted to win over those who remained by building roads and funding development projects, including a dam in Mota Khan, just north of a Soviet Army garrison outside of Sharana, the provincial capital. But their efforts were doomed from the start: Paktika was crisscrossed by mujahideen "ratlines," the supply routes that sustained the insurgency. Moscow learned the hard way that no overarching authority, and certainly not one imposed by a foreign empire, could secure those smuggling routes or win over the allegiances of villagers living alongside them.

The Soviet war's most enduring legacies, however, could be found in western Pakistan. With money and assistance from wealthy Saudi families (including the bin Laden construction dynasty) and the GID, the Pakistanis turned the Afghan refugee crisis into a strategic opportunity. Young Afghan men were recruited from the overfilled settlements along the border in Pakistan's Federally Administered Tribal Areas (FATA). Properly indoctrinated in mujahideen camps and madrassas, they were sent back to infiltrate the Afghan battlefields. No matter how many insurgent fighters the Soviets killed, the Pakistani operation supplied more. It was a simulacra of the Soviet and Chinese efforts in the Vietnam War's safe havens of Laos and Cambodia, an irony not lost on the Pentagon. A 1989 Army report made the point clear: The Soviets' failure to learn from the U.S. example "caused them to make many of the same errors."

The seed Brzezinski planted with Carter grew into the largest and longest covert operation in U.S. history. Who Washington recruited to the Afghan insurgency, or by what methods, was secondary to what Brzezinski identified as the greater purpose: "to make the Soviets bleed for as much and as long as possible."

Half a world away, his ambitions stymied by geopolitical events beyond his control, Bob Bergdahl decided it was time to move on from his Olympic dreams. He was back in Santa Barbara and working in construction when he and his high school girlfriend, Jani Larson, heard from a friend who had moved to Ketchum, Idaho. There was a crew from Santa Barbara there, outdoor junkies like them, intoxicated by the open spaces and abundant cheap land. With a job building a log cabin waiting for him, Bob and Jani packed his pickup truck and a horse trailer and drove north for a new life.

WHEN THEY ARRIVED in the fall of 1980, Idaho's Blaine County was home to just ten thousand people scattered across an area larger than Delaware—a rugged and picturesque stretch of valleys and canyons carved by the clear rivers that flow from the peaks of the Pioneer and Boulder Mountains in the north to the irrigation canals on the Snake River Plain in the south. They settled in the Wood River Valley, a thirty-mile artery of former mining camps and sheep-ranching towns: Gannett, Bellevue, Broadford, China Gardens, Hailey, Bullion, Greenhorn, Triumph, Ketchum, and Galena. After weathering the early 1980s recession, the valley started growing fast, splitting into two identities defined by the land as much as its people. In the south, where the valley walls taper down to an open prairie and the car radios could pick up the AM stations from Boise and Idaho Falls, it was alfalfa and barley, horse and cattle ranches, churches and churchgoers. After payday at local ranches, cowboys in chaps and spurs stood in line at the liquor store.

At the valley's north end, the resort towns of Ketchum and Sun Valley were something else: seasonal playgrounds for people from the coasts who played golf and bought private, daylong ski lessons for their kids, for families who would come and go on private jets and schedules determined by things other than work. The towns had been dependent on outside money since they were settled in the 1880s, when the gold bugs and bankers from California and London turned them into the biggest boomtowns in Idaho Territory. The second boom came in 1936, when Union Pacific chairman W. Averell Harriman built his vision for an Austrian-style ski *berg* deep in the Rockies, and Sun Valley became a magnet for generations of self-styled American aristocracy. But as much as their cash supported the economy and their sensibilities rubbed off on the locals, the wealthy had always been a minority, interlopers in a community that both needed and distrusted them.

"The youngsters get a big kick out of seeing the movie stars and rich people," Ketchum's Jack Lane, who owned the biggest ranch supply store in town, told a reporter in 1938. "But many of the older folks don't exactly approve of those who spend their time playing, drinking, and dancing." Tourists were a good thing, Lane said, "but our main interest is still sheep. That's where we make our money."

By the late 1980s, sheep had given way to real estate brokers, and Lane's grandkids had turned the family business from saddles and wagons to ski boots and goggles. After a trip home to get married, Bob and Jani decided to stay in Idaho for the same reasons as the ten thousand or so other Californians moving there each year: elbow room, postcard views, and a simpler, more affordable life. Bob took a job at the Elephant's Perch, a mountaineering and bike shop where his coworkers knew him as an easygoing natural athlete with a serious work ethic and a spark in his blue eyes. He tuned skis and bikes, worked construction, and provided the steady voice at the other end of 911 calls as a dispatcher with the Ketchum Fire Department.

In 1983, the year they had their first child, a daughter they named Sky, the family's combined income was seven thousand dollars. They were paying the hospital bills with twenty-dollar deposits and living in a rent-stabilized, plywood-sided starter home in a former immigrant enclave known as China Gardens, when Bob decided it was time for a salaried job. He got lucky and was hired as a delivery driver for UPS, which offered a decent wage and benefits in return for long shifts and military-style diligence. Drivers were expected to follow strict codes of conduct and efficiency that dictated how to pack the truck (front to back), how to lift heavy packages (bend the knees), and when to put the truck in reverse or make a left-hand turn (never). In twenty-eight years, Bob missed two days of work.

His ski and bike buddies saw a more serious side of Bob as he settled into life as a homesteader in an isolated canyon west of Hailey. His father had helped him buy forty acres of rangeland for $50,000, and Bob started building fences and horse corrals and improving irrigation ditches in the sagebrush and high grass. He and Jani had both grown up around horses and had visions of a working ranch. But no bank would give them a construction loan for a house on such an isolated property, so paycheck by paycheck they built a 1,600-square-foot, metal-roofed barn outfitted with electricity and a wood stove to accommodate the horses and their growing family. Their son Robert Bowdrie Bergdahl was six months old when they moved into the converted barn full time in the fall of 1986. Ten feet of snow fell that winter; just getting into town could be a day's work.

They had named their son Robert after his father and grandfather but called him Bowdrie, a tribute to Chick Bowdrie, the Texas Ranger hero of Louis L'Amour's pulp westerns. In Croy Creek Canyon, Bob started Bowe with guns early, first with BBs and pellets when he was still a shy, towheaded toddler, and then with a .22, which he could handle and sight in by age five. They chopped and stacked wood for winter and shot target practice when they felt like it. They had a chicken coop, six or seven horses, a sheepdog named Freckles, and half a dozen cats. They taught their children that the goal of life wasn't to acquire material things. Bob put two hundred thousand miles on his blue Toyota pickup truck, then drove it for another ten years.

"We don't have safe deposit boxes; we keep ammo boxes," Bob once said. Beyond their home, the dirt road rose west toward the open range, where a boy could walk eighty miles without seeing another person—just rocks and dirt, sage and tumbleweed, and the occasional abandoned miner's cabin. They packed the green metal ammo boxes as backcountry kits for weekend camping trips into the Smoky Mountains with some church friends who had a son Bowe's age. They brought picnic lunches, fishing poles, and extra meals for the shepherds who spent the summers in the high country, Peruvian Quechuas who followed the same grazing routes as their Basque predecessors had a century before—north to the alpine meadows in the summer, south to the Snake River Plain in the fall. Neighbors were few, and the shepherds became their close friends. Bob and Jani invited them in to shower, do their wash, and call their families in Peru. Bowe and Sky grew up listening to their broken English and sending them off with secondhand clothes when they returned to the range where they slept by their flocks in horse-drawn wagons, went weeks without seeing another soul, and didn't seem to mind.

Like the shepherds, the Bergdahls spent more time outdoors than in. On camping trips, they hiked for days through meadows of wildflowers that bloomed in Technicolor each June. They caught the dry, sweet smell of sage rising from the sunbaked hillsides and listened to the sounds of the high desert soundlessness—a lone bee buzzing in a patch of lupine, the Mormon crickets clicking from rock to rock, and the lodgepole pines groaning in the wind. At six thousand feet above sea level, they looked up to a night sky that filled in with a dense screen of stars and the slow, steady crawl of satellites. Sometimes, on a cold, clear winter night, they could see the green and yellow ribbons of the

Northern Lights spilling across the black horizon. It wasn't the frontier, but it was close. In the silence and the space, Bob focused his energy and his children's attention on what he saw as life's essentials: work, God, ethical living, and self-reliance.

They decided to homeschool the kids. Jani led them through six hours of daily lessons, and while Bowe had trouble spelling, Jani encouraged his tendency to get lost in wry comic-strip books like *Calvin and Hobbes*, *Heathcliff*, and *Garfield*. One of his favorites was *Beetle Bailey*, the 1950s strip that follows the travails of an Army private bumbling through life in the service. Bob supplemented the comics and homeschool curriculum with readings from his favorite Christian philosophers, Thomas Aquinas and St. Augustine. They taught their children that their conscience was their most precious and sacred possession.

On Sundays, they drove to Bellevue Community Church, a small congregation south of Hailey. Families who recognized Bob learned that their UPS driver was also a religious man, an active church volunteer, and a Sunday school teacher who led Bible study groups from well-thumbed volumes of writings by Christian thinkers. Jeff Gunter, a Hailey police officer who also attended Bellevue services, saw Bob as a devoted father of well-mannered children held to higher standards than most kids. Gunter watched Bowe and Sky at church potlucks, compared them to his own nieces and nephews of similar age, and wondered how Jani and Bob raised such polite children.

Bob shielded his children from the world but also insisted that they learn how it functioned. As had his own parents, he encouraged his kids to keep up with current events and analyze history with a critical eye. On a road trip to Big Hole National Battlefield, fourteen miles west of Wisdom, Montana, Bob explained that in 1877 the U.S. Army had attacked an encampment of Nez Perce at dawn. After a pitched battle, upward of ninety Nez Perce lay dead—men, women, and children. The tribe had been headed toward the national border, which they called "the Medicine Line," after being chased for months by battle-hardened veterans of the American Civil War and earlier Army campaigns against the Apaches, Kiowas, and Comanches in the Southwest. "They were just trying to get to Canada," Bob told his children.

Bowe came to understand that his history textbooks presented just one version of the story. When his parents taught him about colonialism, Bowe joked that the United Kingdom should have been called "Not So Great Britain." At home and at church, he was told to place the word of God above the claims of powerful men. Bowe had worn out his first Bible by the time he was a teenager. In his second, he drew a box around Ephesians 2:10: "For we are his workmanship, created in Christ Jesus for good works, which God prepared beforehand, that we should walk in them."

Bowe worked as a teenager, earning his own money doing maintenance at the private jet hangar in Hailey and at a motorcycle shop in Ketchum. The job he took to best was at the Blaine County Gun Club, a public shooting range tucked halfway up a cul-de-sac canyon next to the county dump. He didn't talk much at work, but he liked working. He knew more than the other teenagers on staff about how things operated—how to load the clay pigeon traps, how to set and clear the rifle range, and how to keep everyone safe. The younger kids looked to him for guidance, and after a couple of summers he was the one showing them how to do things.

Aside from when he biked to work, his parents didn't like his going into town on his own. The valley had a seedy side that they had known about since they'd moved there in the early eighties. About fifteen miles north of Hailey, professional (and successful) drug dealers lived in Ketchum's Warm Springs neighborhood. Some got away with it and bought homes in Fiji and Kauai; others got caught. The valley's moneyed north end was snow-dusted in ways that didn't make the travel brochures. There was always a party to go to, the bars were crowded six nights a week, and the town was protective of its rougher edges. When cowboy pranksters Sheldon Yonke and Pat Ryan rode their horses through the swinging doors of the Pioneer Saloon during dinner hour, the well-groomed young ladies from Connecticut gasped, the bartenders told the cowboys to ride out the way they'd come in, and the next year they did it all over again.

Valley kids grew up around partying as a way of life, and in turn many started early. Booze, sex, and weed for twelve-year-olds wasn't uncommon. On the front porches of his delivery route, Bob heard casual talk about drugs and infidelity, and he didn't like it. He and Jani hadn't moved to Sun Valley to do cocaine with supposedly glamorous people, and Bob hadn't built his own home miles down a mountain canyon to watch his only son be corrupted.

When Bob read his Aquinas—"Better to illuminate than merely to shine, to deliver to others contemplated truths than merely to contemplate"—he acted on it too. He shared a disturbing story at church one Sunday: The convenience store on the north end of Hailey, a popular teen hangout that sold candy, slushees, and cigarettes, was openly displaying raunchy pornography. Wasn't this the creeping moral sickness they had all sought refuge from? Were they as Christians supposed to roll over and accept it? Bob started a petition, recruited church friends to help gather signatures, and persuaded the storeowner to get rid of the smut. Most of the congregation applauded Bob's selfless efforts. But one congregant grew tired of the pious displays and vented to his own family: "Bob thinks he's the only one going to heaven."

Bowe was impressionable. And while Bob saw in his son a soulful seeker who reminded him of his younger self, he also saw a child whose imagination and impulses sometimes ran wild. At thirteen, when Bowe started hanging with a crowd of bad-seed local kids—as different from his church friends as he could find—Bob came down on him hard. Bowe needed clearer boundaries. The family turned to religion for answers and began driving to an Orthodox Presbyterian Church in Boise—five hours round-trip—every Sunday whenever they could make it. A Calvinist sect with an austere reading of scripture, the OPC holds every believer and nonbeliever to the same unforgiving standard: Mankind arrived on Earth depraved and riddled with sin, and there are few paths to grace and God's mercy. Bob translated the message for his son: Hard work and humility are mandatory and nonnegotiable.

At the end of Croy Canyon, there was the right way to live, there was the wrong way, and then there was what Sky called "the Bergdahl way"—the hard path of taking on the most work and the biggest challenges and never complaining. In a valley full of clashing values and temptations, Bob would keep his son on the narrow path of what was right, good, and in God's plan.

TWO
BLOWBACK

"The United States is now at war. But not a war that can be fought or won by conventional military retaliation or diplomatic negotiation," Ketchum's *Idaho Mountain Express* declared in an editorial on September 12, 2001. One week later, President George W. Bush addressed a joint session of Congress and the nation. He condemned the Taliban's Islamic Emirate of Afghanistan for harboring bin Laden and al-Qaeda and issued a set of nonnegotiable demands: The Taliban would hand over the terrorist leaders, release imprisoned foreign nationals, protect foreign journalists, diplomats, and aid workers, immediately close every terrorist training camp, and give the U.S. the right to send inspectors to freely and safely travel the country and verify that these demands were met. For the first time since its founding in 1949, the North Atlantic Treaty Organization invoked Article 5 of the NATO Charter—an attack on one is an attack on all—and approved a campaign against the Taliban for all nineteen member nations.

Two days after Bush's speech, the United Arab Emirates and Saudi Arabia withdrew the Taliban's diplomatic credentials, leaving the Islamic Emirate with only one diplomatic home, in Pakistan. The Taliban offered to turn bin Laden over to Pakistan, but leaders in Islamabad said they could not guarantee bin Laden's safety. The Taliban made a final offer: They would detain bin Laden themselves and put him on trial according to the legal codes of Islam, but only if the United States provided evidence that bin Laden had in fact been responsible. The Bush administration rejected the overture on October 7, 2001. American bombing began that night.

"When I said no negotiations, I meant no negotiations," Bush told reporters on the South Lawn of the White House after a weekend with his war cabinet at Camp David. The next phase of the war was a ground invasion with a twist: Rather than send in huge columns of tanks and armored vehicles as the Soviets had, the U.S. would rely on small teams of Special Forces soldiers—Green Berets—entering Afghanistan from Pakistan to the east and Uzbekistan from the north alongside CIA paramilitary units.

Even at the height of its power in the 1990s, the Taliban never controlled all of Afghanistan. In the opening days of the new war, with the American public desperate for an ally in its quest for vengeance, the Northern Alliance became Washington's first partner. Five hundred miles south, in the Pashtun tribal belt, tribal strongmen had been communicating with American teams throughout the fall; they were ready to cut ties with the Taliban as well. CIA officers worked with the most persuadable warlords who could provide manpower and political support. The quid pro quo was access to U.S. air power, equipment, and so much cash it was shipped over on cargo pallets—American greenbacks shrink-wrapped in neat stacks.

Once the CIA secured their cooperation, Special Forces would train the warlords' gunmen and lead them in combat. Multiple Green Beret teams, paired with CIA officers, were assigned to these "Jawbreaker" operations. Some were sent to the north to coordinate with warlords from the Northern Alliance, including the Uzbek General Abdul Rashid Dostum and Tajiks avenging the death of their longtime leader Ahmed Shah Massoud, who had been assassinated by al-Qaeda operatives on orders from bin Laden on September 10. Additional teams were sent into the south and east.

On November 14, 2001, an Operational Detachment Alpha team of Green Berets (ODA-574) boarded a helicopter in Pakistan with two

CIA officers and an exiled Pashtun leader who lived in Pakistan but had traveled extensively in the West to gather support for a post-Taliban government. Hamid Karzai's relatives lived and worked in the U.S., and his American handlers thought he would be an ideal partner to unite Afghanistan under a new government in a way the Tajiks and Uzbeks had failed to do during the decade of post-Soviet civil war. Karzai could rally the southern Pashtuns against the Taliban, whose spiritual home and traditional power base was anchored in Kandahar, the ancient city named after an earlier foreign conqueror, Alexander the Great. Take away that safe space and the Taliban would have no sanctuary.

Karzai had spent October lining up support from Pashtun leaders in the south. At the time of Karzai's insertion in mid-November 2001, the Taliban founder and leader Mullah Omar was bunkered inside his Kandahar compound. It took little more than a week of attacks by local warlords paid off by the CIA and U.S. Special Forces directing bombs from American aircraft to send Omar fleeing. But as the American bombs fell in what Washington believed were Taliban strongholds throughout the south and east, many local tribes didn't understand why they were under assault. Four days after ODA-574 brought Karzai into Afghanistan, a tribal elder in Loya Paktia—comprising the eastern border provinces of Khost, Paktika, and Paktia—spoke to a BBC reporter. "Don't the Americans realise even though we wear turbans and grow our beards long, we're not Taliban?" the elder said.

Though the Taliban's movement had begun in Kandahar in the mid-nineties, and though Loya Paktia was deeply conservative and resistant to outside pressure, not all of Afghanistan's Pashtun leaders were ready to die defending Omar's government. Several saw an opportunity to take control of their own affairs, and if that meant working with the Americans and the incoming NATO-backed government, so be it. The pragmatism even extended to the Taliban itself; several former ministers and mullahs began cooperating. In the south, Omar's exodus had left a power vacuum, which was quickly filled by Mullah Naqibullah and

Haji Bashir Noorzai, a former mujahideen and a third-generation opium dealer and heroin trafficker who seized the opportunity by working for American military units throughout the opening months of the war.

The UN-sponsored Afghan leadership council in Bonn, Germany, named Karzai interim president of Afghanistan. Al-Qaeda was not the Taliban and they could, and would, do what they wanted. For al-Qaeda, that simply meant escaping and regrouping, but the Taliban delegation wanted to bargain. They told Karzai that if he allowed Mullah Omar and the rest of the senior Taliban officials to retire to their home villages and quietly live out the rest of their lives "in dignity," then the Taliban would lay down their arms and accept his new government. They gave Karzai and the Americans forty-eight hours to decide.

The decision didn't take long. On December 7, 2001, the Bush administration rejected the conditional offer. The Taliban could run, or they could fight, but they would never live in peace again. The Northern Alliance, after years of bitter civil war against the Taliban, finally had the upper hand. Under pressure from the Americans, Karzai walked back his earlier offer of a general amnesty for the Taliban. The remaining CIA officers and Green Berets took over Omar's compound in Kandahar, which the CIA renamed Camp Gecko and quickly turned it into a black site—an officially unacknowledged facility. The head of the CIA's Counterterrorism Center, Cofer Black, had told Bush before the bombing kicked off that "When we're through with them they will have flies walking across their eyeballs," and so far, they had kept their promise, dropping bombs and killing every mass formation of Taliban that resisted the invasion. Why would they need to negotiate a separate peace with Mullah Omar and senior Taliban officials when they could just kill them instead? This approach didn't bode well for long-term reconciliation.

The 2002 State of the Union Address was President Bush's second major speech in the Capitol since the 9/11 attacks; the first had resulted in a war. In four short months, Bush said, the United States and their allies in Afghanistan had made incredible progress. They had "captured, arrested, and rid the world of thousands of terrorists, destroyed Afghanistan's training camps, saved a people from starvation, and freed a country from brutal oppression." But had they? To some Afghan eyes, they had merely exchanged one oppressive government for another. In November 2001, two Taliban leaders in the north, Mohammad Fazl and Norullah Noori, surrendered themselves and their men to Dostum and cooperated with CIA officers to pacify pockets of Taliban support. Dostum was brutal to his prisoners. Some were left in oven-hot shipping containers until nature took its course and they baked to death, while others were consolidated into the former Taliban prison at Qali-i-Jangi. But after a decade of bloody civil war, Dostum was ready for peace, and he accepted Fazl and Noori's surrender. "We should not wash blood with blood," he said.

In exchange for their surrender, Noori and Fazl expected amnesty and safe passage to their homes in the south; they had been told that they could work with the new government. Fazl even vowed to help track down bin Laden for the Americans.

But in the north, as in the south, the Taliban didn't get what they wanted. Word came back from Washington: It is useless to work with these men. Bring them in and sweat them. Fazl and Noori were bound for Guantanamo Bay, Cuba. On December 20, they were transferred to U.S. custody. By January 11, 2002, Fazl and Noori were in orange jumpsuits at Guantanamo's Camp X-Ray. It would be more than twelve years before the prisoner exchange that freed them in 2014.

IN 2002, the first full year of Operation Enduring Freedom, the United States spent $36 billion on Afghanistan and forty-nine service members died. Following the 2003 invasion of Iraq, resources and personnel were diverted to the new war, and Afghanistan was quickly forgotten, its budget slashed to a scant $17 billion the next fiscal year. Afghanistan was left with a skeleton force of U.S. troops—around twenty thousand to secure a country of nearly thirty million. The official mission statement remained "to deny sanctuary to the enemy, disrupt the ability of al-Qaeda and the Taliban to plan and execute operations, and destroy enemy forces when in contact." The longer-term American strategy remained nebulous.

The rush to judgment on victory was premature. The Taliban hadn't been eliminated nor had their sanctuary been denied. After the United States and Karzai refused to negotiate, Omar and his inner circle had merely retreated over the border into Pakistan, where they licked their wounds and, with guarantees of support from the ISI, prepared to fight back using the strategies and tactics perfected by the mujahideen against the Soviets. Now in its fourth decade of war, Afghanistan was devastated, the population torn apart, families spread asunder, infrastructure so destroyed that U.S. pilots joked they were just making rocks bounce when they bombed the country.

There was little to work with to rebuild. Rural Afghanistan's demographics were an inverted bell curve; there were little children and there were old men—*spinghira*, Pashto for graybeards, elders. A glimpse of a young, partially veiled woman was rare. So, too, was a glimpse of a young man. Once old enough to fight, they were recruited (often by force and threats of violence) to join the fighting ranks in Pakistan, just as their mujahideen elders had been before them. Starkly beautiful the land may be, but little grew in Paktika but timber in the hills and violence in the valleys.

The timber market in Paktika wasn't a viable job market, given that it was strictly controlled by the Haqqani Network, an armed mafia-militia syndicate that did off-the-books work—assassinations, terror attacks, bombings—for Pakistani intelligence. Jalaluddin Haqqani had been the heavyweight in Loya Paktia and North Waziristan since the mid-seventies, when he first set up training camps to wage jihad against the secularist Afghan president Mohammad Daud Khan. But it wasn't until Operation Cyclone—which courted, armed, and funded Haqqani as Washington's favorite mujahideen commander—when his legend was made and his power solidified. When Osama bin Laden settled in

Peshawar in the mid-eighties, it was Haqqani who permitted him to build al-Qaeda's first training camps in the Pakistani mountains. And in the chaos that followed the Soviet withdrawal, both the Taliban and bin Laden sought his allegiance.

In the mid-nineties, Haqqani joined Mullah Omar's government as the Taliban's minister for tribal affairs and minister of borders. Given the porousness of the border he controlled, it was a logical appointment. Known as the Durand Line, Afghanistan's eastern border was named after Sir Henry Mortimer Durand, the British foreign secretary who had drawn it up in a one-page treaty with the Afghan king whose tribal territories had dealt Queen Victoria's armies their worst colonial catastrophes. To the people who had lived there for centuries, the 1893 border was little more than an abstraction. By design, the Durand Line had disempowered the Pashtuns. By accident, it had given generations of militants a conveniently ill-defined, mountainous redoubt.

Following al-Qaeda's 1998 bombings of two U.S. embassies in East Africa, Haqqani agreed to a meeting at the U.S. embassy in Islamabad, where the Americans pressed him on extraditing bin Laden. Haqqani replied that the Taliban had thought about it, but asked the Americans where they would like to see him go. "Iran? Iraq? Sudan? Would that help you?" he asked. Maybe the best solution, Haqqani said, was for bin Laden to remain in Afghanistan, where the Taliban could keep an eye on him.

After 9/11, Haqqani once again stepped up as bin Laden's protector, ensuring his safe passage out of Tora Bora and through the FATA. Karzai made repeated attempts to court Haqqani into joining his government, each time losing out to the far better arrangement the famed commander enjoyed with the Pakistani government. From his redoubt in Miran Shah, North Waziristan, Haqqani had turned his network into the Taliban's most effective and ruthless fighting force. Thirty years after the CIA chose him as its best proxy, Haqqani would become one of Washington's worst enemies.

To fight him, the United States used cash and contracts to rent their own proxy armies in Paktika. Paying minor warlords protection money and renting their gunmen was cheaper and easier than training indiginous forces from scratch. Over the course of the war, this led to Washington's own Soviet-esque profligacy: American money bought security on American-funded roads by paying middlemen who in turn paid Haqqani. At Forward Operating Base Orgun-E, one of the largest U.S. bases in Paktika, the practice led to financing a warlord named Zakeem Kahn, and his militia of soldiers who did not exist.

Kahn was a truck driver, criminal, and murderer who'd recruited a small army of enforcers before the U.S. war had begun. After the fall of the Taliban, Zakeem rented his gangsters to the Americans, who paid him on a per soldier basis. Sensing a business opportunity, Zakeem padded his ranks with large numbers of "ghost soldiers," men who never showed up to formations but were cut Department of Defense paychecks nonetheless. One month in 2003, Zakeem's money never arrived; the CIA had cut off funding with no warning or explanation. According to one CIA officer who worked in Paktika, it was standard operating procedure. But it also put Zakeem's actual gunmen back on the job market. Concerns that these militiamen—trained by the CIA and Green Berets—would now earn their living by freelancing for the Taliban, Haqqani Network, or al-Qaeda, went unheeded. It was a microcosm of the entire war: After training and funding Zakeem's soldiers, the Pentagon abandoned them to become mercenaries hired by the enemy.

The term for it was "blowback": when secret operations came back to bite the nation that initiated them. The CIA first used the term in a 1954 report on Operation Ajax, the covert operation that overthrew Iran's Mohammed Mossadegh. Agency analysts cautioned that the operation—then viewed as a wild success—would haunt the United States. It would take twenty-five years, and the Ayatollah Khomeini's 1979 revolution, until history proved them right.

THE UNITED STATES Central Command is headquartered in Tampa, Florida, across the bridge from the Salvador Dali Museum in St. Petersburg.

Things are surreal on both ends of the bridge. CENTCOM commanders ran two desert wars from a massive headquarters visible to boats in the emerald-tinted Hillsborough Bay and briefed the commander in chief once a week via an hour-long secure video teleconference (VTC). As Iraq spiraled into chaos, Afghanistan faded almost to black. In 2006, the president's hour-long weekly briefings were devoted almost entirely to the situation in Baghdad; just five minutes, at the end, were set aside for Afghanistan, a five-year-old conflict that was already America's forgotten war.

It was also a time of crucial transition in the war as NATO began to play a more prominent role. By the end of 2006, most American troops in-country—except for the special operators—were serving under NATO's International Security Assistance Force (ISAF), which American soldiers joked stood for "I Suck at Fighting." By this point ISAF, the CIA, and the State Department had become the shadow government of Afghanistan, a troika of rivals seeking to manage a population of thirty million that had not known a stable central government in more than a quarter century, and a Western-backed regime in Kabul that the majority of Afghans did not trust or respect.

Counterinsurgency (COIN) was the new buzzword in Washington, the new path to victory. It was marketed less as a specific way of fighting a war against an unconventional foe and more as an intellectual framework for transforming a whole country. Chairman Mao described guerrillas as fish and the population that supported them as the water in which they swam. In Paktika, that water easily sustained Haqqani and Taliban guerrillas. But in the logic of American counterinsurgency, the local population could be persuaded through a variety of incentives to flip allegiances and support Karzai's government. The Afghan counterinsurgency campaign would be won only with a hybrid warfare-meets-welfare strategy: a combination of combat, diplomacy, civil affairs, and propaganda intended to destroy opposition on an organizational, physical, and mental plane.

It was easier to talk about than it was to execute. "Counterinsurgency places great demands on the ability of bureaucracies to work together, with allies, and increasingly, with nongovernmental organizations," stated the State Department's *Counterinsurgency Guide*, published in January 2009. In order to win in Afghanistan, the U.S. needed to know what counterinsurgency mavens called the "human terrain"—the needs of their friends and the weaknesses of their enemies. Then they simply needed to wait for it all to work and "have the patience to persevere in what will necessarily prove long struggles."

From Fort Leavenworth, Kansas, the Old West frontier base that held the military's largest prison, two generals, David Petraeus and James Mattis, had directed the writing and publication of a joint manual, *FM 3-24: Counterinsurgency*, published in late 2006. It was the first military publication to focus on counterinsurgency since Vietnam. It was intended as a guidebook for soldiers in the field but was hard to read and even harder to implement. There was nothing new about what the United States was doing. The techniques were older than America and had been practiced during the French and Indian War, the American Revolution, the Apache wars in the American West, and the Spanish-American War: Bring in guns and bags of food from half a world away, carried by men without knowledge of the language or culture, who would squeeze, coerce, or cajole the local population into going along with the American-backed government. "We can do this the easy way, or we can do this the hard way" went the implied message of counterinsurgency. In Paktika, all ISAF gun trucks had to be spray-painted with the acronym on turrets and doors before rolling outside the wire. ISAF was written in Latin script rather than the Arabic-derived Pashto or Dari alphabet. Thus, only the few literate Afghans who also knew the Western alphabet could read it. As a public relations gesture, it was as puzzling as the billboard at the traffic circle by Sharana's district center that proclaimed, in English, "Welcome to Afghanistan."

THREE

ADJUSTMENT DISORDER

If Bowe knew his father was going to be home, he made plans to be out. Bob's tough-love Christian doctrine felt like a prison, his high standards impossible to satisfy. Bowe didn't like how his father treated his mother either. She should stand up to him, Bowe would tell his friends, and he was doubly angry when she stood by and defended Bob's demands. Years later, when Bowe would cite the unhappiness of his childhood and the tyranny of the household, his family would feel hurt and confused. His sister didn't share his feelings, and his parents did not understand.

Bob and Jani knew that most teenagers turn on their parents at some point. But with Bowe it was extreme. He was bullheaded about seemingly irrational things, like refusing to sleep on a mattress. He told his mom that he didn't believe in such comforts. He would sleep on the floor. At home, nothing seemed to go his way. When foxes and coyotes came at night for the family's pets, it was always Bowe's kittens that turned up dead in the morning. They lost more cats to violent deaths than they could count.

When he could no longer stand it, he packed his wilderness kit—compass, knives, water, food, journal—and fled into the backcountry. He rode the dirt bike he bought with his own money, brought a sleeping bag, and if he wanted to spend the night under the stars with no one around for miles, that's what he did. He escaped into his imagination too, writing stories in his journal that occupied his mind for days. Alone in the mountains, he felt calm and safe.

Bowe had a driver's license, and his parents told him he could borrow their trucks to drive to work. But he preferred riding his bike, sometimes pedaling forty or fifty miles a day. He spent hours in Ketchum's Community Library, where the valley's other drifters sat alongside the retired New York executives who came to read the *Financial Times* in front of a stone fireplace. He lost himself in historical epics about ancient civilizations and adventures on the high seas, and he checked out books and DVDs on martial arts, wilderness survival, and Bear Grylls, the former British Special Air Service soldier who turned complicated survival scenarios into slick videos.

Bowe knew his social skills were lacking, so he signed up for an afternoon fencing class at the Sacred Cow, a mixed-use yoga and dance studio in a Ketchum building owned by the actress Mariel Hemingway. (On his way to class, he pedaled past Hemingway Elementary, the school named after Mariel's grandfather Ernest, who killed himself with a shotgun in the mudroom of his Ketchum home on July 2, 1961.) At fencing, Bowe made new friends, including Shane and Kayla Harrison, whose mother, Kim Harrison, was an old friend of Mariel's.

Shane and Kayla weren't like other kids Bowe knew. They were homeschooled but not religious. They lived in Idaho, but they didn't go camping and shooting, and they never went to church. One year their mom took their homeschooling on the road, backpacking through the old cities of Europe and searching for coffee shops where they spent their days reading and talking and writing.

As exotic as the Harrisons were to him, Bowe was an equal novelty to them. He was chivalrous and polite to a fault. He didn't drink or show any interest in drugs. Where others would swear, he said "gosh" or "good grief" and had a goofy sweet smile. Kim and Kayla doted on him.

On days when he arrived early to fencing, he watched the end of the Sun Valley Ballet School classes that shared the Sacred Cow studio. He saw the concentration on the girls' faces as they struggled with positions requiring strength, balance, and flexibility. One day he asked the teacher, Anna Fontaine, if he could sit in on a class; he told her he might even want to give it a try. He was seventeen years old, tall, wiry, and strong—the perfect build for a lifter, she thought. First she put him with the other teenagers, but when he didn't know the basics, Bowe volunteered to start with a beginner class. With deep focus and an uncanny devotion that made him a teacher's favorite, he stood at the barre practicing his *plie* and *releve* in a line of nine- and ten-year-old girls in tutus.

Before earning his GED, Bowe signed up for summer-school courses at the public school in Hailey. He loved his teacher, but when he saw a bully harassing a smaller kid, he confronted him—with his fists. The bully had it coming, and the teacher turned a blind eye to Bowe's vigilantism, but he told his mom he'd seen enough of public school.

The following summer, Kim bought an old cabin in downtown Ketchum with plans to build a sophisticated coffee and tea shop like the places she and her kids had discovered in Europe. They would teach people the differences between oolong, lapsang, and sencha; there would be a café and creative performances. Everyone was welcome. It would be "a community place," Kim said—something different and new for teens tired of pumping quarters into the *Big Buck Hunter* up the road at Lefty's Bar & Grill.

Kim was a Wiccan, so she named the place Strega, Italian for "witch." As the scope of the cabin remodel quickly exceeded their abilities and budget, Bowe volunteered to do the work for free. After a day ripping out drywall and sawing lumber to build the ornate tea bar, Bowe would ride his bike nearly twenty miles home—past the hospital and the trailer park, the millionaire's enclave at Gimlet, the mid-valley country club, and the convenience store that used to sell porn. He hung a right at the UPS distribution center where his dad went to work each morning, crossed the Big Wood River, and climbed for miles on gravel and dirt to the house where he no longer wanted to be. Kim made him a deal: As long as Bowe worked at Strega, he could sleep there too. Every night he unrolled his sleeping mat, and each morning he packed it back in his green ammo box, as if he were never there.

If the move bothered Bob, he didn't show it. He shrugged it off, framing it as a natural, if somewhat sudden, step in his son's maturing process, like going off to college. Jani took it harder. It was a rupture in the family, a rejection without explanation. But Ketchum was a revelation to Bowe. Leaving the silence of the canyon and his father's rules, he moved into a kind witch's tea shop tucked between modern art galleries that sold six-figure paintings to second-home owners from Brentwood and Chappaqua. Strega shared an alleyway with the Board Bin, a punk-inspired skate and snowboard shop and cradle of the local counterculture. The valley's newspaper, the *Idaho Mountain Express*, was two blocks north. Two blocks south was the Davies-Reid Tribal Arts building, a South Asian imports bazaar stacked with rugs and shawls woven in small indigenous factories in Peshawar and Swat in Northwest Pakistan.

Comfortable in the woods, Bowe was a naïf in town. Ketchum had an energy that was bigger than its three thousand people, and he studied the daily habits of European ski instructors and art gallerists who spoke many languages and traveled the world. It was also a ski bum town where freak flags flew. The newspaper deliveryman was an Air Force veteran and a tinkerer named Mickey, and when Mickey ran for local office (which he did every election) he campaigned by riding around town in extravagant patriotic regalia on an electric tricycle he built for himself.

Strega was a hit with college kids home on break and cliques of twentysomethings who worked at Ketchum's restaurants, bookstores, and galleries. Bowe joined Kim's gaggle on an oversized, unstructured staff. He sat on a stool by the stove and studied the rich kids and self-styled artists for clues about how to act. Mariel Hemingway used the kitchen to test recipes for her gluten-free cookies. Bowe tried goth—Kayla painted his nails black, and he let his blond bangs hang over his eyes. Kim was hands-off, the cool mom of the whole gang, and the place ran like an artists' commune with teens journaling in leather-bound notebooks and talking about their feelings. Profits were an after-thought. As the lunch orders stacked up, the cooks sent their friends running to the store for bread and tomatoes.

Compared to the binary codes of right and wrong at his parents' house, Kim's world held multitudes. She talked about her Hollywood days doing design work for Oscar-winning blockbusters like *The Night-mare Before Christmas* and *Toy Story.* She spoke the mystical languages of many faiths and filled the store with the spiritual accoutrement of Buddhism, Hinduism, Zen, tarot cards, and astrology. The bulletin board that hung by the door was jammed with business cards from massage therapists, reflexologists, energy readers, energy healers, Ayurvedic advisers, doulas, and yogis. Bowe still checked in with his parents, who always invited him for church on the weekends. Jani was worried. Her son's faith, which she thought had been strong, seemed to be washing away in a muddled New Age flood.

Kim decided that it no longer made sense for Bowe to sleep at Strega, so she invited him to move in with her family. They had an extra room in their house, a funky artist space with a riotous overgrown garden in the front yard, marbles and mosaics embedded in poured concrete floors, and a bathroom covered with her own dark versions of classic Portuguese tilework. Houseguests were encouraged to express themselves on a chalkboard wall, and Bowe became a regular at boisterous family dinners with Kim's brother, Mark Farris, and a rotating cast of friends.

Farris and Kim's grandfather had been a union organizer in Chicago and Los Angeles, and in their home, "socialism" was never a bad word. As the wine flowed, Kim and Mark and their friends let loose on George W. Bush, the lies used to sell the Iraq War, and the inherent evil of the American Right. Mark was an industrial designer with the sensibility of an artist and the only guy at the table who could speak Bowe's language about tactical gear, motorcycles, guns, and outdoor adventures. They took Bowe in without asking who or what he was running from.

"He was obviously struggling to feel comfortable, but he was also obviously a really sweet guy," Farris said. Kim tried to help him build a new emotional foundation. "He learned basic things with me, like he was not going to get in trouble if he ate all the peanut butter," she later told Army investigators. She thought she was enriching him in ways his parents hadn't. She believed that Bowe was socially underdeveloped because his parents never taught him how to discuss his feelings.

Jani and Sky had a bad feeling about Kim. Who was this person, they wondered, indoctrinating an impressionable boy with her own worldview? Kim seemed intent on encouraging his worst instincts about his own family, magnifying the negative moments until they defined the entire relationship. The Bergdahls didn't like it, but they knew that Bowe needed to leave the house at some point. He was a work in progress, and he needed to figure himself out on his own terms.

Where the new adults in his life saw a vulnerable and kind young man, his peers saw a stranger side. At the gun club one afternoon, he jumped from a thirty-foot platform onto hard ground, laughing as he walked away from his stunned coworkers, apparently uninjured. As his social confidence at Strega grew, so did his antics. He didn't talk much, but when he did it was in great detail about weaponry and martial arts to people who he couldn't see weren't interested. He tore phone books in half and told his new friends that he liked to test out burning his hands on the kitchen stove. Why? they asked. To make them tougher, Bowe said. He would disappear into the bathroom and emerged in skin-tight compression shirts with sheathed knives strapped to his body.

"It was like, 'Great, you do that.' Our friends just let him do whatever," said Kyle Koski, one of the Strega crew. "What he actually did with it all, I have no idea. But he looked prepared for something."

Bowe discovered zazen, a meditation discipline that teaches students to control their thoughts, and he devoted himself to it with his usual absolute dedication. He modeled himself on Bruce Lee, the Kung Fu legend who wrote, "Do not pray for an easy life, pray for the strength to endure a difficult one." Despite the social appeals of Strega, and despite Kim's gravitational pull, he hungered for a greater purpose. Along with Bear Grylls, he had been fascinated by a series of British military history books that his parents had lying around the house as collectibles, and in his heady teen years, he began to see himself as a warrior and a protector.

He bought a samurai sword, which he carried around Ketchum "for protection," he said. When his friends asked about the rows of cuts on his arms, he explained them away with different stories to different people. The cuts on his face were from a trip to New York City, he claimed, where he had gone walking around bad neighborhoods to find people to start knife fights with, and the scars on his arms were from experiments with self-surgery. No one called it "cutting." He never saw a therapist. He was training, he said. He started stashing his weapons in Strega's hidden crannies: throwing knives, a garrote, a medieval flail, and in case of a holdup, a gnarled Irish shillelagh under the cash register. Strega's manager, a hip Michigander named Chad Walsh, told Bowe one day that he was giving him a new job as head of security. Strega didn't need a bouncer any more than a person in Ketchum needed a sword for protection, but they all liked Bowe, and Chad wanted him to feel included. On open mic nights at the café, when the college kids tested out their free-form poetry, Bowe stood by the door, scanning the crowd for trouble that never came.

IN A REMOTE MOUNTAIN town where the nearest shopping mall is a seventy-mile drive away and the U.S. Postal Service mail is notoriously slow, everyone knows their UPS man. "Seeing the UPS truck was like Christmas all the time," said John Shaw, a federally licensed firearms dealer who depended on UPS for receiving regular heavy shipments of rifles, pistols, shotguns, and ammunition at his home in Hailey. When

"Shooter Shaw" moved west from his native Memphis, Tennessee, in the mid-nineties, his legend as a self-taught champion marksman was already made. Bob knew whom the gun deliveries were for before they even met.

Shaw had plans to open an Idaho outpost of his Mid-South Institute of Self-Defense Shooting, the successful shooting academy he founded in northwest Mississippi and developed into one of the top military and law-enforcement training centers in the country. In Hagerman, Idaho, he bought a spectacular piece of property with panoramic views of the Snake River and Hagerman Fossil Beds National Monument, where he built a gun lover's Shangri-La.

Bob was generous with local hunting tips and welcoming in ways the Southern transplant never forgot, and, in the late nineties, Shaw counted Bob as one of his first Idaho friends. Their families had dinner dates in Hailey, where Shaw met Jani, Sky, and Sky's boyfriend, Michael Albrecht. The son of a social worker in a family of devout Christians who moved frequently from job to job, Albrecht had also been homeschooled. When Shaw met him, he had recently earned his high school degree from a Bible school in North Dakota and had earned a spot at the U.S. Naval Academy in Annapolis, Maryland, where he was planning a career as a Navy pilot.

"It sounded like a great all-American family to me," Shaw said. He spent hours with Bowe at the Blaine County Gun Club, Shaw's favorite local range. "I noticed his work ethic," he said. "That got my attention for sure. He liked to work. This day and age you sure don't see kids doing that. Even then you didn't see kids doing that. That was a little unusual, just how dedicated he was."

Shaw preferred shooting when his friend's son was working. Of all the kids who pulled trap there, Bowe knew the most about how the targets flew and how much lead to give each clay. "It was a pleasure having somebody like him with me," Shaw said.

John Shaw had an idea for Bob: "If [Bowe] really likes shooting this much, we could use that help back in Memphis." Mid-South was a place where SWAT and SEAL teams went to train, but there were also twenty acres of grass that needed mowing, as well as ranges and target machines that needed maintenance and upkeep. Shaw knew Bowe was a hard worker who didn't have a solid plan for his future. He could live right on the range, he told Bob. He could see a different part of the country, where he would meet new people, including some of the best-trained operators in the U.S. military. Bob liked the idea, and in spite of the tension between them, Bowe still sought his father's advice. Shaw had seen something in him, and Bob encouraged his son to take the job.

John Shaw's Mid-South is in Lake Cormorant, Mississippi, on the Delta, just east of the massive river. It is flat, hot, wide-open country—the opposite of Hailey, Idaho, in almost every way, except for its even greater isolation. Bowe stayed in a small room in a building next to one of several shooting ranges surrounded by miles of cornfields that backed up to a narrow creek called Dead Negro Slough. Poor black communities lined Route 61 north to Memphis. To the south was Tunica, where the gold windows of the Gold Strike Casino Resort were the most notable features in an otherwise featureless landscape. The job was tedious. Shaw and his manager at Mid-South, an Alabamian named Ross Sanders, agreed to give Bowe the same initiation as every other new hire: "Three months of manual labor before you even get a gun in your hands," Shaw said. Sanders handed Bowe a weed whacker and a paintbrush and put him to work, which he did well, earning their trust. Some employees in years past had turned out to be thieves. High-end weapons and expensive tactical equipment had gone missing. But Shaw knew that Bob had an honor code, and he never doubted Bowe. "I don't think he would ever steal from anybody," Shaw said. "I don't think he cared about anything with materialistic value."

When he saw Bob in Hailey, Shaw passed along the report from Sanders: Bowe was happy with the work. He was reclusive, but a reliable part of the team and seemingly dedicated to Shaw's mission. Kim Harrison heard a different story. Bowe called her and vented about the people he didn't like and parts of the job that were terrible, like having to shoot stray dogs that roamed onto the property. She had thought the job was questionable from the start, a strange and isolated pursuit surrounded by, as she saw them, a bunch of gun nuts. The lone bright spot, Bowe told her, was the time he spent with Delta Force and SEAL teams who came for training between deployments. On calls with his parents, Bowe talked about the elite soldiers he was meeting and his goal of joining them one day. But when Bob asked for details, Bowe said he couldn't talk about it. It's classified, he said. Top secret.

In reality, Bowe spent his days mowing grass and greasing the hinges on rusty gun targets. When he did hang out with the SEALs and Delta Force guys, it was as their designated driver for drinking and gambling trips to the casinos twenty minutes south of the range. They knew he wanted to be like them, and they discouraged it in the strongest terms possible. If he so much as tried, the SEALs told him, they would blacklist him from BUD/S, the twenty-four-week Basic Underwater Demolition initiation training every SEAL must complete. "They didn't want to see him go in," Bob said. "He was too good a kid."

But their warnings didn't faze him. He had a goal now. He was just about finished with his weed whacker and paintbrush initiation, and Shaw was planning to start training him for a position as a shooting instructor. "There was no indications at all about him leaving or doing anything, then all of a sudden, just one day, he said he was joining the Foreign Legions."

Bowe craved action, and if the SEALs would block him, like they said they would, then surely, he reasoned, the French Foreign Legion would welcome him with open arms. It would be the ultimate adventure. The French Foreign Legion is a legendary combat outfit. Though it was part of the French military, its soldiers (but not its officers) were from elsewhere. The French Foreign Legion didn't care who you were or where you came from; if one could make the cut and sign the five-year contract to fight for France, France would supply a new identity—a nom de guerre—and guarantee a constant rotation through troubled spots around the globe.

Bowe told only a few people about his plan. Kim thought it was crazy. Bob knew it was doomed. Still, he bought a one-way ticket and made his way to Fort de Nogent, where potential legionnaires are first screened. At the time, with battle-hardened former soldiers from the Eastern Bloc and Africa streaming into the service, the French Foreign Legion did not have any trouble meeting its recruiting goals. They gave Bowe a basic physical exam and told him it wasn't going to work out. He felt that they were laughing at him. It was his eyesight, they said.

Bowe returned home devastated and smoking French cigarettes. He told his mom that his soul was crushed. In truth, he was relieved. From the moment he stepped off the plane, nothing had gone as he had expected. Navigating the foreign city was completely overwhelming. He hadn't anticipated, for instance, that everyone would be speaking French. To his friends, there was no accounting for such surprised reactions to predictable outcomes; it was just Bowe being Bowe.

Back in Idaho, his conversations turned dark. He told his mom that if he ever had children, he didn't want a son, "because he'll be just like me." He looked at job listings in big cities, a process that reaffirmed his disinterest in a normal life. "I am not the type of person that is going to get a job because it has a good paycheck," he told later General Dahl. "I want a job where I can see my effort and see that I am making a difference." In October 2005, he thought he'd found what he was looking for and asked Kim to drive him to the Idaho National Guard recruiting office in Twin Falls. He had decided to join the United States Coast Guard. He didn't tell his parents this time.

THREE MONTHS LATER, the January wind whipped off the Delaware Bay in twenty-mile-per-hour gusts in Cape May, New Jersey. Bergdahl was wearing the same blank gray T-shirt, blue shorts, and white Coast Guard–issue sneakers as every other blank-faced seaman recruit standing in line waiting to piss in a cup. Already, this wasn't what he thought it would be. The company commanders didn't offer him calm or patient instructions. They got right up in his face and screamed.

"Seaman Recruit Bergdahl! Why are you here?!"

Bergdahl froze up. Twelve years later, he tried explaining it to General Dahl. He was fascinated by the ocean and loved boats. (His email address was cutlassclipper@hotmail.com.) The Coast Guard defended America and saved lives every day.

Eye contact with company commanders was forbidden. The slightest deviation from orders could bring them back, red-faced and screaming. Nervous recruits were singled out for special treatment, put on the spot in the middle of drills and in front of their peers with crude questions and sexual innuendo—whatever worked to rattle the new arrivals. Company commanders also knew tricks to impose order. When one recruit forgot to shave one morning, or ran out of time, every man in Quebec Company was ordered to go back, shave again, and line up for inspection. A single missed whisker restarted the entire process. Only after the full company had lathered up and shaved six or seven times, their faces and necks raw and bloody in the winter's ocean wind, did the torment finally stop.

The nights were rarely peaceful. Sleep was interrupted by fire drills, sometimes just one, sometimes one after the other after the other until dawn. When the lights flashed on at 2:00 a.m., the recruits scrambled out of bed, hurried into their socks and the sneakers the commanders called their "go-fasters," and ran outside to line up in tight formation, "nuts to butts," and count off in the thirty-degree night. Then it was back to their bunks, shoes off, socks off, lights off. Forty minutes later, as sleep washed over them, the lights and sirens flashed and the whole exercise unfolded again.

On the night of February 15 the drills started right after supper. At the second formation, one recruit from Quebec Company was missing, and the company commander wanted answers.

"I think that's Seaman Recruit Bergdahl," one recruit said.

Two recruits sent to retrieve him found him curled in a ball in the corner of the bathroom, hugging his knees tight to his chest, crying, tears mixing with blood. "There's blood on the mirror, blood on the sink, on the counter. Blood on the fucking walls," said John Raffa, one of the men who found Bergdahl. Bowe wasn't bleeding out, and Raffa didn't think it was a suicide attempt. He asked him what had happened. Bowe told him to go away and leave him alone.

As it had in Paris, the gap between his expectations and reality had proved unbridgeable. Prior to boot camp, he had meditated to quiet his mind and had run through the steps of what would be required of him. And yet, he had arrived into a situation entirely out of his control. This was real pressure: It was as if every moment of anxiety from when he was a kid and his father had been angry with him had compressed into an unbearable wave of panic. He thought of himself as a failure, he told Dahl. "And suddenly, I am responsible for someone else's life."

Bowe was loaded into an ambulance and driven to the Samuel J. Call Health Services Center, the Coast Guard's largest hospital. "I can't do this," he told the doctors, visibly shaking. They determined the bloody scene was the result of a nosebleed. He was prescribed Tylenol, Ativan to calm him down, and Ambien to help him sleep. The next morning a Coast Guard psychiatrist examined him and recommended a discharge on medical grounds. "Disqualified for continued service in the U.S. Coast Guard due to the following condition(s): ADJUSTMENT DISORDER WITH DEPRESSION," it read.

On February 25, 2006, they issued him a Department of Defense Form 214 (DD-214), making his release from active duty official. Should former Seaman Recruit Bergdahl want to try boot camp again, he would need stress management counseling and clearance by a psychologist prior to reenlistment.

EVERYTHING WAS UNDER CONTROL, Bowe said. Kim was shocked. A few weeks earlier, he had sent her ten pages of scrawled and incoherent journal entries torn out of a notebook. She had been worrying about him ever since, and now he was standing in her kitchen talking about the mental breakdown that he had *faked* to get out of the Coast Guard.

She didn't believe him. "I don't think anyone believed him," she told General Dahl's investigators eight years later. Kim asked Bowe to be honest with her about what had happened in New Jersey. He didn't like it anymore, so he got out of it, he said. "You don't just 'get out of it,'" she told him. That wasn't how the military worked.

Bowe went back to Strega. There was more work for him there in the winter, and only a few people knew where he had been or what he was doing on the East Coast. The winter of 2006 was a big snow year in Idaho's capital ski town: Sun Valley set a single-season record with 360 inches, and at Strega, Bowe was in charge of snow removal. While his friends lingered over earthenware mugs of yerba mate, he shoveled. He cleared the walkway through the courtyard to the street, then he cleared the sidewalk along Second Avenue. When he was done with the grounds, he climbed the building and shoveled the roof. In the back alley, he sculpted the snow and ice into the tables and chairs of a fully functioning smokers' lounge.

There were new people in Strega that winter, and Bowe was making an impression. "I never met anybody who had so much self-discipline," said Matt Larson, a local photographer who helped organize classic film nights at the tea shop. Larson didn't know anything about Bowe, but watching him shovel for hours, he had seen him turn the common chore into a monastic ritual, "like a purification of self through physical activity."

When the snow melted, Bowe saw an ad for an apartment in Hailey, and at twenty years old, decided it was time to live on his own. The landlord happened to be the county sheriff, who, as an old acquaintance of Bob's, made an exception to rent his apartment to a tenant so young. Even as Blaine County Sheriff Walt Femling explained his rules—no partying, no loud music, no mess—he realized Bowe wouldn't be a problem. A few weeks later, Femling was driving through a cold spring downpour when he saw Bowe walking without a coat. He pulled over, rolled down his window, and offered his new tenant a ride. Bowe said thank you, but he couldn't take the offer. He didn't want to get the sheriff's seats wet. Femling looked at his dogs in the cab of his truck and then back at Bowe. "Hey, this is a truck!" he said. "You're not going to hurt it. Jump in!"

Bowe again politely declined, and Femling drove away confounded, watching him in his rearview mirror walking alone in the rain. Days later at the apartment, Bowe told Femling that he was thinking about either joining the military or going to work in Alaska on a commercial fishing boat. He loved the ocean and big ships, he said. One day, he wanted to sail around the world.

Femling told Bowe that when he was eighteen, he'd had the same impulse and regaled him with stories about the summers he had worked in Bristol Bay to pay his way through college. He told Bowe to go for it.

FOR BOWE, Alaska was not a great experience. Yes, he and his friend Dylan Fullmer, who also grew up in the Wood River Valley, were hired for two months to work on Bristol Bay. As the strongest man on the boat, Bowe did most of the heavy labor, pulling and cleaning lines and hauling vast numbers of fish. He breathed the ocean air all day and was rocked to sleep by its swells each night. But the realities of the work, killing so many creatures for human appetites, sickened him. He and Dylan shared cramped living quarters with the boat's captain, a heavy smoker and drinker who passed the time with crude jokes about women and started charging Bowe for trifling expenses, cutting into his paycheck. As they fell asleep one night, Bowe told Dylan that he had better journeys in mind: His next plan was to ride his bike around the world. Dylan thought it was absurd. But Bowe was serious. It would be simple, he said: He would use boats like bridges to span the continents.

When fishing season was over, Bowe returned to Idaho, confusing the kids at Strega with his constant coming and going. Hadn't Kim just thrown him a going-away party? He continued to boomerang, telling different stories about the places he'd been and the things he'd done. He had been piloting a speedboat running boat parts between South

Padre Island and Mexico, he told one friend. His motorcycle broke down in California, he reported to another. When a shooting instructor from Mississippi called to catch up, Bowe told him that he had been working as a bodyguard for a rich man sailing around the world. Bowe got shot in the leg, he claimed, so the job ended, and he came back to Idaho to cool off and lie low.

"There were a lot of unfilled blanks," said Mark Farris. "He would just be 'Some Where Else,' doing 'Some Thing Else.' And there would never be a cogent narrative or explanation."

There was one adventure that ended well. In the summer of 2007, he was hired onto a boat crew that sailed from the East Coast to California through the Panama Canal. When they disembarked in San Francisco, he bought a new bicycle with his paycheck and rode the Pacific Coast Highway to visit his grandparents in Santa Barbara. Sleeping in a garbage bag by the side of the road, he was content. But when his bank account ran dry, he returned home and moved into a spare room at his ballet teacher's place in Hailey. Anna Fontaine was twenty years older than him, like a big sister, and had a habit of staying out late at the bars. Bowe fell into a routine as her designated driver. As usual, he needed a new plan.

With winter approaching, he decided to chase the sun and ride his bicycle from Idaho to Tierra del Fuego, the farthest accessible point by land. He packed his bike and saddlebags with the minimal gear and no end date in mind. He made it as far as Northern California when he was clipped by a tractor-trailer. He was stoic when he called Anna with the damage report: He was fine, but the bike was trashed. Well, she said, rehearsals for the annual Christmas performance of *The Nutcracker* had started, and she always had a role for her best male dancer. Great, Bowe replied, and he headed home.

FOUR

AN ARMY OF ONE

Two years after the incident at Cape May, Bowe's failure still ate at him. He never told his parents what had happened. "The day they shipped me out, a thought occurred to me and it stayed in my mind whenever I thought about the Coast Guard," he told General Dahl, "and that thought was, I wanted to fix that."

Those who knew him knew Bowe was struggling with something. He would never say what it was, but the tension was plain. He spent more and more time in his room at Anna's. There was no bed, no couch, no TV, but on his days off from work, he stayed there, sometimes for days at a time. Fontaine and her other new roommate heard him yelling at himself.

"I can't believe you did that!"

"That was so stupid!"

Some of his friends worried. But Bowe never complained, and, around men in particular, he carried himself with stoic severity. Women saw a more concerning aspect. In the Harrison's kitchen, one of Kim's friends grabbed his hand, flipping his forearm over to reveal the neat rows of cuts. "You have such nice arms," she said to him. "What the heck are you doing to yourself?"

"I'm getting ready," he told her.

"What are you getting ready for?"

"Pain."

"Bowe?! What on earth! What are you talking about?"

"I'm just getting ready."

"Enough time had passed where I got uncomfortable again with not doing something that was making a difference," he told Dahl years later. His parents put him in touch with their pastor from Boise, Phil Proctor, who was ministering with seminary students in Northeastern Uganda. Bowe told his parents it sounded interesting; he could go to East Africa and teach villagers self-defense techniques. But the timing didn't work out; all the seminary spots were taken.

That spring, Bowe's seeking came full circle. He remembered meeting another Coast Guard washout who told him that if he wanted to, he could reenlist: The Army was stressed for new warm bodies.

His family knew he had been thinking about it.

"Whatever you do, don't join the Army," his sister and Albrecht told him. It was a bit of the old Army–Navy rivalry coming through, but Sky also believed that the Navy took care of its own in a way the Army never had. His mother agreed, but didn't think Bowe would actually enlist. Days later, when she saw him on the highway driving back from Twin Falls on his motorcycle, she knew he had.

At the Army Recruiting Station, Bowe was a young man in a hurry. He told the recruiter that he wanted to become a scout, a soldier who takes risky missions to track down enemy positions. The recruiter told him there were no more slots available for scouts, but he had three openings in the infantry, which would fill up fast if Bergdahl didn't act quick. He offered him a five-thousand-dollar signing bonus to sweeten the deal.

In the spring of 2008, the Army had lowered its recruiting standards to levels not seen since the end of the draft. Five years earlier, at the start of the Iraq War, 94 percent of new recruits had high school diplomas. By 2005, that number had dropped to 71 percent. New soldiers with what the Army defined as Category IV intelligence (those who'd scored in the thirtieth percentile or below), were accepted. As Iraq burned, their numbers rose, rising from just 0.06 percent of new recruits to 4 percent. Convicted felons who could secure a waiver from a sympathetic officer were accepted too. Physical fitness standards dropped. Recruiters fudged paperwork and coached problem cases like Bergdahl through background checks. His Coast Guard diagnosis was no longer disqualifying; he simply signed a form prepared by his recruiter stating that he had overcome his earlier issues. Bergdahl's waiver was approved in late May 2008, and he was issued orders to Fort Benning, Georgia, for Infantry One Station Unit Training (OSUT), where civilians were turned into infantrymen.

His parents didn't take the news as badly as Bowe had feared. Jani was relieved that he would no longer be traveling the world alone. Bob thought the structured life would do him good. Reading the news at the time, he also believed that the Taliban was on the run and the risk of serious combat was low.

"He's barely going to get in on the war in Afghanistan," Bob recalled thinking at the time. "It's almost over."

Kim and her brother took it much worse. Mark Farris's heart sank at the news. The last they had talked, Bowe was planning a two-week wilderness trip on the Yellowstone River in a sea kayak. It was a wild idea and would be a tough trip, but Farris thought it could work; the Army would not.

"If there was a human being unfit for the Army, who should never have joined the Army, it was Bowe," said Farris. "He was naive, idealistic, good-spirited. A very gentle person and a gentle soul."

Anna Fontaine was equally concerned. Why was this a better idea than the Coast Guard? "You tried this before. It didn't work. Why are you putting yourself through it again?"

Bowe told her that he was older now and had matured. "I was naive then. Now I know what to expect." Anna had grown up in the South near Army bases and told him he wouldn't like the rough culture. It didn't matter. "He was dead set on it," she said. "He was gung ho." Her parting words to him were: "Keep your head down. Don't be a hero."

AN ARMY OF ONE

DURING TWO WEEKS of in-processing as an infantry trainee at the Army's 30th Adjutant General Reception Battalion, Bergdahl learned that the Army didn't care for his feelings, his opinions, or his time. He stood in one line after another for physical exams, for drawing equipment, and for having his head shaved. His free time was spent in an open-bay starship barracks filled with bunk beds and his fellow recruits.

Second Battalion, 58th Infantry ("House of Pain") was one of six training battalions on Sand Hill, the section of Fort Benning reserved for basic training. Each battalion was led by a lieutenant colonel. Within the battalions were six companies, each led by a captain and a first sergeant. There were four platoons in each company, led by drill sergeants. Some drill sergeants took pleasure in the sadism of the job or were coming unglued after combat tours in Afghanistan or Iraq. On graduation day, one drill sergeant assembled the soldiers he'd spent the last fourteen weeks training and told them one thing: that he couldn't wait to see their names among the death notices in the *Army Times*.

But Bergdahl was assigned to Alpha Company, 2/58, the "AlphaGators," and his drill sergeant was different. Sergeant First Class Olivera was a no-nonsense combat veteran focused on preparing soldiers for war. Olivera felt that screaming and bluster was a waste of time. He was there to train, not to bully. When he saw a private make a mistake, he would tell him to stop, then walk him through the problem and the best way to fix it. Bergdahl would have followed Olivera anywhere. "You wanted to take his orders," he later told General Dahl. His peers were a different story. He thought a quarter of the soldiers who graduated from basic training with him should have failed. Some went out and got drunk on their one all-night pass, returned to base with beer, and abandoned the empties in the laundry room. One soldier with a chipped tooth went on sick call to Salomon Dental Clinic, got the tooth fixed, and said, "Well, I got what I wanted out of the Army," a sentiment Bergdahl found as offensive as the trainees selling contraband tobacco at ridiculous markups.

"Yes, my standard was high," Bergdahl later admitted to Army investigators. He didn't think the Army should keep people who didn't want to serve. Still, they all graduated together, and when Bergdahl invited his parents to the ceremony, he allowed himself a rare moment of happiness when they said they would come. On Fort Benning, Olivera congratulated Bob and Jani for their good work. "Bowe was good to go when he got here," he said.

BERGDAHL WAS ASSIGNED to a paratrooper unit in Alaska that needed soldiers for an upcoming deployment to Afghanistan. Soldiers assigned to the legendary 1/501. Parachute Infantry Regiment were normally required to have attended Airborne School, the three-week course on Fort Benning that qualified soldiers as paratroopers, but the Army was so desperate for soldiers, it waived internal standards and Bergdahl never attended Jump School.

The forerunner of all the Army's airborne units, 1/501 had adopted the Apache warrior Geronimo as their mascot, wearing his stylized profile on the unit crest pinned to their red berets above the right eye. When deployed to Afghanistan, 1/501 became "Task Force 1 Geronimo."

Despite its historical lore, the unit's recent past was as troubled as Bergdahl's. In 2007, the 1/501 completed a rough deployment to Iraq in Iskandariyah, thirty-five miles south of Baghdad. "It is really fucked-up here," 1/501 paratrooper Gabe Trollinger wrote to a friend over email. "There is nothing to be accomplished here other than see people you care about hurt, usually due to the complete lack of imagination of your officers."

In May 2007, a sniper from 1/501 named Evan Vela shot and killed an unarmed captive Iraqi man with a 9mm pistol—twice in the head—

on orders from Staff Sergeant Michael Hensley. The Army considered it murder, and Vela was court-martialed, convicted, and sentenced to ten years in the United States Disciplinary Barracks on Fort Leavenworth, Kansas. Strangely, Hensley escaped punishment for anything but planting a drop weapon on the Iraqi after the murder and disrespecting an officer.

A year later, Private Bergdahl arrived at 1/501 and was assigned to 2nd Platoon, Blackfoot Company. He was crammed into a room in the overstuffed Geronimo barracks with two other soldiers: a personable but chronically unwashed private, and Cody Full, a tough-talking Texan who attracted both drama and dirt. Bergdahl, who didn't drink or swear or dip chewing tobacco, stuck out. He tried to roll with it, but several soldiers would recall that he looked "lost." Joseph Coe, a fellow private who grew up as a Christian missionary, thought Bergdahl was a Mormon. While the other guys went out to drink at strip clubs, Bergdahl and Coe went to Barnes & Noble with Gerald Sutton, another private in 2nd Platoon.

Bergdahl was getting better at making friends but was still an oddball doing his own thing—a sin in the infantry. He knew he wasn't like the other guys, and to him that was a good thing. They goofed off. He used his downtime to learn new languages he downloaded from Rosetta Stone, study maps of Afghanistan, and read the ways of the warrior from lofty texts like *The Book of Five Rings*, Miyamoto Musashi's seventeenth-century treatise on swordsmanship, martial strategy, and samurai honor. "I will learn Russian I will learn Japanese. I will learn French. I will learn Chines [*sic*]," he wrote in his journal. He embraced the discomforts of soldiering, training himself to sleep on the concrete floor, wake up at 5:00 a.m., and breeze through the formation runs that left others winded. When the men lined up in the barrack hallways before morning PT, he closed his eyes and sat in motionless meditation.

"He was different, which is why the other people didn't like him," said Coe, one of the few who did. "He wasn't well accepted."

But Bergdahl wasn't a total outcast in Blackfoot Company. Sutton admired his fitness and strength, Coe related to his strict Christian upbringing, and Private First Class Odilon Nascimento was impressed by Bergdahl's moral code. "If he found a million dollars, he would find the owner," Nascimento later told General Dahl's investigators. Bergdahl's bunkmate, Cody Full, was less impressed and did not hide his disdain. When Bergdahl closed his eyes to meditate amid the barracks' ruckus, Full threw bottle caps at his head, and Bergdahl responded by not responding at all.

BERGDAHL LEARNED that his battalion would spend a month at Fort Irwin National Training Center in California's Mojave Desert. They would prepare for deployment by playing war games that the Army ran for $25 million each. The OPFOR—opposing force—at Fort Irwin was the 11th Armored Cavalry Regiment, who knew their terrain in the Mojave Desert the way Taliban fighters knew theirs. It was a point of pride for a visiting unit to beat the OPFOR. Ambitious units arrived prepared, having studied maps and reports of prior engagements: They knew the best spots to hide in Bike Lake, lie in ambush among the Valley of Death, escape along the John Wayne Foothills, or mask movement for a counterattack in the shadow of Furlong Ridge. But even the best-trained units usually lost.

To Bergdahl, NTC seemed like a $25 million dollar waste. His platoon fared badly in mock battles, the inevitable result of what he saw as a lack of discipline, exacerbated by weak leadership. He couldn't believe that these men were preparing for war. But he carried on, reading and rereading the *Ranger Handbook* and Army field manuals, studying maps, sharpening other soldiers' knives, and taking pride in keeping his equipment clean. At NTC, when leadership noticed that Bergdahl was in shape, a good shot, and "squared away" (a good soldier), they made him a SAW gunner. He carried the Squad Automatic Weapon, the M-249 light machine gun. This seventeen-pound, belt-fed machine gun could fire two hundred 5.56mm bullets in less than fifteen seconds, though soldiers were trained to use shorter bursts to prevent the barrel from melting. Carrying it meant Bergdahl had the most firepower in his four-man fire team. He took to the weapon—always had it clean and in better shape than anyone else's in the platoon.

Second Platoon returned to Alaska before deploying. During an inspection back on Fort Richardson, Command Sergeant Major Ken Wolfe, a career soldier in his mid-forties and the battalion's senior noncommissioned officer, gave a speech to his men about the war they were headed to fight. "I know you all joined because you want to rape, pillage, and kill. That's why I joined," Wolfe began in his Texas drawl. "But you need to think about COIN." Wolfe emphasized that in Afghanistan they would be as focused on winning over the local Afghan farmers, merchants, and truck drivers as they would be on killing the Taliban.

COIN was an impossible contradiction for infantrymen who, from their first day at Fort Benning, were trained to kill. It was something that Bergdahl couldn't have missed in fourteen weeks on Sand Hill, marching in formation, shouting, "Kill," in unison each time his left boot struck the ground. Another marching cadence in the Infantry Training Brigade went: "Trained . . . to kill . . . kill . . . we will." Army indoctrination was not subtle; Wolfe's point was that the war in Afghanistan would be.

Bergdahl didn't get it. He was so stunned by Wolfe's opener that he missed the rest. "I didn't join to be a rapist, murderer, and killer," he thought, and wondered how many of his new comrades had. Before he returned home for Christmas, he learned that sexual assaults and rapes had become rampant at Fort Richardson. He was appalled. His notion of war came from his books, where warriors were held in higher esteem because they lived by a higher code. Now the code was gone.

"These soldiers that we're supposed to be relying on for support, they don't even have the ethics not to rape a woman," he told General Dahl.

As Christmas approached, Bergdahl's attention turned to his own health. Just before break, he had cut his hand on a metal bunk-bed frame, a minor wound that by the time he reached Idaho on December 25 had turned into a staph infection. At 2 a.m. on December 27, with his arm red and swollen up to his elbow, he drove to the emergency room south of Ketchum and was administered IV antibiotics. As doctors ordered him back for twice-daily IVs, he applied iodine and his usual stoicism. When he visited his parents for what they all knew could be their last time together, his father reminded him that some men don't come home from war, and he reminded his father that he wanted to be buried at sea. His sister said she would pray for him.

Back in Alaska, Bergdahl regained his strength and prepared to deploy with the rest of Task Force Geronimo in February. With a new pair of boots that he wanted to break in before he left, he packed his rucksack and went for a two-mile march—and managed to get a massive blister on his left heel. The barracks were filthy, and with deployment approaching he grew increasingly worried about another infection. One morning as he was changing his socks, Sutton and the others took one look at his swollen foot and took him to the emergency room.

There, doctors cut out the infected tissue—a chunk the size of a half dollar—and marveled at Bergdahl's luck. The surgeon said if he'd waited a couple more days, the infection would have spread into his ligaments and bone—he would have needed an amputation. The battalion deployed to Afghanistan the next day, without Bergdahl.

BY LATE SPRING, Bergdahl was well enough for combat. "The closer I get to ship day, the calmer the voices are," he wrote in his journal. "I'm getting colder. My feelings are being flushed with the frozen logic and the training, all the unfeeling cold judgment of the darkness." On May 9, 2009, he boarded a commercial flight to Kuwait and traveled on to Bagram Airfield, the largest American base in Afghanistan and the war's logistical hub, built on the bones of a Soviet airfield outside Kabul.

Bagram was bursting with activity. Three years earlier, as a resurgent Taliban streamed across the border, the United States had responded by sending more troops. Worried about a potential Taliban buildup, President Bush and the Pentagon had approved the first mini troop surge at the end of 2006, extending the tour of soldiers from the Army's 10th Mountain Division for four months to temporarily double combat strength in-country. When Bergdahl joined the Army, there were just under thirty thousand U.S. troops in Afghanistan. By the time he arrived in Bagram, there were forty thousand. The number was expected to top one hundred thousand by the time President Obama's new strategy to recover the drifting war was implemented.

In transit at Bagram, Bergdahl slept on a cot in a commercial circus tent crowded with soldiers in limbo: sleeping, playing video games, and horsing around between smoke breaks. That was a nice diversion from the mandatory briefings, where officers and sergeants gave orientation talks to soldiers new in-country. Using PowerPoint, the briefers droned on about the rules of engagement (when soldiers could shoot, when they couldn't, whom they could legally kill, how they could get in trouble for killing the wrong person), and briefings on ISAF's strict prisoner policy (upon capture, detainees had to be processed and sent to Bagram within ninety-six hours). There were briefings on when soldiers could cross the border into Pakistan—generally only in hot pursuit. "Don't take cross-border lightly" was the message to the soldiers headed out to the FOBs (forward operating bases).

Officially in-processed into Operation Enduring Freedom, Bergdahl flew to FOB Sharana in Paktika Province. Sharana seemed like a mirage, a bustling port city in the middle of a lifeless desert. It was the biggest base in Paktika and one of the major hubs for the war on the border. It, too, was built on the bones of a Soviet base. In 2005, FOB Sharana became the staging point for military engineers overseeing road construction in Regional Command East (RC East). From 2006 to 2007, it grew sevenfold in size and population, and then kept growing as the war expanded under the Obama administration. Rows of shipping containers—"connexes" in military lingo—stretched for nearly a kilometer: red and blue and gray rectangles lined up like Legos, filled with ammunition, humanitarian aid, lumber, spare parts, communications equipment, donated books, pallets of water, cans of tomato sauce. The air hummed with the constant activity of helicopters, airplanes, generators, and rumbling gun trucks.

Bergdahl thought he was going to be taking cover behind sandbags, roughing it out in the desert—dirty, sweating, a soldier. But Sharana, despite its physical isolation, was not the frontier he had envisioned. It was Little America in Eastern Afghanistan. He was shocked by the creature comforts, like air-conditioned barracks with spring mattresses on bed frames, DVD players, hot water showers, and porcelain toilets. And he was appalled by the luxuries: a computer lab, a phone bank, a basketball court, coffee shops, and convenience stores, just like the post exchange in Alaska. At the chow hall, soldiers could have all the food they wanted, any time they wanted, free of charge. "I'm looking at this, and people are complaining to me that life is so hard over here. I'm going, 'Are you serious?'"

Rules on FOB Sharana could be absurd, requiring that soldiers wear reflective belts over camouflage uniforms, shave before entering the chow hall, and keep their pockets buttoned and their boots bloused at all times. The American logistics system, after eight years, could accomplish minor miracles—like transporting weekly steak and lobster dinners to one of the most dangerous and inaccessible locations in the world. Yet there remained the question, asked from both the bottom and the top: What good was that incredible network, which brought in everything American soldiers and contractors needed, if they couldn't win the war?

Bergdahl's first night at FOB Sharana, his platoon was sent out. They were on duty as the quick reaction force (QRF) ready to roll out the gate if anyone outside the wire got into trouble. Bergdahl doesn't remember the exact details of the QRF mission, but he knows he was a "little overwhelmed." He'd only just arrived when the call came, his sergeants yelling, "We're leaving now! You're on patrol with us." The mission was uneventful—no firefights or explosions—but it left a strong impression. Dangerous or not, it was his first combat mission, and he got almost everything wrong. He had forgotten to put fresh batteries in his night vision goggles. When the QRF convoy stopped, his squad leader ordered him out of the mine-resistant, ambush-protected armored vehicle (MRAP, pronounced "em-rap") to check and clear culverts of IEDs, he obliged, even though he had no idea what he was doing and couldn't see. When the squad leader told him to hurry up, Bergdahl thought his leadership was reckless. It was only then, outside the wire, in a combat zone, that he realized he was afraid and unprepared.

A FEW WEEKS into Bergdahl's deployment, 2nd Platoon received another QRF call. A platoon had hit a bomb near Omna, a district on a high plateau in central Paktika. Omna was east across the valley from the Taliban-dominated town of Yahya Khel, a way station southeast of FOB Sharana, accessible only by a thin dirt road up steep mountain switchbacks. No one had been hurt in the blast, but the platoon couldn't tow their hulking MRAP down the switchbacks with just a tow bar or rope—they needed a wrecker, a tow truck on steroids. The Army normally hired local Afghans for that kind of work. But Bergdahl's platoon was ordered to escort a wrecker to Omna, load up the damaged vehicle, and return it to Sharana. On the way up the switchbacks, they hit another bomb in the road. No one was killed, but now two vehicles were disabled on a mission that was rapidly bogging down.

When 2nd Platoon finally reached the initial bomb site, the MRAP wouldn't fit on the wrecker and they wound up spending six days on the mountain road trying to find a solution. They were sleeping five men to a truck, ran out of food and water, and had to be resupplied by a low-altitude airdrop. What should have been a routine six-hour mission had turned into a tortured week-long ordeal. Eventually a team of mechanics arrived and cut the MRAP into metal chunks with acetylene torches, and 2nd Platoon returned to base.

The breakdown in Omna had given the Taliban plenty of time to set traps and lie in ambushes on the convoy's likely routes back to the FOB as they crawled home. The Americans were predictable that way. A Taliban triggerman remotely detonated a bomb buried in the road, blowing up the explosive ordnance disposal (EOD) team's truck. Again, no fatalities, but the explosion was the signal for more Taliban lying in wait to attack—a classic ambush. The disabled EOD vehicle was stuck in the kill zone.

Bergdahl heard gunfire and the distinctive *pop-whiz* of rocket-propelled grenades as they flew past his bulletproof window. It was both exciting and terrifying: armor-piercing bullets burned through the MRAP's quarter-inch steel plates. The gunner in Bergdahl's vehicle tried to return fire with his .50-caliber machine gun, but it malfunctioned, and Bergdahl passed him his SAW. Even though there was no way to shoot back from inside the truck, he felt vulnerable without his weapon. This, then, was Bergdahl's first taste of combat: sitting useless in a million-dollar, up-armored, mine-resistant vehicle, watching through the portholes as his comrades tried to push the EOD truck out of the kill zone while returning fire and counterattacking in a maneuver the soldiers knew as Battle Drill Four: React to Ambush. Then, they heard hope from above: Close Air Support (CAS), the reason Americans rarely lost a long firefight in Afghanistan. Cuting their losses, the Taliban retreated back into the countryside.

But the day could always get worse, and it did. Returning to base after their week outside the wire, exhausted but still coming down from the adrenaline high of their firefight, 2nd Platoon was greeted at the gate by their battalion commander, Lieutenant Colonel Clint Baker. The first thing he noticed was the stubble under their nylon chinstraps. "What, you couldn't shave?" Baker demanded. Bergdahl was incredulous. This was Baker's leadership? After their harrowing mission, in which any one of them could have died, how hard was it to say, "Good job out there"? The soldiers wanted to park their trucks, clean their weapons, use a real toilet, eat, sleep, shower, check email, or call home, but Sergeant First Class Hein passed down the first order from Baker: Before doing anything else, the soldiers would shave.

FIVE

OP MEST

Lieutenant Colonel Clint Baker faced his own pressures. His battalion, Task Force 1 Geronimo, reported to Task Force Yukon, which was responsible for all operations in RC East, one of the military's five regional commands. Task Force Yukon was commanded by Colonel Michael Howard, who ran his sector of the war as a sort of regional CEO, making his decisions after consulting his board of directors: civilian representatives from the United States Agency for International Development (USAID), the Agriculture Department, the State Department, the Education Department, and every branch of the military.

Also at Howard's disposal were Human Terrain teams, anthropologists working for the Army to map the tribal and ethnographic structures of Afghanistan; and provincial reconstruction teams (PRTs), a hybrid military, State Department, and USAID development organization. Beyond even these, Howard had law enforcement liaisons from the FBI and DEA, bomb specialists, special operations troops, intelligence teams to help with targeting and detainee ops, and military THT units—tactical human intelligence teams—who kept an incentive drawer of illicit goodies for Afghan sources (liquor and porn were especially popular). It was all ad hoc—they'd never been organized quite this way before. Howard seemed to see all and know all, and he used that perceived omniscience to intimidate his younger officers, who called him Sauron, though never to his face.

But despite all those resources, the Taliban in Paktika were proving maddeningly difficult to subdue. With orders from Howard to improve security, Baker directed his subordinates in Blackfoot Company to send out platoons and build an outpost nineteen miles southwest of FOB Sharana along a well-trafficked smuggling route. The idea was to man it with a combination of U.S. and Afghan troops who would intercept the arms, explosives, and Taliban foot soldiers that streamed in from the Pakistani border, roughly fifty miles to the east. They would establish security, identify the Taliban, separate them from the local population, and show the villagers that even here in Paktika they were better off with Karzai and the Americans in charge. With security thus established, the Americans would turn it over to the Afghans to run by themselves. First the small observation posts (OPs); then the FOBs like Sharana, Chapman, and Salerno; then the country. In the spring of 2009, with more than thirty thousand fresh troops on their way, this was counterinsurgency on the ground. This was the newfound commitment to what Obama called "the good war."

That had been the hope. The reality was that Bergdahl and 2nd Platoon had been ordered to dig bunkers for the new OP in what was clearly an Afghan cemetery, and no one seemed to care. The second, more shocking reality came when Bergdahl saw Lieutenant Colonel Baker kick one of the graves in a fit of rage. Bergdahl had already made his mind up about his battalion commander, and he shouldn't have been watching him anyway. He should have been pulling security for the other guys working in the heat on the desolate hillside. The Army named it OP Mest for one of the Taliban-controlled villages nearby: Mest Malak. Only the Army would pick this spot for an OP. The men dreaded staying there, and after a few rotations, some of the guys in Bergdahl's platoon started calling it OP Joke.

To Bergdahl, everything in Afghanistan felt like a bad joke, starting with Baker himself. He commanded the entire battalion, and here he was throwing a tantrum like an angry child. He was screaming at Sergeant Greg Leatherman, getting right up in his face, chest to chest, for an old-fashioned Army ass chewing. An Afghan National Police (ANP) commander stood by his side, and Bergdahl thought Baker was putting on a little show for him. The show ended when he kicked the grave so hard it sent rocks clattering down and little clouds of moon dust puffing up like smoke from the sun-baked desert floor.

The platoon shared the OP with the dead, and when they didn't feel like walking down to the latrine, some soldiers would shit between the graves. The cemetery was little more than piles of stones harvested by leather-skinned old men who drove battered trucks around the desert, combing for scrap. The families of the dead stacked stones around the bodies in rectangular mounds and hung multicolored flags and rags from sticks to mark the area, like flowers in a place where nothing grows. These people have been fighting off foreign armies for generations, Bergdahl thought, and now they have to watch Americans desecrate their graves.

The Army either didn't understand or didn't care what message it sent by building the OP on a sacred graveyard. As soon as they got there, the villagers complained. They told the interpreters, young Afghan men with American haircuts and American names like "John" and "Jack," to tell the soldiers that this was a problem. The men didn't like it, but the chain of command wanted this outpost built on this exact spot, graves be damned. The bad mojo might have been worthwhile if the OP were in a good tactical location, but it wasn't. It was fully exposed to gunfire, mortars, and rockets. The natural cover provided by the surrounding hills and wadis worked both ways; there were huge blind spots where anyone could sneak on, or off, the base.

To control the high ground and fortify the position, Sergeant Leatherman ordered his men to dig a bunker big enough for six men and their gear, high on the hill. It was early June, and it was hot. One soldier from another platoon had already been evacuated for heat sickness. Leatherman's men were drenched in sweat as they shoveled the dirt and filled the prefabricated blast barriers with sand. After checking with the sergeants on the other side of the hill and hearing no objections, he let them shed their gear and strip down to T-shirts and uniform trousers. Rules were looser on the frontier.

Baker was in a convoy driving toward the hill when he spotted them: 2nd Platoon, Blackfoot Company, 1/501. This wasn't the first time he had seen these particular young men behaving like jackasses on his watch. Second Platoon was his problem child. Not a month had passed since he had written up a bunch of them for their performance in front of a British photographer with *The Guardian*. They had been out of uniform then too, lazing around and complaining about the mission in a video broadcast around the world. In several photos, one of the men—Bergdahl—was smoking a pipe.

To Baker, *The Guardian* incident was a symptom of deeper problems. If soldiers couldn't do basic things right, how would they do the more complex tasks the war demanded? How could they win the respect of the Afghan people and carry out the more nuanced requirements of the counterinsurgency mission? Baker handed out Field-Grade Article 15s to the two sergeants in charge, the most severe punishment he could administer shy of a court-martial. He told them that their conduct had endangered the entire mission and was no different from the child rapists who had destroyed the Army's reputation at My Lai. Baker thought this was a clear message, and he thought it was received.

And yet here he was, looking up at the hilltop OP in disbelief. According to his own command sergeant major, 2nd Platoon was the worst unit in the entire battalion. Now they were disregarding his authority again, dressed in a mishmash of half uniforms, none of them in body armor or helmets. Baker ordered the convoy to stop, invited the ANP commander and his men to join him, and charged the hill. Bergdahl knew that whatever was about to happen wasn't his business. But as Baker stormed and raged, he couldn't look away. Baker finished screaming, turned his back, paced and trembled with a terrible rage, and then wound up and kicked the grave with such force that his boot sailed chest high and the pile of stones went tumbling down.

Bergdahl saw the young ANP soldiers turn to their own commanding officer with looks of shock.

"What're you doing!?" the Afghan officer shouted at Baker. "This is a graveyard!"

It made no sense to Bergdahl. Had Baker intended to kick the grave to make a point? Defiling the dead was low on the list of ways to win friends and influence people. And if so, he proved that the COIN doctrine and the "cultural training" they had been force-fed since Alaska was bullshit. All of it. The whole idea that they were there to "help people," the idea he had signed up for, was a scam. A grave is sacred in any culture. A life here is worth the same as a life back home. To desecrate a grave as an American, as the people who were sent here to spread liberty and fight oppression, was incomprehensible to Bergdahl. Which raised the second possible explanation: that Baker was not in control of his actions, unfit for leadership, and quite possibly insane. He was going to get them all killed, Bergdahl thought. Someone needed to do something.

BACK AT FOB SHARANA, Bergdahl sent a coy Facebook message to Kayla Harrison. Her mother, Kim, was listed as his next of kin, to be notified if anything happened to him. If it did, he asked, could she please keep her mother calm?

"Actions may become . . . odd," he wrote. "No red flags. I'm good. But plans have begun to form, no time line yet. . . . I love you! Bowe." He had been in Afghanistan less than a month.

The message worried Kayla. She wrote back that she would do her best if and when that time came. "Exactly what kind of plans are you thinking?" On June 9, Bergdahl responded with a string of code intended to avoid triggering keywords—emails to and from soldiers in Afghanistan were scanned by both software and human analysts for violations of operational security, or OPSEC.

"l1nes n0 t g00 d h3rE. tell u when 1 ha ve a si coure 1ine about pl/-\ ns," he wrote. Kayla told him there was still time for thinking and asked him not to do anything "stupid or pointless."

"You know I plan better than that," he responded. On June 14, Bergdahl requested an Eagle Cash debit card, the kind used by soldiers in Afghanistan at restaurants, coffee shops, and stores on base, and to withdraw money. On June 20, he took out three hundred dollars, and went to the on-base bazaar, which permitted Afghan merchants to sell trinkets, pirated DVDs, clothing, and blankets to GI's. He bought a *shalwar kameez*, a long flowing shirt and loose-fitting pants, and a typical Afghan headscarf. The next day, he sent another email to Kayla. "How far will a human go to find their complete freedom?" he mused. "For one's freedom, do they have the right to destroy the world to gain it?" On June 26, two days before the platoon rotated back to OP Mest for the final time before handing control to the Afghans, Bergdahl visited the FOB post office and mailed his laptop, journals, some books, and a Kindle to Kim. He followed this with a long email to his father's account for both his parents to read. He didn't mention the Article 15 he'd received for appearing out of uniform in *The Guardian*, but it was clearly front and center in his thoughts: Bergdahl called Baker "a conceited old fool" and worried about the fact that the good sergeants, like Leatherman, had lost their jobs. He continued:

"In the U.S. Army you are cut down for being honest . . . but if you are a conceited brown nosing shit bag you will be allowed to do whatever you want, and you will be handed your higher rank. . . . The system is wrong. I am ashamed to be an american. And the title of U.S. soldier is just the lie of fools. The U.S. Army is the biggest joke the world has to laugh at. It is the army of liars, backstabbers, fools, and bullies." As a signoff, he wrote, "I am sorry for everything."

His parents were immediately worried; it sounded like Bowe was coming unspooled.

Before his platoon left for OP Mest, Bergdahl wrote more emails to his friends back home.

"Hey there may be a shift in events at some point," he wrote in a June 27 email to Monica Lee, a childhood friend from church. They'd grown closer after he joined the Army, and she'd become a sort of long-distance, wartime sweetheart. She had sent a letter and photo of herself to him at Fort Richardson before he deployed. "Its awesome. I love it. I love you. I will Carry it with me," he wrote. To Lee, he came closest to articulating his plan: "Fear is only in your head, and it only has power over your mind if you allow it. I am going out of the wire again, but this time i am not sure when i'll get back and online to talk to you. There are things i need to do, though this system i am in will not let [it] happen. This problem will be resolved. The afghan people do need help. Conceited soldiers from a failing country is not the answer."

That night at FOB Sharana, he posed a question to Sutton and Coe: "What do you think would happen if I walked off towards the mountains near Omna?" He told them he wanted to walk to India. He would go through Pakistan. It was about fifty miles to the border. He could do it. He said he was going to do it.

Coe didn't take it seriously. Escape fantasies were one of the platoon's favorite topics. No one wanted to be dodging bombs in Paktika Province; they all would rather have been somewhere else. They schemed novel ways out. A guy could shoot himself in the foot, or run into the aid station with a grenade and pretend to have gone insane. Coe and Sutton had heard this sort of thing from Bergdahl before. "We thought he was just venting," Coe said. "It was like, 'Whatever, you're full of shit. You're venting, you're bitching, and you're releasing stress.'"

On June 28, Bergdahl rode with his new lieutenant, John Billings, and three other soldiers from the FOB to the OP. They arrived at Mest, unpacked their gear, and settled in for their last rotation. Bergdahl asked Specialist Shane Cross, who had been issued a sidearm in addition to his heavy machine gun, what would happen if his M9 Beretta pistol went missing. Cross told him the consequences would be severe.

Lieutenant Fancey had been removed from command for less. Bergdahl had thought about taking it with him, but decided then to leave Cross's 9mm pistol alone.

On the night of June 29, Bergdahl and Coe went up the hill for a meal with the Afghan soldiers. Other guys in the platoon blanched at the thought, but Bergdahl made a point of eating with the Afghans whenever possible. Bergdahl felt that Coe—who had grown up as a Christian missionary in the jungles of Northern Venezuela, nearly three hours by bush plane to anything resembling a town—intuitively understood why it was important. It wasn't for the okra stew; it was both the right thing to do and a commonsense precaution. The Afghans had been there before 2nd Platoon arrived, and they would be there after they were gone. Bonding with them could prevent the next not-so-accidental "green on blue" case, the Pentagon's term for the epidemic of Afghan soldiers and policemen killing their American allies. Plus, the Afghans at OP Mest were mostly friendly; the platoon had given them nicknames like "Ice Cream" and "Crazy Eyes."

Seven years later, the dinner burned into Coe's memory. He remembered the menu: tomatoes, okra, bread and cucumbers, onions, pickles, and fish from an aquafarm in Sharana. Later that night, Bergdahl gave him a memory card filled with photographs. The pictures were mostly of Alaskan and Afghan skies, clouds, sunrises, and sunsets. Bergdahl was "obsessed with the sky," Coe recalled. It had seemed like the end of a normal day, or as normal as Coe could expect five months into his tour. As a late deployer, Bergdahl had been there just five weeks.

BEFORE HE STEPPED OVER the wire and into the quiet dark of the Paktika night, Private First Class Bowe Bergdahl had a plan. As he saw it, there was an epidemic of moral corruption in Task Force Geronimo. He had seen NCOs routinely violate their oath. The battalion commander appeared to be unstable and seemed to care more about his men's shaving habits than their safety. Orders for the next suicide mission could come any day. Bergdahl wasn't the only man in the platoon who worried about Baker. But no one cared. The other guys were happy eating Burger King and sitting around the PlayStation back at the FOB. Something had to be done, and if Bergdahl didn't act, no one would.

More than three years had passed since his stress-induced breakdown in Coast Guard boot camp. Since then, he had built himself back up with a self-designed regimen of mental, physical, and spiritual training. That failure in New Jersey was a private matter he didn't discuss with anyone, and with each new day of training he pushed it deeper into a locked compartment in his mind until Seaman Recruit Bergdahl, the one who couldn't hack it in the Coast Guard, no longer existed. Drill Sergeant Olivera had seen the results at Fort Benning. Bowe's success in infantry school at Sand Hill told him that he was right to trust himself and his instincts, and that his family and everyone else who doubted him were wrong. He was a natural soldier, a warrior-monk uniquely suited for this life and bound for even greater things.

Bergdahl had also become impatient with the pace of his military career. He felt that his advanced soldier skills were being squandered pulling guard shifts in a regular infantry unit. After Fort Benning, Fort Irwin, and Fort Richardson, he was eager to attend Special Forces selection. He would easily pass it, of course, and then move into the yearlong Special Forces training at Fort Bragg known as the Q Course. The Green Beret he would earn after Q Course was the next step on the climb he envisioned for himself. Army Special Forces were good, but they were not the most elite. The SEALs back in Mississippi may have blacklisted him from BUD/S, but he could also try out for Delta Force or pass selection for Task Force Orange or another black ops unit. For now, he was stuck in the regular infantry, wasting his time. He'd gone out on patrols and earned the "mark of a man," as Army recruiting posters described the Combat Infantryman's Badge (CIB), for the firefight near Omna. It was a fraction of what a typical infantryman in Afghanistan did over the course of a yearlong deployment, and he had complained in earlier messages to his parents and in bitch sessions with the guys in the platoon that he was ready for more action.

But in those same emails home, he was also repulsed by what he had seen. The war he had been sold was a lie, he thought, a con spun from the desire in the American heart to spread freedom and liberate the tyrannized peoples of the world. *De oppresso liber*—to free the oppressed—that was the Special Forces motto, written on the metal crests every Green Beret wore above his left eye. That had been Bergdahl's hope too, and he had a role to play in the epic he had written in his imagination and signed up for at the recruiting office. But then he saw his deployment for what it really was: not just lame but perverse. Here, it was normal for soldiers to mock and ridicule the Afghans they had been sent to help, and his own battalion commander had desecrated a graveyard to make himself look tough. Here, the U.S. military provided cash, weapons, and support to corrupt strongmen. This wasn't the war story Bergdahl had written for himself, so he decided to write his own.

"I had to do something," he confessed to Dahl in the Army office building more than five years later in Texas. "Happily with my ignorance, from a young man's mind and my imagination, I came up with a fantastic plan."

The plan wasn't complicated. He had run the simulations in his mind, visualizing and scrutinizing every step and potential outcome until he knew it would work. Along with wilderness survival and knife fighting, he told Dahl, running simulations was one of his most prized skills. He would leave OP Mest at night, when most of the men were asleep or on guard shift. He knew the gaps in security and would slip off near the blind spot in front of OP4, climb the hill through the graveyard, drop down the other side, and run through the moon dust to FOB Sharana. It was about eighteen miles, roughly the same distance from his parents' house in Croy Creek Canyon to Strega. He'd been on tougher solo treks at the same altitude in Idaho, and since arriving in-country, he'd kept in shape at FOB Sharana by running laps for miles along the fence line by the airfield. Distance and terrain weren't going to be a problem.

The Army would say he was missing. But he had studied the maps and would have his compass and would not get lost. Before daybreak, he would find a place to hide, and when night fell again he would finish the run to Sharana's front gate. He planned for every possible risk he could imagine. He'd bought his disguise, and he had three hundred dollars in cash, split between afghanis and U.S. dollars. If a Kuchi nomad spotted him in the desert, he would buy the man's silence. Bergdahl had never worn a disguise to blend into a population of nomadic herdsmen, and he had never paid a bribe, but he knew from books and movies that these tactics would work.

He knew the radio call would go out when they noticed he was gone. He had learned the term at one of his first rotations at Mest, when they were digging out the first guard tower bunkers. One bunker, which they later abandoned, was in a terrible location, out of sight from the rest of the unit but in clear view of the village and the Taliban fighters who overnighted there. During radio checks, soldiers in the isolated, exposed, and ultimately pointless bunker would identify themselves as "OP DUSTWUN."

Bergdahl, new to country, had asked his sergeant what DUSTWUN meant. It's the code for when a soldier goes missing, Sergeant Louis told him, like an Amber Alert for a war zone. A DUSTWUN was no localized event. The call would go from Mest to Sharana to every FOB and OP across Eastern Afghanistan, lighting up the vast network of American installations and triggering a massive reaction, not only within the Army, but in the Navy, the Marines, and the Air Force too. Every node in the military matrix would go on high alert.

Bergdahl didn't press Sergeant Louis for more details. He grokked the scope of the thing immediately. A DUSTWUN was a rare thing in the military—a "flash" signal that went straight to the top, bypassed blockages in the chain of command, and could not be ignored, suppressed, or covered up. It reminded Bergdahl of a familiar idea, similar to what he had struggled to explain to friends in Idaho years ago and then rediscovered again in the character of John Galt in Ayn Rand's *Atlas Shrugged*, which he had brought with him to Afghanistan. With the DUSTWUN, he could bring the great and terrible gears of the machine grinding to a halt.

He would show up to the FOB unarmed and unharmed, an instant Army legend. They might think he was crazy, but they would respect what he had done and hear his concerns. "I'm not saying anything until I see a general," he would say to the FOBBITs at the gate. The Army would have no choice but to investigate how he slipped off the OP without anyone noticing. A general would come see him, and Bergdahl would explain everything—that Baker needed a full psychological evaluation, that the Task Force Geronimo chain of command was rotten through and through. They would purge the unit. Any officer or NCO unable to carry out their responsibilities and meet the leadership standard set by Drill Sergeant Olivera would be relieved of duty.

He assumed there would be a price to pay. They would probably throw him in prison. He didn't think they would charge him with desertion. Deserters run away from danger, not into it. They might strip his rank with another Article 15, he thought, but as a private first class he didn't have much rank to lose. He might live or he might die, but he would *act*, and such were the sacrifices that warriors had made throughout history. He wasn't too concerned about the personal costs. Any punishment the Army dealt was better than looking down at the blood-clotted moon dust and the mangled pieces of what used to be Sutton or Coe, knowing he could have done something.

The day after he shipped his things home, he sent an email from Sharana to a group of friends in Idaho with the subject line: "who is John Galt?"—the mantra of Rand's book. "It is not the being of value who fails the system. It is the system that has failed the man," Bergdahl wrote, and then declared:

For man should not stoop to fit the system, but the system should be made and remade, to fit the man who holds value as worth. I will serve no bandit, nor liar, for i know John Galt, and understand. This life is too short to serve those who compromise value, and its ethics. I am done compromising.

ACT II.

LOST

SIX

DUSTWUN

June 30 couldn't come soon enough for 2nd Platoon. The men just wanted to make it back to Sharana, where they could finally shower, rest, and relax. Third Platoon would rotate in to replace them at OP Mest and then the miserable and isolated base would be turned over to the Afghans to run on their own. The two units switched off every three or four days, according to a schedule designed by battalion headquarters to be patternless and unpredictable. Under ideal conditions, driving fast on Route Audi—the Army named routes in the area after cars, among them Audi, Dodge, and Viper—without stopping to check culverts for hidden bombs, it was possible to make it from OP Mest to the gates of FOB Sharana in less than an hour. But conditions were never ideal; Route Audi was a magnet for Taliban bombs, and the fourteen-ton MRAPs were too big and heavy to maneuver with any speed along the mountain switchbacks and dry riverbed wadis that Lieutenant Billings preferred as alternate routes. On the afternoon of June 29, Billings canceled the next morning's foot patrol from Mest and directed his men to focus on packing up and clearing out.

Billings was a career soldier, a by-the-book officer, and a prior-service NCO. His men liked him, and his commanders trusted him to get the misfit 2nd Platoon back on track. Billings considered every step outside the wire a potential combat operation. He was conditioned to look out for his men's well-being before his own, and he did not send out patrols every day. If the weather wasn't right or if the men were tired from the grueling work of building up the fortifications at the OP during the day, he would call it off. The village of Yahya Khel, a known enemy safe haven and home to the Afghan government's district center in a mud-walled compound off the main bazaar, was less than three miles away, but Billings had not yet sent his men there on patrol.

Inside the wire, Billings expected the men to stick to the buddy system they had all learned in basic training. If his soldiers wanted to visit the Afghan detachments at the top of the hill, as Bergdahl and Coe did most nights, they would only do so with another member of their squad, and they would stay close, never more than six feet of space between them at any time. The contained, Americans-only section of the hillside base was the one area where Billings was lax. The men were always within his line of sight or earshot, and soldiers were free to walk alone to the latrines or the burn pit, where garbage smoldered at all hours.

That night, Bergdahl pulled guard duty as he always did. He stood in the turret of Billings's truck, and with his night vision goggles he scanned the darkness of the Paktika countryside. Behind him the men rested—the guys he trusted and liked, and the guys he didn't. There were Full and Gerleve from Texas, Coe and Sutton from Michigan, and the private first class who smelled bad but was so loyal and kind everyone liked him anyway. That night, Billings reported in to his immediate superior as he did every night: "Green One Up," he wrote to Captain Silvino Silvino, company commander at the Blackfoot Tactical Operations Center (TOC) at FOB Sharana: All personnel and equipment were present. Captain Silvino passed the personnel and equipment reports from his four platoons to Lieutenant Colonel Clint Baker, who compiled them with reports from his four companies and passed those on to his superior, Colonel Michael Howard at FOB Salerno. It was a basic function of the chain of command and a key part of the leader's task list—a combination inventory and attendance roster reported every morning and every night until the compiled statistics reached the senior officer in Afghanistan, General Stanley McChrystal.

Bergdahl returned to his shelter from his guard shift around 2130 hours. He organized a kit of essentials by the light of his headlamp. Water: a CamelBak bladder filled with enough water to last him a day or two. Food: some nuts from a bag of trail mix and a sealed packet of chicken meat from an MRE. Tools: knives and his compass; his digital camera and journal; and for inspiration some old torn-out journal entries, a couple of poems, and a newspaper clipping about a man who set a world record for sailing around the world alone. Bergdahl knew that three or four soldiers, at most, would be awake, along with a roving sergeant of the guard who supervised their rotations. The times and manning of the guard shifts varied by the day, scribbled out in marker on a piece of waterproof Rite in the Rain notebook paper. Every hour, the soldier on guard in Billings's truck would check the FBCB2—the Blue Force Tracker, a networked GPS, map, and text messaging system that commanders used to track and communicate with all of their units in real time.

His things in order, Bergdahl shut off his headlamp and waited. The guys would assume he was in his tent for the rest of the night. He would slip off by OP4 and walk to the top of the hill, where the Afghan guards didn't have night vision goggles. No one would be looking for him until dawn.

COE WAS IN HIS bivouac sack and sleeping bag when Cross shook him awake.

"Hey, you seen Bergdahl?" Cross whispered.

Coe knew instantly. "He's gone," he said. "He's fucking gone."

He told Cross to go check the latrine, and he radioed up to the guard tower at OP1, closer to the Afghan detachment. Maybe Bergdahl went for some predawn chai, he told himself. But in his gut, Coe already knew his friend had done something insane. Neither he nor Cross wanted to break this news to leadership, so they played a round of rock-paper-scissors to decide. Coe lost and woke up his sergeants with the update and his recollections of Bergdahl's bizarre vows.

They checked Bergdahl's hooch and found his weapons and sensitive items lined up in a neat row on his cot, as if ready for inspection. His machine gun was there—clean, with infrared sight and daytime optics still attached. Next to it were his night vision goggles, wrapped neatly in a T-shirt, snug in their pouch. The light of dawn was cresting over the Shinkay Hills to the east as Coe and the others woke up Lieutenant Billings. He was groggy; he'd been asleep for less than an hour after pulling his own guard shift. Billings was still new to the platoon, and he was always expecting the guys to pull some pranks. He thought it was a joke, but when he looked at his men gathered around, no one was smiling.

An image of Bergdahl flashed in his mind. He had just seen him and waved to him the night before. This must be a mistake. He told the men to go through the entire OP and systematically check every place someone could hide—check the latrines and the burn pit, make sure he's not stuck under or inside a vehicle. He sent a team up to the bunker at OP1 to check with the Afghans, and then he went to talk to the Afghan commander himself. It was a fruitless search. Bergdahl wasn't in the latrine, he wasn't with the Afghans, he wasn't passed out in a half-filled Hesco. There was no trace of him.

Billings was in shock. This was not a prank, or a drill, or a scenario in a war game at NTC. He had to report the situation to Silvino at Sharana, but he didn't know what to say. He climbed into the passenger seat of his MRAP, where the Blue Force Tracker's display blinked back at him. Sergeant First Class Hein stood by the door, watching as Billings pecked at the rubberized, waterproof keyboard. Six months earlier, one of Hein's young soldiers had been killed in a car accident on his way home for Christmas. That had been bad enough. Losing a private here, with nothing but Taliban villages in every direction, was unthinkable.

Staring at the draft of his message on the Blue Force Tracker, Billings paused. He couldn't fathom what he was about to report. Bergdahl never stood out as a problem. He was quiet, but he was also a fitness stud, a hard worker, and if anything, Billings thought, one of the platoon's most reliable soldiers.

"Alright, I'm getting ready to send this message," he said to Hein. "Is there anything else I need to say?"

Hein shook his head. "Go ahead and send it, sir. You should have sent it ten minutes ago."

IN THE YEARS SINCE his disappearing act, several versions of Bergdahl's walkabout and capture have been presented as fact in government reports, in the news media, on the internet, and in the military's rumor mill. The Eclipse Group, a private intelligence firm under contract to the Department of Defense, reported to their bosses at ISAF Headquarters that Bergdahl, despite his lifelong straightedge reputation, was either high on hashish or looking to score some when he was lured by rogue Afghan policemen away from the base; they justified spreading this purported information on the grounds that it devalued the hostage and would make it easier to negotiate a trade. Blackfoot Company veterans heard similar rumors. Some Taliban fighters would claim that they raided the OP, found Bergdahl squatting in the latrines, and kidnapped him there. The first official Taliban story released to Western media on July 2 was that Bergdahl had been captured while drunk and lagging behind a patrol.

In his sworn statement more than five years later, Bergdahl said that he exited OP Mest unassisted shortly after midnight. He walked over a plastic crate that the Afghan soldiers used as a makeshift bridge over the razor wire separating the two sections of the base and that 2nd Platoon had neglected to remove overnight. From there, he walked into a shallow gully that he knew was a blind spot for the guards in the bunker at OP4. If his comrades were inattentive, as Bergdahl assumed they would be, the blind spot was even bigger. He passed through it unnoticed and worked his way to the top of the hill, where some of the Afghan soldiers heard him. He saw their flashlight beams pierce the dark, and he knew there was no turning back. He hadn't brought a radio. Trigger-happy Afghans sat in the guard towers smoking charras, jumping at shadows, sometimes burning though whole magazines of ammo firing at stray dogs that came to the OP looking for scraps. They might mistake him in the dark for an enemy sapper. Trying to sneak back on base was now more dangerous than pressing on.

He started down the backside of the hill toward the village of Mest Malak, an enemy way station where Taliban troops bivouacked in private compounds for a night of rest before moving on. He skirted the edges of the village, crossed through an alleyway, and then sped away from any buildings he could make out in the darkness on a parallel track to the north-by-northeast arc of Route Audi. He had his camera and his disguise and his bribe money in his pockets, along with his water, food, and tools. He would tell Major General Dahl that it took him about twenty minutes to fully appreciate the gravity of his situation. Bowe slowed to a walk.

"You just gotta stay in the game," his father would say. He had said it when they last saw each other in Croy Canyon at Christmas. It was a family mantra from his grandfather's days as an all-star running back for the UCLA Bruins. Don't get in your own head, it meant. Be alert to what's happening around you. Always know the score. The score, right now, was not in Bergdahl's favor. He was AWOL in a war zone, and if he made it to Sharana, the Army was going to come down on him hard. It struck him that he needed to prove himself beyond the plan's basic elements. He needed something more—a piece of intelligence or information collected outside the wire, something he could parlay into leniency. He thought about other soldiers who had been in situations like his own: the Office of Strategic Services' (OSS) Jedburgh teams, men and women who had parachuted into France to organize insurgencies against the Nazis with nothing but their courage, skills, and savvy. The

OSS had been Special Forces and CIA before Special Forces and CIA even existed. They didn't have night vision or GPS. He thought about the snipers sent into the Vietnamese jungle. They were told to do a job and they got it done. They succeeded by adjusting their mission plans as necessary. He needed to adjust his.

Bergdahl changed directions and went back toward Route Audi. If he could do some scout work and collect information about the greatest threat 2nd Platoon faced—IEDs—maybe he could change his circumstances again. He needed to stay calm, use his skills, and get lucky. He might spot a Taliban team planting bombs in the night, track them from a distance, and see where they stored their explosives. He would take pictures, draw a map of the spot. When he brought this irrefutable intelligence to the general on FOB Sharana, the Army would have no choice but to forgive him.

More than five years later, he marveled at the simplicity of it. "Stupid actions. Stupid young man," he told Dahl. "I had always been a failure. I knew the Army. I knew weapons. I knew soldiers. I knew how to do that. This was my chance to prove I wasn't just a failure."

The old plan was to stay on flat ground, hide during the day, and run again at night. The new plan required sneaking around the hills and gulches where the Taliban hid waiting to plant their bombs. He climbed to the top of a high ridge, descended, and then climbed another. After a few hours he checked his compass. He wasn't lost, but he was growing disoriented. He looked toward the night sky to find his polestar and navigate by its light.

He was still following the stars when the gray light of the approaching dawn broke over the valley. Bergdahl put on his headscarf and shalwar. He was now more than ten kilometers, or six miles, from the OP. He walked at a steady pace, and as the inky sky surrendered to the brilliant reds and yellows of daybreak, he knew his plan was failing. He was in over his head, and now he was lost. He scanned the ground for footprints or vehicle tracks, any clues in the dust. Conscious that he was now visible to anyone passing by, he focused on not looking around too much or acting suspicious. In the distance he saw a shepherd. Keep moving, he told himself. It was close to noon when he heard the motorcycles.

CAPTAIN SILVINO SILVINO was drinking his morning coffee in the Blackfoot TOC at FOB Sharana when Billings's message came through. The TOC was Silvino's domain, a concrete building wired with FM and satellite radios and a hardened computer terminal called the "Command Post of the Future," on which he could read all of his platoons' Blue Force Tracker messages in one place and keep track of their movements. On the morning of June 30, 2009, his men were spread out over five districts and twelve hundred square miles. Leading Blackfoot was a hard job, but Silvino was no amateur. He'd commanded the same company at the tail end of its 2007 Iraq deployment, the tour that had given Gabe Trollinger and Evan Vela so much grief. All told, Silvino was Blackfoot Company's commander for thirty-four months, an extraordinarily long time for a captain to spend in command of the same company. He took the job so seriously that he declined a promotion, because it would have meant moving into a staff position and leaving his men just as they headed back into combat in Afghanistan.

"Sir, you've got to take a look at this," his radiotelephone operator (RTO) said, pointing at the emergency message from 2nd Platoon on the Command Post of the Future.

"Looking for one more person. We're not up," Billings wrote.

"Check again," Silvino typed to Billings over the Blue Force Tracker. "Must be a mistake."

"Not a mistake," Billings typed back. He identified the missing soldier by his battle roster number, sending his initials and the last four digits of Bergdahl's Social Security number over the encrypted FBCB2 link. Silvino's RTO checked the battle roster and filled in the gaps.

Private First Class Bowe Bergdahl was a late deployer and somehow already missing after less than two months in-country. Silvino called in his first sergeant, his company staff, and 3rd Platoon's leadership and issued orders: Get the men and the trucks ready, have everyone mount up, do it double-time. They were going out to OP Mest.

Next, Silvino walked over to battalion headquarters, the Task Force Geronimo TOC, where most mornings he would find Lieutenant Colonel Baker barking orders at troops or briefing Colonel Howard at FOB Salerno over the satellite radio. But this morning Baker was absent, out on patrol near an outpost south of Mest called FOB Kushamond, overseeing a gravel delivery to a new OP. It was a first sergeant's work, not a typical mission for a lieutenant colonel in command of hundreds of infantrymen, but after an earlier logistics patrol that he had sent to deliver the gravel was hit by thirty-seven Taliban bombs in succession, Baker decided to accompany this one himself. Sharing the danger with the men under his command helped morale and made sure things were done right. When he left Sharana, Baker put his executive officer (XO), Major Larry Glasscock, in charge.

Glasscock looked Silvino dead in the eye when he heard the news. "You'd better be damned sure that this is what you're saying it is," Glasscock said. He knew that once the battalion activated DUSTWUN protocols, there would be no way to stop the cascade of events that followed.

"Sir, it is. Unfortunately. I'm going to go out there. We're going to look for him."

Back at OP Mest, the men of 2nd Platoon were already looking. After alerting higher headquarters, Billings called together his men and delivered the morning's mission in a quick burst briefing called a FRAGO (a fragmentary order): He needed a nine-man squad to head outside the wire and start looking for Bergdahl. Maybe a dirt farmer saw something from his dirt field and invited him in for tea. It wouldn't be much to go on, but they couldn't just sit on their hands.

They marched down the hill, skirting the edge of Route Audi, and made their way to the American-built school in the village, where they met an Afghan boy. Their interpreter, an Afghan from Baghlan Province who had taken the Americanized name of John, asked if the boy had seen an American. John was careful about phrasing the question, fearing that the news of a missing soldier would spread through the village. Who knew how many degrees of separation there were between this child and the Taliban? "A soldier went out for milk this morning," John lied. "Did you see him?"

Yes, the boy replied. He *had* seen an American. In fact, he saw an American today, as he was walking to school. He even knew the exact time: 0602. "How does he know the exact time?" Billings asked. John said a few words and the boy pulled up his sleeve to reveal a digital Casio watch strapped to his wrist. Billings thought it was strange, as such luxuries were rare in this part of Afghanistan, even for adults. But it gave him hope. Bergdahl was alive and they were on his trail. Inside the school, the students were less helpful. A preteen boy warned his classmates not to talk. "No one has seen anything," he told John. Facing a wall of adolescent silence, they moved on to another class, where John bribed them with coins from his pocket until finally another boy spoke up.

"Yes! He was there," the boy said, pointing to a spot of green in the fields away from the village. John asked the boy to describe Bergdahl. Tall, blue eyes, carrying a flashlight, the boy recalled. Did he have a gun? No, the boy said, and stopped talking, silenced by another student. The foot patrol left the school, circled through the surrounding fields, dropped in the wadi toward the intersection of Routes Audi and Dodge, and headed back to the OP with no real leads.

Billings couldn't help but think this wasn't how the morning was supposed to go. He'd planned for it as a rest period, an opportunity to organize and relax before they returned to the FOB. Now everything was chaos. On the OP, Billings's Blue Force Tracker was lit up with messages from higher headquarters, and his mind was abuzz with the implications of the clues from the Afghan school boys. He wished the children were more reliable, but he understood the Taliban's proclivity for reprisals against those who cooperated with the Americans. His commanders demanded updates, issued new orders, and when he responded, asked follow-ups that he could not answer. To Billings's growing horror, his little outpost had become the focus of his entire chain of command.

Command's eyes were already watching Billings through the orbital cameras and sensors on a Predator drone buzzing ten thousand feet overhead, call sign VOODOO—it had come on station at 11:37 a.m. The military and CIA had dozens of different unmanned aerial vehicles flying over Afghanistan with sinister names attached to bland alphanumeric designators: MQ-1 Predators, MQ-9 Reapers, RQ-7 Shadows, RQ-4 Global Hawks, and others that only a select few with high security clearances knew even existed. If a drone's designator began with an R, it was unarmed and strictly a reconnaissance platform. R drones could look but they couldn't kill. M drones were armed with the AGM-114 Hellfire (heliborne, laser, fire, and forget) missile, a weapon originally developed so gunners in AH-64 Apache helicopters could destroy Soviet tanks without exposing themselves to antiaircraft fire in the process; once locked onto its target, the Hellfire adjusted course along the way until impact. Armed or not, drones would stay overhead Mest and western Paktika for weeks.

Lieutenant Billings received his new orders: Command wanted him to set up blocking positions—essentially traffic stops, like a DUI checkpoint with fourteen-ton vehicles mounted with machine guns and grenade launchers—on Route Dodge past the graveyard. To do that, he would have to split his platoon, a security risk well outside his usual comfort zone. He was sending the men out when the first helicopter landed near his truck, coughing up a soldier who ran over to Billings and began shouting. The man was a pathfinder from the 101st Airborne Division, sent by division headquarters. Billings couldn't hear him over the roar of the rotors, but nodded along anyway before the soldier ran back to his helicopter, lifted up, and flew away.

Billings didn't know what the man had said, but he knew what it meant that he was here. The pathfinders were under the direct control of Colonel Howard's boss, Major General Curtis Scaparrotti, commander of the Combined Joint Task Force 82. If the pathfinders were already at Mest, that meant Scaparrotti had sent them. If he knew about the DUSTWUN, then that meant everyone else knew, right up to General Stanley McChrystal, who was settling into his second week on the job at ISAF Headquarters.

SEVEN

THE LOST PUPPY

It was a sunny Tuesday morning in Kabul as Major General Michael T. Flynn arrived for a meeting in one of his two new offices at ISAF Headquarters. In his previous job as director of intelligence for the Joint Staff at the Pentagon, Flynn had sat through endless meetings and briefings, which he learned to hate, and it didn't seem like Kabul would be any better. Staff officers presented classified PowerPoints, briefing slide after briefing slide, that all seemed to say the same thing: The war was going badly, the structures and strategies in place to fight it weren't working, and the Taliban were growing stronger and launching more deadly and sophisticated attacks from their sanctuary across the border in Pakistan, where U.S. troops could not venture. Nothing came from these meetings—if good ideas did emerge, they were stymied by an unending bureaucracy. "I spend 80 percent of my day, easily, fighting our own system," Flynn would tell *Rolling Stone* writer Michael Hastings in 2010.

Flynn was just two weeks into his new dual-hatted job—as both the war's senior U.S. military intelligence officer and as the director of intelligence for NATO's ISAF coalition—and he was just now developing a clear picture of the war's dysfunction, which he discussed in late-night chats and on early-morning runs with his boss, General Stan McChrystal. In March 2009, President Obama had tapped McChrystal to replace the previous commander, General David McKiernan, the first four-star general in the field relieved of duty since Harry Truman fired MacArthur during the Korean War. Obama had given McChrystal total discretion to assemble his command staff, and McChrystal had known and trusted Flynn for years, since they were paratroopers in the 82nd Airborne. They'd grown even closer over their shared deployments to Iraq, where McChrystal commanded the Joint Special Operations Command (JSOC) black ops units that included Delta Force and SEAL Team 6, and Flynn served as his senior intelligence officer. In Iraq, Flynn deepened the wild-card reputation he'd had since Operation Just Cause, the 1988 invasion of Grenada, when he'd flown his signals intelligence platoon into the fight without authorization. After the four-day operation was over, Flynn escaped punishment because he, by chance, was setting in eavesdropping positions on the coast and spotted two soldiers flailing in the Caribbean Sea. Flynn, who'd been a lifeguard and passionate cold-water surfer growing up in Rhode Island, jumped into the water and dragged the men back to the beach. Flynn's colonel admonished the young lieutenant for disobeying orders and sneaking into Grenada, but thanked him for saving the soldiers. Flynn was a good officer with the makings of an excellent leader—the kind of officer who deserved to be protected, even from himself.

Over the course of his career, Flynn demonstrated a knack for cutting against the grain of both the Army and the intelligence community, angering his civilian counterparts in the CIA and its military analog, the Defense Intelligence Agency (DIA) in the process. He kept getting promoted into better and better assignments because sometimes Flynn's brand of crazy was the only way to get things done. He was lauded for putting together the team that developed rapid-fire targeting and intelligence gathering methods for the special operations strategy that allegedly decimated al-Qaeda in Iraq during the 2006–2007 surge. There was some merit to the argument: JSOC kills included Abu Musab al-Zarqawi, the founder of Iraq's preeminent terror franchise, AQI (al-Qaeda in Iraq). Yet these oft-repeated claims that McChrystal, Flynn, and JSOC were incredibly successful in their secret war against

AQI were rarely scrutinized. Instead, politicians on both sides of the aisle repeated their praise ad nauseam as they sought any good news from a bad war that could dazzle and distract their constituents from the coffins coming into Dover Air Force Base in Delaware. The role that McChrystal and Flynn played in pacifying Iraq was further exaggerated by a breathless national security press seduced by the mystique of special operations. Al-Qaeda in Iraq was never destroyed and would eventually rebrand itself as ISIS. By the time he arrived in Afghanistan in 2009, McChrystal had a reputation as a snake eater, a killer, a tough guy who could sell the gentler aspects of the Army in Afghanistan's new old way of war: counterinsurgency.

McChrystal knew how to sell the war, but that didn't mean he could win it. Now, as the director of intelligence for ISAF, Flynn would oversee NATO and the U.S. information operations and intelligence gathering in both the acknowledged battlefield (Afghanistan) and the unofficial war in Pakistan, where only the CIA was authorized to capture and kill.

As wanting as the Pentagon was for reliable intelligence in Afghanistan, the situation in the FATA was worse. Nearly eight years after Osama bin Laden disappeared into the mountains of Tora Bora, Flynn inherited what looked to him like a dysfunctional intelligence apparatus. It was the same CIA that had lost a U-2 spy plane after it took off from a CIA airfield in Peshawar in 1960, missed the Pakistani underground nuclear tests in 1998, and failed to stop Islamabad from using nuclear scientist A. Q. Khan as a cutout for proliferating weapons-grade plutonium and nuclear technology to aspirational regimes in North Korea, Iran, and Libya. Pakistan was a mess, and Flynn believed it was predominantly CIA's fault, and that he and the Pentagon could fix it. If he could show up his CIA rivals, like Kabul Station Chief Greg Vogle, all the better.

Flynn's meeting on the morning of June 30 had been called to address these exact concerns. A retired Army colonel named Michael Furlong, now a civilian in a position funded by the Defense Intelligence

Agency, was in from San Antonio, Texas, pitching unconventional solutions in Afghanistan. Furlong had ideas that would fill the tactical intelligence gaps that bedeviled the troops on the ground. Tactical intelligence—the type that saved soldiers' lives on the battlefield, rather than the type that informed politicians of the price of barley in Bahrain—was why McChrystal's predecessor had signed Furlong on in the first place. After an American outpost in Wanat was nearly overrun in July 2008, General McKiernan had demanded new approaches. Furlong had plenty of ideas, including information operations, kill/capture campaigns, and deception operations. Furlong was just getting started with his pitch when Flynn's executive officer, Colonel Andrea Thompson, came to the door with the morning's news: A soldier was missing. It was one of the Alaska paratroopers assigned to work with the Afghan security forces in the Eastern Provinces, a twenty-three-year-old who vanished overnight from a small observation post in Paktika, leaving his weapon behind.

Their meeting had been scheduled that morning to address the sorry state of U.S. intelligence. Now that they had a fresh crisis, Flynn and Furlong formed an unlikely yin-yang duo. Flynn, who was intense, thin, and wiry verging on gaunt, woke up every morning at 0430 for five-mile runs around the ISAF compound with McChrystal. Furlong was built like a former NCAA lineman gone to seed and was perpetually patting at a pack of Marlboros in the chest pocket of his rumpled shirtsleeves. Where Flynn was all confidence and edge—like a "rat on acid," as one of his own staffers put it—Furlong had the desperate staccato delivery of a used-car salesman. McKiernan had called him, with no disrespect intended, "the fat sweaty guy."

With a mind that sparked in rapid-fire bursts, Flynn had little patience with colleagues who couldn't keep up with his bang-zoom thought processes. In Furlong, he found a man tuned to the same wavelength, and one of the best bureaucratic knife fighters the Pentagon had produced in years. In the 1980s, when Furlong was an OPFOR (opposing force) officer with the 11th Cavalry ("Ride with the Blackhorse!") at the National Training Center, he won so many mock battles in the Mojave Desert that the Army named part of Fort Irwin after him. Furlong Ridge was one of the terrain features that Private First Class Bergdahl had studied in California, a procession of linked hills that Furlong used to conceal his men as they moved into place for a counterattack. It also didn't hurt that Furlong, Flynn, and McChrystal had known each other as young lieutenants at Fort Bragg. McChrystal's brother even bought a house in North Carolina from Furlong. This was before Furlong moved into a series of strange jobs he wasn't supposed to talk about.

In the early 1980s he parlayed a yearlong tour helping out the Defense Department's end of the Russian nuclear talks into a series of odd jobs. From there, he helped rebuild a clandestine Army unit called Yellow Fruit, which served as a sort of ultra-secret Army/CIA front during the Iran-Contra affair. He then worked on the Joint Staff and in special technical operations centers, where black ops coordination cells were embedded in a general's staff in a way that ran both under the radar and under parallel command circuitry to the rest of the military. He returned to the regular Army in 1995 as the commander of a Psychological Operations unit at Fort Bragg before retiring from active duty as a colonel.

For Furlong, rank didn't really matter, because he had something better: He knew secrets and he knew the sources of those secrets. His power came from the information he knew, the information he had access to, and the sources of that information. In the intelligence community, access depended on three things: security clearances, needs to know, and higher-ranking officials approving undercover proposals. Furlong's power was ascendant. He'd come back into the federal government as a GS-15—the civilian equivalent of a colonel—after trying his hand at government contracting by running an American-backed Iraqi media company into the ground post-invasion. He did it in style, though, tooling around Baghdad in a civilian Hummer he imported from Maryland, the same model that Arnold Schwarzenegger drove to the ski slopes in Sun Valley.

When Furlong had worked for General McKiernan, he was often one of the last people to speak in daily briefings in the secure room at ISAF Headquarters in Kabul. The briefings continued according to sensitivity, and as the classification markings on the PowerPoint slides became longer, the mandatory fine print specifying the punishment for revealing the information became increasingly severe: *UNCLASS. For Official Use Only. Confidential. Secret. Top Secret: Special Compartmented Information. Special Access Programs. Top Secret: NOFORN (No Foreign Nationals). Top Secret: Five Eyes Only*, and on and on. Some information the U.S. government considered so sensitive that even the code names designating the clearance levels required to view it were classified. An information security officer in the room had access to each briefing officer's clearance level through a networked computer system called JPAS (Joint Personnel Adjudication System) and monitored who could listen to what, inviting those without the proper clearance to clear the room. As the room emptied, Furlong stayed, sometimes until only he, the general, and a trusted aide remained. After Colonel Thompson delivered the news, Flynn looked at Furlong.

"What can you do for me?" Flynn asked, the implied question lingering in the air: *What can you do for me, Mike, that the others can't, that the CIA won't?* He wanted an answer by 9:00 p.m.

"I was going to be there for the rest of the summer to build the strategy, and then this happens, my first meeting," Furlong said. He worked his phone and poured over his classified spreadsheets all afternoon. A missing U.S. soldier could have catastrophic consequences. At best, it would be a public relations nightmare that could embarrass the Army. At worst, this DUSTWUN could have political fallout that reached all the way to the White House—a captured hostage soldier could be a devastating domestic distraction and cripple McChrystal's efforts to turn the news of this war around. They needed to contain the story, find the soldier, and get back to the mission at hand.

One of Furlong's first phone calls was to another major general, this one in Tampa, Florida, at the headquarters of the Special Operations Command (SOCOM). The general had an idea of who might be able to help. He told Furlong to call a retired CIA officer, Duane "Dewey" Clarridge, who was now running a private intelligence company, the Eclipse Group, from his home in San Diego, California.

Clarridge was a living legend, aging but still in the game, receiving raw intelligence reports poolside from agents in the field and from his extensive network of contacts in foreign governments via encrypted email, which he read, collated, and sent off to his clients in the U.S. government and private industry. Furlong told Flynn he was bringing Clarridge on board. There was just one problem: Clarridge would arrive with heavy political baggage, and Furlong wanted some guidance on how to proceed.

CLARRIDGE'S BAGGAGE, as fate would have it, came from cases like Bergdahl's. While he was a CIA officer in the 1980s, hostages were at the center of his most notorious missions. Clarridge was the first chief of the newly formed CIA Counterterrorism Center in 1986, where he planned and supervised the 1987 ruse that brought Hezbollah operative Fawaz Yunis, one of Imad Mughniyeh's soldiers on the TWA 847 operation, to American justice via "extraordinary rendition"—government-sanctioned kidnappings of foreign nationals from third-party soil that even a federal appeals court had deemed within the bounds of U.S. law. When Clarridge was head of the CIA's Latin America Division, he was a key player in the Iran-Contra affair. He was investigated by Special Counsel Lawrence Walsh and indicted on seven counts for lying in his sworn testimony about his role helping Oliver North arrange a covert shipment of Hawk missiles to Iran in 1985 in a scheme designed to free American hostages in Iran and Lebanon. Clarridge was indicted but never convicted; President George H. W. Bush pardoned him in 1992 before his case went to trial.

In the written pardon statement, President Bush justified executive leniency for Clarridge and other senior officials involved in Iran-Contra on the grounds that the "common denominator" of their motivation—"whether their actions were right or wrong"—was "patriotism." He explained that no one charged with a crime related to Iran-Contra was corrupt, as none of the indicted government officials he was pardoning (which included a former secretary of defense, a former national security adviser, a senior State Department official, and two CIA executives) made any money for themselves or personally profited from the illegal weapons transfers. That part of the case was arguable (the finances were murky), but it was clear the weapons were sold at enormous markup, some of which made its way to the U.S. Treasury, while most of the profit was consumed by payments to arms-dealing middlemen contracted by the five men pardoned. Bush, a former CIA man himself, argued that Clarridge and the other indicted men had long records of service to the country, and for that reason, "all five have already paid a price—in depleted savings, lost careers, anguished families—grossly disproportionate to any misdeeds or errors of judgment they may have committed."

Seventeen years later, Clarridge was still in the game, running a network of human intelligence assets on both sides of the Afghan-Pakistan border. Eclipse was a small organization, and an unusual crew ran its intelligence-gathering operations. There was a plastic surgeon from Texas who did overseas charity work repairing cleft palates in Kurdistan and the FATA. Another Eclipse operative was Tim Lynch, a retired Marine lieutenant colonel who'd become a private security contractor in Jalalabad and maintained a blog devoted to Afghanistan called *Free Range International.* Lynch was a Marine Corps princeling—his father was a retired major general—with connections throughout the military and the FATA and a sideline smuggling alcohol through Haqqani-controlled territory. He'd once appeared on the cover of *Soldier of Fortune.* Eclipse also used a Pakistani national as what Furlong described as a NOC (Non-Official Cover Agent), and who was as capable as any CIA officer.

Flynn had no objections to Furlong's plan to recruit and pay the old spymaster for help. "I'll do this on good faith right now," Clarridge told Furlong, but reminded him that he had his needs too. "I'll get my guys working on it, and you see what you can do on the contract." Tracking Bergdahl became the priority on the pool deck of the once-in-never-out spy legend in San Diego, but that legend needed concessions. Furlong scoured his spreadsheets for the black budget money he needed. He diverted $200,000 from another contract and was ready to get Clarridge, a retired, indicted, and pardoned ex-CIA officer, on the Pentagon payroll. Furlong recalled how easy it was; he would eventually scrape together $24 million for Eclipse and his other private intelligence operations, deliberately keeping it under the threshold of $25 million that would trigger congressional oversight. Pentagon lawyers could parse whether this was technically legal. They had a soldier to find and a way to do it. It was legal enough for Furlong.

BERGDAHL SAW THE MOTORCYCLES turn off the main road. His first thought was, "There's nothing I can do." If he had a gun, if he had taken Cross's 9mm, maybe there would have been a chance to escape. But he hadn't, and there wasn't. There were five motorcycles and six guys in their early twenties with AK-47s and one with a longer rifle. They blindfolded Bergdahl, tied his hands behind his back, put him on the back of one of the bikes and drove him to a two-story home where they emptied his pockets, and refastened his wrists with heavier, tighter straps. They drove him to a village, where it sounded to Bergdahl like the whole town had turned out to see their quarry. The villagers laughed and shouted. Children threw rocks at him. Then they were moving again and his captors made what sounded like excited radio calls looking for someone who could speak English. Finally, they found someone, and met an educated man by the ruins of a mud-built compound.

"How are you?" the man asked pleasantly. Through the cracks in his blindfold, Bergdahl saw that the man wore glasses.

"I am fine," Bergdahl replied.

The man with glasses looked at Bergdahl's swollen hands and told the gunmen to loosen the straps. Bowe felt the blood flow back into his hands, which the men then wrapped in a metal chain and fixed with padlocks. The gunmen produced the wallet they'd taken from his pockets earlier and handed it to the man in glasses. He examined it, saw the Army ID card, and told them what they already knew: They had hit the jackpot. Their hostage was an American soldier.

Next came another townsite, where the elders gushed over the young captors to such a degree that Bergdahl suspected it was their home village. Here, they threw a blanket over his head and left him kneeling on the dirt outside, while the men presumably discussed the opportunities and dangers their precious cargo represented. As Bergdahl knelt in the dirt and children gathered and again threw rocks, he worked his eyebrows and cheeks to budge his blindfold. He bent his face to his knees, nudging the fabric until he could see that the village was surrounded by steep hills. Maybe he could make it.

He stood and ran, and cleared about fifty feet before a gang of men tackled him mid-sprint and began beating him. One struck him with the butt of a rifle with such force the weapon broke, wooden stock shearing from the metal receiver of the AK-47. Now knowing he would run, Bergdahl's captors took precautions. They locked him in a small room where he was watched over by an old man with a gray beard. From there they drove him to a tent, where they used a cell phone to record a ten-second video: Bergdahl, cross-legged, hands bound behind him, leaning over. It was their first proof-of-life video, saved on a SIM card, which soon after was delivered via courier to Major General Edward M. Reeder Jr. in Kabul, along with a message seeking a ransom and the release of prisoners in return for the American hostage. At dusk, the gunmen stashed Bergdahl in the bed of a pickup truck under layers of blankets. "If you move, I am going to kill you," a man said to him in broken English. "But don't worry. We take you to another place."

THE AMERICAN OPERATIONS OFFICER, Major Ron Wilson, sat cross-legged and barefoot on woven rugs at the Tribal Liaison Office in Kabul when he felt his flip phone vibrate in his pocket. He was there for the day's *jirga*, a traditional assembly where leaders gather to discuss the issues facing their tribes and make decisions by consensus and according to the codes of Pashtunwali. Wilson wore his usual work clothes for Afghanistan—jeans, a long-sleeved shirt, and a ball cap—and the tribal elders sat in a wide circle around him, wrinkled men in black turbans with flowing dark beards, and for the oldest men, white beards dyed with henna. Back home Wilson was clean-shaven. Here he grew his beard to show respect—not as long or full as the elders', but a small gesture to the people whose trust was the currency of his work.

The jirga was held in the big room on the building's second floor. Tribal leaders arrived in little yellow taxis. The larger the gathering, the farther they traveled. Some had been driving for days. After they arrived, they performed *wudu*—ablutions of their feet, faces, and hands—they prayed, and then they talked. They talked about the new school being built, the well being dug, the goat that was killed by the American bomb, the government collaborator who was killed by the Taliban. Talking was why they were there, along with the tea and the food, a generous spread of dried fruits, nuts, and sweets to fuel the hours.

Wilson was there to listen. About fifty tribal leaders were gathered, many of them Kuchis from the violent border provinces of Paktika, Paktia, and Khost—the "P2K" of ISAF parlance. There were some Zadran leaders too, recognizable by their jet-black hair and dark eyes. Based in the southeastern provinces, their tribe was one of the country's most mercurial. They shared ancient ties and kept strong ongoing relationships with the Afghan Taliban and the Haqqanis. (From 1994 to 2001, Jalaluddin Haqqani, a Zadran, had served as the minister of tribal affairs for the Taliban's Islamic Emirate.) Wilson knew the Zadrans at the jirga were "friendlies," and they seemed more interested in the hashish and scotch stashed in an upstairs room than they were in him.

Wilson stood up and walked out of the main jirga, past the pile of plastic sandals the Afghans left by the entrance, and stepped into the hallway to take the call.

"Hey, we got a lost puppy," his boss at ISAF headquarters said on the other end.

He listened to the news and peered down to the courtyard where the younger men helped with chores while their elders met upstairs. The competing smells of burnt goat fat and hashish mixed in the air. A twenty-three-year-old Army private lost near the Pakistani border was bad news. Receiving the call at the jirga, surrounded by tribal leaders from the districts where kidnapping was a thriving business—that was just good timing.

Wilson walked back into the room and got to work. He raised the subject of kidnapping for profit with the elders. Was it a problem they were familiar with? Wilson didn't mention the missing soldier; he didn't need to. The elders had an unparalleled institutional memory, and if they didn't know the answer to Wilson's questions, they would help him find someone who did. A Kuchi elder from the east told his story about how three of his own men were recently taken hostage as a moneymaking venture for a local criminal gang. When the captors killed one of them, the elder paid twenty thousand dollars apiece to save the other two. Wilson posed a hypothetical: "If an American was kidnapped in Paktika, what would happen to him?"

Wilson was joined at the jirga by Robert Young Pelton, a Canadian writer who had been traveling to Kabul since the mid-nineties, attending all manner and makeup of tribal jirgas and *shuras* (smaller, routine meetings like American town halls) and befriending everyone from foot soldiers to national power brokers. Charismatic and built like a lumberjack with a mop of salt-and-pepper hair, a musketeer goatee, and twinkling blue eyes, Pelton lived and worked like a conflict-zone wizard, appearing and reappearing over the years whenever there's trouble to document, dangerous groups to study, powerful men to chase.

Pelton was in Afghanistan for his new venture, an information subscription service called AfPax Insider, which he had launched with former CNN executive Eason Jordan. They were looking to re-create the success they had found in Baghdad with IraqSlogger, an online compendium of "Insights, Scoops, and Blunders" written by a squad of local reporters and sources they had recruited around the country during the war. But in Afghanistan, the demand for good, raw, well-sourced information was higher than it had been in Iraq. Their timing for the Kabul spinoff was not incidental; American generals had been making public complaints for years about the lack of reliable intelligence in the region. In July 2008, after the battle at Wanat, Pelton pitched AfPax to General McKiernan as the solution. AfPax launched to an insatiable audience. "We had subscribers from every venue: media, State Department, NGOs," Pelton said. According to one U.S. officer who worked in classified information operations under JSOC command in the summer of 2009, Pelton's outfit was the best source at the time for fresh, clean, unprocessed intelligence.

With Pelton and Jordan's venture thus established, Wilson was tasked by his superiors at ISAF to work as a liaison between the U.S. military and AfPax, to bridge the gap between the consumers and the purveyors of raw information in the Afghan intelligence labyrinth. The tribal leaders explained the kidnapping business model in their home provinces. They named specific individuals and villages that formed the nodes of an illicit underground ratline network that used taxicabs and safe houses to stage and move weapons, drugs, and valuable human cargo. The kidnappers would make frequent stops, never driving more than an hour or two, and they would make a predictable sequence of calls as they sought payment to process the hostage up the Taliban's regional chain of command.

"Where would they take him?" Wilson asked.

There was no ambiguity. Every scenario led to the same destination: Bergdahl would be delivered to the Haqqanis in Pakistan.

It was as predictable as it was discouraging. Once Bergdahl crossed the border into the FATA, there would be no straightforward way to bring him back. Wilson and Pelton knew they didn't have much time. They thanked the elders, left the jirga, and started making calls to Pelton's network, regardless of affiliation or background. They called Taliban lawyers, friendly mullahs, and officers in the notoriously corrupt Afghan Border Police. The more people Wilson called, the more he learned. He was told which models of deception the Taliban would use to mask Bergdahl's movement, how they would spread invented stories designed to embarrass the Americans, and how it would end: "a ransom, a prisoner trade, or a high-profile execution video."

This was how human intelligence worked. Rather than avoid men with questionable associations, he pursued them, seduced them, and flipped them to support the American mission using the four principal motivators that case officers kept in mind when handling their espionage agents. MICE was the mnemonic, drilled into CIA, DIA, and JSOC human intelligence officers throughout their training at the CIA's yearlong spy course at Camp Peary, Virginia: Money. Ideology. Coercion. Ego. Decipher which of these motivated an agent, use it to your advantage, and he would do what you wanted. Spies did not deal with the world's nice people. They were tasked with protecting America from those that would do her harm. In America's post-9/11 Global War on Terror, "We don't negotiate with terrorists" is an oft-repeated government mantra. It's also an idea that Wilson characterized as a political nicety, divorced from the reality in Afghanistan. Wilson cites an Afghan saying—"There are no bloodless hands"—as a truism that applied to his work. "We talked to guys who were clearly Taliban. They would tell you. They believe in the mission and the goals of the Taliban."

By the end of the first day of the DUSTWUN, Wilson had a multi-sourced and corroborated forecast for the Army's missing soldier. "We knew how they were going to move him, where they were going to move him. We figured it would be forty-eight hours at the most before he was across the border."

EIGHT

RIVER CITY

On June 30, 2009, at 4:42 p.m. local time, Colonel Mike Howard punched the panic button. Howard was ninety miles away from Kabul on FOB Salerno in Khost Province, north of Paktika, issuing orders to his brigade and directing searches on the ground. Over the American satellite radio network linking all units in RC East came a message from Howard to every soldier under his command: "All operations will cease until the missing soldier is found. All assets will be focused on the DUSTWUN situation and its sustainment operations." Translation: Everyone, stop what you're doing—this is your new priority, your only priority. The troops were now incommunicado with anyone but each other, a condition known to the soldiers as River City.

For Howard, cutting external communications was a way to control the flow of information. For soldiers on the ground in Afghanistan, it put an even further distance between them and their families and friends back home. The troops were accustomed to the rules of River City, which were generally imposed for seventy-two to ninety-six hours after a fatality in-country, intended to prevent a mother in Arkansas or Detroit from learning of her son's death from a careless Facebook post before the Army could properly notify next of kin by sending soldiers in dress uniforms to break the news.

Less than an hour after Howard's message, the Navy arrived over Paktika with two F/A-18 Hornet fighter/bombers launched from the

USS *Dwight D. Eisenhower* in the north Arabian Sea. They circled over OP Mest with bombs hanging from hardpoints on swept wings while the pilot and the weapon systems officer sat over a 20mm cannon peering out from under a bubble cockpit, waiting to kill Taliban on the ground the moment the infantry called in an airstrike. By nightfall, they were relieved by Air Force pilots in F-15s flying from Bagram Airfield, who flew under the uniquely Air Force call sign DUDE-21. Earlier that afternoon, at 2:15 p.m., a second drone, call sign PHINGSTON, had arrived to replace VOODOO, joining several intelligence, surveillance, and reconnaissance (ISR) aircraft already over Mest or en route. Th military's reflexive saturation of the airspace above Observation Post Mest paid quick dividends. It lifted morale—nothing raised the spirits of weary infantrymen quite like the sight of close air support overhead—and gathered intelligence as the spy planes intercepted chatter between Taliban elements on the ground. These smaller ISR aircraft flew at lower altitudes and lower speeds, equipped with a variety of cameras and sensors sucking up cell phone and radio conversations, which were then bounced back to earth, where teams of interpreters and analysts processed and pored over the transcripts looking for clues on the missing soldier. The first was intercepted at 2:42 p.m. by a Northrop Grumman RC-12X plane (call sign GUARDRAIL) from an unidentified male:

> UIM INDICATES THAT AN AMERICAN SOLDIER IS TALKING AND IS LOOKING FOR SOMEONE WHO SPEAKS ENGLISH. INDICATES AMERICAN SOLDIER HAS CAMERA.

At 8:13 p.m., the Americans intercepted a transmission from a Taliban soldier who claimed they'd captured three Afghan civilians and one U.S. soldier. Bravo Company's quick reaction force, which Captain Silvino had launched from FOB Sharana that morning, had already hit its first compound twenty minutes before that, then raided another, and came up empty both times. No Bergdahl. No clues. "Nothing significant to report," they had radioed back.

The Americans weren't the only ones confused and scrambling. That night, there were more intercepts from the Taliban. The Afghan National Police gathered around the iCom radio scanner, something they did most nights, toggling through frequencies to pick up Taliban walkie-talkie conversations and trade insults and threats. At 10:50 p.m., as Billings hosted nearly his entire chain of command on the OP, the ANP chief called down to the Americans. The Taliban were on the radio. They had an American soldier and they wanted to speak with a "Son of Bush," their name for Afghan interpreters working for the Americans. The Taliban told the ANP they would come back on the radio in ten minutes.

EIGHT YEARS AFTER the overthrow of the Taliban, native Dari and Pashto speakers were in constant demand in the military and the intelligence community. One CIA case officer who spoke Pashto and worked at a black site in Paktika recalled being an anomaly; he could count on one hand the number of case officers who spoke Pashto well enough to spy in the language. The Pentagon threw money at the problem, hiring contractors to serve as translators for American troops. L3 Communications (a publicly traded multinational corporation with thirty-eight thousand employees in eight countries, headquartered three blocks from the United Nations building in Manhattan) and Mission Essential Personnel (a global outfit with offices on five continents, based out of a nondescript glass-paneled office building adjacent to Washington Dulles International Airport) were two of the largest of these interpreter "body shops." Both organized their labor into three categories: Category I were local Afghan nationals without a security clearance, assigned to conventional units for patrols outside the wire; Categories II and III were American citizens with secret and top-secret security clearances respectively. Educated and skilled interpreters could earn incredible wages; several thousands of dollars per month was not unusual.

"I didn't go to spread democracy," one Afghan interpreter who was assigned to Australian troops said after he moved to the U.S. several years later. "I went because they paid me so well."

The interpreters had a dangerous and impossible job. Unlike the soldiers they served, they had no other country to call home. They spent most of their time with American forces on the FOB or on patrol, but were never fully integrated into the close-knit units. Rare was the American service member who trusted an interpreter like a fellow soldier. Because they worked for the Americans, their fellow Afghans also distrusted them. On patrol, they wore masks or bandanas to hide their faces, hoping to remain anonymous and keep their families and themselves from becoming targets of Taliban reprisals. In their downtime, most interpreters remained on American installations, happy for the protection from the constant Taliban threat, only traveling home for brief rest and relaxation visits, during which they were careful not to stay too long or say too much. A common Taliban tactic was to target interpreters for recruitment as spies or informants, and, if that failed, begin kidnapping members of their families.

When their contracts ran out, many feared that moving to their home villages put their families at too much risk. Most stayed in Afghanistan, hiding out and waiting for permission to begin new lives in the United States. That had to come from the Afghan Special Immigrant Visa office, run by four employees in New Hampshire known for turning back paperwork for typos. The situation discouraged countless qualified Afghans from working with the Americans, except for those who sufficiently hated the Taliban for their own reasons.

The interpreter who had joined 2nd Platoon on the first searches that morning went by the name John Mohammed. He was born in the north to a Pashtun man and a Tajik woman and grew up speaking both Pashto and Dari. He learned English from two main sources: his father, an English teacher in the village school, and Hollywood. *Rambo III* was one of his favorites. He had no prior connection to Paktika, and he never traveled alone from Sharana into the surrounding villages. If he were ever caught, he assumed he would be beheaded after the captors extorted ransom money from his family.

TEN MINUTES LATER, John was listening to the iCom radio scanner and heard the Taliban come up on the net.

"We have one of the infidels with us," the Taliban said over the radio. "He's a good guy. He's not rude, he's not bad like the others. He's a quiet guy. We are good hosts. We can feed him well. We will be a good host because he's our guest." They said complimentary things about Bergdahl's looks, his facial features. Then they asked John what their prisoner would like to eat. John asked the men to put Bergdahl on the radio. When the Taliban said no, Bergdahl's fireteam leader and first line supervisor, Sergeant Evan Buetow, told John to try a different tack.

"Tell him Buetow says hi," the sergeant suggested. Maybe that would elicit something. It did. The Taliban response came: "Evan Buetow makes me happy."

That sealed it. Using Buetow's first name in the reply was no accident, and there was no way the Taliban could have known it without having Bergdahl. Then the Taliban began telling John awful things, boasting that they were holding their prisoner down and sodomizing him. Neither John nor the soldiers knew whether to believe it. Maybe it was part of a Taliban psych-out strategy to throw the Americans off balance ahead of negotiations for his release. As quickly as it turned dark, the conversation flipped again, lighthearted now, back to how hospitable the Taliban were to their new hostage.

"We have to feed him," the Talib said. "He looks hungry. I'm sure he would like chicken, flatbread, and rice." John Mohammed again asked to speak with Bergdahl. No luck. The Taliban made their offer for an exchange—fifteen Taliban prisoners for the one American soldier—promised to feed Bergdahl, and then dropped off the frequency. The conversation lasted less than five minutes, and it left Bergdahl's platoonmates more confused than before. That may have been the goal all along.

At 7:04 a.m. the next day, July 1, a twin-engine Beechcraft King flying low over the ground under the call sign REDRIDGE recorded radio chatter between Taliban fighters:

> UNIDENTIFIED MALE 1: I SWEAR THAT I HAVE NOT HEARD ANYTHING YET. WHAT HAPPENED? IS THAT TRUE THAT THEY CAPTURED AN AMERICAN GUY?
>
> UNIDENTIFIED MALE 2: YES THEY DID. HE IS ALIVE. THERE IS NOWHERE HE CAN GO [LOL] BUT I DON'T HAVE THE WHOLE STORY. DON'T KNOW IF THEY WERE FIGHTING. . . . ALL I KNOW THAT THEY CAPTURED HIM ALIVE AND THEY ARE WITH HIM RIGHT NOW.

Three minutes later, a third Taliban entered the conversation with a brutal directive:

> UNIDENTIFIED MALE 3: CUT THE HEAD OFF.

Tactically proficient Taliban used false reports on the missing soldier as a lure for baited ambushes. The concept was simple: Make the Americans think Bergdahl was in one location, plant bombs in the roads along obvious routes, and send fighters to lie in wait. On July 1, less than twenty-four hours after Billings first tapped out the message to Silvino that his soldier was missing, spy planes and ground-based sensors stole more signals and confirmed this ruse.

> UNIDENTIFIED MALE 1: [LOL] THEY KNOW WHERE HE IS BUT THEY KEEP GOING TO THE WRONG AREA.

> UNIDENTIFIED MALE 2: OK, SET UP THE WORK FOR THEM.
>
> UNIDENTIFIED MALE 1: YES WE HAVE A LOT OF IEDS ON THE ROAD.
>
> UNIDENTIFIED MALE 2: GOD WILLING WE WILL DO IT.

After the two unidentified males finished this portion of the conversation, a third Taliban voice chimed in over his radio. The Taliban, lacking the material wealth and firepower that American soldiers took for granted, did not lack initiative—particularly when there was money to be made or a bargaining chip to be seized.

> UNIDENTIFIED MALE 3: CAN YOU GUYS MAKE A VIDEO OF HIM AND ANNOUNCE IT ALL OVER AFGHANISTAN THAT WE HAVE ONE OF THE AMERICANS?
>
> UNIDENTIFIED MALE 1: WE ALREADY HAVE A VIDEO OF HIM.

The next morning two tribal elders from Mest met with Task Force Geronimo's third-highest-ranking officer, Major Jeff Crapo, just east of the Yahya Khel district center. The elders came with a message for the Americans: Their lost soldier was alive and unharmed. They also explained that their status as *spinghira*—white-bearded wise men—gave them prestige in the Taliban's eyes, and they could help broker a deal for the soldier's safe return. The Taliban who held Bergdahl had already contacted them, they said, and were ready to negotiate. They wanted fifteen of their Taliban brothers held in American prisons released and an unspecified amount of cash. Crapo had no authority to release prisoners on his own, and no one up the chain of command took the elders seriously. Crapo's superiors told him to make a counteroffer of MREs, medical supplies, and blankets. When he did, the elders laughed, and the meeting ended with no deal.

IN THE E-RING of the Pentagon, Secretary of Defense Bob Gates was briefed on the DUSTWUN. He would be updated for several days on the situation via secure video teleconference from leadership in Kabul and CENTCOM headquarters in Tampa. It was only a few minutes out of his day, but to Defense officials on Gates's staff, who were already working overtime to manage the surge, even that was unthinkable.

"It doesn't sound like much, but in a war like that, two to five minutes is a lot of goddamn time," one former Gates staffer said. "It was a distraction of the highest order."

Bergdahl's disappearance brought an entirely different war to Eastern Afghanistan. Within hours of the DUSTWUN call, half of the U.S. military's airborne assets in the country were redirected to Paktika. Colonel John White, a career Army aviator and commander of a FOB Salerno-based helicopter unit, later testified that in his career he'd only seen that much airpower amassed one other time, during the opening salvo of Operation Desert Storm in 1991.

No sector of the Army saw their lives more radically altered than soldiers on the ground in RC East, where Colonel Howard had a clear mission with a new name: Operation Yukon Recovery. Gone were the days of relaxed afternoon shuras with elders over tea, or of sergeants fighting boredom by going on missions to the village bazaar to buy goats to roast for dinner back on the FOB. That hearts-and-minds COIN mission was over. The DUSTWUN brought on an entirely different war, and in the span of just a few days, Task Force Geronimo was cranked into a manic tempo none of the soldiers had ever before experienced. Suddenly, their once nebulous mission snapped into clarity: They were looking for Bergdahl.

Sutton and Coe and 2nd and 3rd Platoons were ordered to blocking positions in far-flung parts of the province they had never seen. They were instructed to stop passing cars and question civilians about Taliban activity and the missing American and to continue doing so all hours of the day and night until they were told to stop. They drove to locations where battalion supply trucks didn't hold enough fuel to reach them, and when they ran out of food and water, deliveries arrived from wild-eyed Russian pilots flying vintage helicopters that were older than most of the soldiers themselves. Or they shopped in nearby villages, where Sutton assumed the local fare would bring another round of the diarrhea that plagued their deployment, but found instead that living on orange soda and fried potato cakes was an unexpected DUSTWUN highlight.

They were told to stop civilians, but the blocking positions were so isolated there was no one around to question. At one, Sutton saw a single Afghan over the span of three days. With nothing else to do, they sat inside their trucks playing video games on their handheld PlayStation Portables. *Monster Hunter* was the most popular. They slept on the ground, and when they were called back, they drove ten, fifteen, or twenty hours to the FOB, where they were given ninety minutes to shower, devour hot meals, and stock up on gum, candy, and cigarettes before heading back into the desert to start again. They held this pace for thirty-five days straight. Sleep deprivation set in, and time passed in blurs of confusion. With five men packed into a truck that had lost power to its ventilation system after it was shot up by Taliban bullets, temperatures hovered in the low triple digits, and things stopped making sense. Coe was behind the wheel when he began hallucinating and asked Sutton where they were and what was happening. "We're looking for Bergdahl," he said.

The soldiers hypothesized about why he had done it. Maybe Bergdahl's weird shtick was an act; maybe he was CIA or a JSOC operator on a covert mission. They agreed that Bergdahl was peculiar, but he wasn't dumb. He knew the danger outside the wire. Everyone knew that what he'd said about walking to India was nonsense. The idea wasn't just stupid; it was so absurd that it didn't rise to the level of discussion. Except . . . it was Bergdahl. They remembered how he had talked, his fantasies about shedding his gear and uniform to join the Kuchis in their giant tents and learn their ancient goat-herding ways. It was all ridiculous. There were so many ways to get out of the war; walking alone and unarmed into Taliban territory was not among them. There was no explanation. But Coe knew his friend, and his gut told him what Bergdahl had done. Bergdahl had something to prove, and he would show the rest of them that he was what he claimed to be: a warrior and survivalist without peer who could withstand any hardship.

"He thought he was Lone Survivor," Coe said, referring to Navy SEAL Marcus Luttrell, who, four years before Bergdahl's walk, had found himself alone, wounded, and helpless on a Kunar Province mountain in enemy territory after a SEAL reconnaissance mission had gone wrong. In reality, Coe figured that Bowe had "grossly underestimated what he was doing," stepped outside the wire, and then realized, "Oh shit, I made a monumentally horrible decision."

Now that Bergdahl had shown everyone what he could do and how insane he could be, it seemed to the men in his platoon that questionable decisions were being made all around them. They were sent on their endless drives to futile blocking positions, Coe thought, because leadership needed to please their own superiors. If the Army had an actual idea where Bergdahl was, Sutton said, they would send in another unit like the SEALS for the recovery. Coe felt it was all for show.

At least one officer above him was more skeptical than that. Lieutenant Colonel Stephen Smith was thinking about his retirement and was preparing for a routine day at FOB Salerno when the DUSTWUN came in. Smith, who commanded the Task Force Steel artillery battalion out of Salerno, told his driver that their usual thirty-minute convoy had been rerouted to Camp Clark, a base on the high road carved into the mountains just south of the Khost-Gardez Pass. They sped along the newly paved stretch of highway to get there on time, but within minutes of their arrival, Smith stormed out of the meeting, kicking rocks as he hoisted himself into the passenger seat and told his confused driver to turn back the way they'd come. For the ninety minutes back to Salerno, Smith ranted about the crisis unfolding around them.

"If they knew the kid was fucked up, why didn't they send him home?" Smith asked, not expecting an answer. He had gone into the briefing at Clark knowing that a soldier was missing; what he had not expected to hear was that Bergdahl had been informally discussed as a potential mental-health case months before he ever arrived in Afghanistan. If his leadership knew it then, Smith said, then Bergdahl "had no business being here now." An unstable particle within his own unit, Bergdahl had broken loose and triggered a chain reaction explosion. People were going to get killed, he said. The search teams would be turned into so many Taliban targets. If Geronimo battalion leadership had been so incompetent as to bring over a kid who never belonged here in the first place, Smith said, then it should be Geronimo soldiers out there looking for him.

Sergeant Johnny Rice—Blackfoot Company, 3rd Platoon—had already started. Rice had been awoken early at Sharana, ordered to drive south immediately, and was halfway to OP Mest before he knew why. That afternoon and in the marathon that followed, he led search patrols in an expanding radius that brought him to villages where Afghans told him they hadn't seen an American in more than a year. Operation Yukon Recovery was an all-hands-on-deck event, and as Colonel Howard's troops swarmed the farthest reaches of their territory, his staff called on a psychological operations team to design and print single-page leaflets as simple tools of communication. Several editions were printed, each carrying a different message: One showed the blank silhouette of a U.S. soldier sitting with a group of smiling Afghan children. Another had Americans kicking down a door. "If you do not release the U.S. soldier, then you will be hunted," the caption read.

Where COIN had made cultural sensitivity a priority for years, the DUSTWUN replaced such niceties with sustained aggression. The soldiers stormed impoverished villages and fortified *qalats* to search for weapons, signs of Taliban activity, and information about Bergdahl. When they found locked doors, they broke them down. In most cases, they only found old men and children, bags of rice, and huddles of women cowering in corners, shielding their faces. The interpreters told the women to show themselves. When they didn't comply, soldiers acted on orders to check behind every veil. The Taliban, they had been told, might be hiding Bergdahl in a burka.

Sergeant Rice had never met Private First Class Bowe "Special Forces" Bergdahl, as the guys in his platoon called him, but he had seen his type in the Army before. The nickname told him everything: In Rice's experience, the guys who start out super gung-ho are usually off balance to begin with. He figured Bergdahl was one of those who wanted to re-create his identity by carrying a gun, and the Army was the only institution willing to let him try. Nor did Rice think they would actually find him; if the Taliban hadn't killed him, then Rice assumed they had already whisked him far away. "Common sense dictates that they aren't going to keep him around for long." As Rice stood guard on one patrol after another, he looked around and didn't see anyplace where a deserter could even desert. He saw a wasteland, where every Afghan he met hated him and no American could possibly survive on his own. *Hopefully he's dead,* Rice thought about the soldier who had abandoned his own platoon. *But he's not here.*

NINE

DIVERSIONS AND DECEPTIONS

Less than forty-eight hours after he took the call at the jirga, Ron Wilson was coming to the same conclusion: If Bergdahl wasn't already dead, he was on his way to the wrong side of the border and out of reach of the U.S. military. On July 2, the Taliban identified Bergdahl's captor as the Haqqani-linked commander Mullah Sangeen Zadran, confirming what Wilson's contacts had predicted. The soldier had been sold by a local gang that had captured him in Paktika, fed him into a sophisticated network of safe houses and taxis, and would deliver him to the Haqqani doorstep in Pakistan as quickly as they could. But as the days ticked by, Wilson kept reading overly optimistic statements from ISAF officials spinning the information he had been passing to his superiors about tracking the Army's missing soldier.

U.S. and Afghan forces had "fanned out" across Eastern Afghanistan "to shut down routes the kidnappers could use," unnamed officials told *The New York Times*. One anonymous senior defense official said that the Army had the Taliban "pretty boxed in, with not a lot of room to maneuver."

For two days, Wilson worked his contacts to find out how to stop Bergdahl's captors from sneaking him over the border, and he soon realized that his question was absurd. "It's the Silk Road, for God's sake," Wilson said. "It's been a smugglers' transit route for thousands of years. So the Taliban better be pretty good at it. And they are." Sangeen was

On a still winter's day near their home in rural Idaho, Bob Bergdahl teaches his son, Bowe, how to shoot.

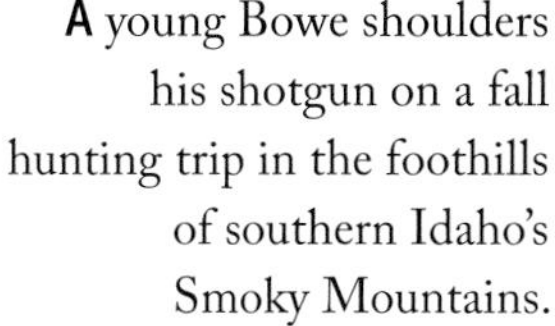

A young Bowe shoulders his shotgun on a fall hunting trip in the foothills of southern Idaho's Smoky Mountains.

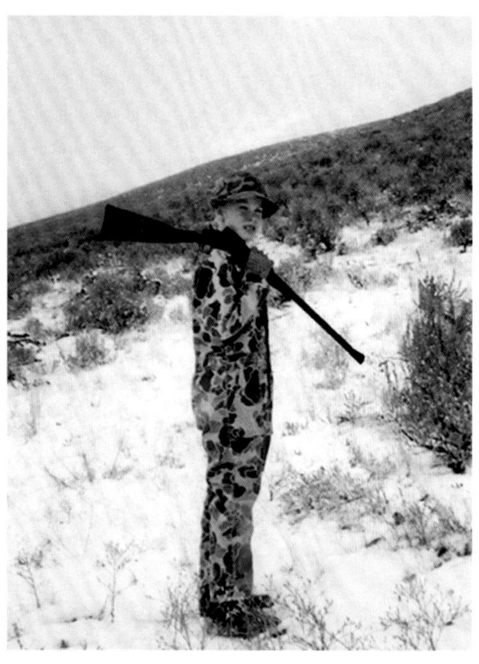

Bob and Bowe Bergdahl (second and third from right) with Peruvian shepherds in Blaine County, Idaho, in the early 1990s. When the Bergdahls moved to a remote mountain canyon, they came to count the shepherds as close family friends.

Private Bowe Bergdahl at Fort Benning after graduation from Infantry One Station Unit Training with his drill sergeant from Alpha Company, 2/58, Sergeant First Class Olivera.

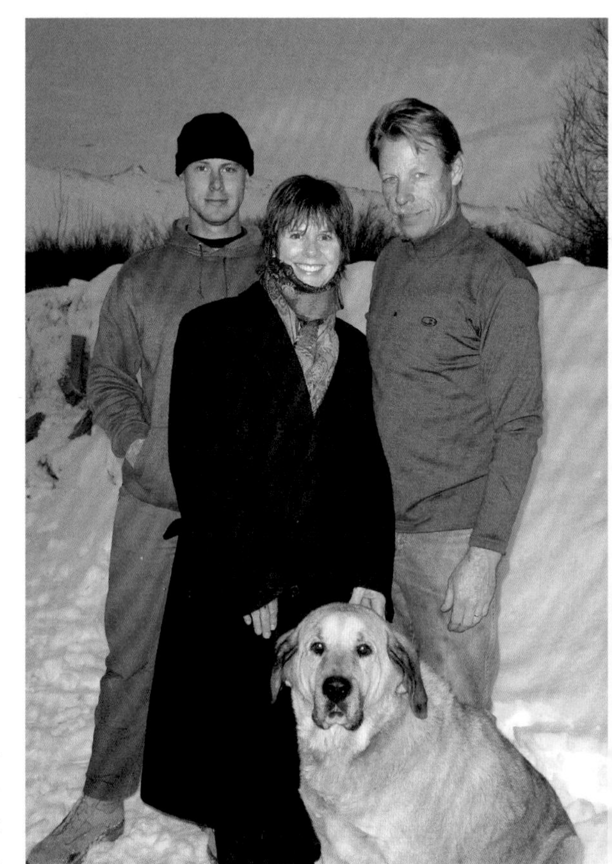

Bowe, Jani, and Bob Bergdahl—with Rufus the dog—in Idaho during Bowe's pre-deployment leave, December 2008.

Bowe Bergdahl at OP Mest, June 2009. Upon publication in *The Guardian*, these photographs resulted in disciplinary action against Bergdahl and other soldiers for uniform violations.

Made for the Bergdahls by Keith Maupin, whose son had been captured and killed in Iraq, stickers bearing Bowe's face were ubiquitous in southern Idaho during his captivity.

Bergdahl begs for his release in an April 2010 Taliban proof-of-life video.

In the summer of 2010, Bergdahl escaped his captors for eight days. Soon after he was recaptured, his guards photographed him with Badruddin Haqqani, a senior commander in the Taliban-aligned Haqqani Network and the son of legendary Pashtun warlord and former CIA asset Jalaluddin Haqqani. Badruddin was killed in a drone strike in 2012.

Black Hawk helicopter from the U.S. Army's Task Force 160 lands with Special Operations Forces to recover Bergdahl from the Taliban on May 31, 2014. A Taliban media team filmed the handoff, which was broadcast worldwide later that day.

Bob Bergdahl grasps the hand of POW activist and actor Gerald McCullar at the Rolling Thunder rally on the National Mall in Washington, D.C., May 27, 2012.

Bob and Jani Bergdahl address the crowd gathered at the Bring Bowe Home rally on June 22, 2013, in their hometown of Hailey, Idaho, as the four-year anniversary of their son's capture approaches.

Bob Bergdahl poses with a POW-MIA wreath at the Vietnam Veterans Memorial in Washington, D.C., April 9, 2013.

Special Forces Captain Jason Amerine with future Afghan president Hamid Karzai in 2001. Amerine's Special Forces team provided security for Karzai in southern Afghanistan during the opening phase of the war to overthrow the Taliban. In 2012, as a lieutenant colonel at the Pentagon, Amerine was tapped to develop options to recover American hostages from northwest Pakistan.

Bob and Jani Bergdahl join President Barack Obama for a ceremony in the White House Rose Garden on May 31, 2014, shortly after their son's release.

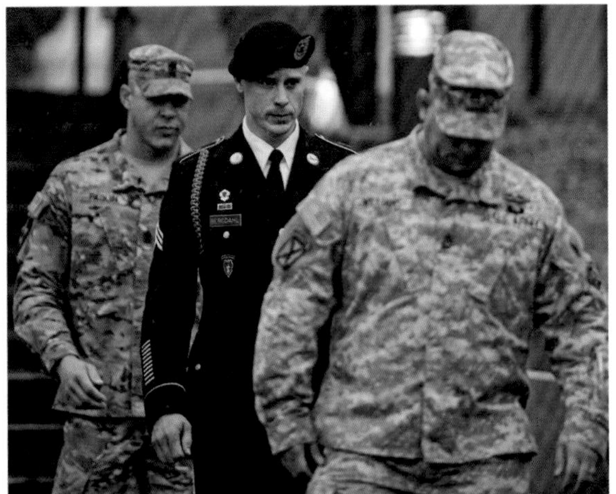

Sergeant Bergdahl leaves the courthouse on December 22, 2015, after his arraignment at Fort Bragg, North Carolina.

Eugene Fidell, Bergdahl's civilian attorney, speaks to the media following his client's sentencing at Fort Bragg, November 3, 2017.

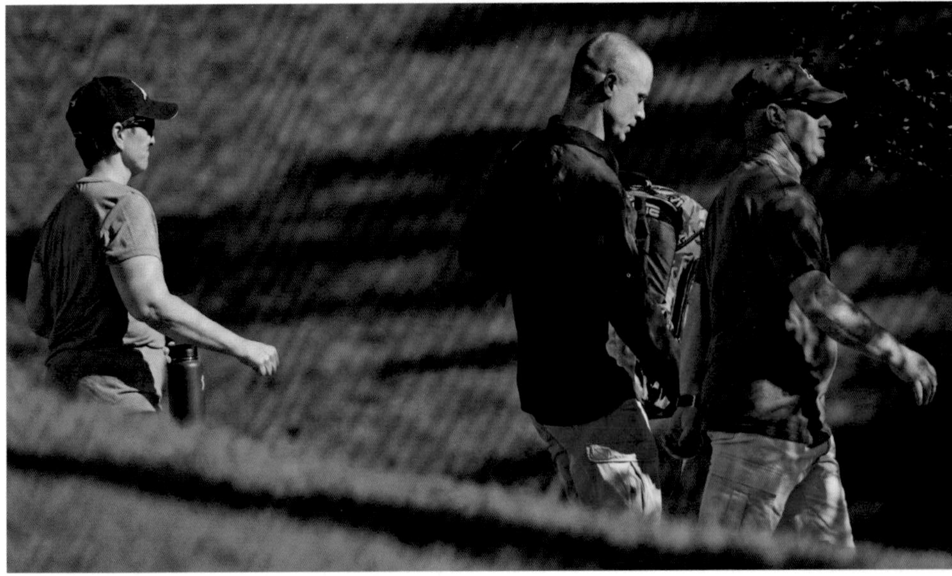

Bergdahl leaves the Fort Bragg courtroom on November 3, 2017, after his sentence was read: dishonorable discharge, a reduction in rank, and a forfeiture of pay—but no prison time.

a known quantity, a wily commander and Taliban shadow governor who had survived targeted airstrikes—false reports of his death had merely fed his legend. With Sangeen in charge of the operation, Bergdahl was as good as gone.

During Bergdahl's first thirty-six hours captive, Taliban gunmen shuttled him between multiple holding locations. On the night of July 1 or 2 and into the early hours of July 3 or 4, they hid him under blankets in the flatbed of a pickup truck, parked, took him out, and hiked him through the darkness into Pakistan, where they met Sangeen. By the third day after the DUSTWUN, Furlong was privy to the classified updates that search units had detained Afghans in RC East whom the Taliban had provided with cell phones, scripts, money, and instructions for acting out calls designed to outmaneuver the American surveillance dragnet.

One of the first tips shared by search units on July 1 was that the Taliban was planning to move him northeast, to the provincial capital in Gardez. Before noon the next day, there was a report of a sighting of Bergdahl's body, just east of a search patrol. A flood of tips began pouring in that afternoon, sending ground units, air-assault teams, and reconnaissance aircraft chasing down intel placing Bergdahl in Kuchi tents and Afghan trucks scattered across Paktika. On the afternoon of July 4, Task Force Geronimo thought they finally had a breakthrough: A report came in that Bergdahl had been spotted in a village near Ghazni, about fifteen miles northwest of Mest, with a bag over his head, dressed in dark clothes, and riding in a black Toyota Corolla with a conspicuous entourage of Taliban motorcycles.

Five years later in Texas, General Dahl explained to Bergdahl and his lawyer, Eugene Fidell, how the Army had been misled. Within twenty-four hours of the DUSTWUN call, Taliban in the area knew that the Americans were searching for a soldier, and as soon as they did, the intelligence was "all over the map," Dahl said. Dahl's team determined that most of what ended up in U.S. intelligence reports was unreliable. A report from the day he went missing said that "an American soldier with a camera is looking for someone who speaks English." This mistranslation—produced by an analyst's read of an interpreter's translation of overheard Taliban radio chatter—would be cited for years as proof that Bergdahl had sought out the enemy. In reality, it was the kidnappers who were looking for an English speaker with a camera. Bergdahl was blindfolded and bound on the backseat of a motorcycle racing across unmapped dirt tracks southeast of OP Mest when he heard their excited calls. They needed someone who could speak to and record a video of their new prize.

With each day the DUSTWUN dragged on. As Colonel Howard's Task Force Yukon called in additional assets, the dubious intelligence reports multiplied. It wasn't just Blackfoot Company platoons searching now; every available unit in RC East was mobilized, spanning the Army's spectrum of preparedness, from teams of multi-tour Green Berets to freshly arrived National Guardsmen still adjusting to the altitude at the start of what they had been told would be COIN-oriented missions training Afghan National Army soldiers.

"Unequivocally—all of my sources, all embedded forces, all trainers—stop what we are doing, pivot, and devote every asset we had to this search," said Michael Waltz, an Army Special Forces major in-country before Bergdahl went missing. Between deployments, Waltz had worked in Washington, D.C., on counternarcotics and counterterror policy, and in one job as an adviser to Vice President Dick Cheney. During the DUSTWUN, Waltz said he was not given time for proper source vetting. Faced with conflicting reports that had Bergdahl on either side of the border, Waltz ordered his men to track down leads in Afghanistan, the only territory where they were legally permitted. When he ordered his men to search a compound in Ghazni, they walked straight into an empty building booby-trapped with packs of C-4 explosives lining the ceiling.

"By the grace of God, it didn't go off," Waltz said later, but the close call left him with no doubt that the Taliban were spreading false information to lure American soldiers into baited traps.

In other parts of the province, Task Force Geronimo soldiers driving million-dollar MRAPs and carrying briefcases of cash arrived in villages that had never had running water or electricity and doled out money in exchange for information. Even somewhat credible indicators could fetch thousands of dollars, and U.S. intelligence was soon overwhelmed with hundreds of tips from Afghans claiming to know something about the missing soldier.

"The data was a nightmare," said Amber Dach, the CENTCOM lead intelligence analyst on the case. "He's here, he's there, he's dead, he's not. There was no way to find two validated pieces." Within hours of the DUSTWUN call, Dach and her team of analysts at CENTCOM had already arrived at an unofficial conclusion that Bergdahl would be smuggled over the border as fast as his captors could get him there. The analysis was based on recent kidnappings, open-source reporting, and common sense. On May 4, 2009, a front-page *New York Times* story had announced: "Porous Pakistani Border Could Hinder U.S."

Bergdahl's abduction also played out against the backdrop of the high-profile kidnapping and stunning escape of *New York Times* reporter David Rohde. Rohde had been captured in November 2008, but his employers, the government, and his family had kept his captivity secret as they attempted to negotiate his release. On June 20, 2009, the dramatic details of his escape were plastered across newspapers around the world. Eleven days later, the galling reality of Rohde's imprisonment in Miran Shah was still fresh in Dach's mind. Nevertheless, her superiors told her that her team's analysis on Bergdahl would not be accepted until it was corroborated by two independent, validated sources, and she returned to sifting through the unending flow of contradictory tips.

At the highest levels of the U.S. command, the crisis was amplified by an organizational lag. McChrystal's team was in the first month of his second war in three years. Iraq had been the gravitational center of the U.S. military for more than six years, and in Kabul, commanders had done the best they could with limited assets and personnel. When

Bergdahl triggered the DUSTWUN, there was no designated personnel recovery (PR) cell on the ground in Afghanistan to manage the event. His capture should have been processed through the same clear hierarchies that worked to find missing soldiers like Private First Class Jessica Lynch, who went missing in Iraq in 2003. But absent a PR cell in Kabul, the crisis ascended the chain of command and then dispersed into ad hoc, hydra-headed disarray. Without the proper intelligence architecture in place to coordinate efforts, Dach said, the DUSTWUN turned into an "organized free-for-all."

At ISAF Headquarters, Pelton watched the spiral in disbelief. He was invited into military offices to discuss the situation. "They had maps on the wall," he said, "and I would point to Pakistan and say, 'He's going that way.'" Meanwhile at ISAF, Wilson was told to drop his efforts four days after the first call. The lost puppy was someone else's problem now. As an "unconventional warfare" officer who rode around Kabul in unmarked cars, dressed in civilian clothes, and called lists of Taliban contacts from his flip phone, Wilson knew that there was a finite number of U.S. government entities doing similar work, and an even smaller number operating under Pentagon authorities. When Wilson heard that the Joint Special Operations Command (JSOC) had also been told to stand down on the DUSTWUN, he knew that Bergdahl was in Pakistan.

In Washington's post-9/11 era, and particularly under McChrystal and Flynn in Iraq, JSOC had become the Pentagon's cleanup crew for the Global War on Terror's messiest problems. But there were some places that even JSOC couldn't go; according to the federal laws governing military and espionage, Pakistan was strictly CIA territory. As far as the Army was concerned, Wilson thought to himself on July 5, the search for Bergdahl was over.

BY THE JULY 4TH WEEKEND in Kabul, Furlong also had corroborating reports from Pelton's AfPax and Clarridge's Eclipse that Bergdahl was across the border. He updated Flynn with these reports on a daily basis. But the CIA disagreed; at classified meetings, they told Furlong that they had cell phone intercepts indicating Bergdahl might still be in Afghanistan. Furlong knew they were wrong, but said nothing.

By the summer of 2009, both Furlong and Flynn had come to see the CIA not only as incompetent, but also as their nemesis. At Langley, the feelings were mutual. CIA officers who crossed his path had seen Furlong as a threat for years, a once-Army-always-Army former ranger who believed in his bones that the military was better at intelligence than the Central Intelligence Agency and who was habitually conjuring new ways for the Pentagon to do the CIA's job. But between Furlong and the generals he worked to please—McKiernan in 2007 and 2008; McChrystal and Flynn in the summer of 2009—it was widely accepted that the CIA was being outmaneuvered by the ISI. To the procession of frustrated generals in Kabul, Furlong was an appealing, if mystifying, government creature: a useful minotaur in the Pentagon's labyrinthine bureaucracy. As one officer who worked with him said, Furlong spoke at Pentagon meetings in such complex jargon that "nobody would ask any questions because they didn't want to appear dumb and admit that they didn't know what he was talking about."

But Furlong's prior approval from McKiernan to fund AfPax had done little to assuage Langley's concerns. Agency officers in Kabul knew that Furlong had schemes that went beyond AfPax; by the time he hired Clarridge and tried to package all of his intelligence efforts into a top-secret program he called Capstone, the agency considered Furlong not just reckless, but dangerous. If he were permitted to run a parallel spy ring in Pakistan, CIA assets could very well be killed in the process. And if he succeeded, it would prove that the CIA had fallen behind and endangered their share of spook funding in Washington. In July 2009, after years of tension, meetings that sometimes blew up into screaming matches, and an exchange of terse memos from Langley to the Pentagon, Furlong knew he needed to choose his battles. In Kabul, he was finally doing what he had set out to do. As the CIA and CENTCOM pored over the intelligence reports that Furlong already knew were Haqqani deception tactics, he decided not to press his case. Rescuing Bergdahl wasn't worth triggering the battle with Langley that could bring it all crashing down.

Pelton was confused. He had thought Furlong and Flynn wanted to find their missing soldier. But when he passed along AfPax reports that Bergdahl had arrived in North Waziristan, Furlong told him to stop. "We have natural enemies because we are good," he wrote to Pelton on July 17. The next day, as he sensed the walls closing in, he wrote Pelton again: "Keep doing what you are doing. . . . I am building an enduring program that will continue without me. . . . Move forward even if I am fired."

Furlong's insistence that his operations were legal enough didn't satisfy everyone. That summer, Furlong had invited an ISAF colonel to lunch at the ISAF Joint Command (IJC) headquarters in Kabul. He was hoping to persuade the colonel's boss, Lieutenant General David Rodriguez, who as IJC commander ran day-to-day operations for ISAF, to support his projects. Furlong started telling the colonel about this "intel ring" he was running. The colonel, who had spent his career alternating between regular infantry duty and classified staff assignments, grew concerned. It was unclear what authorities Furlong had secured for his "intel ring"—but the law (i.e., Title 50 of the U.S. Code), was clear: Outside the powers granted to the CIA and the Department of Defense, there were strict limits about who was authorized to engage in espionage in countries where the United States was not at war. Eclipse was clearly engaging in espionage; the Eclipse Group helped Furlong build a parallel target list—a kill list complete with phone numbers, physical addresses, and email addresses—to rival CIA's while still meeting the agency's criteria for extrajudicial killing. Furlong claims he passed his spreadsheet to Flynn with the intent that it be merged into intelligence databases as if it had come from a CIA or military case officer. Furlong thought it was a model spying system: "It's brown people talking to brown people—it ain't a bunch of white Special Forces running around."

"Mike, are you SOCOM?" the colonel asked.

Furlong told him he wasn't.

"Mike, are you working with the CIA?"

Hell no, Furlong wasn't working with CIA; if anything, he worked against them.

"Mike, who are you working for?" the colonel wanted to know.

To run such an operation, Furlong would have needed a signed authority from a high-ranking official—the secretary of defense, the director of the CIA, or the president. But Furlong wouldn't say who provided his authority, and to the colonel, who had worked with three secretaries of defense, it sounded like a rogue program. The colonel ended the lunch and went straight to his boss, Lieutenant General Rodriguez, the ISAF joint commander, who in turn called Flynn and asked him to handle the problem, assuming that Flynn would send Furlong home. But he didn't; he sent him south to run operations in Kandahar. When the ISAF colonel learned years later that Furlong was allowed to continue operating, he was stunned. "If Mike Furlong's not in jail—and he's not in jail—that means this program was sanctioned. So who the fuck sanctioned that negligence?"

Eventually, the CIA finessed its Furlong problem with a series of apparent leaks to *The New York Times*. The best way to eliminate shadowy figures was to shine a light on them, and after the front-page story broke about his secret spy ring in March 2010, Furlong was shut down and sent home.

Despite the bad press, Furlong was proud of what he had pulled off—cobbling together a spy organization in the FATA, feeding the data back to Flynn in a deliberately byzantine way that made everyone assume it was authorized. Under the cover of the "white" (unclassified) contract for media support from Robert Young Pelton and Eason Jordan, Furlong funneled money instead to the "black" (classified and unacknowledged) portion of the contract. The AfPax work was a diversion to get funding to the real mission: using Eclipse to gather names for the kill list. It was a crafty scheme, but it was dangerous. If no one knew

Eclipse was feeding data into the kill list, one of the dead targets could turn out to have been innocent, or an agent of another intelligence service. After it went public, an alphabet soup of federal agencies investigated Furlong and several Eclipse agents for years. One, a former Green Beret turned security contractor, was sent to prison for procurement fraud in 2015. Furlong, however, was never formally charged, and the investigations into his activities remain classified. For the Pentagon, the best thing to do with Furlong was pretend that he hadn't existed at all.

ON JULY 13, Bergdahl's captors dressed him in a light-blue salwar kameez and sat him cross-legged in front of a small table with a black microphone and a glass of neon-yellow soda. While the camera rolled, an unseen man asked him questions in accented English and held his dog tags up to the camera lens. When the Taliban released the video for worldwide broadcast six days later, U.S. intelligence analysts noted that his captors had had time to dress him in clean clothes, shave his head, make a show of feeding him on camera, and record, edit, and distribute a twenty-eight-minute video. Clearly, they were in a safe place.

The day after the video aired, ABC News cited military sources involved in the search who said that Bergdahl was already in Pakistan. The Pentagon insisted that he was not, and in an interview later that day in New Delhi, Secretary of State Hillary Clinton dodged the question entirely. "We are attempting to do everything we can to locate him," she told ABC's Martha Raddatz. By July 18, nearly all U.S. intelligence agencies monitoring the case updated their assessments to reflect the new reality: Bergdahl was in Pakistan. CENTCOM was the only holdout.

At Bergdahl's court-martial more than eight years later, Dach testified that when she updated her team's assessment after the video's release, her superiors at CENTCOM did not accept her analysis and instead demanded an unprecedented level of certainty. Dach had joined the Army shortly after 9/11, and in a sixteen-year career that had taken her to assignments at the Pentagon, Guantanamo Bay, and Afghanistan, this was the only time her chain of command had rejected her analysis. She was frustrated.

"You pay us to tell you what we think, then you tell us you don't want to know what we think," she said.

Dach started getting calls from analysts at other agencies, grilling her about CENTCOM's balking. The implications were obvious. The War in Afghanistan was being fought in Afghanistan, and when all available intelligence pointed to the fact that Bergdahl had been moved to the wrong side of the border, into a country where the Pentagon was not at war, CENTCOM withheld its own analysis and continued to carry out searches for the missing soldier in the only battle space where it legally could.

AS THE SEARCHES CARRIED on past the time when military and government leadership knew that Bergdahl was almost certainly in Pakistan, the Army began focusing on information control. Task Force Geronimo soldiers were given nondisclosure agreements (NDAs), agreeing to never discuss the DUSTWUN searches. Joshua Cornelison, the platoon's medic, remembers being in a manic haze, rushing around Sharana for food and a shower when an officer told him and his comrades to line up and sign the agreements. The contract was written in awkward legalese, but the point was clear: "We weren't going to talk about it." In the weeks and months that followed, the NDAs would reach thousands of personnel. Some men were told that if they didn't sign, they wouldn't fly home.

As the DUSTWUN spun into its third and fourth weeks of what most soldiers saw as sustained madness, Sergeant Rice discerned the logic at work. He was leading his men into raids, air assaults, and "hard knocks"—kicking down doors and stirring up Taliban before sunrise.

Early on in his deployment, Rice had been frustrated by COIN's stringent rules of engagement, the extensive intelligence needed to detain suspected Taliban. But during the DUSTWUN, his superiors approved every raid.

"If it was a mission to retrieve Bergdahl, it was an instant green light, get it done as fast as you can," he said. "From an infantryman standpoint, we were doing our job for once."

Rice was hit by eight IEDs in two months, and the brain injuries sidelined him from a month of patrols.

"It was extremely tiring. It was terrible. But it was the right thing to do as far as using the opportunity," he said. "They took the opportunity and I one hundred percent stand behind it."

For officers and mission planners, the vanished soldier had taken on a new life as an internal military tactic. "'Bergdahl' became a language tactic to get assets," one former Blackfoot Company officer explained. For officers sending their men on dangerous patrols in a confusing war, "it was easier to say we're looking for a guy, rather than another pointless order mission." He said the ruse went on for months.

For the men in his own platoon, Bergdahl became the war's central unreal reality, the embodiment of the contradictions and confusion that had surrounded them from the start. But even when they knew the DUSTWUN had become a sham, they embraced it.

"We tried to do every mission to the best of our ability," Cornelison said, "even when we knew that Bergdahl wasn't even in Afghanistan."

ACT III.

TRAPPED

TEN

NOT THE WORST NEWS

Jani Bergdahl heard Rufus, the family sheepdog, barking and looked out the window to see three soldiers at the gate. *But he just got there!* she thought as she opened the door and greeted them, an officer, a sergeant, and a chaplain, all in their Class A uniforms: polyester green suits with multicolored ribbons on their chests next to precisely arranged badges and coded epaulets. It was almost four in the afternoon in Idaho, less than twenty-four hours since the DUSTWUN call had gone out from OP Mest.

"Is your husband home?" the soldiers asked.

He was not.

"Do you have anybody home with you?"

She did not.

"Is there some way to get in touch with your husband?" Bob didn't carry a cell phone on his delivery route, but she could reach him in an emergency through UPS central dispatch. She told the men from the Army that she would make the call, but first she needed to know if her son was dead. They would not say. "You can't tell me anything?"

Army policy was to not break the news to unaccompanied next of kin. After notifying thousands of soldiers' families that their sons and daughters were dead, the Pentagon learned that people break down in different ways. "It's not the worst news it could be," one of the men offered, finally, and then refused to say another word.

Jani decided to drive into town and meet Bob at the UPS lot. The soldiers followed her in their government car on the drive she had made countless times before, down the gentle grade toward the Big Wood River, past the alfalfa fields, with the jagged and still-snowcapped peaks of the Pioneer Mountains looming above the valley to the east. Bob saw the message flash on his UPS terminal—"Jani wants you to call her"—and turned the truck back to the distribution terminal, about a fifteen-minute drive from the other side of town. "Oh crap," he said to himself as he pulled into the dusty gravel lot. Jani was already there, the soldiers by her side.

"Are you ready for this?" he asked as he walked to her. "Do you know what this means?"

"No, not yet," she replied.

As of that morning, the Army men told them, their son was "DUSTWUN."

"That was the beginning of the endless acronyms," Jani said later.

The soldiers explained as best they could. He's missing. That's all they knew, their information no more or less complete than the radio calls still going up at that moment from the Blackfoot Company elements seven thousand miles to the west, raiding compounds, looking for Bowe, telling their superiors "Nothing significant to report."

Not knowing what else to do, Bob climbed back in his truck and finished his route. That was his job. He told himself what he had told his son at Christmas before he deployed: "You've gotta stay in the game." Bob had delivered boxes with a broken rib and with pneumonia. He could work, and the work needed to be done, so he did it. That night they called their pastor in Boise, Glenn Ferrell, who drove two and a half hours across the Camas Prairie the next morning so Jani wouldn't be alone while Bob was at work. They showed Ferrell the last batch of emails Bowe had sent from FOB Sharana. Even before the Army's green suits arrived, the Bergdahls' "greatest concern about Bowe was his spiritual condition," Ferrell said.

They didn't tell anyone else at first, and it was a lonely four days.

They knew this was going to ruin Sky's 4th of July party in Twin Falls with Jani's mom, the kids' grandmother. Still, Independence Day seemed like as good an opportunity as any to break the news to family and friends: Bowe had gone missing in Afghanistan. Now he was a hostage of the Taliban. It would be all over the news soon.

Jani said later, "We thought they'd get him within the week."

As that hope vanished, they knew their anonymity wouldn't last. Bob prepared for unwanted attention. He took down the big Ron Paul yard sign facing the road. He received a call from Lieutenant Colonel Tim Marsano, a former Air Force intelligence officer and Idaho National Guardsman who volunteered to work as the family's on-loan military public affairs officer (PAO)—Bob dubbed him "the media mediator." Bob and Marsano decided they needed someone from the community who could speak for the family, and they chose Sue Martin, the owner of the popular local coffee shop, Zaney's, where Bowe had last worked before he deployed. Bob had known her for years.

Martin understood inexplicable tragedy; she had opened her shop with her son, Zane, a Ketchum firefighter and EMT, in 2004. Zane's namesake business had quickly become an institution when, in 2006, he was killed in a motorcycle accident north of Ketchum. Sue decided to keep the business running. It was a scrappy operation where every employee was at some point called on to do every job. Bowe's quiet aptitude was a good fit. He only needed to watch her balance out the register and make a soy decaf latte once, and he knew it cold.

Bob knew that putting Martin in this position was a big favor to ask, but he trusted her as a neighbor with solidity, grace, and grit. She agreed, and from then on, Zaney's served as the town's ad hoc Bergdahl shrine and media operations center. Soon, Martin found herself taming all manner of creatures and queries at the center of the family's media circus, a spectacle that brought phone calls from Oprah Winfrey and Christiane Amanpour, a bouquet of flowers from producers at *Good Morning America,* and news correspondents by the dozens.

While they avoided the press, the Bergdahls began building a local network of military and government connections. Bob's UPS customers included two retired Navy admirals and a family that had made a small fortune in commercial real estate in Washington, D.C. Jani cleaned houses in Sun Valley as a side job and knew that one of her clients was a former Marine Corps captain who had been wounded in Vietnam and stayed close with a circle of veterans, including several POWs. After surviving the war that killed two-thirds of his Marine Officer Candidates School classmates, Hayward Sawyer had traded in his fatigues for a suit and tie in the insurance industry in Connecticut. He became wealthy and settled into a gentleman rancher's retirement in Sun Valley. The day the Taliban posted its first proof-of-life video, Jani was cleaning Sawyer's house and saw him watching the news.

"I know you're a praying man," she said to him. "That soldier you heard about on TV this morning is our son."

Stunned, Sawyer started making calls to his cadre of former POWs. Bob and Jani knew that they needed friends who understood the military but weren't beholden to it. Sawyer was the perfect advocate, down to the Purple Heart ribbon he pinned on his blue blazer and, when in Idaho, his Purple Heart belt buckle. "We knew we were going up against the military complex," Bob said. "We brought [Sawyer] for shock and awe," Jani added.

Once the first proof-of-life video was broadcast and Bowe became the most famous soldier in the world, his hometown rallied. A July 22 vigil in Hailey was one of the largest impromptu town gatherings in memory. Hundreds of locals turned out, most of them on bicycles, to honor the local boy who was perpetually riding his. They carried homemade signs that said "Support Our Troops" and "Bring Bowe Home," and they fixed American flags to their handlebars for a mass walk from Zaney's, past Bob's UPS lot, and down the hill to Hop Porter Park, alongside the Big Wood River.

It was a somber Idaho night, and as the crowd walked into the park under the tall cottonwoods and the cool shadow of Carbonate Mountain, the mood was serious but upbeat. "We're a very small community.

We're very tightly knit," Chamber of Commerce Director Jim Spinelli said. "If you don't know Bowe, the person you talk to knows Bowe." They lit candles, prayed in silent unison, and hoped that positive thought would bring a positive outcome.

That Sunday, July 26, Sawyer chartered a jet to fly in retired Navy pilots Jerry Coffee and Render Crayton, both of whom had spent more than seven years as prisoners in and around Hanoi, to meet with Bob and Jani and speak at another smaller vigil. Coffee and Crayton didn't soften the hard realities of the situation. They told Bowe's friends the same thing they told his parents—to steel themselves for what would likely be a long and painful process. No matter what they heard on TV, bringing Bowe home was not the Army's top priority. Later, away from the crowd, they encouraged Bob and Jani to lobby the military brass and plead their case on a personal level, as parents of a soldier who had volunteered (twice) in service for his country. They also warned them: Do not trust the Pentagon.

ON JULY 19, the confusion and anger that coursed through the ranks burst onto the national airwaves and out of the mouth of Fox News strategic analyst, retired Lieutenant Colonel Ralph Peters.

"We know this private is a liar. We're not sure if he's a deserter. But the media needs to hit the pause button and *not* portray this guy as a hero," Peters told Fox anchor Julie Banderas. The July 14 video was proof, Peters said, that Bergdahl was not only lying but guilty of "collaborating with the enemy, under duress or not."

Banderas looked stunned. The network had decided not to air the video in full, she said, because it was deemed to be enemy propaganda. "They wanted that message to get out there, and we're not going to do the Taliban any favors here," she said. Banderas referred to emails from viewers who wanted to know how something like this could happen, how a soldier could simply walk away on his own. It sounded like a failure of leadership, or at least of the military's buddy system. But now that Bergdahl was confirmed captured, she asked Peters, "How do we get him back?"

Peters, who in addition to his two decades of military service was also a popular writer of spy novels, assured Banderas and Fox viewers that Bergdahl was too valuable for the Taliban to kill. Special operations and surveillance would track him down, but actually retrieving him would come only at great expense and effort. That outcome did not sit well with Peters, so he shared his vision for a simpler remedy.

"If, when the facts are in, we find out that through some convoluted chain of events, he really was captured by the Taliban, I'm with him," Peters said. "But if he walked away from his post and his buddies in wartime, I don't care how hard it sounds. As far as I'm concerned, the Taliban can save us a lot of legal hassles and legal bills."

It was a historic moment in television punditry. Banderas, taken aback, reminded her viewers that Bergdahl was "one of ours" and that Fox News did not, in fact, wish to see him harmed. Wars may create their own cruel logic systems, but Peters's call for peremptory judgment was, at the time, far outside political norms—and it did not go unnoticed. Two days later, a group of twenty-three veterans serving in Congress wrote an open letter to Fox News CEO Roger Ailes to lodge an official public complaint. The congressmen had watched Peters "with incredulity and disgust," accused him of behavior unbecoming a former officer, and attacked his apparent historical ignorance.

"Soldiers are often forced to make statements contrary to their beliefs simply to stay alive," they wrote. The most obvious reminder of this fact was the most powerful veteran in Congress. "Perhaps Mr. Peters would choose to question [Senator John McCain's] patriotism as well," the congressmen wrote.

For the fourteen Democrats and nine Republicans who signed it, the Ailes letter was low-risk theater, a signal of patriotic virtue against Peters's toxic noise. If anyone had provided aid and comfort to the enemy, they wrote, it wasn't Bergdahl but retired Lieutenant Colonel Peters.

Following the brief controversy, Peters found himself on the receiving end of some "screwball death threats from 'patriots,'" as he deemed them. While he later conceded that he had spoken out of anger, Peters was a reliable advocate for the rank and file, and the mission he had set for himself that day had been clear: to speak for voiceless soldiers, men he saw as the real victims of Bergdahl's mess. "Julie, think about his buddies," Peters said, wagging his finger at Banderas at the end of the segment. "Remember his buddies."

By July 19, these sentiments were already widespread. From OP Mest to Sharana to CENTCOM headquarters in Tampa Bay, men in uniform struggled to defend or even explain what Bergdahl had done. In the absence of facts, a swirl of rumor and grievance filled the void. In Paktika's villages, intelligence gatherers bearing cash rewards asked Afghan sources leading questions: Is it true that the missing American soldier wanted to join the Taliban? Soldiers were warned that if they found Bergdahl, he was unlikely to go with them peacefully. Some of Bergdahl's own self-aggrandizing tales, spread from the guys who had met him, mingled with the rumors.

"He was very good with knives and trained to throw and fight hand-to-hand with knives," one anonymous soldier wrote in an email to the conservative commentator Michelle Malkin during the DUSTWUN. They didn't know anything about Bergdahl's mental status, but it seemed safe to assume that it was not stable.

In civilian society, a person's reputation is a complex and constantly evolving composite. In the Army, Bergdahl's character had been settled. "The U.S. Army is an organism, like any organization," said David Sedney, a senior Pentagon official who was in Kabul that summer. "And it rejected Bowe Bergdahl. It rejected Bowe Bergdahl as an alien object from the very beginning."

Sedney's official title was deputy assistant secretary of defense for Afghanistan, Pakistan, and Central Asia. He had spent the decade following 9/11 on the diplomatic front lines. In 2002, he first went to Kabul as the deputy chief of mission—rebuilding the U.S. presence for the first time in the twelve years since the Soviet withdrawal—and returned to Washington to join George W. Bush's National Security Council as the director for Afghanistan. As Sedney's government postings continually intersected with Bergdahl's five-year captivity, he viewed the case through a lens of social anthropology. To Sedney, the loner private with the Kiplingesque fantasies was doomed from the start.

Bergdahl might have forged real bonds with Coe and Sutton, but more relevant was the fact that "he was surrounded by scores, hundreds of thousands of other people who were not his friends." What struck Sedney most was the speed and consistency with which even the false rumors spread. "It's a real testament to organizational groupthink. I talked to a lot of people in the Army, almost the day after Bergdahl left his post, who were just convinced that this guy was a traitor."

There was never any reliable intelligence to back up the claim. As another Pentagon official pointed out, it was based on nothing more than wild speculation, and stories from Afghan sources who knew they could make the most money by regurgitating tales that American soldiers most wanted to hear. And yet the smear was irrepressible, quickly spreading from the conventional infantry units patrolling RC East to military leadership in Kabul. There, General Mike Flynn told a reporter during the first year of Bergdahl's captivity that the captured soldier was "a jihadi."

In the fall of 2009, the Pakistani journalist Ahmed Rashid was in Kabul meeting with American officials about a range of topics, including the captured soldier. To Rashid's surprise, no one he spoke to seemed to care about Private First Class Bowe Bergdahl.

"I met with people in the U.S. military who were extremely dismissive of him as an individual," Rashid said. "One wonders, if he had been a SEAL or a Special Forces guy, whether the attitude would have been different."

Though the hive mind had rejected him, Bergdahl remained CENTCOM's responsibility, and even after Ron Wilson was told that

JSOC had been called off the search, the Pentagon ordered special operations commanders to draw up options for cross-border recovery missions. It was inevitable that they would be given the task; hostage rescues were this secret army's origin story. JSOC was created after the failure of Operation Eagle Claw to rescue fifty-two Americans held in Tehran in April 1980. Following 9/11, Secretary of Defense Donald Rumsfeld, angry that the CIA had taken the lead at the start of the War in Afghanistan, oversaw the buildup of Special Operations command (SOCOM) of which JSOC is part. By the end of the decade, JSOC was a bigger and more capable paramilitary than what the CIA could muster on its own.

JSOC was home to the military's best-trained killers, "operators," known by their secret, color-coded units: SEAL Team 6 (Task Force Blue), Army Delta Force (Task Force Green), and JSOC's intelligence support activity (Task Force Orange). They functioned as Washington's secret army in countries where the United States was at war—officially or unofficially—including Yemen, Somalia, Nigeria, Mali, and the Philippines. Lethal missions in different countries required authorization at different levels of government. To go into Pakistan, JSOC required direct approval from the president.

Any cross-border mission would have confronted the "10–50 dance," as covert operators in Kabul called the legal lambada wherein Pentagon and CIA lawyers found workarounds to the federal codes that govern overt military action in Afghanistan (Title 10), and covert paramilitary operations run by the CIA in Pakistan (Title 50). When President Bush had ordered a handful of such raids in 2008 and helicopters full of elite operators crossed the border, the military personnel became employees of the CIA in midair, a practice known as "sheep-dipping."

JSOC mission planners drew up two options for rescuing Bergdahl—one "high" and one "low." The high option called for eight MH47 Chinook transport helicopters carrying upward of two hundred special operators. The low option would have sent a small SEAL team over the border in stealth helicopters. One Navy SEAL team involved in the planning nicknamed the low option Objective Cat Stevens, after the British pop star who became a Muslim, changed his name to Yusuf Islam, and sold all of his guitars. From what the SEALs knew, it seemed like an apt description. Their commanders were less amused.

Both options carried huge risks—a diplomatic crisis with Pakistan at worst, or a limited but bloody shootout against Haqqani or Pakistani soldiers at best. No one at the Pentagon believed either was worth the gamble.

"We're not going to utilize all of our resources to save Bergdahl and lose the War in Afghanistan as a result," said Sedney. At the very least, a rescue mission would have risked the lives of elite operators, which no commander deemed acceptable.

According to Sedney, not a single mission order, for either the Army's conventional units or JSOC's special operators, was ever sent out with the specific order to find and rescue Bergdahl. "It was never the primary purpose or one of the top two or three purposes of any operation that took place," he said.

Still, the Pentagon always plans for every contingency, and the classified Bergdahl rescue missions were put away in a locked file. Less than two years later, the plans were updated, adapted, and re-tasked again, this time for Operation Neptune Spear, the May 2, 2011, mission to assassinate Osama bin Laden.

ELEVEN

THE PAKISTAN PARADOX

Pakistan is the pivot of the world," Muhammad Ali Jinnah, Pakistan's founding father and first governor-general, declared in 1947. More than six decades later, the country's pivotal status would make everything connected to Bowe Bergdahl's captivity and recovery vastly more complicated and difficult.

Jinnah had made his pronouncement to Margaret Bourke-White, the *Life* photographer and journalist who had traveled to South Asia to interview the leaders of the world's youngest and largest Muslim nation. Documenting the vast emigration of India's Muslims that followed the partition of British India, she captured the iconic images of the time: Mahatma Gandhi sitting cross-legged with his spinning wheel, scenes of disease and death among the refugees, and an arresting close-up portrait of Jinnah, Pakistan's severe, skeletal leader.

"America needs Pakistan more than Pakistan needs America," Jinnah told her. He was speaking then of the exigencies of the developing Cold War, when Pakistan could serve American interests as a counterweight to the Soviet and Chinese Communists to the north and India's leftist regime to the east. But Jinnah also understood that his country's spiritual role transcended its geographical borders. To a fragmented and dispossessed Muslim world partitioned by Western powers after every great war, Pakistan was an inspiration. For the international Muslim community, the Ummah, it was an organizing principle.

In 1949, the Constituent Assembly, Pakistan's first parliament, made this purpose explicit: The nation would be a refuge for the persecuted Muslims of South Asia to live their lives "in accordance with the teachings and requirements of Islam." That same year, the president of the Muslim League party took it one step further, proclaiming that his country would unite the Muslim world—if not in space, then at least in spirit—by renaming itself "Islamistan." The passions of these Muslim identity politics were often expressed as grievance. The country was less than a year old when, in May 1948, following Israel's formal declaration as an independent state (and another refuge for a persecuted religious minority), three thousand Pakistanis descended on the U.S. Embassy in Karachi to protest American recognition of Israel.

Nevertheless, Pakistani officials were confident that the United States would finance their country's defenses. At diplomatic meetings in both countries, they reminded the Americans that if Washington didn't step up and help build Pakistan's military and intelligence infrastructure, Moscow would. Educated Pakistanis vouched for the sanctity of their democracy, as had Jinnah—"Of course it will be a democratic constitution," he told Bourke-White, "Islam is a democratic religion"—while downplaying the fervor in their streets and the clerics who clamored for the rule of Sharia law. While hard-liners at home called on their government to send troops to liberate Palestine from the Jews, diplomats traveled to Washington to lobby the Truman administration for military aid.

Jinnah, keenly aware of his geopolitical advantage, leveraged both sides to his benefit, a strategy that became a staple of Pakistani politics. Rather than commit one way or the other, generations of Pakistan's political class stoked the fires of anti-American Islamic populism, all the while relying on Washington's largesse to build a massive military and spy agency designed to deter India, its original and eternal foe. Less than a year after Truman signed his own National Security Act, the legislation that formed the Defense Department and the CIA,

Washington bankrolled the founding of Pakistan's Inter-Services Intelligence (ISI).

The country's main Sunni party, Jamiat Ulema-e-Islam, ran on platforms of domestic "Islamization" and regulations of everything from women's clothing to music and entertainment. Over the years, the terminology changed—from "Islamic constitutionalism" to "Islamic democracy" and "Islamic socialism"—but the reactionary fervor persisted. When it raged out of control, the Pakistani government could point to its domestic political unrest as just cause for increased American aid.

Washington complied, and Islamabad continued to rely on foreign money to build out its defense and intelligence capabilities. By the early 1950s, the country was spending 60 percent of its annual GDP on defense. A civilian and military ruling class lived affluently, while most of the country remained mired in poverty. The contrast wasn't lost on American jazz trumpeter Dizzy Gillespie, who visited Karachi in 1956 on a State Department–sponsored goodwill tour. Gillespie was appalled that tickets to the Pakistan show were priced so high that "the people we were trying to gain friendship with couldn't make it," and he refused to play until the doors were opened to the lower classes and street children gathered outside.

The following year, James Langley, President Eisenhower's new ambassador, challenged Washington's prevailing assumptions about Pakistan shortly after his arrival. A newspaper publisher from Concord, New Hampshire, and an outsider to the culture of government policy groupthink, Langley asked whether his colleagues were accepting Pakistani reports about their own affairs "as gospel truth without sufficient periodic scrutiny." He described the popular notion that the country was pro-Western as "wishful thinking." In Pakistan, Langley wrote, "We have an unruly horse by the tail and are confronted by the dilemma of trying to tame it before we can let go safely."

Pakistani turmoil over American influence came to a head in November 1979, when a mob stormed the U.S. Embassy in Islamabad. It was just three weeks after Iranian students had done the same in

Tehran and one week after Saudi fundamentalists took over the Masjid-al-Haram in Mecca, taking hostages at the holiest site in Islam during the Hajj. When Iran's Ayatollah Ruhollah Khomeini spread the rumor that the Americans were behind the attacks at the Hajj, protests erupted throughout the Muslim world. The next day, the mob in Islamabad burned the American Embassy to the ground as police stood by.

Over the course of the Cold War, Washington's leniency enabled Pakistan's worst impulses. Islamabad learned to stop worrying about its own economic output (or repaying foreign loans) and to start loving high-tech weaponry. The national quest for nuclear parity culminated in the 1998 test of the Muslim world's first atomic bomb. Indulged by American dollars and complacent about its internal dysfunctions, Pakistan at the end of the Cold War had grown into the West's problem-child state, perpetually oscillating between its roles as Washington's military vassal and a quasi theocracy that wielded Islamic populism as a weapon it couldn't fully control.

September 11, which was masterminded by the Pakistani terrorist Khalid Sheikh Mohammed, only amplified these dynamics. Even as President Pervez Musharraf vowed to be Washington's indispensable partner in the War on Terror, bin Laden and Ayman al-Zawahiri were provided safe passage through the tribal areas. In March 2004, Secretary of State Colin Powell designated the country as a "major non-NATO ally," a label that, as *New York Times* reporter David Rohde noted at the time, "added diplomatic prestige and greater access to American military technology, surplus defense equipment, and training." Between 2001 and 2011, Islamabad received more than $20 billion in U.S. aid, the bulk of which was earmarked for the FATA, which, after decades of neglect and political disenfranchisement from the British Raj, India, and most recently Pakistan, had emerged as the nexus of global terror. Assistance from Germany, the U.K., Japan, the World Bank, and the Asian Development Bank added about $10 billion more. Still, the Pakistani military was not content.

Days after *The Wall Street Journal*'s South Asia bureau chief Daniel Pearl was abducted in a Karachi restaurant in late January 2002, his captors released a photo of their hostage with a gun to his head, along with a list of demands. Writing from the email address kidnapperguy@ hotmail.com, they had two ultimatums: first, that the U.S. government release all Pakistani detainees from Camp X-Ray at Guantanamo Bay; and second, that Washington fulfill its promise to send the Pakistanis several F-16 fighter jets purchased in the late 1980s and held up by sanctions over the country's rogue nuclear program. It seemed like an awfully specific and sophisticated demand from kidnapperguy, and to many observers, evidence that elements of the Pakistani military, or at least a few bad actors in the ISI, were complicit in the Pearl atrocity.

As the Taliban insurgency gained strength in the waning years of the Bush administration, Washington placed hope above experience and poured millions more into western Pakistan. In 2007, the State Department announced a five-year, $750 million Security Development Plan aimed at a range of social and economic initiatives, including infrastructure, women's and children's health care, and education; the Pentagon kicked in an extra $200 million to shore up Pakistan's Frontier Corps (FC), the paramilitary force composed of soldiers recruited from the Pashtun provinces they were meant to patrol and whose sympathies the Pakistani Army struggled to retain. (Fliers distributed in Waziristan warned FC soldiers, "We know that you have become America's slave . . . a traitor to your religion for food, clothes, and shelter.")

Washington's investments were tied to the explicit goal, as then Deputy Secretary of State John Negroponte told the Senate Committee on Foreign Relations in May 2008, "to bring these remote areas into the Pakistani mainstream and render them permanently inhospitable to terrorists and extremists." Negroponte spoke frankly about the challenges—no clean drinking water, no public education, and a female literacy rate hovering around 3 percent made the western frontier provinces one of the most neglected and destitute places in all of Asia. The good news, he said, was that "nowhere are common U.S.-Pakistan interests more in evidence than in the [FATA]."

Whether Negroponte believed his own pronouncements was unclear. He was privy to U.S. intelligence reports that told a starkly different story: Even as the State Department money was spent (along with the roughly $2 billion in annual military aid), the militias, terror groups, and Taliban only grew stronger. For President Bush, the final insult arrived on the Monday following the July 4, 2008, holiday weekend, when a twenty-two-year-old Pakistani detonated a Toyota Camry laden with explosives at the front gate of the Indian Embassy in Kabul. Fifty-eight people were killed, mostly Indian government and military personnel.

There was little question who had been behind the attack. Bush and his national security team already knew that an ISI colonel was cozied up to Sirajuddin Haqqani, the son and commander of the Taliban faction named for his father, the CIA's former favorite warlord, Jalaluddin. "We're going to stop playing the game," Bush said to aides at the time. "These sons of bitches are killing Americans. I've had enough."

Three decades after Washington first saw his clan's utility, American spy-craft was once again focused on Haqqani. The same man whom Democratic congressman Charlie Wilson once described as "goodness personified" and whom the CIA entrusted with frequency-hopping radios and heat-seeking, man-portable, anti-aircraft Stinger missiles was now a critical threat—and the ISI's most effective proxy. Haqqani operated under the private approval and public denials of a rotating cast of Pakistani politicians and generals. Just as the Americans had used the mujahideen during Operation Cyclone, now the ISI turned to an assortment of mercenaries to carry out its hard-line policies. Lashkar-e-Taiba was another remnant of the Soviet War that the ISI had repurposed for a new era. In November 2008, ten Lashkar fighters staged a bloody four-day siege in Mumbai that left hundreds dead and wounded. The Pakistani authorities detained the group's founder and leader, Hafiz Muhammad Saeed, permitted him to hold an indignant press conference, and then held him under house arrest in his own upscale Lahore neighborhood. A Pakistani court acquitted him six months later.

In 2008, Senator Barack Obama had no illusions about the war's central shaky alliance. "Make no mistake," he said during his presidential campaign that summer, "we can't succeed in Afghanistan or secure our homeland unless we change our Pakistan policy. We cannot tolerate a terrorist sanctuary, and as president, I won't." It was the kind of hopeful talk that got him elected. But Obama entered the White House knowing that finding common purpose with Islamabad could prove impossible. During his presidential transition, Obama read intelligence reports detailing the same stark realities that had so outraged Bush—former president Musharraf and the chief of staff of the Pakistani military, General Ashfaq Parvez Kayani, were personally authorizing ISI officers to work with the Haqqanis, the Quetta Shura (the Taliban's government in exile), and Lashkar.

Obama launched the most aggressive diplomatic campaign since Pakistan's founding. Defense Secretary Robert Gates, a Republican who would go on to deride Obama's team for what he saw as a string of rookie foreign policy mistakes, credited the young Democratic president's approach. "No administration in my entire career devoted more time and energy to working the Pakistanis," Gates later wrote in his memoir. Between 2008 and 2011, Chairman of the Joint Chiefs admiral Michael Mullen led the diplomatic charge, traveling to Pakistan twenty-seven times to meet personally with General Kayani and turn what had been an essentially transactional relationship into a truer partnership. Even when their meetings failed to produce concrete agreements, they helped Mullen discern the limits of Pakistani allegiance. When Mullen offered to send U.S. advisers to train Pakistani Army formations to fight extremists in the FATA, Kayani declined, saying his country would sooner go to war with India than launch such a massive assault on its own people in the territories.

Kayani earned his master's degree at the United States Army Command and General Staff College on Fort Leavenworth, Kansas, in 1988, just as the CIA and ISI were assessing their victory over the Soviets. He wrote his thesis on the "Strengths and Weaknesses of the Afghan Resistance Movement." There was no way to see that conflict without appreciating the CIA's central role. Thirty years later, he had become the most powerful man in his country, and together with ISI director general Lieutenant General Ahmed Shuja Pasha, perpetuated their delicate liasons with Washington. Early in Obama's first term, they shared ISI intelligence about radicalized Muslims from the U.S., U.K., Germany, Canada, and Sweden arriving in the FATA to train in al-Qaeda camps. In February 2009, Pasha even vowed to senior White House and State Department officials that he would clean out his agency's "rogue elements." As Obama ramped up the CIA's drone assassinations, Pasha's ISI shared more intelligence on al-Qaeda and Haqqani fighters who had joined forces in North Waziristan. Even as Pakistani president Zardari publicly vented that the drones were a violation of his nation's sovereignty, Kayani and Pasha allowed the CIA to launch its drones from Shamsi Airfield in Balochistan.

These were positive steps, but the Obama White House let Kayani and Pasha know that they would need to go further, publishing a tough-love policy report in March 2009 that addressed the issue bluntly: "The core goal of the U.S. must be to disrupt, dismantle, and defeat al-Qaeda and its safe havens in Pakistan," it said. Terror networks must be confronted "in Afghanistan and especially Pakistan." Global stability depended on it; the possibility of extremists obtaining a nuclear device "is all too real." Instability in the FATA wasn't simply an American concern about winning the War in Afghanistan, but an imperative of far greater consequence—saving Pakistan from itself. Even a limited nuclear exchange between India and Pakistan would cause a temporary nuclear winter, threatening the lives of a billion people.

Ambassador Langley's unruly horse was slipping away. Were it lost, the best outcome would have Islamabad falling under heavy influence from Moscow and Beijing, potentially in open war with India. The worst-case scenario—with men like Haqqani, Saeed, and their hard-line ISI enablers in control of the world's only Muslim nuclear arsenal—was unthinkable.

THE FACT that the only American POW in the Afghanistan war was being held inside the borders of America's key ally in that war meant a rescue raid was out of the question. With thousands of U.S. troops arriving at Bagram each month, the risk of triggering a larger regional conflict, or worse, destabilizing Islamabad's own shaky hold on power, was simply too great. With each new proof-of-life video, U.S. officials issued the same vows to find Bergdahl and bring him home. But there was no actionable plan or coherent strategy to back up those promises. Bergdahl had been sucked into a geopolitical black hole. Held captive by America's enemy under the protection of her ally, his plight mirrored the self-enforcing illogic of the entire war.

Private First Class Bergdahl may have been the first U.S. soldier detained long-term in Pakistan, but he was not the first American, nor the Taliban's first high-value hostage. Kidnapping was a business in Afghanistan, and during the war, business was good. More than one hundred foreign citizens were abducted between 2001 and 2011, including a dozen journalists. During the summer of 2007, Taliban gunmen stopped a bus carrying nearly two dozen South Korean missionaries on the road between Kabul and Kandahar. Before the nearly six-week crisis was over, two missionaries were executed; the Korean government in Seoul vowed to withdraw its two hundred troops from Afghanistan, stop sending missionaries, and according to various Taliban claims, paid $10 million or $20 million dollars to bring home the survivors.

The Taliban called their hostages "golden chickens" or "golden sparrows." For the Haqqanis, the chicken trade was brisk, and along with extortion, chromite mining, and fund-raising from Jalaluddin's roster of Saudi benefactors, hostage ransoms provided the network with substantial revenue at little cost. Overhead was low, logistics straightforward: Taliban operatives used elaborate promises for high-level meetings to lure Western journalists into vulnerable settings. Once they were bound, blindfolded, and rendered docile, the captives were smuggled over the border and locked away in safe houses while Haqqani leadership haggled with the hostages' families, insurance contractors, or governments over the price of their freedom.

Several Taliban factions carried out abductions, but the Haqqani captor network that nabbed Bergdahl was the most sophisticated operation of the bunch. In 2008, it snatched three consecutive high-profile Western journalists: Jere Van Dyk, a CBS and *New York Times* contributor (held for forty-five days); BBC filmmaker Sean Langan (eighty-six days); and *New York Times* reporter David Rohde (two hundred twenty-two days). All three had years of experience in Afghanistan.

Bergdahl was a hostage far longer than Langan, Rohde, or Van Dyk, but like them, he had fallen victim to his own hubris. Bergdahl would later acknowledge the ignorance and absurdity of his "fantastic plan." Rohde called his own kidnapping "the stupidest disaster of my career." Langan said that he "felt like Icarus," and that interviews with dangerous men had become the sun around which not just his life, but his family's lives, had come to revolve. Van Dyk knew the region better than most, and he would later say that he should have known better. In 1973, he and his brother had traveled the hippie trail through Afghanistan in an old Volkswagen. During the Soviet War, he had written about Haqqani's military prowess and stayed as a guest on his property. But in February 2008, he ignored his gut and numerous warnings from his Afghan contacts, and traveled in disguise into the FATA. He was kidnapped after one day, held for forty-five, and released without explanation.

Langan had covered kidnappings for years. In 1997, he filmed a three-part BBC series tracking two British tourists abducted in Kashmir. Four years later, just before 9/11, he was in Kabul, sneaking his forbidden cameras into meetings with Taliban officials. When the U.S./U.K.-led wars broke out, Langan was in them. In 2003, he was an embed in Fallujah, shuttling his cameras between U.S. combat patrols and Sunni insurgents in Iraq's Anbar Province. Then it was back to Afghanistan, where Kabul became a second home, and his risk taking was rewarded with years of access to otherwise inaccessible subjects. Langan sat down with a company of Taliban fighters in Helmand Province, met masked Hezbi-Islami guerrillas infiltrating the border in the mountains of Kunar, and in a haunting 2006 conversation, chatted with an adolescent boy who had been packed with explosives and smiled serenely as he discussed his imminent martyrdom. With his career in full stride, Langan aimed higher. He wanted the stars of the insurgency—Siraj Haqqani and Baitullah Mehsud—and he wanted them on camera. His local fixers assured him it was possible, made all the arrangements, and sent him into a trap for a commission.

By the time he was released on June 21, 2008, Langan had lost forty pounds from dysentery and malnutrition. He returned to London, where he found himself on the wrong side of the camera lens. There were rumors that his employer, the publicly funded Channel 4 Television Corporation, had paid a six-figure ransom. Tory politicians and Fleet Street columnists charged Langan and Channel 4 with incentivizing more kidnappings and questioned whether he had been worth the price. In public statements, the British Foreign Office said it discouraged paying ransoms, but unofficially the Foreign Office also told hostages' families to do whatever they needed to do to bring their loved ones home; they would not be punished. Citing a Foreign Office source, *The Times* later reported that Channel 4 had paid £150,000 each for Langan and his translator. In a final dose of irony, Siraj Haqqani sat for an interview with an NBC producer at a safe house in Khost the following month.

That summer, Rohde was nearing the end of his time as the South Asia bureau chief for *The New York Times*, newly married, and worried about his career. He had planned to write a book about the reporting that had taken him from the falling towers in Lower Manhattan to the front lines of the wars that followed. But in those years of work and dozens of bylines, he had never interviewed a Taliban commander and was anxious about returning home and being seen, as he later put it, as "a New York–based journalistic fraud." When an opportunity arrived to meet a commander named Abu Tayyeb, Rohde told himself not to let the story fall victim to his own fears.

The night before his appointment with Tayyeb, Rohde met with colleagues at a restaurant in Kabul's international zone to discuss the plan. He noted the new blast barriers that had been set up following a wave of Haqqani-directed bombings, signs of the Taliban's growing impunity. Rohde's friends had mixed opinions about his scheduled interview. The gossip in Kabul was that Langan and Van Dyk had been reckless; no fair-skinned, blue-eyed American or Brit could go wandering alone and unarmed into the border's lawless frontier. But Rohde wouldn't take that kind of risk. His Afghan fixer, Tahir Luddin, was one of the best; he had worked for the *The Times* of London and arrived with glowing references. Luddin assured Rohde that Tayyeb was a known commander who had conducted on-camera interviews with European journalists before. He was a moderate Taliban, Luddin said. The biggest risk would be bandits on the road.

Rohde and Luddin never did meet a commander named Tayyeb in Logar Province. Their car was hijacked at gunpoint that November morning, and they spent days stashed among blankets and rugs in the back of a Toyota station wagon that cruised the dusty desert back roads of southeastern Afghanistan. Their captors hiked them overnight through the mountains and through a small village. Rohde suspected he knew the moment when they had crossed the Durand Line; he saw his guards' body language visibly relax. When they put him in another car that started driving down the left-hand lane, British style, he knew he was in Pakistan and assumed that he would be killed.

In *A Rope and a Prayer*, the 2010 book about the ordeal he coauthored with his wife, Kristen Mulvihill, Rohde called his plan "a bachelor's decision." His regret and guilt were compounded by the uncanny fact that it was not his first experience as the highest-value American hostage of a foreign war. In 1995, he was reporting from Bosnia and asking too many questions around the Srebrenica massacre when Serbian authorities locked him up, sparking a minor international crisis that ended only after substantial diplomatic pressure from U.S. envoys, including Secretary of State Warren Christopher and UN ambassador Richard Holbrooke. Thirteen years later, when Rohde told the legendary diplomat that he was headed to Afghanistan, Holbrooke quipped, "Don't get captured again."

Six days after the 2008 presidential election, Rohde had done just that, and Holbrooke was wondering whether his own career was finished. He had been a leading contender for secretary of state under what would have been his second Clinton administration—had Hillary Clinton won the nomination and the election. Instead, after Obama named his former rival to be the country's chief diplomat, Clinton hired Holbrooke for what was arguably the State Department's most difficult job: special representative to Afghanistan and Pakistan, or SRAP.

Rohde's captivity was one of the better-kept secrets in Washington that winter, his case kept under wraps by an extraordinary international media blackout led by his editors and publisher at *The New York Times*. For the senior Bush and Obama officials who tracked his case—including Hillary Clinton, who as secretary of state made a personal pledge to Mulvihill to get her husband out—Rohde was a living reminder of the limits of Washington's power, influence, and logistical capabilities in Pakistan.

The day he was abducted in Logar, Rohde assured his captors that he and Luddin were worth more alive than dead. It was a reflexive act of survival that he only later realized encouraged wild overspeculation about what he might be worth; his captors opened negotiations at $25 million and the release of fifteen Taliban prisoners from Guantanamo and Bagram. That was $5 million more than even the highest estimates of what the South Korean government had paid to release more than twenty missionaries, and far from realistic. The kidnapping and ransom (K&R) insurance policy of *The New York Times* covered just $2 million, his family had no such sums, and releasing prisoners was a nonstarter. Negotiations dragged on for months.

In the Haqqani safe house where he was imprisoned, Rohde found a ten-foot section of dirty rope tied to a three-foot metal chain on a shelf full of wrenches, motor oil, and spare car parts. Each day, when he could, Rohde loosened the rope from the chain, terrified the noise would give him away. On June 19, while the guards slept, he and Luddin climbed down a twenty-foot wall and ran.

For Kayani and the Pakistani government, the fact that Rohde ran to a Frontier Corps base just down the road from a Haqqani prison was deeply embarrassing—and made their denials of coddling extremists that much more implausible. For the Haqqanis, Rohde's escape was a humiliating end to what had been their most successful American kidnapping, eight months of work literally out the window. Less than two weeks later, Bergdahl was their stunning redemption.

THREE DECADES OF CONFLICT had taught Pakistan's generals and spymasters that the benefits provided by their resident extremists outweighed the risks. Context mattered; the mujahideen ideologies and capabilities had been forged in the crucible of the Soviet War and the CIA's massive covert response. From Islamabad's perspective, Washington was demanding a Pakistani solution to an American-made problem.

By the spring of 2009, however, the once-isolated infection of radicalism in the FATA was no longer contained. The number of fighters and independent militias, each with its own goals, had reached unprecedented levels. While Lashkar operated under the nominal control of Pakistani authorities, and Haqqani ruled North Waziristan, a new and different threat emerged in South Waziristan: the Tehrik-i-Taliban Pakistan (TTP), a confederation of roughly forty tribal militias that had joined together under the revolutionary banner of the Pakistani Taliban led by Baitullah Mehsud. Unlike Haqqani and Gulbuddin Hekmatyar, the legacy mujahideen warlords in the north, Mehsud's worldview wasn't formed by the Soviet War—when he had been just a child—but by 9/11. As he watched the Pakistani government collaborate with the Americans against the Taliban, Mehsud decided the problem was the Islamabad government itself. He announced his upstart terror group's arrival with the December 2007 assassination of Benazir Bhutto.

Mehsud claimed to have forty thousand fighters at his command, and in the late summer of 2008, his Pakistani Taliban had done the unthinkable and seized power in the Swat Valley. For decades the valley had been a bucolic mountain getaway for upper-class Pakistanis escaping the summer heat and smog in crowded Islamabad and Rawalpindi (home to the government and military, respectively). The Switzerland of Pakistan, as local tourism bureaus touted it, Swat had been a popular stop along Central Asia's Hippie Trail in the 1970s; its local weavers were some of the same artisans exporting cashmere shawls to Terry Reid and Sharon Davies's import bazaar in Ketchum, Idaho, a few hundred yards from where Bergdahl had worked at Strega. There was a ski resort in Swat at Malam Jabba, built in the 1980s with financing from the Austrian government. Its hotel was burned to the ground in August 2008 as Mehsud's fighters moved in. Skiing, they declared, was un-Islamic.

Swat became a Taliban safe haven and a clear sign that Islamabad was losing control. Between 2007 and 2009, the TTP burned down nearly two hundred girls' schools and beheaded dozens of local government officials and Frontier Corps soldiers. The Swat Taliban was led by Maulana Qazi Fazlullah, a ski-lift operator turned radio demagogue known as Mullah Radio for his pirate FM broadcasts. In local newspapers, Swat police officers took out ads to publicly renounce their secular authorities and save their own lives.

After a failed attempt by the Pakistani Army to take back the valley, the provincial government struck an appeasement deal with Mullah Radio—permitting him to impose his authority in exchange for peace.

The government's legitimacy had never been less certain. When Ahmed Rashid went to see President Zardari in Islamabad in July 2009, the presidential palace was surrounded by concrete blast barriers and more than a half-dozen checkpoint perimeters. But Zardari (who was Bhutto's widower), downplayed the threat. Instead, he framed the problems facing his country in more historically familiar terms.

"We have no money to arm the police or fund development, give jobs, or revive the economy. What are we supposed to do?" the president asked. Musharraf had been lavished with $11 billion in U.S. aid, Zardari noted, while he had been given far less. If his country failed, the president told Rashid bluntly, it will be America's doing. On May 7, 2009, the standoff in Swat erupted into a full-blown air and ground war. Kayani sent in thirty thousand Army soldiers along with heavy artillery, fighter jets, and helicopter gunships. In an unprecedented decision, supporting troops were called in from the border with India, where the government in New Delhi vowed not to exploit the situation with an attack. By the time fighting subsided that summer, three hundred Army soldiers and ten times that many militants had been killed.

As the fighting spread, upward of three million civilians fled their homes, and they took shelter with host families registered by the UN or in dozens of hastily built camps on the lowland plains to the south. By the time the fighting subsided, it would be the largest internal displacement of refugees in Pakistan's history. In Washington, U.S. officials were both satisfied with Kayani's results and alarmed by the Pakistani Army's indiscriminate violence. "The British at least forewarned us and they never targeted innocent women and children. The military was ruthless," Waziri writer Ghulam Qadir Khan Daur reported. Hundreds of Pashtun villagers were killed in the fighting, and rumors swirled among them that the slaughter was arranged by the Haqqanis and ISI under a false flag designed to produce a new generation of militant recruits.

On the night of August 7, a CIA drone guided by ISI intelligence launched two Hellfire missiles at a remote South Waziristan farmhouse, killing Mehsud and eleven others. The Pakistani military, after three years of near chaos, was finally regaining control. But as Kayani's offensive extended from Swat into the FATA that fall, it was also notable for what it didn't do: Pakistani pilots flying American F-16s hit more than a hundred targets in Waziristan, but Haqqani property was largely unscathed.

Obama wrote a personal letter to President Zardari in November, urging the Pakistani president to make a real move on Haqqani's domain in North Waziristan, where U.S. intelligence believed Bergdahl was being held. Zardari didn't write back for several weeks, and when he did, his response was vague and evasive. Obama's demands went ignored.

TWELVE

FIXING INTEL

On Christmas Day 2009, the Taliban paraded their American prisoner in a confident and ambitious new global broadcast. It was Bergdahl's second public appearance, and the Taliban media affairs team had raised its technical game since July with a variety of slick edits and deft embellishments. Al-Emara, the logo of the exiled Islamic Emirate's propaganda channel, floats in the upper-right corner in English and Arabic. The video features quick cuts and bullet-hole graphics with whooshing sound effects, split screens, and a backdrop image of a U.S. soldier standing alone in a dark desert sandstorm. Arabic captions identify him as "the witness of his people."

Bergdahl is seated in front of a red and gold tapestry, wearing an army combat helmet. Beneath the helmet, he wears mirrored sunglasses, a prop he would later tell intelligence debriefers was meant to hide his eyes as he read from his captors' scripts and cues. He's dressed in an Army combat uniform shirt stripped of identification—no private first class rank insignia, no BERGDAHL name tape, no 25th Infantry Division "Electric Strawberry" patch—much like the "sterile uniform" that the Delta and SEAL operators he admired wore on missions where anonymity was key. Bergdahl's face is thin, his cheeks hollowed out since July. The skin on his neck is pale and wan, and when he moves and shifts his weight, the shirt betrays his now-bony frame. When his parents saw the video, they guessed he had lost twenty pounds. The Taliban production team may have intended the getup to make him look intimidating, like a real American soldier. But his physical decline is evident, and the overall effect is closer to a cancer patient on Halloween.

The POW ritual begins with Bergdahl confirming he is who he is: name, birthplace, blood type, mother's maiden name, Army rank and unit. His mouth cracks in a downturned grimace, his voice a narcotized monotone—just like the crew of the USS *Pueblo* and Daniel Pearl before him, and James Foley and Kayla Mueller after.

> I came to Afghanistan on May 3, 2009, and was positioned in the Paktika Province of Afghanistan, in the district of Sharana.

As Bergdahl speaks the screen splits, revealing footage of American soldiers shackling, hooding, and caging detainees in the Global War on Terror. He narrates the indignities suffered "by Muslim prisoners in Bagram, Guantanamo Bay, Abu Ghraib, and many other secret prisons hidden around the world," against a backdrop of hooded prisoners, piles of men stacked in a grotesque parody of the classic American cheerleader human pyramid, and naked men cowering before snarling dogs. Another prisoner stands with arms stretched behind his back, his back and shoulders splattered with feces. Alongside them, American military police prison guards pose and smile.

> Knowing the brutality and inhumane ways my country has ravaged the land and the people of my captors, the Taliban, one would expect that they would justly treat me as my country's Army has treated their Muslim prisoners . . . but I bear witness. I was continuously treated as a human being with dignity.

There are distinct forms and functions to POW testimonials. First, they present proof-of-life, the baseline for further negotiations. They critique specific policies and are crafted to inspire and outrage targeted audiences—in Bergdahl's case, Taliban foot soldiers, aspiring mujahideen, and persuadable Americans. The Christmas Day video shows the casualties of U.S. foreign policy: the frozen faces of dead children and a frail elderly corpse in a white death shroud, all allegedly killed by American bombs; YouTube footage of an American civilian rapid-firing his pistol into a Koran as it skips across the ground. The arc of Bergdahl's testimony follows the classic conversion story: the confession of sin, an awakening to higher truths and newfound sympathies, and ultimately, gratitude to the captors.

> Far from the continuous brainwashing and false hype-up and propaganda that the Army drowns us in, I had the chance to actually see with my own eyes the people that I was supposed to consider my enemy. . . . Even though I'm a prisoner of war, I had a chance to rethink a lot of things, and to ask myself questions that I never asked myself before.

As Bergdahl reveals his own supposed awakening, his clothing changes from a soldier's uniform to a simple cloth shirt and no helmet.

> And so, do I, my family members, my fellow soldiers in the army and their families, and all the regular Americans—do we or even should we trust those that send us to be killed in the name of America? Because aren't our leaders, be it Obama or a Bush or whoever, aren't they simply the puppets of the lobbies that pay for their election campaigns in the first place?
>
> I'm afraid to tell you that this war has slipped from our fingers. It's just going to be the next Vietnam unless the American people stand up and stop all this nonsense. And as a soldier in the U.S. Army and just as an American person here, I find it as my duty and responsibility to let my people

> know exactly what the truth is behind this facade that is the Army and, uh, and to let them know the truth behind, you know, these wars that our governments just keep throwing us into.

Interspersed between his testimonies, the video cuts to snippets taken from American television of U.S. military veterans urging President Obama to de-escalate the war, including former Marine captain and State Department official Matthew Hoh, whose bold resignation letter had gone public a few months earlier. The Taliban had taken Hoh's clip from a November 10, 2009, interview he did with CNN's Wolf Blitzer. Earlier that day, anonymous news leaks, likely from the Pentagon itself, had suggested that Obama had already approved the surge that McChrystal wanted. Blitzer asked Hoh to address the president's apparent decision, and to "look into that camera" and talk to Obama directly. Hoh took the direction:

> Mr. President, I understand the domestic political concerns that you have. However, this is an opportunity to be a great leader, to recognize the challenges that we are facing and the fact that it's a civil war. American combat troops are not defeating al-Qaeda by their presence in Afghanistan. All they are doing is just fighting people who are fighting us because we're occupying them.

Hoh wasn't surprised that the Taliban used him in the Bergdahl tape. Their messaging had been effective for many years, Hoh said, noting that the Taliban was broadcasting on Facebook, in English, years before social media became the central venue for foreign propaganda in the United States. Before the Christmas Day video ends, Bergdahl's testimony grows more dogmatic—and more absurd. The split screens runs footage of burning MRAPs, dead ISAF soldiers, and video of IED attacks enhanced with postproduction death-porn touches: Humvees disappear from the road like ghosts, trucks explode, and alleged flying body parts are highlighted in red circles, like a slow-motion NFL replay, for easy home viewing.

As the video progresses, Bergdahl's delivery improves. He grows more animated and adds hand gestures, his statements veer away from the demonstrable evidence of U.S. military prisons to the dubious claims that circulate on the streets of Kandahar and Peshawar. The real numbers of children killed by American forces are hidden, and once revealed will "have surpassed Hitler." American bombs are disrupting Afghan fertility, leading to miscarriages, birth deformities, and babies forced to live "wretched lives as retarded children." American power, in this telling, is transcendent—not just cruel, but an omnipotent power that compels Muslims to jihad. "We," Bergdahl says, the Americans, "have forced them to strap large amounts of explosives to their precious bodies, to leave their homes and their children to kill us."

The tape reaches peak implausibility when Bergdahl describes his own health and well-being. The split screen shows an American military interrogation. Soldiers hold a man's head under water in a red plastic bucket, and we hear audio of his grunts, wretches, and screams. Cut to Bergdahl: "No, the mujahideen have not tortured me," he says, his voice falling away on the final words. He says that he has a toothbrush, toothpaste, and shaving equipment, that he takes regular showers. Cut to Bergdahl sitting comfortably at a table covered with fruit and glass-bottled beverages. He wears a shalwar and a small red *taqiyah* cap, has a blue pen in his shirt pocket, and eats rice with a fork. He sips from a white cup and nods in exaggerated appreciation. "As far as chains, yeah I'm in chains. I'm chained to where I sleep . . . but it kinda comes with the area of being a prisoner of war."

The chains, he said, "haven't inhibited my movement in a huge way that causes my body to degrade." Intelligence analysts only later realized he was trying to drop hints about his condition. He tells the world he is being treated according to the ethical codes of Pashtunwali. "I'm healthy and being taken care of as a guest in someone's home." He apologizes to his parents in a passing moment of candor that they said stuck with them for years. "That's all we had to go on," Jani said. The video ends with a statement by Taliban spokesman Zabihullah Mujahid with a scrolling English translation:

> The Islamic Emirate of Afghanistan has demanded and still demands release of limited number of prisoners in exchange for this American prisoner, Bowe Robert Bergdahl. Unfortunately, the arrogant American rulers are not ready to take any step in this regard.

In the nine and a half months since the golden sparrow had flown into their hands, the Taliban had been reaching out through numerous channels to negotiate. Major Jeff Crapo fielded the first attempt from the village elders near Mest the day after Bergdahl was captured. That same day, Taliban commanders, including Sangeen himself, called journalists with their opening bid. In calls with CBS and Agence France-Presse, they said they spoke for Siraj Haqqani and Taliban leadership. "We would not mind a prisoner exchange in this case," one commander said.

Those were the public tactics. Privately, also in the first weeks of the DUSTWUN, Haqqani delivered their first proof-of-life video on a cell phone SIM card, along with ransom demands to General Reeder, commander of the Combined Joint Special Operations Task Force-Afghanistan. The captors wanted $19 million and twenty-five Taliban prisoners from Guantanamo in exchange for Bergdahl (less money but more prisoners than their offer for Rohde a few weeks earlier). Reeder didn't respond. A few weeks later, motivated to make a deal, the Haqqanis followed up with a better offer: five million dollars and no prisoner exchange. More than most generals, Reeder had formed close relationships with a wide array of former Taliban officials, and one told him that Bergdahl was already in Miran Shah. Reeder passed the messages up his chain of command, to Flynn and McChrystal, where they promptly disappeared. He later told a journalist that he was surprised that none of his superiors acted on the information. Six months later, with the Christmas video, Haqqani tried again. As with each prior offer, the U.S. military did not respond.

IT HAD BEEN eight years since the Taliban were routed from Kabul and Kandahar and bin Laden vanished into the mountains and cave complexes of Tora Bora. The CIA needed a win and thought they had one with a Jordanian doctor named Humam Khalil Abu-Mulal al-Balawi. Balawi was just what the CIA had been missing: a mole with intimate access to core al-Qaeda leadership. Since early 2009, his handlers in Amman had been passing along his covert reports to their CIA counterparts, and, with each new dispatch from the FATA, Balawi's stature grew, from merely a promising asset to a mole with historic potential. In August, he sent a short video clip of himself alongside Atiyah Abd al-Rahman, a thirty-seven-year-old al-Qaeda commander, explosives expert, and the man bin Laden had tasked with managing Abu Musab al-Zarqawi, the Jordanian leader of Al-Qaeda in Iraq (AQI). Most compellingly, Balawai also had access to Ayman al-Zawahiri, on whom the last tips were at least two years old.

The Jordanian General Intelligence Directorate, or Mukhabarat, was upfront with the Americans about Balawi's checkered background. He had been recruited by a young GID officer, a cousin to King Abdullah II, who discovered Balawi through his online alter ego as a prolific jihadi named Abu Dujana al-Khorasani. After the Mukhabarat hauled him in for interrogations, Balawi flipped allegiances and agreed to help the Mukhabarat track down terrorists. Still, there were doubts about his reliability. He needed to be vetted by the CIA directly. In mid-

December 2009, Langley issued orders to Jennifer Matthews, the senior officer in Khost Base, and one of the agency's most experienced al-Qaeda experts, to find out if Balawi was what he seemed.

Matthews and her team decided to bring him across the border from the FATA into Afghanistan and drive him the ten miles to Camp Chapman, the CIA annex on FOB Salerno, one of the largest U.S. bases east of Kabul and, as brigade headquarters for Colonel Howard's Task Force Yukon, the command center during the midsummer DUSTWUN. After two weeks of negotiations, the meeting was set for December 30. The White House was briefed. Matthews told her team that if they wanted Balawi to trust them, they needed to show him trust as well. They ordered the driver not to search him. They even baked him a cake, which awaited him in the debrief room. Most of the agency's staff at Chapman, fourteen people in all, gathered for the meeting. The red Subaru station wagon arrived after 4:00 p.m. The driver passed through three security checkpoints without stopping for a search and parked in front of the annex's central compound. Balawi stepped out of the car with his hand in his pocket, said the Shahada, and detonated. Six people were killed instantly. A mortally wounded Matthews was loaded onto a medevac helicopter and died in the air.

Six months into his Kabul mission, Major General Mike Flynn saw a war in tailspin. Rather than gifts, Christmas had brought a slick propaganda video of Bergdahl as a POW, a deadly CIA disaster, and, in early January, a posthumous martyr's video from the suicide bomber al-Balawi, broadcast across the globe by Al Jazeera and on YouTube. The wise men in the White House, the Pentagon, and the State Department did not comment. In early February a secret report arrived at Bolling Air Force Base, the Defense Intelligence Agency headquarters in southwest Washington, D.C. It said that Haqqani had carried out the attack at Chapman after it was initiated, directed, and funded by Pakistani intelligence. ISI spies had met twice with Haqqani commanders in the month before the attack, once to hand over the operation's seed money and once with operation orders. It didn't cost much. Two hundred thousand dollars went a long way in the FATA, covering overhead and bribes for an Afghan Border Police commander in Khost. When a heavily redacted portion of the U.S. intelligence report surfaced in Western and Indian media, Islamabad denied everything.

Of Chapman's many tragedies, its preventability was the most demoralizing, and Pakistani complicity the most infuriating. The hard truth was that the enemy had outmaneuvered the Americans both on the battlefield and in the ISI-CIA shadow war. Throughout 2008, Chairman of the Joint Chiefs of Staff admiral Michael Mullen had devoted himself to building trust with Pakistan's generals and spymasters. Lieutenant General Asad Durrani, the ISI director general at the time, gave Mullen the same old promises, vowing to take incremental steps to rein in bad actors in the FATA, while, in the same meeting, denying that the Quetta Shura, the Taliban's government in exile, had sanctuary in Quetta, or even existed at all. Mullen knew it was a brazen lie. The shura not only existed, but U.S. and British intelligence had high confidence that Pakistani intelligence was represented within the Taliban's leadership council. The power dynamic between them, however, was difficult to pin down.

Three days before Bergdahl's video was released, General Flynn's staff updated their "State of the Insurgency" PowerPoint briefing in Kabul, noting the enemy's growing capabilities: The average size of IEDs on the Afghan battlefield had increased dramatically. These cheap armor-defeating bombs had become the weapon of choice for the Taliban, the new iteration of the Stinger missiles the CIA had provided to the mujahideen to defeat the Soviets. Slide twelve concluded, "The Afghan insurgency can sustain itself indefinitely."

It had been nearly thirty years since Washington spent billions teaching the mujahideen how to fight and win against a larger, richer, and more technologically advanced "Evil Empire," as President Reagan had labeled the USSR. The Islamic guerrillas had incorporated and passed down the lessons and tactics to a new generation. Meanwhile, America's future generals had turned their attention to another battlefield: politics. David Petraeus's 1987 Princeton doctoral dissertation examined how the media's representation of the Vietnam War had been the real impediment to victory. A decade later, H. R. McMaster's 1997 book, *Dereliction of Duty,* studied the machinations within Washington and Robert McNamara's Pentagon that had led the country down the path of catastrophe in Southeast Asia. The Vietnam War continued its blind escalation, he wrote, "without a vision of how military action might actually achieve the goals of the war."

Like Petraeus, McMaster, and his commander Stanley McChrystal, Flynn knew that COIN was the product of political logic as much as, if not more than, military strategy. In practice, it could even undermine the mission. Yet here he was, delivering yet another slideshow, touting COIN as a panacea six months after he and McChrystal had already seen its futility in southeastern Afghanistan and went gunning instead for the more immediate results of special operations night raids. COIN was the public face of the new way to victory in Afghanistan, but it didn't match reality on the ground, or the intent of the command structure in Kabul. COIN was every bit the mirage that Bowe Bergdahl had suspected.

IN THE CIA'S SIXTY-TWO-YEAR existence, only one attack had been worse than Chapman: On April 18, 1983, a Hezbollah truck detonated in front of the U.S. Embassy in Beirut with what the FBI later described as the largest man-made nonnuclear explosion since World War II. Sixty-three people were killed, including seventeen Americans, seven of whom worked for the CIA. But the Chapman attack was different—if Beirut was an Achilles frontal assault, Chapman was a Ulysses Trojan Horse. The Hezbollah driver had crashed through three armed checkpoints and heavy gunfire; Balawi just walked in for cake. The central lesson from Chapman was also the lesson of the war surrounding it, as obvious as it was maddening: The United States government was dumping trillions of dollars and tens of thousands of lives into a war against an enemy it had trained and an ally it had financed, and there was no way out.

The attack also opened a new round in the eternal and bitter feuding between the Pentagon and the CIA. Before Langley could write and disseminate its after-action report about the causes and implications of the attack, the Pentagon delivered its own indictment of the agency's practices. Five days after the blast, Flynn published *Fixing Intel: A Blueprint for Making Intelligence Relevant in Afghanistan*. Rather than submit the paper to a military journal where no one would read it, Flynn sent it to the Center for a New American Security, a Washington, D.C., think tank that was a popular way station for hawkish Democrats between political appointments. Flynn's coauthor was Matt Pottinger, a former *Wall Street Journal* reporter turned Marine Corps intelligence officer.

"Eight years into the war," the paper began, "the U.S. intelligence community is only marginally relevant to the overall strategy." American spy agencies, despite their multibillion-dollar budgets, were "unable to answer fundamental questions about the environment in which we operate and the people we are trying to protect and persuade." *Fixing Intel* was more than a diagnosis; it was an attack on the status quo in an intelligence community dominated by civilians. The CIA had tried and failed in Afghanistan, and now it was the uniformed Pentagon's turn to take over and fix the problem. The paper quoted McChrystal on the heart of the problem: "The chairman of the Joint Chiefs of Staff, the secretary of defense, Congress, the president of the United States—are not getting the right information to make decisions."

The basic intelligence failures were all the more remarkable in light of the immense technological gap between the U.S. and the Taliban. At any given time, American spies could access all cell phone, radio, and electronic transmissions in the country; watch live and recorded video from drones, blimps, airplanes, and satellites covering wide swaths of the rural Afghan countryside; and read constant Blue Force Tracker position pings and situation reports from troops on the ground. Still, the Taliban grew.

Fixing Intel urged the military to approach intelligence in a new way. The paper imagined teams of brainy analysts "empowered to move between field elements, much like journalists," Flynn and Pottinger wrote. "Microsoft Word, rather than PowerPoint, should be the tool of choice for intelligence professionals in a counterinsurgency." In short, they imagined a military intelligence model that looked less like the mind-numbing COIN lectures and more like Robert Pelton's Afpax Insider, the very program that McKiernan had contracted after the Battle of Wanat in the summer of 2008, and which Mike Furlong would ultimately bring crashing down with his extracurricular activities.

As much as Flynn claimed to hate the bureaucracy, publishing the paper when and how he did was a savvy bureaucratic move. In a speech a few weeks earlier at West Point, President Obama had vowed not only to deploy an additional thirty-thousand troops to the war, but also to commit another $30 billion to the problem. To Flynn and Furlong, it was a fresh line of credit and an opportunity to seize control of the CIA's rice bowl in Afghanistan.

Predictably, reactions to *Fixing Intel* were split according to institutional loyalties. In his memoir, Secretary of Defense Robert Gates wrote that Flynn's diagnosis and recommendations were entirely astute and sensible. His sole point of dissent was with Flynn's decision to publish his assessment in public and expose American weaknesses to the enemy in Afghanistan. At Langley, CIA director Leon Panetta and agency rank and file read it as a ruthless attack from the military on the CIA when they were at their most vulnerable. "Flynn was a guy who thought he could make anybody walk on water," a CIA officer reflected, but ultimately he was "a neophyte in the intelligence game.

Flynn never got the big strategic picture." In the end, his paper's greatest accomplishment seemed to have been aggravating the existing divisions within the national security apparatus.

Neither CIA nor DoD had a way to solve the war's fundamental problem: the fact that the Taliban knew the terrain better than their enemies and would never give up fighting as long as the American invaders occupied their land. The U.S. Army worked *against* the land, bombing it from the sky and shielding its fighters in fourteen-ton armor-plated trucks. American soldiers were both protected and weighed down by their "battle rattle"—sixty pounds or more of body armor and gear, while the Taliban fought in flip-flops and loose-fitting cloth shalwars, using the terrain as their armor. The Taliban saw American soldiers as soft, predictable targets, unable to function for long stretches of time without supplies from their support bases. Taliban commanders didn't try to compete with American firepower or technology; they didn't need to. They would wait and plan, attacking, melting away, and regrouping to attack again when the time was right. They struck at the weakest joints in the lumbering American war machine. After an airstrike, they looked out for unexploded bombs among the NATO ordnance, collected them as gifts from above, and used the material to build their own homemade bombs. Unlike the American-propped Karzai government, the Taliban had no need to enforce nationwide rule. In a country the size of Texas, where hundreds of tribes and subtribes spoke more than two dozen languages and decades of war had divided them further, national unity had always been a lofty aspiration.

In nineteen pages of text, Flynn and Pottinger used the words "fail" and "failure" sixteen times. Noting that "revenge-prone Pashtun communities" are unlikely to work with the same people they view as indiscriminate killers, the paper concluded that "merely killing insurgents usually serves to multiply enemies rather than subtract them." It was as true for the U.S. as it had been for the USSR, which despite killing several hundred thousand Afghans, "faced a larger insurgency near the end of the war than they did at the beginning."

Even in the national security state that he was trying to shake up, Flynn's alarm was not unique. Matthew Hoh, the former Marine Corps officer featured in the Taliban's Christmas Day video, had resigned from his State Department post in Zabul Province in September 2009 with similar concerns of inevitable failure. In his resignation letter, Hoh wrote that "the insurgency fights not for the white banner of the Taliban, but rather against the presence of foreign soldiers and taxes imposed by an unrepresentative government in Kabul." The Karzai regime was seen as corrupt because it *was* corrupt. Hoh doubted not only the way the U.S. was conducting its war, but also its greater purpose.

Secretary of State Hillary Clinton had similar questions after her own deputy warned her that the Pentagon lacked a clear goal and had put Washington on the path to quagmire. Speaking via video teleconference with Admiral Mullen weeks after Hoh's letter went public, Clinton relayed a recent report from the State Department's senior representative in RC South, Frank Ruggiero, who could not safely venture into Kandahar from a nearby U.S. base. This sorry state of affairs, Clinton noted, persisted even after troop levels in the area grew tenfold. Clinton asked Mullen to explain: Why, after the troops that were requested to secure RC South were provided, wasn't the situation under control? Because, Mullen answered, McChrystal didn't have enough troops. The answer was as obvious as it was insane, and it followed a basic rule of bureaucratic logic: Failure was the evidence that more effort, more manpower, and more funding was needed. For Mullen and McChrystal, the problem was that fewer and fewer U.S. officials were buying the argument.

That winter, Flynn traveled to Pakistan to meet with his Pakistani counterparts. If *Fixing Intel* was seen in Washington as a breach of intelligence service etiquette, his efforts to salvage the mission in-theater were even less polite. The most urgent topic, as it had been before he and McChrystal arrived and would remain after they were gone, was Pakistan's inability or unwillingness to control the terror groups operating with impunity on Pakistani soil. Being lied to by Pakistan was no longer a glitch; it had become the central feature of the relationship, a dysfunctional codependency that twisted further as the war escalated. How could Flynn, the career intelligence officer who had built his reputation by bending the rules, continue to go along with this Pakistani charade? Flynn was known for his temper and his apparent attention deficit disorder. In a meeting with the ISI, this was a dangerous combination. Perhaps Flynn didn't intend to tip his hand and reveal highly classified information to the Pakistanis, but in this winter meeting he did. While the exact information he revealed remains classified, his breach was serious enough that, in a rare event, a lower-ranking Naval Intelligence officer present reported Flynn for a security violation. A CENTCOM investigation concluded that Flynn had revealed government secrets to Pakistan, but it was inadvertent and did not threaten national security.

The Washington Post cited a separate incident in 2009 in which Flynn had disclosed sensitive information to Pakistan about "secret U.S. intelligence capabilities being used to monitor the Haqqani network." It was more than a breach of protocol; it was a heedless attack on rivals within his own government. A CIA officer in the meeting was so aghast at the disclosure, he promptly reported it to headquarters in Langley, which relayed the officer's concerns to officials in the Defense Department. The investigation put Flynn's future job prospects in limbo for a year before CENTCOM commander General James Mattis cleared him of the charges.

After Michael Hastings published "The Runaway General" in the June 2010 issue of *Rolling Stone*, Stanley McChrystal was fired for his loose lips and insubordinate attitude toward the Obama White House, and he retired. Mike Flynn remained in the Army. In September 2011 he was promoted to lieutenant general and appointed assistant director of national intelligence for partner engagement at the Office of the

Director of National Intelligence. This man, chronically frustrated by intelligence bureaucracy and with a documented history of revealing classified information to foreign governments, was now in charge of a branch of U.S. intelligence devoted to partnering with spies from allied nations. In the lawless regions of one of these ostensible allies, Bowe Bergdahl remained in chains.

THIRTEEN

MEANS OF ESCAPE

Bergdahl's guards feared that he would escape again. He had done it twice in the first week they held him, and the second time he proved that he could break out of a locked cell. It was just two or three days after he had left OP Mest. After they had hiked him through the night to Pakistan and presented him to Mullah Sangeen, his guards brought him to a low-ceilinged cell on the ground floor of a private home. In broken English, they pointed to the corner of the dirt floor and told him he could relieve himself there.

Once they were gone, with his blindfold off, he realized that he could see their comings and goings through the cracks in the wooden door. Whenever water was delivered to the home, his guards would leave his area for about ten minutes. They had chained his hands and tied his feet with rope, but he managed to twist and wriggle his way free of both. When the guards left for water again, he squeezed his hand through the door jamb, unwrapped the heavy wire they used as a lock, and, as quietly as possible, pushed the door open and ran. He was, for the moment, free.

Outside Bergdahl's cell, life went on. Children were playing. He saw a woman with a broom, and she saw him too, freezing in place before she began screaming. He kept running, cutting his bare feet as he reached a road and picked up speed before darting into a thicket of short trees and thorny bushes. His feet now punctured and bleeding, he realized that he wasn't fully concealed, and sprinted to a nearby single-story home and climbed to the roof, which was puddled with mud from a recent rain. He got down and rolled in the muck to camouflage himself, but it was all for naught. A few seconds later, a man climbed to the roof, followed by another with an AK-47. They seized him, punching him as they chained his hands behind his back and stuffed him into a waiting car. He had been free for less than fifteen minutes.

Blindfolded again, Bergdahl heard his captors talk among themselves and then yell out in a group cheer. They drove him to a larger compound, fortified with iron gates, metal shutters, and bars across the windows. In the middle of the room that would become his cell was a stripped bed frame—just pipes held together by string. There was no mattress, just bare springs. They shackled his wrists to the top of the frame and padlocked his leg chains to the sides. Aside from trips to the latrine and filming propaganda videos, he would remain splayed this way for the next three months.

When the Pentagon's Joint Personnel Recovery Agency (JPRA) compiled the official government record of his captivity five years later, it divided Bergdahl's treatment into three distinct categories: torture, abuse, and neglect. The torture was concentrated in the early months. At night, an English speaker carrying a length of rubber pipe came in to interrogate him. He asked who had helped him escape. Was it the woman he had seen? They also wanted to know about America. Why were so many Americans so fat? Is Obama gay? Where do the U.S. officers in Afghanistan get their prostitutes? When he couldn't answer, the man twirled the hose in the air, making it whir before striking him, the sound becoming a feature of the routine. Guards held AK-47s to his head, took off his blindfold to show him videos of beheadings, and told him that he was next. They whipped his feet and legs with copper cables and plastic pipes, gradually rendering them useless. One guard entered each night with a razor, kneeled on Bergdahl's chest, and made small slices—eventually hundreds of them—in his torso.

The first months were designed to initiate him into the long-term captivity that awaited him, breaking him physically so he could not escape again. Sores opened on his ankles and wrists where he was chained, and on his forehead and eyelids under the blindfold. His muscles atrophied, as intended, and when his captors saw that he could no longer stand on his own power, they unchained one arm so he could sit up to eat. They fed him elbow noodles, rice, and a bottle of water twice a day. Later recalling the chronic dysentery that started then, Bergdahl suspected that they had also poisoned him. Looking at the sores on his ankles, he thought that his staph infection from the prior winter had returned. He cut away the dead flesh with scissors borrowed from his guards and packed his wounds with sand before they shackled him to the bed again.

In Pakistan, Bergdahl would spend four years and eleven months in isolation. He only knew that he was an American soldier held by the Taliban, and that he needed to escape.

THEY WOULD MOVE him over that time to at least nine locations: rural and urban, single-story mud huts, and forty-foot-tall concrete compounds. When it was time to move, his guards blindfolded him, dressed him as a woman in a burka, or bound his wrists and ankles and stuffed him under blankets and rugs. He was always accompanied by at least one man carrying a pistol or an AK-47 as they drove in circles to disorient him. When he arrived at a new location, a new set of people would cycle through to ogle and taunt.

"I was the new, shiny thing, and they'd come and try to talk to me," Bergdahl said later. Women and adolescent children were among the guards assigned to feed him and to walk him by his chain, handcuffed and shackled, to a toilet each morning. They were no more lenient than the men and, in some ways, more cruel. The women would spit in his food and slap him. The kids would whip him with his chains and toss cups of urine at him. One school-age boy was kinder than the rest, and he scolded the others for their pranks and shooed them away. He wanted the prisoner to teach him English. Bergdahl had nothing against the kid, and they exchanged words when they could.

"It was usually about a week before they started getting bored, before they started getting careless and forgetting about me," Bergdahl recalled. Whether intentionally or from negligence, his guards would leave glaring electric lights on in his cell for days, then leave him for even longer periods in total darkness. The perpetual light was worse, but most maddening was the random flickering between light and dark that destroyed his sleep patterns and concept of time. Seldom was there a guard who spoke conversational English. But when Bergdahl motioned that he wanted a flashlight after days of darkness, his guards refused and explained by running in place, a charade of their fear that he would escape again. When they brought food, they would toss it on the ground and deny his requests for a plate or bowl for the same reason and with the same pantomime: he might somehow use it to escape.

Into his cell walls, Bergdahl scratched the evidence of his time: his initials, the letters P-O-W, and his unit's name and insignia. The guards gave him a blanket or a mat to sleep on mud or concrete floors. "Mud [floors] were easier. It allowed me to dig holes to try and escape, and to dig holes to hide diarrhea," Bergdahl later testified. His illnesses had become chronic, and when his diarrhea was impossible to control, his guards grew furious. They threatened to cut off his nose and ears if he did it again. Some days they told him that he would be freed imminently. Other days they told him that he would die there.

As his body wasted from dysentery, they denied him access to a bath or shower for about four months, and he lived in his own filth. But he realized that the fouler he smelled, the less often his guards came to see him and the more time he had to work on escaping. In one compound, he spent months digging a tunnel into a mud wall at night, replacing the loose dirt by morning, and urinating on the debris to smooth away all traces of disturbance. He hid the evidence of his excavation in his clothing and deposited what he could carry to the toilet each morning. After several months, he had dug four or five feet into the wall and was worried that he had produced too much dirt to hide. But just then, they moved him again.

BERGDAHL ENDURED HIS ISOLATION by focusing on the smallest details of his surroundings and the largest unseen powers of the universe. He blocked his mind from heading down paths of nostalgia and sentiment. Early on, he realized that his friends and family back home could not save him and that thinking about them would only cause more pain.

"You can't go insane if you're talking to God," he would later tell Pentagon debriefers. But for the most part, "what helped keep my mind occupied was the effort of constantly trying to solve the puzzle of getting out." The idea that his guards could go on tormenting him with impunity and denying him his freedom enraged him. "In so many ways, letting them win was not an option," he said.

As he had done in the Army, he scrutinized the system that held him for seeking out even the smallest flaws. He listened to footsteps to learn his guards' routines. He studied his chains and shackles for spots of rust and the ropes for frayed places that he could work over until they broke. By spitting on a link in his hand shackles for a few months, he rusted it until it snapped, then hid the damage by piecing the mechanism back together with shreds of wood and fabric. Later, when a small boy unknowingly dropped a key from a ribbon, Bergdahl grabbed it and discovered that it opened most of the cheap padlocks that were used on his chains. He hid the key in the cuff of his pants, and when he was taken to meet Badruddin Haqqani, Jalaluddin's son and the operational commander for his captivity, he swallowed it, knowing he could retrieve it later in his own cell.

In early 2010, the Haqqanis moved him to his sixth location, a large, remote home that he and his Pentagon debriefers would later call the Mountain Fortress. Here, he was kept on an upper level in a spacious room with a fire pit in the middle of a dirt floor, and was chained to a wooden column that stood next to his blankets and mat. There was no latrine for him; the guards pointed to the floor. They left him alone for longer and longer periods until he realized that on some days the only people present were women, children, and old men. Dysentery had withered him, and as he looked at his protruding ribs and bulging joints, he decided there were only two ways left to die.

"I said to myself, 'I can either die here from illness, or escape. You have to try.'"

He began preparing by collecting tools. Pulling a nail from the wall, he sharpened it with a rock and stuck it in the sole of his rubber sandal. He found a piece of plastic pipe and hid it in the nest of linens that were so filthy he knew no one would touch them. When his guards brought bread, he set aside rations for his journey. Night after night, he rehearsed opening his shackles and tying his bedding to the pipe as a makeshift rope. As the day approached, he unlocked himself from the chain and walked to the window: He could see that he was in the mountains and hear the distant whine of U.S. surveillance drones. When a boy spotted him at the window, Bergdahl leapt back and hurriedly rechained himself.

"I let my guard down too much," he recalled thinking as an old man entered his room with an AK-47. The boy shortened his chain and the old man motioned that he would shoot him if he tried to get loose again. It was now apparent that aside from the boy and the old man, the house was empty. Bergdahl decided that he would have to leave that night.

"There was no doubt in my mind that jumping out that window and trying to run for it was suicide," he said later. Dying from exposure was likely, he figured, but that was better than "sitting in a locked room at someone else's mercy and dying that way."

When the house was quiet and dark, he removed his shackles quietly, hands first, then his ankles. He lashed the purloined PVC pipe to a stick, tied a rope around this improvised grappling hook, and wedged it into the window frame. Carrying his blanket, sandals, and the plastic soda bottle they put his water in each morning, he climbed to the sill, stood there for a moment, and then rappelled to the ground. For the first time in a year, he was free.

Bergdahl walked through a night so dark he didn't realize that he had come to the edge of a deep wadi until he was already falling. He fell for so long, he had time to be surprised that he was still falling—and hit the ground with such force that some nearby dogs started barking. He struggled to his feet, walked to the creek in the riverbed to fill his bottle, and realized that he couldn't open his left hand. Limping far up the hillside away from the dogs, he dug a trench at the base of a tree and buried himself in dirt and pine needles as the gray light of dawn broke on the horizon. He remained there for the day and rose to walk again at night, the same schedule he had laid out when he had left Mest more than a year earlier. For the next eight nights he continued this way, his face camouflaged with mud, steering away from signs of people as he searched for water and food. The saved bits of bread had turned to mold. He saw berries growing on bushes, but didn't trust them. With no other options, he started eating grass and drinking putrid water. Disoriented, he walked in wide circles that brought him back again and again to where he had started. Throughout, he heard the drones buzzing, and, one day, saw six of them in the sky.

Lost alone on a ridgetop in the most surveilled sector of South Asia, Bergdahl knew that at that moment, on the other side of the world, American pilots and intelligence officers were scanning real-time video of the ground where he stood. If only he could get their attention—if only someone would notice him. But as he searched the sky where his salvation hovered obliviously overhead, there was no way to reach out.

His body began to fail. Trying to stand, he would black out and fall over. One time as he came to, he heard a sound approaching and saw a lone Taliban emerge from the nearby bushes. Thirty seconds later, some fifteen or twenty more men followed behind him. Bergdahl assumed that they would kill him. Instead, they grabbed him, slung him over their shoulders, and moved quickly off the mountainside, fearful of drones. They slapped and punched his face and tore at his hair and beard. Then they loaded him into a truck and returned to the Mountain Fortress. When they saw his condition—ribs and clavicles protruding, feet cut open and full of thorns, big toenail ripped off—they stopped beating him.

They drove him to a new place and fitted him with heavier chains and bigger shackles. Then they brought the cage: elevated eight inches off the ground, constructed of quarter-inch iron bars crosshatched and welded about three inches apart. There was a small door at one end. A Haqqani commander who spoke English arrived to inspect his most valuable prisoner in his new home.

"He told me the cage was specifically built for me."

ACT IV.

BRING BOWE HOME

FOURTEEN

PAWNS

The United States does not negotiate with terrorists. This has long been an effective bit of American political rhetoric, but it's never been accurate. The first U.S. president to pay ransoms for hostages was George Washington, in 1792, and the practice of negotiating, paying, and bartering for prisoners has continued ever since, regardless of the label applied to those who held them. Washington and the 2nd Congress appropriated $642,000 to free forty-two American sailors held in Algiers by the Barbary pirates, the Ottoman Empire's non-state terror proxy. Seven years earlier, before the Constitution had even been ratified, the Continental Congress had paid $80,000 to appease the pirates and bring home the captive crew of the merchant ship *Betsey*.

In the centuries of American wars that followed, few prisoners' lives were valued that highly again. The Revolutionary War was the most brutal; some twenty thousand soldiers and patriotic insurgents were held captive, more than half of whom perished in squalid British prison ships anchored in the estuaries of New York Harbor. Roughly eleven thousand men died inside those ships, more than the total killed in the war's seven years of fighting. Twenty years after the war ended, as President Thomas Jefferson ordered the dredging of the Brooklyn shoreline to build a Navy yard, thousands of skeletons were found and collected from mass graves in the tidal muck.

The parlay over prisoners of war is as old as war itself. In Greek mythology, the ten-year Trojan War of Homer's *Iliad* began with the kidnapping of Helen of Troy; it was expected that prisoners would be treated humanely and ransomed after conflicts had ended. During the Middle Ages, when war became an occupation of the landowning nobility, non-heir sons were sent away to fight external enemies, lest they threaten the internal order. These young noblemen were coveted hostages, and their capture resulted in handsome profits. If their families could not or would not produce payments, execution was common.

Prisoners, hostages, and detainees—whether military or civilian, active participants in the conflict or innocent bystanders—have almost always found their lives commodified. Sacrifices to the greater conflict, they live in chains while distant scales measure their worth, whether in cash, as barter for political concessions, human shields, or tools of propaganda. As the United States gained power and prestige, the early practice of paying ransoms to pirates was deemed less and less politically acceptable and presidents sought out alternative methods. They often settled on military rescues. When those failed—as with the elaborate April 1980 unraveling of Operation Eagle Claw in the Iranian desert—several presidential administrations have made political compromises and paid secret ransoms to bring Americans home.

Civilian hostages lucky enough to be freed rarely faced any sustained scrutiny. But for returning POWs, American attitudes shifted from war to war. After World War II, POWs who had been held in German and Japanese camps were respected, if pitied, for their service and their suffering. It wasn't until the Korean War that perceptions changed. GIs captured in Korea were seen as tainted by a distant conflict in an obscure nation that, so soon after the victories of 1945, few Americans had paid attention to. The Forgotten War, as Korea would be called, took the lives of more than 36,000 Americans, and some 4,714 were held as POWs. Their plight was severe: More than a third died in captivity. By September 1950, three months after the war had begun, the CIA estimated that there were five hundred American POWs in Seoul, held in makeshift detention centers. They were visited daily by agents of the North Korean Internal Affairs Office, who worked to indoctrinate their American captives with Communist ideology and forced them to sign confessions and read propaganda scripts. When prisoners refused, they were beaten, tortured, and eventually moved en masse to Pyongyang.

From the beginning of truce talks on July 11, 1951, and for more than a year that followed, the U.S. government sought an agreement to bring home sick and wounded POWs, raising the issue a dozen times in both formal and informal negotiations. As the prisoners were gradually released and debriefed by U.S. intelligence, concern grew within the CIA about Communist brainwashing, which, in the era of McCarthyism, was understood as an insidious psychological infection that could spread like a virus within the American public at large. The Communists, the logic went, were sending back our own men as mental time bombs with fuses lit by masters in Pyongyang and Beijing.

A shadow fell over the POWs, and men were judged harshly for their behavior in captivity. But how much was treason and how much was coercion? What should be expected of soldiers or sailors under duress? To answer those questions, the U.S. military drafted a code of conduct and adopted a range of training programs falling under the rubric of Survival, Evasion, Resistance and Escape (SERE). The training was often brutal. Even when they knew that their SERE training was a simulation, most men broke, proving that the code of conduct itself was unrealistic.

The modern movement to rehabilitate the American POW began with the wives of the men held in Vietnam, and most prominently with Sybil Stockdale. Her husband, naval aviator Commander James Bond Stockdale, had been shot down and captured in North Vietnam in September 1965. He would spend seven and half years in the colonial-era stockade known as the Hanoi Hilton, and as its highest-ranking prisoner, he was in command, teaching newcomers the coded alphabet of coughs and taps the men used to communicate. When Commander Stockdale learned about his captors' plans to film him for propaganda, he slit his scalp with a razor and bashed his face into a fifty-pound stool until his eyes were swollen shut. For these and other insubordinations, he was routinely tortured and spent about four years in "Alcatraz," a separate block of six-by-nine solitary confinement cells.

Despite her husband's rank, the Pentagon stonewalled Mrs. Stockdale, offering opaque statements and instructions not to talk about him—not with her friends, not with other military wives, and definitely not with the press. Making a fuss, they told her, would only delay her husband's homecoming. Seeking special attention would only bring him worse abuse, even torture.

In May 1966, more than eight months after her husband had disappeared over North Vietnam, Sybil found her first Pentagon ally in Naval Intelligence officer Commander Robert Boroughs, who encouraged her to go public, organize, and lobby the chain of command. She quickly recruited a network of wives, including Evelyn Grubb and Shirley Stark, whose husbands had also been shot down. The Army had denied benefits to Grubb and her four children until it was convinced that her husband had not been brainwashed in captivity into a Communist sympathizer. To Stark, it was the Pentagon that appeared to have been brainwashed into madness. "We were bombing their country, and they were shooting us down," Stark said. "What was the big secret?"

Withholding information from POW families was standard government procedure, and it triggered the rise of one of the largest and most successful grassroots lobbying campaigns in U.S. history. By the time Operation Homecoming brought 566 POWs home from North Vietnam in 1973, the issue had become one of most politically charged of the war and carried a legacy of betrayal that would haunt the Pentagon for decades. Gradually, and for reasons both noble and politically expedient, the Defense Department spent thirty years after Vietnam writing policy and building agencies to address the issues first raised by Stockdale. The reforms would be far from perfect—and the Pentagon would never lose its taste for secrecy—but the changes helped ensure that POW-MIA families of the future would not be ignored. But Stockdale, Stark, Grubb, and the families who joined them only won these concessions after years of persistent lobbying and an excruciating struggle against their own government.

Ahead of the 1968 election, President Lyndon Johnson saw no political upside on the issue. Young Americans he had sent to war were captive in unspeakable conditions. Why publicize it? It looked especially toxic ahead of the 1968 election, with even Republican challengers like Michigan governor George Romney promising a radical reassessment of the war. (Romney had been for the war before he was against it, but he told a television reporter that he had been "brainwashed" by American generals into thinking Vietnam was a good idea.) As the war's chaos spread that fall, Sybil Stockdale and Evelyn Grubb formally organized the National League of American Prisoners and Missing in Southeast Asia, taking their plight and claims of government deception mainstream. In the name of patriotism, the National League accused the military of hypocrisy: Leave no man behind?

By the time Johnson left Washington for his terminal exile in the Texas Hill Country, more than three hundred men were confirmed captured and nearly six hundred were missing in Southeast Asia. Four years and two heart attacks later, Johnson was dead, and Nixon abruptly turned the POW-MIA crisis into a political opportunity. In the spring of 1969, Nixon directed the Pentagon to take the lead on what the administration would call the Go Public campaign. On May 19—four days after police killed one college student and sent dozens more to the hospital during antiwar riots in Berkeley, California—Nixon's secretary of defense, Melvin Laird, unveiled Washington's new POW policy in an emotional presentation. Building his argument from the bedrock of universal human rights, he declared that the North Vietnamese were guilty of war crimes and holding POWs in violation of the Geneva Conventions. The U.S. government demanded a large-scale prisoner release.

Wire stories from the Pentagon press conference ran nationwide. The *Chicago Tribune* reported that demands for prisoner releases had actually begun years earlier, when W. Averell Harriman, as Johnson's envoy to the Paris Peace Talks, had threatened American retaliation if the prisoners were mistreated. But when Harriman—a former New York governor, ambassador to the USSR, and founder of Idaho's Sun Valley Resort—heard about Nixon's plans to use the POWs to his political advantage, he was appalled. He called Laird at the Pentagon to lobby him against parading captured Americans into the political arena.

But Nixon and Laird's Go Public campaign was already in motion, and the May 19 press conference kicked it off in the most explosive terms possible, displaying a series of poster-size photos of captured men in Hanoi starving and disfigured behind bars. In a savvy move, Laird had hired Dick Capen, a *San Diego Tribune* reporter, to help sell the Pentagon's new policy. In his prior newspaper job, Capen had already interviewed the families of almost fifty captured servicemen; following the press rollout, Laird sent him on a forty-five-stop tour to lavish publicity on POW families nationwide and bring them onto the right side of Nixon's domestic battle lines.

Where the Pentagon had only recently used threats and fear to discourage Sybil Stockdale and her allies from talking, now the Defense Department encouraged them to protest Hanoi in the most public ways possible. Prisoners' wives traveled to North Vietnamese embassies to deliver morose personal pleas, preferably on camera. Congress followed Nixon's lead and passed unanimous resolutions condemning Hanoi for its treatment of prisoners, and in a burst of creativity, even hijacked a Communist holiday to further the cause. Congress declared May 1, 1970—International Workers Day in the Communist sphere—as "a day for an appeal for international justice for all the American prisoners of war and servicemen missing in action in Southeast Asia." POWs were honored with a week of remembrance, a day of prayer, a commemorative postage stamp, and an Air Force flyby over the Super Bowl. Letter-writing and petition campaigns were launched by the American Legion, the American Red Cross, the Veterans of Foreign Wars, and local chapters of the Jaycees, Rotarians, and Elks. The Air Force grew especially fond of POW-wife Mrs. Shirley Odell of Mount Clemens, Michigan, and her letter-writing campaign; it even published her phone number in promotional newsletters, encouraging other families to reach out and join Odell's cause.

On April 28, 1970, President Nixon approved a full invasion of Cambodia, justifying American expansion into a third Southeast Asian country in an April 30 television address. He then declared May 3, 1970, a National Day of Prayer for all American soldiers missing or captive in Southeast Asia. At the Paris talks, North Vietnamese negotiators agreed to begin releasing American prisoners as soon as Nixon set a firm date for withdrawal. Nixon replied to the offer with a public tautology: "As long as the North Vietnamese have any Americans as prisoners of war, there will be Americans in South Vietnam."

Following the news of the North Vietnamese offer and Nixon's refusals to negotiate, Mrs. Odell stopped sending her letters to Hanoi and started sending them to the White House instead. "How many more men must die before you make a decision?" she wrote on July 17. A few weeks later, she mailed the president a care package of toothpaste, soap, vitamins, hard candy, and a personal note—the same supplies she sent to her husband every other month. "I hope you can survive on this till I can send you another package," she told Nixon.

The movement she had started would eventually have five million remembrance bracelets on American wrists, bumper stickers on about fifty million cars, and, twenty years later, a black flag of mourning at every federal building in the country. But in the fall of 1971, Stockdale still had no idea whether her husband would ever be free. "I've never left Washington without someone taking me aside and telling me in confidence, 'In two or three months we expect a development of a substantive nature.' Now I say, 'Don't tell me. I don't believe it.' But I don't believe the Vietcong either."

JANUARY 2010 BLANKETED CROY Creek Canyon and the high Idaho foothills in several feet of fresh snow. Bob and Jani had spent Christmas with a harrowing video of their son, pale and gaunt and reading anti-American screeds on a Taliban propaganda tape. They hung a Christmas wreath on the metal rungs of their cattle gate. In front of it, one of Bowe's friends left candles half buried and glowing like lanterns in the snow.

The Army hadn't provided his family any new information in months. Sky Bergdahl had been a Navy wife for nine years, and she watched in amazement as the Pentagon shut down requests even from her husband, a naval aviator with a top-secret security clearance. She was torn between the informed opinion that "the Army has been feeding us a whole lot of doublespeak" and the sense that the secrecy was in the interest of protecting those sent to rescue her brother. She remained optimistic.

"We have to hope," Sky said. "I believe that we were created by a loving God. I know everything happens for a reason and for the good of those who believe." This is how the months passed—Bob driving his delivery route, Jani talking for hours on the phone with family and their pastors in Boise. Prayer carried them through.

They had also been lifted by support systems that they never saw coming. Three weeks after Bowe's name was first broadcast on July 18, 2009, the first hundred bikers rolled into Hailey for what the Pocatello POW-MIA Awareness Association had named the Bowe Prayer Run. Saturday, August 8, carried the first chills of autumn in the Idaho desert, and the black-leather-clad bikers rode for three to five hours from Pocatello, Elko, and Boise through the cold needling rain and temperatures in the high forties. They crested Timmerman Hill in formation and rode north into Hailey, converging at Zaney's.

Word had spread that the captured soldier's parents were wary about attracting much attention; they were private people, and the Army had already warned them against it. But the bikers felt compelled to do something. Many had fathers, uncles, and brothers who had served and never returned from the jungles of Southeast Asia. Some had lost family to more recent wars.

"We live in an NFL and an *American Idol* world, and people don't even realize there are soldiers, sailors, airmen, and Marines out there," Roy Breshears, one of the Pocatello organizers, said later. The men fighting the War in Afghanistan and the families who waited for them had been forgotten, he said. "If nothing else, we needed to show his parents and each other that we still have the humanity to care about that."

The bikers parked in formation in front of Zaney's with "colors out": the POW-MIA, U.S. Marine Corps, U.S. Coast Guard, and U.S. flags flapping in the cold August wind. Bob and Jani had only just begun to process the reality of their ordeal. They put on black clothes that morning and the bikers pinned yellow ribbons on their chests. Bob hadn't shaved in more than five weeks, and the stubble on his chin had grown almost as long as his moustache. He said a few words of thanks to a huddle of bikers and friends that tightened around him and his family, and when they asked if he knew anything beyond what they could read in the news, Bob said he did not.

The Bergdahls' brain trust of politically connected Vietnam veterans told them not to believe what they heard from Washington. But there was no avoiding the Pentagon. It is the node through which all U.S. military stories must pass. And things had changed since the 1970s. For all of its flaws, the Defense Department had evolved and internalized the lessons of Vietnam in this regard: The families of the missing and captured could not be ignored.

Even as Sky and her husband marveled at the familiar modes of military obfuscation, her parents were provided with support plans and personalized attention that would have been unheard of in earlier wars.

The Joint Personnel Recovery Agency (JPRA) was designed to track down all missing and captured servicemen and women, and it was equipped to help their families for the duration. A family assistance team flew to Idaho, laid out the logistical and medical plans for reintegrating Bowe back into the Army, and treated their son's homecoming as a guaranteed outcome.

The team was headquartered at Brooke Army Medical Center (BAMC) in San Antonio, Texas, and led by Colonel Bradley Poppen, the Pentagon's senior SERE (Survival Evasion Resistance Escape) psychologist. Poppen, whom everyone called "Doc," had been through these cases before; he exuded an academic and professional calm. In 2003, his team had managed Jessica Lynch's recovery during the Iraq War; and in 2008 they welcomed home three Pentagon contractors held in chains for more than five years by leftist rebels in the mountains of Colombia. Even in darkness, Poppen would tell Bob and Jani, the human animal—and surely a young man as independent as their son—is more resilient than most people think.

Bob and Jani felt they were in good hands and were comfortable in the military community. In addition to his brother-in-law pilot, Bowe's maternal grandfather had served in the Navy, and one of Jani's cousins was an Army helicopter crew chief who'd been killed in Nicaragua. Bob's grandfather had served in the Merchant Marine, and his great-uncle, Corporal Frank Powers, had fought with the 3rd Armored Division near the German-Belgian border, where he was killed by an artillery shell in 1945. Before he died, Corporal Powers had written a letter home about an incident with a German officer who crossed Allied lines to negotiate an off-the-books prisoner swap. To Bob, it was an instructive artifact of history; if only some commander in RC East had had such clout (and a briefcase full of cash), his son might have been freed within days. Instead, he was in a true no-man's-land, trapped by a non-state actor inside the disputed borders of an unconvincing ally. The very fact of his being located in Pakistan, obvious to anyone with an internet connection, was classified, its very discussion by anyone in the military or intelligence community punishable by federal law.

Bob and Jani didn't know what had happened at Mest, but they knew their son. Despite the tension between them, Bowe had written to his parents from Afghanistan, and over the course of six weeks, emails that had started out with humor and aplomb quickly turned dark and dispirited. They worried that he was psychologically isolated and ethically confused about his purpose there. Bob saw clues in the videos shot by *The Guardian*'s Sean Smith, who had embedded with 2nd Platoon at Mest in June 2009. He watched them over and over: Bowe digging out a bunker while the other soldiers stood around watching, Bowe speaking with a young Afghan from a nearby village, Bowe posing with a pipe on the hilltop at sunset. In one scene, the soldiers talked about the Taliban planting IEDs in the road at night. Bob suspected that his son might have been slipping off the OP on solo missions to gather his own intelligence. "Maybe that's how it went down," he said to Jani.

All of it had Bob torn. On the one hand, he was proud of the all-or-nothing resolve that had driven Bowe to volunteer twice for the U.S. military. At the same time, he couldn't shake the feeling that if Bowe didn't survive this, it was somehow his own fault as a parent.

Before Bowe had deployed, Bob followed the news and emailed him stories about the war he was headed into. After the DUSTWUN, Bob's reading consumed him. He was a lifelong autodidact, and he dove into fathoms of academic and historical research and contemporary policy analysis. In the evenings after his work shift and in the mornings before, his studies grew into his own all-or-nothing mission. He read nineteenth-century British writers who surveyed the tribal dynamics of the Raj's North-West Frontier Province, and he pored over colonial maps that laid out where each tribe had lived. Comparing these with present-day analysis, he was struck by how little had changed.

In 2009, the Obama administration devoted countless hours and hundreds of millions of dollars to shore up the partnership with the

Pakistani military and ISI. But the expected outcome of that effort—that the Pakistanis would restrain the Taliban and promote reconciliation in Kabul—had not materialized. After a decade of war, Washington still had no viable diplomatic channel to Mullah Omar and the Quetta Shura. And after Chapman, the CIA and the Pentagon were in no mood to talk.

Plenty of Americans communicated with the Taliban, but not at the levels where policy was decided and applied. Clandestine Army officers like Major Ron Wilson had Taliban contacts, but no authority to negotiate. The CIA had the authority but was focused on droning Haqqani commanders and finding bin Laden, not Bowe Bergdahl. Aside from firing missiles from remote-controlled robots in the sky, the United States government had no power over the men who held Bergdahl, no method of contacting them, and only vague sketches of a plan to begin trying. When a reporter at a White House press conference asked if the president or his staff had contacted the family, Obama replied, coolly, that he would, when he had good news.

"I'm going, 'How much intel do we have in that area? How is this going to be reconciled? Is CIA going to be in on this? Is ISI going to be in on this? Can we trust the Pakistanis?" Bob didn't need a classified briefing to tell him where his son was, but after six months, he and Jani did need something they were not getting: reassurance that the U.S. government would or even could do anything about it.

Retired Navy captain Jerry Coffee and his wife, Susan Page, had been wondering the same thing, and the meeting they had with Bob and Jani in July 2009 had spurred them to action. From Idaho, Coffee and Page had traveled east to Annapolis, where the former POW had made speaking at the Naval Academy Plebe Summer a yearly tradition. The couple also made plans for lunch with an old friend, Senator John McCain. They knew John, as they called him, as a man with a conscience and a code.

"I don't have the authority or the information to tell John McCain anything," Page said later. "But I could just feel for these parents. My son is a Marine. I would feel so desperate."

McCain was skeptical. From what he knew, he told his old friends, Bergdahl had "just walked away." Coffee and Page couldn't speak to that. But they believed that the Bergdahls were good people, that they were being left in the dark, and that they were suffering. McCain said he would look into it. The next Page heard from Jani Bergdahl, it was in an email that winter, thanking her and her husband. The Bergdahls had been invited to the Pentagon.

As Bob and Jani prepared for the trip in February 2010, the backdrop of the war was grim. In February, the Dutch government had collapsed over the future of its two thousand troops in Afghanistan and became the first major NATO ally to announce a pullout. Then, in March, British journalist Jerome Starkey published an exposé in *The Sunday Times* about a botched February 12 night mission in Paktia Province that left five civilians dead. U.S. Special Forces acting on false intelligence had stormed a home in Gardez and opened fire on two pregnant women (one a mother of ten, the other of six), a teenage girl, and two men working for the Afghan government, killing them all. At first, ISAF claimed that the women had been found in an apparent Taliban murder scene. Starkey's reporting revealed the story of an American atrocity, complete with U.S. soldiers digging their own bullets out of the walls of the home and the dead women's bodies.

The incident in Gardez capped off months of bad news for McChrystal and the Pentagon. Obama's surge had sent civilian deaths into record numbers, and even though the Taliban was responsible for the vast majority, perceptions tilted against Western troops. "We're going to lose this fucking war if we don't stop killing civilians," McChrystal had barked at an early-morning staff meeting in August 2009. Six months later, ISAF was caught in a lie about why five innocent people in Gardez were dead.

Bob and Jani weren't expecting a cheerful reception at Army

headquarters. But a strange thing happened in Arlington. They walked under the twin flag poles at the building's entrance (one flying red, white, and blue; the other POW black) and came out with something they hadn't anticipated: a real human connection with the chairman of the Joint Chiefs of Staff.

Admiral Michael Mullen invited his wife, Deborah, who'd worked for years as an advocate for military families, to join him for the meeting, and the two couples quickly bonded over their common roots: Bob and Mullen had graduated from rival Catholic high schools in Los Angeles, and both men's parents had long careers in the entertainment industry. Whether McCain had pulled any strings was not discussed. Rather, the two couples marveled at a more uncanny connection. The day Bowe's identity had been released, Bob's uncle had called up Mullen's mother; the two were old friends from Los Angeles.

The Bergdahls saw the coincidences as providence, proof that a higher power was guiding them. Mullen had expected a relationship defined by compassion for suffering parents, but as time passed, he grew increasingly impressed by Bob's research and analysis of the FATA. "There were many times when he knew more about it than I did," Mullen said.

After they left, Mullen called then Joint Forces commander General James Mattis, and the two agreed to give the family a security clearance. Mattis and his staff took the lead on managing the relationship, which, as with Mullen, grew into a bond based on common histories. For Mattis, it was growing up without a television and surrounded by books in the farmlands of Washington State's Columbia River Valley. On a 2012 trip to CENTCOM, Bob brought Mattis a horseshoe that belonged to his son. "Good luck, sir," he said, handing it to him. "You're gonna need all the luck you can get to fix Afghanistan." Mattis hung it on a prominent wall outside the operations room at CENTCOM headquarters.

Mullen reminded Bob that their relationship, and the quiet arrangement with Mattis's staff, was not unconditional; he needed to keep a low profile and show them that he could be trusted. Bob understood. "I give Bob a lot of credit for this," Mullen said. "His commitment to not be out in public with everything we were telling him facilitated a long-term comfort with each other."

Mullen had heard the rumors about Bowe's allegedly nefarious motives and considered it a matter that the military courts would resolve. On this issue, Mullen and the parents agreed: "Nobody is going to be able to tell us exactly what happened until we hear from Bowe Bergdahl."

They all heard from him just a few weeks later. On April 7, 2010, the Haqqanis released their first proof-of-life video since Christmas. Their prisoner was skinny and bearded, wearing camouflage pants and a gray long-sleeved Army PT shirt. In the seven minutes of footage, he performed a few push-ups, deep knee bends, and leg lifts for the camera. In stilted language, odd syntax, and, to those who knew him, exaggerated emotion, Bowe pleaded with the U.S. government.

"Please! I'm begging you, bring me home!" he said with his hands clasped in front of his face. "Let me go! Get me to go. Just . . . release. Get me . . . to be release."

He didn't look good, but he looked alive. The Haqqani's April 2010 video ended the same way as the July and Christmas 2009 videos had before it, with a call for a prisoner swap. Taliban spokesman Zabihullah Mujahid told the Americans to "use their rationale and show readiness to release our limited prisoners in exchange for their prisoner."

There was fresh diplomatic momentum following a UN conference in London that winter, where Karzai made a bold call for the Taliban to enter peace talks. The Pentagon visit had brought some solace to Bowe's parents, and as the one-year anniversary of his capture loomed, the calls for negotiations brought them hope. Strangely, so, too, did the propaganda videos of their son, conveniently uploaded to YouTube. Bob would stay up all night watching them, thinking about how to get his son home, and about what, if the Pentagon failed, he alone would do to make it happen.

UNBEKNOWNST TO HIS FAMILY the video of Bowe doing push-ups and deep knee-bends was just the public half of a two-pronged Haqqani negotiation strategy. The same week the video was released, a private letter from Mullah Sangeen arrived at a U.S. military base, delivered by one of the only couriers still trusted by both sides.

Sangeen had written the letter himself. The ISAF interpreters took one look at his messy scrawl and could see that the powerful Taliban commander had little formal education. At the upper right-hand corner, he wrote the date as "10/4/15"—a confused mash-up of the Europeans' day/month/year and Pashto's right-to-left.

"I have something with me from the Americans," Sangeen wrote. "We will talk about it."

Sangeen had done nothing prior to this letter to ingratiate himself with U.S. forces. In his last public statement, a September 2009 interview with al-Qaeda's main propaganda channel, he had declared that the Taliban and al-Qaeda were fully united. "Just as the infidels are one people, so are the Muslims, and they will never succeed in disuniting the mujahideen," Sangeen had said.

It remains unclear how far up the chain of command Sangeen's letter was reported. (The White House was not aware of it until years later.) A U.S. government entity in Afghanistan responded with their own letter, written in Pashto script by an interpreter, but it was not the reply that Sangeen—or Siraj Haqqani—had hoped for:

> *Greetings and peace and Allah's blessing be upon you, Moulavi Sangeen,*
>
> *Many innocent Afghans and your friends get killed because of your activities and their children become orphans. You are the only one responsible for all these deaths. Because of your activities against the Afghan National Army and Coalition Forces, we are very obliged to kill and/or capture your friends.*

> *If you don't decide to quit your activities, we will target you and your friends.*
>
> *You still have one last chance to make your choice to abandon your activities.*
>
> *Now this decision is in your hand to make.*

The reply didn't tell Sangeen anything he didn't already know; the Americans were hunting him and his comrades from the sky and didn't care what he wanted to talk about. Nine years after George W. Bush first explained it, U.S. policy toward the Taliban remained unchanged: no negotiations. Shortly after the letter exchange, a U.S. drone strike killed the courier, and along with him, one of the only open channels between the Americans and the Taliban.

WHEN BOB ACCEPTED an invitation from the Idaho Republican Party to speak at a fund-raiser at the Sun Valley Resort on June 10, 2010, he knew that his son's captors wanted to make a deal. He did not know that Sangeen had reached out with a personal letter, or that the U.S. government had followed up by literally killing the messenger. But he was a lifelong Republican and had been invited to speak alongside RNC chairman Michael Steele and Idaho senator Jim Risch. Though wary that the party was using him as a political prop, Bob was more concerned that the Pentagon was intentionally suppressing his son's case in Washington.

Spring had been full of the usual up-and-down news from Afghanistan. In late May 2010, ISAF airstrikes had killed the ranking al-Qaeda leader in the FATA and another Taliban commander in Kandahar. President Karzai had successfully convened the largest peace summit in years, a massive *loya jirga* that gathered roughly sixteen hundred delegates under a giant tent at Kabul Polytechnic University. Security ahead of the June 2 event was tight; homes in the area were searched, Afghan police were positioned at the top of a hill overlooking university grounds, and a Turkish commando team was in the neighborhood on standby. But just minutes after Karzai began his opening remarks, a rocket attack issued its rebuttal.

The ranking Americans in attendance, McChrystal and U.S. ambassador to Afghanistan Karl Eikenberry, were hurriedly escorted out, and Karzai pleaded with his audience to remain calm. The Taliban was not his enemy, he said in the spirit of the day. "They are the sons of this land," he said, and repeated his standing invitation for Taliban leaders to return from Pakistan and join his government. The attack was quickly contained (four would-be suicide bombers disguised in burkas had not detonated; two were shot and two were captured), but it was an embarrassment nonetheless. That weekend, Karzai accepted resignations from his interior minister, Hanif Atmar, and, more worryingly for U.S. observers, from Amrullah Saleh, the Northern Alliance veteran who had gained the Americans' trust as Karzai's steady intelligence director since 2004. To Washington, Karzai's shakeup looked like an act of vanity, more proof that the "Mayor of Kabul," as Vice President Joe Biden had dismissively called him, was not a reliable partner.

Bob had been immersed in Karzai's struggles for nearly a year, but as he walked into the Sun Valley ski lodge his mind was on his own government. In addition to Steele, Risch, and the Idaho GOP, he knew that several wealthy and connected donors from his UPS route would be in the audience. These were the people he and Jani needed to mobilize.

A small table had been set in front of the speaker's podium with a white tablecloth and the symbols of the Vietnam-era POW-MIA ceremony: empty chair, empty glass, burning white candle, one red rose, one Bible, and the POW-MIA black flag. Bob hadn't shaved in eleven months and ten days, and as he approached the podium his audience went completely still. He paused, gazing into the distance with a sad, heavy gaze. Then, in a low steady tone like an incantation, he began a meandering sermon on the vast suffering of war and the shame of wounded American soldiers who return home only to fall through the cracks of government-run Department of Veteran Affairs health care. He broke into a wry smile explaining how his own background had led him to accept the invitation to speak at a partisan fund-raiser. "I grew up in a conservative family in Los Angeles," he said. His parents were for Goldwater and Nixon. He was the only surfer at UC Santa Barbara who voted for Reagan. Bob might have found his crunchy libertarian side in Idaho, but he was still a Republican. As for Bowe, he told them, "Everything that can be done has been done. I have Admiral Mullen's cell phone number on me right now." Several people in the audience began to cry.

From there, Bob made his pivot: "The man who we believe holds Bowe grew up on the lap of his mother learning the Koran. He is a powerful man, a man of faith. We pray for him. He recently lost a son to a CIA missile drone strike. The fact that he didn't kill Bowe right then is incredible. So we pray for him."

The room's silent respect turned to quiet confusion. A prayer for the Taliban? A secret CIA assassination? No one knew what he was talking about. The failed February attempt to kill Badruddin Haqqani—which ended up eliminating his younger brother, Mohammad, instead—was not public information. But Bob and Jani had spent months talking with their pastor about the unappreciated overlaps between Calvinism and Islam. If Bob was going to lend out his family's suffering for political exploitation, he would do it on his own terms and deliver his own message: Peace would not come without understanding the men who held his son, and without peace, his son would never come home.

After the event, Risch and an aide asked to speak with Bob in a private corner of the room. The senator told him that he shared his concerns, particularly regarding Pakistan. Though Risch sat on the Senate Foreign Relations Committee, he could not publicly discuss it. "You just informed the entire lodge what I can only say in a secure and classified room," Risch confided. Bob was dismayed. It confirmed his suspicions that the Pentagon was burying the central facts of the war and hiding the truth even from lawmakers. By reading Pakistani news websites in his own home, Bob was more informed than the average congressman.

FIFTEEN

THE NO-NEGOTIATIONS NEGOTIATIONS

In the summer of 2010, the Haqqanis' golden sparrow had begun to look like a long-term investment. Taliban officials, spokesmen, and military commanders had been broadcasting a consistent message to the Americans—*let's negotiate a prisoner swap*—through every available channel for more than a year, with no signs of progress.

Robert Pelton flew into Kabul in August 2010, and as he had done on most of his trips to the country since 1996, he paid a visit to his old contact, Abdul Rashid Dostum. After several years of political exile in Turkey, Karzai had invited Dostum to return in the summer of 2009, just before that year's Afghan national elections. Karzai needed the Uzbek strongman as an ally and peace broker in the north. The day Pelton arrived to see him in Kabul, Dostum's guards escorted him to an ornate waiting room where he joined two men with jet-black beards and tremendous pastel pink turbans and who were also waiting for a meeting. Pelton recognized them as members of the Zadran tribe from Khost, and likely Taliban. He felt the men glaring at him, and the air grew tense until one barked out an angry question in Pashto.

"Why don't you want your American back?" a translator asked. It was nearly Eid al-Fitr, he said, the feast days that mark the end of

Ramadan, and Siraj Haqqani needed money for the holiday—$3 million dollars. They gave Pelton their phone number.

Pelton did not officially work for the American government, much less represent Washington in high-level negotiations; he was a contractor and explained that he was not the right person to talk to. The Zadrans fumed. After the meeting, Pelton called his U.S. military contacts to pass along the phone number and the latest Bergdahl update: Siraj Haqqani was so eager to negotiate that he had his henchmen putting out feelers to any random Westerner they bumped into.

Not all of Haqqani's attempts to open dialogue were so clumsy. That same month in Kabul, Miles Amoore, a British journalist with London's *Sunday Times*, secured an interview with a midlevel Taliban commander who went by the name Nadeem and claimed to be one of Sangeen's lieutenants. Amoore had built a reliable roster of Taliban fixers and sources during his five years in the city, and he had been asking around about Bergdahl for months. Nadeem said he knew Bergdahl's captors and said that he had personally spent time with the American soldier.

Amoore and his fixer met Nadeem in a safe house in Kabul, where he told them an incredible story: In the year since Bergdahl had walked off his base, Nadeem said, he had become a fully integrated Taliban collaborator. The U.S. soldier had converted to Islam, taken the name Abdullah, and was leading Taliban strategy seminars. Nadeem had attended one himself, a two-hour training session in Sar Hawza District, just southeast of FOB Sharana. He said Abdullah Bergdahl had taught him how to turn a Nokia phone into a remote control for roadside bombs.

Amoore knew to be skeptical of such tales. Kabul was rife with "shoppers"—sources selling fake stories to mislead Western journalists and intelligence officers, but this one seemed to check out. Amoore compared battle footage with news reports to verify that Nadeem was who he said he was. Next, he ran it by his intelligence sources at the Afghan National Directorate of Security (NDS), who confirmed the basics of Nadeem's story. There was no way to safely verify it, they told Amoore; the Taliban had already killed two of their own for talking about Bergdahl. The American prisoner had become one of the region's most guarded secrets, and Amoore was the only reporter with the story. *The Sunday Times* headline on August 22, 2010, set the tone for years to come:

CAPTURED U.S. SOLDIER HAS JOINED OUR CAUSE, SAY TALIBAN.

It would be years before Amoore realized that he had been conned. The Taliban used disinformation for a variety of reasons. In this case, the fake news was likely meant to goad the Americans into the prisoner exchange or ransom that the Taliban demanded. As a means to spread rumors and set a narrative that would sow political discord in the United States, it would prove incredibly effective; as a method to kick-start negotiations, it was premature.

Twenty months into the Obama administration, Washington still had no coherent diplomatic policy toward the Taliban. The president had spent hundreds of hours managing exhaustive White House policy reviews that assessed every available leverage point, from digging more village wells to incentivizing farmers to replace their opium poppies with cotton or wheat. But in all of the analysis, peace talks were never seriously considered. The no-negotiations Bush-era legacy had left little insight into Taliban leadership, no strategy about whom to communicate with, and no method to even begin.

NEARLY A DECADE of war had taught both the Taliban and the Americans that claims from the enemy could not be trusted. When the mullahs Fazl and Noori surrendered in Mazar-i-Sharif in November 2001, it had seemed briefly possible that some Taliban officials would be permitted to join Karzai's government. Abdul Haq Wasiq, the Taliban's deputy intelligence minister, also turned himself over as a willing cooperator after he was told that he would be granted amnesty. Weeks later, all three were captured by U.S. forces and flown to a makeshift prison aboard the USS *Peleliu*, the amphibious assault ship that had carried the first Marines to the region before it began receiving detainees in the Arabian Sea.

From their prison ship, the men were hooded and restrained, blindfolded with goggles stuffed with cotton balls, sedated with rectal suppositories, strapped into the cargo bay of U.S. transport planes, and flown to Guantanamo Bay, Cuba. In early 2002, they were joined by Mullah Khairullah Khairkhwa, a founding member of the Taliban who, as the governor of Herat Province, had earned a reputation as a moderate among senior Taliban officials. None had been charged with any crimes, but as they shuffled in shackles into the tropical heat and wire fencing of the open-air U.S. detention camp, the lesson was clear: The Americans could not be trusted. The Taliban leadership in Pakistan had been looking for ways to get the men back ever since.

Caught between the ISI and the threat of American imprisonment (or Hellfire missiles), Taliban leaders began telegraphing their desires to the two ISAF nations that showed the greatest diplomatic capacity for peacemaking: Norway and Germany. For three and a half years, between 2007 and 2010, Norway's Minister of Foreign Affairs Jonas Gahr Støre, managed the opening moves in a delicate and at times dangerous diplomatic chess game. Whenever he came close to bringing Taliban and Afghan envoys together, the meetings were blocked by Taliban hard-liners or the ISI—it was often hard to tell the difference. The Norwegian government hadn't told the Bush administration about the Taliban's outreach efforts, and as much as Obama's first year brought hope for diplomacy, his Afghanistan surge had also revealed the depths of American factionalism.

Secretary of State Hillary Clinton had authorized Richard Holbrooke, her special representative for Afghanistan and Pakistan (SRAP), to begin quietly searching for a brokered peace even as the Pentagon and CIA remained confident that they could kill and capture their way to victory. Uncertain which way the winds of U.S. policy were blowing, Støre waited until December 2009 before he told Clinton about his secret

Taliban diplomacy. Even then, and to the evident chagrin of Clinton's deputies, he refused to share his Taliban contacts' names, fearful that they would be snatched by U.S. agents and stashed in Guantanamo alongside Fazl, Noori, Wasiq, and Khairkhwa.

The only party to the war more obstructive to diplomacy than the Americans, and more capable of undermining it, was the ISI. By the spring of 2010, with both the Taliban and Karzai working with the Norwegians to set up peace talks, the ISI was working just as hard to obstruct them. Later that summer, Norwegian diplomats in Islamabad received typewritten death threats, and yet another meeting they had scheduled between the Taliban and Karzai's representatives was derailed at the last minute by shadowy forces. In both cases, it seemed that ISI elements were responsible, and the Norwegians soon accepted that the gears of power driving the conflict were beyond their control. Peace in Afghanistan rested on a catch-22: Without talks, the war would never end, and as long as the war continued, there could be no talks.

RICHARD HOLBROOKE WAS DETERMINED to close out his diplomatic career with an achievement no one else could claim. But from his first days on the job, when he was faced with the déjà vu rescue of David Rohde from a more unreachable captivity than what had trapped him in Bosnia, Holbrooke knew that peace in Afghanistan was a distant dream. He also knew that he needed an expert from outside the Beltway, and before Obama was sworn into office, Holbrooke called Barnett "Barney" Rubin, a New York University professor who he believed could light a path through the Taliban's murky power structure.

Rubin was a senior fellow at NYU's Center on International Cooperation, sometimes working out of the program's Abu Dhabi campus, and had been writing about Afghanistan for nearly thirty years. He could read and write in Arabic; speak Urdu, Hindi, and a bit of Dari; and had access to a broad network of contacts across the Muslim world, especially in Kabul. (Karzai's own spokesman had previously worked for him at NYU.) From his efforts with the UN Development Programme, Rubin had met former Taliban leaders from Omar's inner circle, and when Holbrooke contacted him, he had recently returned from a trip to Pakistan as a guest of a policy think tank working on reconciliation. There, he had met with former ISI directors general and former ISI officers who had worked with the mujahideen, the Taliban, and other militant proxies. Few Americans could match Rubin's insights into the region's obscure social and tribal hierarchies, and Holbrooke told him to begin at the beginning: Find out who speaks for Mullah Omar.

Holbrooke and Clinton saw an opportunity to recreate the aggressive peace-through-strength diplomacy that had worked in their favor in Bosnia. Obama's surge would pin down the Taliban militarily, weaken its negotiating position, and force it to accept American terms up front. Or at least that was the idea. As Rubin began quietly working his contacts in the Middle East, Holbrooke navigated his own channels in Washington. Difficult as it might be to get the Taliban to the table, he knew that convincing the White House, Pentagon, and Congress would be just as hard.

Rubin has a dry wit and wears a white beard and a shock of white hair over wire-frame glasses. His overall effect is more hip rabbi than technocratic wonk. But iconoclasm was precisely why Holbrooke had brought him on—to shake up a war-planning bureaucracy seized by perpetual spasms of internal gridlock. Rubin was dismayed, for instance, that the Obama White House had retained what he saw as an outdated and misguided Bush-era counternarcotics policy of poppy eradication. The U.S. government should focus its powers on heroin traffickers, he thought, not on poor uneducated farmers.

"The peasants that grow the flowers are not our enemy," he said. "In fact, we're trying to win them over, and destroying their livelihood is not a good way to do that."

Living in New York and reporting only to Holbrooke, Rubin conducted his initial outreach more or less in secret. As he explained it to his new boss in a December 2008 memo, some of Rubin's best contacts included people who "might be easier and more effective to utilize from a base partly outside the government."

In April 2009, Holbrooke formalized Rubin's role, hiring him on as a special government employee of the SRAP office at the State Department. He obtained a Top Secret/Special Compartmented Information security clearance and later that month flew to Kabul to meet with Mullah Abdul Salam Zaeef, the former Taliban ambassador to Pakistan and an early associate of Mullah Omar. Zaeef's life told its own story of the war. Following 9/11, he had hosted press conferences as the public face of the Taliban taunting the U.S. government. In December 2001, two weeks after he applied for formal asylum in Pakistan, the ISI detained him in Islamabad; five months later he was shipped off to join his comrades in Guantanamo Bay. Though he was a high-ranking Taliban official deemed to have ties to al-Qaeda, and while his time as a detainee in Cuba was marked by belligerent noncompliance, the Bush administration released Zaeef on September 11, 2005. Back in Kabul, he reconciled with Karzai's government, wrote a memoir, and gained a reputation as the kind of moderate Taliban who could bridge the diplomatic divide.

Zaeef told Rubin that the Taliban wanted to negotiate. They believed that the Norwegians and Germans had been sincere in their peacemaking desires. The problem was the United States, which broke its promises to those who had cooperated and seemed intent on fighting the war forever. Nevertheless, Zaeef said, if and when the Americans were ready to talk, the Taliban was as well—assuming that a few essential conditions were met up front.

First, ISAF troops needed to leave Afghanistan. Second, the Taliban needed assurances that their envoys would not be arrested when they traveled to talks. Third, the Taliban wanted to run a brick-and-mortar diplomatic office—in Saudi Arabia. Finally, the U.S. needed to release six Taliban detainees from Guantanamo; these men would help run the Saudi office.

The Saudi royal family had been pursuing this mediation role for years, with intelligence chief Prince Muqrin bin Abdulaziz leading the effort. The royals saw geopolitical opportunities in peacemaking. Beyond the international prestige, the kingdom could strengthen its bonds with Washington while also weakening Iranian influence in Afghanistan. For Prince Muqrin, however, the main challenge was figuring out what exactly the Americans wanted. Muqrin complained that he was receiving totally conflicting requests from the State Department, which wanted help finding Taliban officials to speak with, and his CIA contacts, who demanded that he detain more of the Taliban officials on its blacklist.

"What am I supposed to do?" Muqrin pleaded to Rubin. "Talk to them or arrest them?"

About two months after his meeting with Zaeef in Kabul, Rubin was back in Holbrooke's office on the first floor of the State Department when he first heard about the captured American soldier. His time with Zaeef had led Rubin to believe that peace and reconciliation talks were inevitable. With Bergdahl in Taliban captivity, a prisoner exchange now looked equally unavoidable.

"I knew before I started that the Taliban, if we ever met them, would ask for the release of those five guys from Guantanamo," Rubin said. Originally, the request was for six, but in 2011, following the death of Mullah Awal Gul, it dropped to five.

Rubin was on vacation in the south of France later that summer when he received a call from a Saudi national and former mujahideen who asked him to fly to Dubai to meet in person. When Rubin arrived, the old soldier said he had a message of peace. Mullah Omar wanted to talk to the Americans, and the Saudis could connect them to the one man with the authority to speak for him: Tayeb Agha.

Rubin knew the name. He had met Agha before; in 1998, the young man had served as an interpreter for an interview Rubin conducted with a Taliban official in Kandahar. He knew that Agha was close to Mullah Omar, had been traveling to the Arab Gulf States on fund-raising trips for the Taliban, and, ergo, was about to be sanctioned by the U.S. government. Rubin told Holbrooke the good news, followed by the bad: Agha was their most promising lead yet, but the Treasury Department was going to ban him from traveling to countries that would work with the U.S. to detain him.

Before the issue could be addressed, Rubin learned that the Saudis had backed out as mediator. There had been a feud between the Taliban and the Saudi royal family; a disagreement had grown into an argument that blew up into a fight, and by the time Rubin heard about it, the Saudis were spreading rumors that Tayeb Agha was an Iranian double agent. But the falling-out proved only a minor setback for the Taliban. The Saudis weren't the only courtiers in their ambit, and Agha moved on to a more reliable mediator: the German Federal Intelligence Service. In January 2010, Bernd Mützelburg, Germany's special envoy to Afghanistan, invited Holbrooke and Rubin to a meeting in Abu Dhabi to share the news.

It was the breakthrough that Holbrooke had been waiting for. The question he couldn't yet answer was how his own government would respond. If the Norwegian efforts had revealed the schism between moderate and hard-line Taliban, Obama's surge had divided the U.S. government in similar ways. With record numbers of young American soldiers and spies fighting and dying, diplomacy was anathema to the Pentagon, CIA, and their oversight committees in Congress. Talks would mean accepting the unacceptable reality that the Taliban would never be defeated.

At the White House, Obama had retained Lieutenant General Douglas Lute as his unofficial "war czar." First appointed by President Bush in 2007 to manage the unmanageable, Lute was seen as a low-key and pragmatic problem solver. Under Obama, Lute formed the Conflict Resolution Cell (CRC), a classified group of senior advisers recruited from the Pentagon, CIA, State Department, and NSC; it was an interagency group that by design represented the full range of policy options and internal conflicts. The Pentagon wanted to keep fighting;

the CIA was having a banner year with its drones; and despite Holbrooke's assurances from the Germans, no one from Langley or DoD had seen any proof that the Taliban was genuinely interested in peace.

Sitting among the military brass, Rubin was out of his academic element, but certain in his belief. "The Taliban want to talk," he told them, and there was no harm in listening.

"WE'RE GONNA NEED YOU full time," Holbrooke barked to Rubin over the phone later that summer. All of a sudden, the White House was ready; Tayeb Agha was ready; and for Rubin, the part-time gig as Washington's foremost secret diplomat wasn't going to fly any longer. He and Holbrooke were on the verge of opening the highest-level wartime peace talks since Vietnam, but almost no one in the U.S. government knew about it. Hillary Clinton had given Holbrooke a long leash, and Lute had granted Holbrooke's request not to share the update from Germany with the Pentagon or CIA. Since Rubin reported only to Holbrooke at the time and enjoyed relative isolation as a special government employee, his was an unencumbered role that drove some bureaucrats mad.

"Once or twice people got wind of my activities and accused me of violating policy," Rubin said. "I asked them to write down what I had done and what policies I had supposedly violated. They had nothing."

In late October 2010, with approval from Clinton, Gates, and President Obama, Holbrooke put the plan in motion. He assigned Frank Ruggiero, the State Department deputy who had been trapped on his Kandahar base a year earlier, as the lead negotiator. He would be joined by two military men on loan from the Pentagon: NSC deputy and DIA analyst Jeff Hayes, and Army colonel Chris Kolenda, one of Gates's most trusted aides. The German intelligence service (the Bundesnachrichtendienst) would handle the logistics, hosting the first meeting on November 28 in a safe house outside Munich.

After years of diplomatic jockeying, the Germans had become the only party trusted by all sides. Afghans had a kinship with the

Germans dating back nearly a hundred years based on their shared histories of going to war with the British and the Russians (and now the Americans)—somewhat awkward facts for U.S. national security meetings. But the Afghans saw the Germans, as NDS chief Saleh told Rubin in a meeting with Karzai, as "a different species" of white Europeans. Scientific accuracy aside, the sentiments were sufficiently widespread to give Karzai and the Taliban some common ground.

Secrecy in Munich was a top concern. At the White House, Obama agreed that Agha could travel without being arrested by U.S. authorities. Despite that direct presidential approval, Lute decided not to share the plans with his Conflict Resolution Cell. Though the group's very existence was compartmented and highly classified, Lute believed—just as Holbrooke, Støre, and Mützelburg had before him—that some elements of the U.S. government could not be trusted.

Three days after Thanksgiving 2010, Ruggiero, Hayes, and Kolenda arrived at a safe house in a sleepy Munich suburb that had been locked down with a security perimeter ahead of the talks. Agha flew in on a German jet in Western clothes, his hair and beard trimmed in the Western style. Though he was one of Mullah Omar's closest aides, Agha was also something of a Taliban rarity: a literate, sophisticated English speaker equally comfortable lingering over a gourmet meal in a luxury Gulf State hotel as he was holding an AK-47 and drinking chai in a mud-walled *qalat* in Quetta.

Before Ruggiero left for Munich, Clinton had laid out her negotiation guidelines, which weren't much different from the demands that President Bush had made in the fall of 2001. If there was to be peace, the United States had three nonnegotiable terms: First, the Taliban would need to stop fighting; second, break off their lingering relations with al-Qaeda; and third, agree to accept and abide by the Afghan constitution. Outside of those redlines, Clinton said she was open to "creative diplomacy." Above all, Holbrooke told Ruggiero before he left, "the most important objective of the first meeting is to have a second meeting."

Both sides had reasons to be nervous. For the Americans, the Chapman attack stood as a testament to the consequences of misplaced trust. For his part, Agha relied on German promises that he wasn't walking into a trap that ended at Guantanamo. Inside the house, Agha changed into his Afghan salwar and introduced the Americans to a Qatari delegate who had traveled with him. "You Americans have your German friends with you," he said, "and we Taliban want to have our Muslim friends from Qatar with us." Ruggiero and Hayes didn't argue the point. Only later, however, did Holbrooke, Rubin, and the rest of the team learn that German and Qatari diplomats had been meeting for months to arrange what was, in fact, a co-mediation.

The meeting began with each side reading statements. Agha's was deeply critical of U.S. involvement in Afghanistan and the injustice of holding the Taliban responsible for 9/11, a crime it neither planned nor committed. The Taliban, he said, are not terrorists. Ruggiero defended the American and NATO response in 2001, but conceded up front that the war was a stalemate. Now, the U.S. wanted peace to come from the Taliban and Karzai's government reconciling on their own terms. In six hours of dialogue over the course of two days, Agha said that a prisoner exchange was one of Omar's highest priorities. There would be no problem delivering Bergdahl from the Haqqanis, he said, because the Haqqanis and the Taliban were one and the same.

Barney Rubin was flying from Washington, D.C., to Kabul on the same day that Ruggiero flew home from Germany. Rubin was headed to Afghanistan in part to brief General Petraeus, and he needed to know what had transpired in Munich. Holbrooke was eager to know as well, so all three met for an impromptu meeting at Harry's Tap Room in the main terminal at Dulles International Airport, where Ruggiero devoured a burger as he recapped Agha's top lines and the next steps.

He told them that there were serious obstacles to overcome. On the question of the Taliban's relationship with al-Qaeda, Agha had been vague. His plans for reconciling with Karzai were equally noncommittal. But both sides had agreed to fulfill a series of confidence-building measures, and the prisoner exchange would be one of the most critical steps toward mutual trust.

Meeting adjourned, Rubin checked in for his flight, Ruggiero went home, and Holbrooke went back to the office. The secret peace process had consumed Holbrooke. His critics saw it as naked ambition, daydreams of a Nobel Peace Prize. But Rubin saw the man who recruited him as driven by a more relatable fear. Holbrooke had confessed to him that he didn't want to end up like Defense Secretary Robert McNamara, with his legacy defined by the historic magnitude of his mistakes. Eleven days later, Holbrooke was with Clinton at the State Department when his face flushed red and he announced that "something horrible is happening." In the ambulance, he continued dictating messages for work. Rubin was back in Dubai for a regional conference when he heard that Holbrooke had died.

Before the holiday recess, Congress passed an updated National Defense Authorization Act (NDAA), the annual legislation that sets the Pentagon's budget (and the attached congressional strings). For 2011, the bill passed with bipartisan approval for a critical amendment that took direct aim at Obama's pledge to close the military prison at Guantanamo Bay. After seven years of regular detainee transfers under the Bush administration, the 2011 update mandated that no more would be released without the full prior consent of the Pentagon and Congress.

Washington hard-liners had their own methods of derailing the peace process. To Rubin and NSC officials dedicated to resolving the conflict, the sudden NDAA change looked like Washington politics at its worst. The same transfer process that had released 532 detainees during the Bush administration would now be tightly managed by congressional Republicans. Obama had been outmaneuvered, and as he signed the NDAA into law on January 7, 2011, he undermined the promise he'd made on his first day in office to shut the prison camp—and lost the best available option to bring Bowe Bergdahl home.

SIXTEEN
BOB'S WAR

Bob and Jani's lives were now fully intertwined with the U.S. government's fiasco in Afghanistan, their son's fate to be determined by the same convoluted calculus that had led the White House to triple the size of the war while simultaneously planning its end. In the November 2010 NATO summit in Lisbon, Karzai and his ISAF backers agreed that Western troops would be out of Afghanistan by the end of 2014; the war had been put on a four-year schedule. In Idaho, Bob and Jani coped through prayer and counsel from their expanding network of Vietnam POWs, Afghanistan policy experts, former hostages, pastors, and for Bob, a tight crew of cyclists who joined him for weekly long-distance bike rides that doubled as foreign policy seminars. Five mornings a week, he put on his brown UPS uniform, a polite smile, and walked his deliveries through the glass doors on Main Street in Hailey, Idaho, all of them bearing the same yellow ribbon sticker framing his son's smiling face and the message:

"CAPTURED IN AFGHANISTAN 6–30–09—PLEASE HELP FIND ME."

The stickers had been sent by Keith Maupin, whose son Matt Maupin had also been an Army private when he was captured by insurgents north of Baghdad in April 2004. When Keith first called Bob and Jani in the summer of 2009, it had been more than a year since his son's remains had been found in Iraq, marking the end of his own ordeal and a tenacious four-year lobbying campaign. Maupin told Bob that he would do whatever he could for them as they endured their similar nightmare. Over the course of five years, he printed about sixty thousand of the yellow-ribbon stickers that would become ubiquitous in Southern Idaho and in POW-MIA chapters nationwide.

The winter and spring of 2011 had led Bob to even greater doubts about U.S. capabilities in the FATA, and a deeper understanding of the power structures that blocked access to his son. "My theory was the U.S. (kind of) controlled the Pakistani military, the Pakistani military (kind of) controlled ISI, and ISI (kind of) managed the Haqqani Network," Bob wrote years later. "(Kind of) simplistic, but more or less true." On January 22, 2011, a front-page *New York Times* story by reporter Mark Mazzetti followed up on his earlier bombshell about Michael Furlong with a front-page exposé about Clarridge's Eclipse Group and the ongoing struggle for intelligence dominance in Afghanistan. His story—"Former Spy with Agenda Operates a Private C.I.A."—made it clear that the seventy-eight-year-old Clarridge was still capitalizing on chaos.

In describing Eclipse's rogue network of pseudo-spies running amok on both sides of the Durand Line, Mazzetti's story had again served the CIA's strategic purposes. One week later, as if by karma, the CIA stumbled into its own flap.

Raymond Davis was a former Army Special Forces soldier turned CIA contractor when he shot and killed two men in Lahore in broad daylight. As an angry crowd circled the scene, he triggered an emergency signal to his CIA handlers, who, fearing an international crisis if Davis was arrested, sent an extraction team to rescue him, which, in its haste, accidentally ran over and killed another Pakistani man en route. Davis was detained for nearly two months before the matter was settled with a $2.4 million payment from the U.S. government to the families of the deceased. (Such blood-money payoffs, known as *diya*, are legal under Pakistani Sharia law.) The families pardoned him, and Davis walked free. Bob and Jani couldn't believe it. "We saw what could be done, if they wanted to," Bob said of the backroom deal. "If you're a CIA Blackwater mercenary, you get the red carpet extraction."

As the CIA and White House scrambled to contain the Davis fallout, Holbrooke's sudden death had left the State Department's SRAP office briefly rudderless. Hillary Clinton worked her way through a list of potential replacements, eventually hiring Marc Grossman, a former ambassador to Turkey during her husband's presidency. A tall, kind-eyed man with a professorial demeanor, Grossman had been heartbroken by Holbrooke's premature end. He had known him his entire career, since Grossman first joined the Foreign Service with a freshly inked diploma from UC Santa Barbara in 1976. Thirty-five years later, Clinton asked him to come back from a lucrative private sector job to take over Holbrooke's quixotic mission.

On February 14, 2011, Clinton announced Grossman's return to the State Department, and Ruggiero and Hayes arrived in Doha for their second sit-down with Tayeb Agha and Michael Steiner, the German envoy who had replaced Mützelburg. They met at a private compound provided by the emir of Qatar. At their first meeting in Munich, Agha had told the Americans that he had traveled to Germany without Mullah Omar's knowledge. In Doha, for the first time, he said that he was negotiating with Omar's direct blessing and authority.

At the White House, one of the Conflict Resolution Cell's first and highest priorities had been identifying who was actually authorized to negotiate on behalf of the Taliban, and who was just a con man. Days before the first meeting in Munich, a story broke in the press about an Afghan who had convinced ISAF officials that he was one of Mullah Omar's closest associates. The Fake Mullah, as he would be known, had been toying with British and U.S. intelligence for months, complete with an ISAF security detail that escorted him to and from high-level meetings, for which he had been paid more than a hundred thousand dollars in cash before he suddenly disappeared.

Jeff Hayes was certain that Agha was not an imposter. "We knew we were dealing with the real guy," he said. What he, Ruggiero, and Rubin didn't know was how much influence Agha actually had within the Quetta Shura, or with the Haqqanis and other hard-line Taliban factions. The Americans asked Agha if he could produce proof that Bergdahl was alive and well. If he followed through, it would clarify the Taliban hierarchies and bolster the chances of a prisoner exchange.

ON THE NIGHT OF May 1, 2011, President Obama was in black tie and owning the room during the White House Correspondents' Dinner at the Washington Hilton. Donald Trump was in the audience, and as Obama mocked the man who would eventually replace him about the weighty decisions he dealt with as the host of NBC's *Celebrity Apprentice*, only a handful of senior White House officials heard the joke behind the joke. Earlier that day, Obama had ordered the assassination of Osama bin Laden. Hours later, jubilant crowds swarmed the streets around the White House after Obama delivered a brief live television address from the East Room:

> I've repeatedly made clear that we would take action within Pakistan if we knew where bin Laden was. That is what we've done. But it's important to note that our counterterrorism cooperation with Pakistan helped lead us to bin Laden and the compound where he was hiding.

Obama's vague language raised instant suspicions. Abbottabad is home to Pakistan's premier military academy. The notion that the ISI had been taken by surprise, as they claimed, hardly seemed plausible.

Bob and Jani watched from Idaho as bin Laden's death triggered mass protests in Pakistan, where politicians decried the violation of their national sovereignty. In the moment of American exultation, the Bergdahls feared that a vengeful ISI officer would order the Haqqanis to kill their son. Bob had to do something. He drafted a statement, combed his hair and beard, put on a black shirt, and on May 6, with the last snow of the heavy winter lingering on the hillsides behind him and a yellow ribbon tied in the branches of an aspen tree, he spoke directly to the men in control:

> I am the father of captured U.S. soldier Bowe Bergdahl. These are my thoughts. I can remain silent no longer. I address the Pakistani armed forces.
>
> I personally appeal to General Kayani and General Pasha. Our family is counting on your professional integrity and honor to secure the safe return of our son, and we thank you. . . . Our family knows the high price that has been paid by your men in the Army and in the Frontier Corps. We give our condolences and thanks to the families of those who have fallen for Pakistan.
>
> Strangely to some, we must also thank those who have cared for our son for almost two years: Mullah Sangeen, the Haqqanis, and the others who have played a role in sheltering the American prisoner.
>
> We know our son is a prisoner and at the same time a guest in your home. We understand the rationale the Islamic Emirate has made through its videos. No family in the United States understands the detainee issue like ours. Our son's safe return will only heighten public awareness of this. That said, our son is being exploited. It's past time for Bowe and the others to come home. To the nation of Pakistan, our family would wish to convey our compassionate respect. We have watched the violence of war, earthquake, epic floods, and crop failures devastate lives all while our son has been in captivity. We have watched your suffering through the presence of our son in your midst. We have wept that God may show his beneficence, his mercy, and that his peace may come upon the people of Pakistan. *Assalamu alaikum.*

> We ask that your nation diligently help our son be free from his captivity. I pray that this video may be shown to our only son. *Assalamu alaikum.* God bless you. We love you. We've been quiet in public, but we haven't been quiet behind the scenes. Continue to be patient and kind to those around you.
>
> You are not forgotten. You are not forgotten.

The video lasted three minutes and nine seconds. Before he posted it to YouTube and sent it to Tim Marsano at the Idaho National Guard for distribution, Bob shared it with his pastor in Boise to make sure he hadn't violated church doctrine. He also cleared it with Admiral Mullen, who assumed that Bob had been coached by the FBI, was astonished that he hadn't, and promised Bob that he would hand-deliver a written follow-up message to General Kayani at their next meeting. Two days later, the Taliban released a proof-of-life video of Colin Rutherford, a Canadian citizen also held by the Haqqanis in the FATA. The Rutherford video was the same three minutes and nine seconds. Bob and Jani tried not to tie their hopes to speculation, but this seemed like more than a coincidence, and a sign that someone had heard their plea.

The day after Bob posted his statement to YouTube, the American negotiators, Tayeb Agha, and his Qatari representatives returned to the Munich safe house where they had first met five months earlier. As the talks entered a phase of gridlock over the prisoner exchange, Agha shifted topics to the Taliban's desire for a physical office; they had chosen Doha as their only viable option.

After the Saudis' diplomatic implosion, Qatar's then emir, Hamad bin Khalifa al-Thani, saw little downside to hosting the Taliban office. The Qatari royal family had cultivated an aspirational foreign policy for years; diplomacy was a chance to match and even exceed the stature of its larger competitors in Saudi Arabia and the UAE. Hosting five aged Taliban veterans and their families was not a high price to pay for the prestige that closing the deal would bring. Later that summer at another meeting in Doha, Agha delivered a letter for President Obama, allegedly written by Mullah Omar, pressing for the prisoner exchange and assuring that the released Taliban would live out their days in peace.

Back in Washington, Lute's Conflict Resolution Cell couldn't agree on the most basic elements of the conflict, much less a deal to free the highest-ranking Taliban in U.S. custody. David Sedney and his Pentagon colleagues suspected that Agha was simply using the pretense of diplomacy to spring his comrades from Guantanamo, and as much as Sedney respected Barney Rubin as a historian and scholar, he saw the process that he and Holbrooke had begun as flawed from the start. Still, Grossman had the authorization he needed, and in August 2011 he flew to Doha to meet with Agha personally, a gesture intended to convey Obama's seriousness. But when Grossman reiterated the White House's preconditions, Agha dodged those issues and pressed his case for trading Bergdahl for the Guantanamo Five.

Bob and Jani first learned about the State Department's proposed prisoner exchange in a private briefing that summer. The broad outlines had been declassified to SECRET for their knowledge, but specifics were left out when Bob was in the room. (Intelligence officers and analysts had grown a bit wary of Bob's hunger for detail.) Agha delivered a new proof-of-life video in October, proving his sway over Siraj Haqqani and his ability to free the American soldier. It was a major breakthrough, and the White House started moving quickly; Lute dispatched Pentagon lawyer Jeh Johnson to travel to Doha to hammer out the terms of an agreement with the Qataris.

At a November meeting in the Situation Room, Deputy National Security Adviser Denis McDonough, along with Ruggiero and Rubin, briefed a wider group of senior officials, including Homeland Security Adviser John Brennan, Deputy CIA Director Michael Morell, and ranking lawyers from the State Department and the NSC. Despite Pentagon and CIA analysis that the Guantanamo Five would try to rejoin the fight, the group agreed that the five men, headed to an air-conditioned retirement with their families under Qatari surveillance, posed a minor threat. The next, and they agreed harder, challenge would be getting the plan through the gauntlet of American politics.

BARNEY RUBIN'S BRIEF GOVERNMENT experience had proved just how far outside of the Washington mainstream he was. Even at the State Department, where he made his first hesitant suggestions that releasing prisoners from Guantanamo could be a constructive step in the reconciliation process, officials looked at him as if he were insane.

"It was incomprehensible to them," Rubin said. Two years later, with his once-crazy ideas put into motion in the Situation Room, the passage of time hadn't made them any more popular. He reminded his colleagues about how the Taliban leaders had ended up in Cuba in the first place. "None of those five guys ever fought the United States. Three of them surrendered, and two of them we detained after they showed up for appointments saying they wanted to help us," Rubin said. These facts didn't seem to matter. "The conventional wisdom was, 'These are the worst of the worst.'" For years, every person he encountered in the national security establishment was against releasing them.

Jeff Hayes, as a DIA analyst, knew that his military colleagues were dismissive of his new mission. As a former Army sergeant, Hayes was something of an anomaly at the Obama White House. He had gained a reputation at the Pentagon as a fiercely intelligent workaholic and an apolitical soldier who could speak plainly to power and had the ear of the principals running the war. His work with Ruggiero might have placed Hayes at the center of history, but it also landed him on the wrong side of the government's cultural divide. At the Pentagon, his old comrades saw the State Department and White House as "peaceniks sitting around smoking dope and trying to give the farm away to the Taliban, while they were out there fighting and dying." Hayes knew that working as a negotiator would cost him with the Army, and possibly even end his career.

Hayes had the highest security clearance available in the U.S. government, was privy to all need-to-know matters about the war, and never believed the reports that Bergdahl was a traitor or that he'd collaborated with the Taliban in captivity. Hayes was also sympathetic to Bowe Bergdahl's plight. Like Bergdahl's own friends in Idaho, Hayes saw him as a clear case of "someone who shouldn't have been in that situation to begin with," he said. "We're responsible as a nation and as an Army for putting him in [there]."

On November 15, 2011, Bob and Jani took their first trip to CENTCOM on four connecting flights from Idaho to Tampa paid for by the Department of the Army. General Mattis and his staff received them warmly. "If I added up all the dumb things I did in my twenties, it would fill a roll of microfilm," he told them. Though they had been invited to attend a formal briefing with intelligence officers and analysts, Bob took the opportunity to brief them, holding forth on what he had learned about the war. At one point he asked if anyone in the room could explain the difference between the Pilgrims and the Puritans. Silence greeted him.

"If you don't know the history of your own country, how do you expect to figure out the theological complexity in Afghanistan?"

Before and after his lectures, however, Bob was affable and disarming with the military, and to the men and women devoted to their son's recovery, effusive with gratitude. It wasn't the individuals whom Bob had a problem with, but the institutions where they worked.

Shortly after their CENTCOM visit, Bob sent his first message to Zabihullah Mujahid, the alias used by official Taliban spokesmen. He had found the obvious email address—zabihullahmujahid@gmail.com—right on the Taliban homepage. Days later in Idaho, he and Jani were visited by two young men from the U.S. government wearing civilian clothes and carrying computers of the same make and model as Bob's. They wouldn't say what agency they worked for, but explained that the family's emails and online activity would now be monitored as part of the government effort to find their son.

On December 7, 2011, the basic facts of Sergeant Bergdahl's week-long escape and recapture broke as a global news story, and Grossman prepared to make the case on Capitol Hill for bringing him home. With Ruggiero and Hayes by his side, Grossman led a classified briefing with a bipartisan group of senators from the defense and intelligence committees in a secure Capitol Building conference room.

"They just blew a gasket," Hayes recalled about the moment the senators heard about the proposed prisoner exchange. Across the room and the political spectrum nearly every senator was skeptical. Congress had passed the NDAA amendment to rein in Obama's desires to close Guantanamo, and they didn't intend to relinquish that power now. One Republican staffer sent Grossman packing with a blunt warning: If Obama went through with the trade, Republicans would frame it as his "Willie Horton moment" in the war on terror.

Grossman continued shuttling between Kabul, Doha, and Washington, D.C., to close the deal. But when he made the abrupt decision to bring Karzai's demands to the negotiating table, he lost Agha and the Taliban as well. With a theatrical public statement blaming their decision on the Americans' "ever-changing position," the Taliban officially withdrew from the peace talks in mid-March 2012.

Days later, Bob and Jani Bergdahl were at the State Department listening to Grossman explain why the process had come to a standstill. To their ears, the senators' rejections were a betrayal. From Foggy Bottom, they took a taxi to Capitol Hill for a meeting with John Kerry, one of the only senators supporting the deal. Kerry ended their thirty-minute conversation with a vague promise: "Leave this to me."

Bob appreciated the sentiment, but as he and Jani walked the marble floors to yet another meeting, this time with Idaho congressman Raul Labrador, he was losing patience with Washington. Labrador was candid about what he perceived as his own powerlessness. "I don't know how I can help you," he said. Bob was wearing a combat service uniform shirt bearing his son's nameplate and hadn't shaved in nearly two years.

"You're a fiscally conservative libertarian. You sit on the House

Appropriations Committee. You hold the purse strings," Bob reminded him. "There is no military solution in Afghanistan! *Defund the war.*"

They returned home despondent, thinking back to the advice from Sawyer, Coffee, and Phil Butler, another former Vietnam POW who had encouraged them to go public. They were coming to see that the controversy and rumors surrounding Bowe's disappearance were impeding his recovery.

Marsano urged Bob to remain patient, resolute, and most important, quiet. But silence wasn't bringing their son home, and he and Jani decided to go their own way. They sat down with Michael Hastings, the *Rolling Stone* writer whose work had brought down McChrystal two years earlier. Beyond Bob and Jani, Hastings found that Blackfoot Company veterans, intelligence officials, and White House staffers all had a story to tell: about the lowered standards for Army recruits that allowed Bowe to enlist in the first place, the NDAs they had been forced to sign in Afghanistan, and Bowe's newfound role as a bargaining chip in a global game. Hastings's feature, "America's Last Prisoner of War," would mark the unofficial end of the Pentagon's three-year cover-up.

After breaking their silence, Bob and Jani cranked the volume with interviews for several print outlets. They were prepared to break Pentagon protocol and sacrifice their privacy to save their son. But Bob still worried. "How deep is the water we are jumping into?" he wrote in an email that spring. "How hungry are the sharks?"

THE BERGDAHLS FLEW EAST again for Memorial Day in Washington. Bob had been invited to deliver the keynote address at the 25th annual Rolling Thunder rally, where hundreds of thousands of bikers were expected to descend on the National Mall in a show of unity and support for the POW-MIA movement. The day before the rally, they were clad in black leather as they were escorted to the White House in a phalanx of Harley-Davidsons for a meeting they anticipated as little more than a photo op. When they arrived, Secret Service whisked them away from the bikers and into a small West Wing conference room where they were greeted by John Brennan and Denis McDonough.

Bob told them he knew that the CIA had assets on the ground in the FATA targeting locations for the drone program. "We need those assets looking for Bowe," he said, heedlessly charging into top secret territory. Brennan, a career CIA analyst with thirty years' experience, including as Riyadh station chief in the mid-1990s, sat stone-faced in response. They couldn't talk about Bob's idea even if they wanted to. Instead, McDonough pledged the White House's faithful support (a promise on which he would make good with years of handwritten updates) and assured them that their son's case was a priority at the administration's highest levels. Before leaving, the Bergdahls gave each man a yellow "Bring Bowe Back" wristband, which Brennan wore on national television at his confirmation hearings to become CIA director later that year.

Bob had made the depth of his knowledge clear at the White House. What he hadn't told them was that he needed better intelligence to inform his own nascent plans to retrieve Bowe himself. The meetings two months earlier with Grossman, Kerry, and Labrador had marked a turning point, the moment when he and Jani realized with sudden clarity that they could not count on the government to save their son. They looked at the calendar. June 30, 2012, would mark Bowe's third year in captivity, and Bob's twenty-eighth year with UPS and the date on which he could retire with a full pension and benefits to sustain them while he committed to the new plan: flying to Pakistan on a one-way ticket and offering himself to Siraj Haqqani in exchange for his son. If anyone had a better idea, Bob hadn't heard it.

Jani knew there was no stopping him and supported the mission, "because it's your child, and you'll do anything," she said. But as they left the White House on May 25, they had not shared the plan with anyone. Nor did they think it was so foolproof that they could suspend their efforts at home. Rolling Thunder was not only the largest POW-MIA event in the country; it had grown into one of the largest motorcycle rallies in the world. In 1988, the first Rolling Thunder drew about two thousand bikers to Washington to protest what organizers believed was ongoing government deception about American POWs still living in the jungles of Southeast Asia. The rally's name was its own subtle protest, a double entendre tribute to the bikers' rumble and a historic U.S. military failure. Between March 1965 and November 1968, Operation Rolling Thunder dropped more than 864,000 tons of explosives and napalm on North Vietnam, killing about ninety thousand people, including some seventy-two thousand civilians, and did nothing to change the war's outcome.

In 2012, the crowd gathered in front of the rally stage at the southeast corner of the Mall, flanked on the east by the Korean War Memorial. The memorial is a cluster of statues, nineteen ghost-faced infantrymen wearing ponchos and marching in patrol formation. They stand beside a highly polished granite wall, their reflections creating an optical illusion that there are actually thirty-eight statues, a reference to the 38th Parallel that separates North and South Korea and the thirty-eight months of the Forgotten War. As the biker hordes circled the Mall, the sky filled with a roar that stretched over the Potomac, a cover band warmed up the crowd with their take on Robert Palmer's "Bad Case of Loving You," and a double amputee in his early twenties walked out of a portable toilet on twin spring prosthetics. Nearby, a single amputee in a wheelchair struggled to roll across the grass until a Rolling Thunder volunteer in a black leather vest helped push him to the sidewalk.

The Rolling Thunder speeches began with the symbolic POW cage presentation: Gerald McCullar, an emaciated, white-bearded, shirtless, and very tan actor wearing a khaki camouflage bandana on his head sat in a bamboo tiger cage roughly the dimensions of a refrigerator box. The cage was carried to its perch in front of the speaker's podium by four Rolling Thunder bikers in their version of full dress: white polo shirts, black pants, black vests bedazzled with pins and patches, wraparound sunglasses, black berets, and white gloves. A color guard advanced to plant flags, the national anthem played, and the men saluted.

The Bergdahls' day had begun at 6:00 a.m. in the Pentagon parking lot, the rally staging ground that by midmorning had become a shimmering plain of chrome and glass baking in the Virginia sun. They had hailed a cab from Washington before sunrise, and when Bob recognized the driver as a Pashtun, he asked him, in Pashto, "Do you understand Pashto?" The driver's head swiveled to the backseat, wide-eyed. "Did you just speak Pashto to me?!" he asked in English. The cabbie told them that he had left Afghanistan years earlier, but his family all remained. "Why does America hate my country?" he asked them, tears welling in his eyes and eliciting more from Bob and Jani as they explained who they were and what they were doing in Washington. At the end of the ride, he refused to take their money.

Thousands of bikers treated the Bergdahls as royalty that day. Rally organizers paid for their airfare and hotel. A North Carolina Rolling Thunder chapter escorted them from the Pentagon to the Mall, where they parked at the Washington Monument and walked the length of the Reflecting Pool toward the Lincoln Memorial and the rally stage. Bob and Jani listened as Rolling Thunder executive director, former Army sergeant Artie Muller, gave his introductory remarks. Muller wasn't happy with the progress of the long wars, noting that America was supposed to be "kicking butt, killing the enemy, and coming home" to live in harmony. "Whites, blacks, reds, and Orientals being together is what America is all about."

The crowd had thinned by the time Bob took the stage. "My son is not in a cage, but he is in chains," he said, unaware that Bowe had by that time been living in a cage for nearly a year. He thanked the organizers, and then he spoke to his son: "Bowe, if you can hear me, you are not forgotten and—so help me God—we will bring you home. Your family has not forgotten you, your hometown has not forgotten you, Idaho has not forgotten you, and thanks to all the people here, Washington, D.C., will not forget you."

Bob knew the value of brevity; his speech clocked in at just under five minutes, most of it directed at his son. "We love you, we are proud of you. Stay strong, never give up. We pray for the day that we welcome you home," he said.

During the opening speeches, Bob had been watching the man in the tiger cage. He knew that McCullar was a paid actor who had done the bit for years, but he was moved by him. He also noted that the other speakers had only addressed McCullar indirectly, as if he weren't there or weren't real. As Bob stepped down from the podium he reached through the bamboo slats, closed his eyes, and held McCullar's hand in solidarity. Years later, he remembered what went through his mind:

"I wanted to start tearing the cage apart with my hands and get him out."

SEVENTEEN
THE FIVE-SIDED WIND TUNNEL

Army leadership at the Pentagon was divided on Sergeant Bergdahl. In casual off-the-record chats with the press, multiple general officers openly referred to him as a traitor. But Lieutenant General John Campbell was not one of them. As the Army deputy chief of staff for Operations, Planning and Training (known as the Army G-3), Campbell had immense global resources at his command. He saw Bergdahl as a Pentagon problem, and in late 2012, he turned to Lieutenant Colonel Jason Amerine to find a new, nonviolent Pentagon solution.

A military rescue raid had been on the table since the DUSTWUN, and after bin Laden's death, a handful of Pentagon officials believed a similar mission could work for Bergdahl. But at the White House, there was scant support for another, bloodier incursion into Pakistan. There was also a significant risk that Bergdahl or members of the raiding party would die in the process. Linda Norgrove, a thirty-six-year-old British aid worker who'd been kidnapped in Kunar in September 2010, was accidentally killed when a Navy SEAL threw an errant grenade during the raid to free her. Bergdahl's parents had opposed such a mission from the start. They preferred to wait for a living son rather than rush the return of a dead one, and they told their military handlers and senior officials as much.

Amerine had spent his career in Army Special Forces and knew what it meant to bring soldiers back from Afghanistan in body bags: He'd been among the first Americans into Afghanistan in 2001, leading the Special Forces team (ODA-594) that infiltrated Hamid Karzai into the south to foment an insurrection against the Taliban in their heartland. He'd lost three of his Green Berets and more than twenty of their Afghan allies when an American B-52 dropped a two-thousand-pound bomb on a suspected militant hideout nearby. Amerine had objected to the bomb in the first place but was overruled by his newly arrived superiors.

In his twenty-five years in uniform, Amerine had served in the infantry, majored in Arabic at West Point, and helped topple the Taliban after 9/11. He had earned a reputation as a reliable troubleshooter, and by 2012, he was also the closest thing to a living GI Joe hero in the Army's ranks; the Army had even modeled an action figure and video game character on him for a recruiting campaign. Eleven years after he was sent home from Afghanistan, the senseless loss of the 2001 bombing and the men and their families who had been failed by their own leaders weighed on him heavily. Bringing Bergdahl home alive was a shot at redemption.

Amerine carefully maintains that when Campbell tasked him to investigate ways to get Bergdahl home, he was merely a strategist on the Army staff. In fact, that dull-sounding job was a cover for the organization Amerine led, a military intelligence office buried within the Army Operations staff whose very existence was unknown to almost all within the building. When President Truman abolished the Office of Strategic Services in 1945 with Executive Order 9621, the Army, Navy, and State Department absorbed the intelligence functions that the CIA would eventually take on when it was created in 1947. What the Army didn't advertise was that it had quietly kept its own unacknowledged spy service in action. Identifying itself by the number on the door on their Pentagon vault, the organization was unusual not because it was so secret—there are many secret organizations buried in the Pentagon—but because it could be tasked to conduct missions that were normally the domain of the CIA.

Amerine and his team began with a full audit of Bergdahl's case: what happened, who was holding him, what options were available to free him. He started with the Defense Department—the Joint Staff, Central Command, Special Operations Command, the Defense Intelligence Agency, the National Security Agency—and then widened his scope to executive branch agencies that had touched the case, including the State Department, CIA, Department of Justice, and Drug Enforcement Administration. The answers disturbed him. Since Grossman's negotiations had stalled, there was no alternative recovery plan in the works. Worse, Bergdahl was not the only Western hostage in the FATA: There were also six civilians, including an infant born in captivity to Caitlan Coleman and Joshua Boyle, a captive American-Canadian couple. Most troubling, there was no single official in charge and no coordinated effort to bring them all home.

Discretion and diplomacy would be essential. "None of this was kicking in doors and saying, 'You're fucked up,'" Amerine said. "Everything we did was with a light touch." Amerine sent one of his deputies to meet with Mattis's staff in Tampa, where he was presented with detailed plans for Bergdahl's reintegration once he was home. Dozens of government personnel from bases across the country had been put on the case and were meeting twice a year to refine and rehearse the script, a procedure that Amerine found as impressive as it was baffling. With such meticulous plans for Bergdahl's care upon his return, he wondered, "How can nobody know that there is no plan to actually get him here?"

Amerine didn't buy the rumors that swirled after Bergdahl's capture. The intelligence reports—most of them filled with unverified tales bought from Afghan story shoppers—were no better. If he had actually joined the Taliban, his captors wouldn't have missed the propaganda opportunity; they would have paraded Bergdahl's alleged conversion publicly, just as the mujahideen had done with Soviet defectors. Amerine didn't care why Bergdahl had left; his job was to bring him home. Still, he understood the skepticism he encountered in the military. One general officer refused to talk about it and told Amerine to leave his office. Traitor or not, Amerine said, "Bergdahl walked off base, and a lot of people went through a lot of hell for a long time."

With each government door he opened, Amerine saw another view of the jurisdictional crack into which Bergdahl had fallen. As a soldier, he belonged to the Army, but the Army had no legal authority east of the Durand Line. Held in the FATA, he fell under the CIA's domain, but he was not a CIA priority. The FBI claimed that since Bergdahl was a U.S. citizen beyond the war's legal borders, he was an FBI concern, which they refused to discuss. The State Department was committed to its negotiations—and had no known contingencies should they fail.

Nearly every person Amerine spoke with assured him that someone else was handling it. He had a surreal conversation with W. Montague Winfield, a retired general serving as deputy assistant secretary of defense for the POW/MIA Accounting Agency. Winfield told him that CIA had Bergdahl covered. "That's not the CIA's job. They're not working on this," Amerine said; he had already talked to agency personnel about it. He and Winfield had a polite argument as Amerine explained that the Taliban and Haqqanis wouldn't let their hostages go for nothing.

The civilian cases shocked Amerine the most. They ranged in age from the captive infant to the septuagenarian Warren Weinstein, a USAID contractor who was working in Lahore mentoring farmers and craftsmen when he was kidnapped by an al-Qaeda affiliate. Colin Rutherford and an unnamed American were also languishing. The FBI had jurisdiction, but as Amerine probed, it became clear that the Bureau was ill equipped and underresourced for the task. If the CIA struggled in the FATA, there was no reason to think that the FBI would fare better. As years passed without progress, some families had even been threatened with prosecution should they attempt to pay for their loved ones' lives. "I had no concept of how little regard we have for our own citizens until I worked my way through this," Amerine said.

When he briefed his findings to his superiors, Campbell was incredulous and told him to do whatever he needed. "I said, 'Okay, we're bringing everyone home,'" Amerine recalled.

For non-American hostages, ransoms were the most common solution. The French, Swiss, and South Korean governments didn't discuss it, but all had evidently paid cash to bring their people home. There were gray areas in U.S. law that federal agencies could have exploited to do the same. After a missionary couple had been abducted by Islamic militants in the Philippines in 2002, the Bush administration had loosened the rules on facilitating payments. But Amerine ruled out ransoms early in his process. Any cash destined for Siraj Haqqani, no matter how elaborate the delivery scheme, carried immense risk not only for Amerine, but all of his superiors.

The precedent for a national political disaster had been set by another lieutenant colonel granted top-level authorities to find innovative ways to end a protracted hostage crisis. But when Amerine studied Oliver North's case and the history of the Iran-Contra affair, he also found some helpful lessons.

"Iran-Contra was a completely out-of-the-box way to deal with a crisis," Amerine said of the secret plan to sell anti-aircraft missiles to Iran and transfer the proceeds to right-wing Nicaraguan guerillas. "Out-of-the-box is good," Amerine said. "But to fight the system you have to play by its rules." In Pakistan, he decided that the boldest move was to play it straight. He would take his plans through the appropriate channels, inform every agency, and rally support within the U.S. government. Within months, he learned that that mission would be impossible.

IN THE FALL OF 2012, General Jim Mattis had a problem, and its name was Bob Bergdahl. Mattis had learned from his staff that Bob had retired from UPS and was making plans to move to Pakistan in a wild scheme to trade himself for his son. He had been doing whatever he could to convince his son's captors that he was serious, including trying to enroll at one of the largest hard-line madrassas in northwest Pakistan, the same religious school where Jalaluddin Haqqani and Mullah Omar had studied. Mattis knew that Bob was desperate and determined, but didn't know if it was a cry for attention.

"I wasn't trying to hide anything," Bob said years later. "The primary message was, 'Look at what the father is doing. What are you doing?' The idea was to push the bureaucracy into action."

But his stated plan to move to Pakistan wasn't a mere bluff. Certain in his belief that the government would fail, Bob applied for a tourist visa at the Pakistani Embassy in Washington, D.C. He would fly to Islamabad and approach the first uniformed soldier he saw with a simple message, which he had memorized in Pashto and Urdu: "Where is the ISI office? I need to talk to somebody." He would then demand to see the chief of the Pakistani Army or the director general of the ISl. They already knew him from Mullen, who had passed along his messages, and from YouTube. He would ask for their help. "I honestly think that Kayani and Pasha would have been sympathetic," he said later. Regardless, Bob had tried for three years with his own government. It was time to seek mercy from the other side.

Just as Bowe had hinted at his plans to Sutton and Coe on FOB Sharana the night before their final rotation at OP Mest, Bob started to broadcast his ideas to his military contacts, including CENTCOM's director of intelligence, Lieutenant General Robert Ashley. On October 3, 2012, Mattis and a plainclothes bodyguard arrived in Hailey, Idaho, in a large black SUV. Mattis had by then spent several hours with the family in Tampa. Now, in their home, he told them what others already had: The Haqqanis didn't play by Bob's rules and would simply kidnap him as well. He stayed until he could see that Bob had been swayed from his plans.

Like Sybil Stockdale's ally in Naval Intelligence, the Bergdahls' active service military advisers encouraged them to take their lobbying up the civilian chain of command. For the generals and admirals at the helm of the war, it was partly an admission of their own powerlessness in Pakistan. But in late 2012—with Grossman stepping down as SRAP, the talks in Doha on indefinite hiatus, and Amerine's audit underway—it was increasingly apparent that nothing was being done to bring Bergdahl home. At CENTCOM in late 2012, General Ashley put it to Bob bluntly: "If it were my son, I'd be asking harder questions."

More than three months later and no closer to answers, Bob spoke at a National League rally on the east end of the National Mall on April 9, 2013. He and Jani were in Washington for meetings at the State Department, Capitol Hill, and the Pentagon, none of which had produced any discernible progress. As he gestured to the Capitol behind him, rage flowed from every pore as he demanded diplomacy in Afghanistan, calling it "a moral obligation placed upon the American people" after decades of Cold War meddling. In June, he and Jani prepared for the fourth Bring Bowe Home rally, the largest the town had hosted. Main Street closed for a procession of hundreds of Harleys led by police cars and Bob, riding solo in an all-black uniform of protest and mourning, complete with a POW-MIA headscarf, and John Lennon–style rose-tinted glasses above the blond beard that had taken over his face. Prior to the event, Bob had learned that a reporter from BBC Pashto Radio would be attending, news he saw as a strategic opportunity.

"Let me say something directly to the Taliban," Bob told the crowd of Pocatello bikers. He began speaking in Arabic with the *bismillah*—"In the name of God, the most gracious, the most merciful"—then spoke Pashto, quoting the Koran for about twenty seconds and translating for the crowd:

"As time goes by, as history passes, humanity is at a loss, humanity loses, lest those who believe encourage one another to do good works, encourage one another in patience, and encourage one another in truth."

Bob seemed on the verge of tears. Few in the Idaho audience knew how turbulent the days leading up to the rally had been. "U.S. to Launch Peace Talks with Taliban," *The Washington Post* had declared on Tuesday morning, June 18. But when the Taliban opened its coveted office in an ornate, high-walled compound in an upscale Doha neighborhood hours later, it broke several agreements with Karzai that Obama, Kerry, Lute, Rubin, Hayes, and the Qataris had been attending to for months. Specifically, the office flew the white flag of the Islamic Emirate of Afghanistan and had affixed a metal plaque to an exterior wall bearing the emirate's name. Karzai went apoplectic at the appearance of a legitimate Taliban Embassy, and the Americans scrambled to mollify him. Rubin, already in Doha, arrived at the compound and did not leave until the plaque had been removed. Kerry called him several times, and for two days global headlines traced the seismograph of Karzai's mood. "The flag remains," the BBC reported Thursday, "albeit on a shorter flagpole."

But it was too late. The talks were off again, and as Bob spoke Pashto in Idaho to what he hoped was a radio audience in Peshawar, his belief that the U.S. government was incapable of diplomacy was reaffirmed, as was his determination to finish the job himself. He amped up his digital activism; he had come to see Twitter as a platform equally suited for antiwar protest and rogue intelligence operations. In a few months, he amassed a following of journalists, policy analysts, diplomats, and Pakistani military officers.

"Twitter was a battlespace," Bob said. If CENTCOM could run Twitter bots to influence the War on Terror in 2012, he saw no reason why he couldn't play the game too, but as an avatar for peace. With targeted messaging and retweets, his NSA-monitored account attracted an audience of suspected militants, Pakistani military officers, and even a few accounts flying the black flag of ISIS. "Finally, a smart American," one wrote. English speakers called him out for talking to the enemy, but Bob saw every follower as a potential intelligence source, and his military handlers didn't disagree. Calling on the sympathies of his Muslim followers with quotes from the Koran, he broadcast his message of radical peace on every channel, including in handwritten letters that he and Bowe began exchanging through the International Committee of the Red Cross in 2012. Bob assumed the letters would be screened by the

ISI and the Taliban, and he reassured Bowe and any other readers that Washington was closing in on the prisoner exchange deal.

Uncertain of that claim himself, he continued to pursue his own plans. In Washington, he visited the All Dulles Area Muslim Society, a thirty-year-old mosque and interfaith center in northern Virginia, and sought counsel from the imams. They taught him how they prayed, and then they prayed together. It fed Bob's mind, prepared him for his planned travels, and offered a quiet place for his fury to rest. It was also strategic: Bob reasoned that spreading the rumor that Sergeant Bergdahl's father was flirting with Islam could inspire the captors to show his son some mercy.

"Know your enemies," Jani said of Bob's transformation. "The Taliban was now a part of our family," said Bob. They knew that Pashtuns followed strict patriarchal codes. To have any credibility with the Quetta Shura, Bob needed to act like them too. "I don't want to look like some soft American man," he told Jani as his beard reached biblical lengths. In every message to Zabihullah Mujahid and his other contacts, Bob reminded them that he was the head of his own clan. "I am the father. Za abba yem. زه پلار يم." Even at church in Ketchum, when Jani would bring her Bible, Bob started wearing a kufi, a Muslim prayer cap, performing ablutions in the bathroom, and removing his shoes at the end of the pew. They didn't care what anyone thought.

In August 2013, Bob and Jani heard an unexpected knock on the door. The man introduced himself as working for OGA, or "other governmental organization," the acronym alternative for the CIA. He had recently returned from the Durand Line, he told them, and he was struck by the similar climate and terrain in Southern Idaho. For an hour, he sat with Bob's Google Maps, showing him the various ratlines one could use, were one so inclined, to infiltrate the FATA. Bob committed the routes to memory. He would go from Kabul to Khost and finally to Miran Shah. He would go slowly, spreading word of his intentions and gaining permissions for safe passage. Or he could go with a group of former Special Forces A-Team members who had served in RC East, where they had flown the POW flag on their trucks and collected their own intelligence on Bowe's location. They were angry about the way their war had been fought and had always wanted to take the fight to the safe havens. They offered to bring Bob to the region while they activated their own off-the-books armed rescue in North Waziristan.

Bob thanked the veterans, but said he was after a peaceful resolution. One of Bob's journalist advisers had put him in touch with a State Department employee who had moved to Washington, D.C., after working for ISAF as a language instructor. Before that job, he had been a member of the Taliban. Bob met him for tea in Falls Church, Virginia, where the man explained the intricate feudal hierarchies that govern the border region. He wrote Bob a note of safe passage to carry with him and deliver to a Taliban commander in Logar Province, south of Kabul. That commander could get him to Khost. A Canadian journalist offered to put him up in Gardez. The plan was coming together.

"Was I gullible? Yeah. Whatever. It didn't matter," Bob said later. "I was going to die trying. I wasn't going to live the rest of my life with woulda, coulda, shoulda. How do you live that way?"

AT THE PENTAGON, Lieutenant Colonel Amerine's plan was also moving forward. Through civilian intermediaries and at least one ISI contact, he opened what appeared to be a new diplomatic channel to the Quetta Shura. The message from the other side was unchanged from what the State Department had been told all along: The Taliban wanted to make a deal, and it was American disorganization that was delaying the process.

A serious trade proposal emerged from the Taliban's wish list. It would have freed all seven U.S. and Canadian hostages—Bergdahl, Weinstein, Rutherford, Coleman, Boyle, their child, and another unnamed American—in exchange for one prisoner in U.S. custody.

In Helmand after 9/11, Haji Bashar Noorzai had been one of the first and most powerful tribal leaders to defect from the Taliban. He was one of the wealthiest men in the country, a successful opium trader like his father and grandfather before him, and in the late 1990s had been one of Mullah Omar's earliest financiers—"the Sheldon Adelson of the Taliban," Rubin called him. In late 2001, Noorzai rekindled his relationship with the CIA, began reporting on Taliban operations, and ultimately delivered more than a dozen truckloads of regime weapons to U.S. forces.

By May 2002, however, the veil had fallen from Karzai's promises of Pashtun unity. Rather than bringing the south together as Washington had expected, Karzai and his allies were using the American military to eliminate their rivals. When a U.S. raid killed one of Noorzai's closest mentors, an elder who had also pledged his support to the Americans, Noorzai feared he was next and fled with his family to Pakistan. Two years later, he was once again talking to U.S. elements and offering his help on diplomacy. He was an optimist, and if Afghanistan had a chance of a better future, he wanted to be a part of it. In April 2005, Noorzai flew to New York with guarantees of safe passage from his American handlers and the understanding that he was being groomed as a Taliban informant. No one told him about the sealed drug trafficking indictment waiting for him in federal court.

The U.S. government was as divided on Noorzai as it was on the rest of the war. The CIA and Pentagon wanted him cultivated as an asset, while the DEA agents who picked him up at JFK airport saw him as a historic catch in the global heroin trade. As the agencies squabbled, for nearly two weeks the DEA put him up in a cushy hotel, encouraged him to order room service, and questioned him on Taliban activities. When they were done, they arrested him.

When his name surfaced during Amerine's negotiations, Noorzai was serving a life sentence in a California prison and reiterating his desires to work for the U.S. government as a Taliban informant, diplomatic mediator—anything to get out. To Amerine, he looked like the perfect tool of diplomacy.

"We would release a guy that never should have been in jail in the first place, who is an ally to Afghanistan, who could help bring stability to southern Afghanistan, and in return I could at the very least get Bergdahl and some or all of the other hostages," Amerine said. His sources in Afghanistan and Pakistan found widespread support among the Noorzai tribe and their Taliban contacts. Indications from the Haqqanis were that the hostages, and Bergdahl in particular, had become a burden. Even the ISI offered indirect help to close the deal.

Amerine gained quick approvals at the Pentagon from the Army staff, which led him to the Joint Staff, where he was told he needed to run it by Special Operations Command (SOCOM). "This all makes sense to me," the general at SOCOM told him, but he couldn't sign off on it unless the State Department did. At State, Amerine met with Ambassador James Dobbins, who had replaced Grossman in May 2013. The two men had a connection: When Amerine was infiltrating Karzai into Afghanistan, Dobbins was in Bonn working with the exiled Afghan leaders who would elect Karzai president. They had, in effect, fought the same war in 2001: the soldier in Afghanistan, the diplomat in Germany. Dobbins listened to the plan receptively then told him there was nothing he could do regarding Bergdahl. "I don't know why you're talking to me. This is a DoD issue," Dobbins said.

With that, Amerine had gone in a perfect bureaucratic circle. He thought of the *ouroboros,* the ancient symbol of infinity, a snake eating itself, and realized he was living it in Washington, D.C.

He pressed on by shifting focus to the civilian cases. He knew the FBI was fiercely territorial over its authorities and budgets and though he still believed that he and the Pentagon had greater resources for the task, he made his case for cooperation. He and the FBI shared the same goal and ultimately played for the same team, he told them. But if his sources and the FBI's sources were unwittingly negotiating with the same Taliban, he needed to know before the crossed wires blew it up on both of them. No, the FBI agents replied, he did not.

"I knew that things were bad, I just didn't know how bad," Amerine said later.

Trapped in his bureaucratic stovepipe, there was a lot that Amerine didn't know. After a series of leaks to the press that had hobbled the talks early in 2013, the State Department and White House shared their progress with fewer and fewer people within the government. Amerine had no way of knowing that when Obama traveled to Kabul earlier that year, he had privately told Karzai that the United States was committed to negotiating through Agha and did not want to introduce any new mediators. But in the months that followed, with almost zero coordination among them, Amerine's office, Special Operations Command, and the FBI would all do just that.

In January 2014, a new proof-of-life video of Bergdahl arrived in Washington, and it was nothing like those preceding it. He looked ghastly: emaciated, shaking, barely able to speak.

"It looked like he was dying," his parents recalled. "Like terminal cancer," Bob said. The tape shattered their concepts of his living conditions. "We were under the delusion that they were taking good care of him," Jani said. In Bob's messages with the Taliban spokesman, he had always quoted the Koran's teachings on mercy and vowed that if the captors lived up to their scripture, he would see to it that his government lived up to its own professed ethics. Across the federal government, the video was read as a clear signal that the Haqqanis were going to close the deal by whatever means necessary, and with whoever could make it happen. It also marked the start of a race between government agencies, each intent on recovering Sergeant Bergdahl their own way.

The FBI had its reasons to keep its case file secret from Amerine. The Bureau had their own sources and methods to protect, which by that winter included Bob Bergdahl himself. After four years of enterprise, Bob's network now spanned the globe, from young Western journalists living in rented apartments in Eastern Afghanistan to former ISI officers retired in posh Washington, D.C., suburbs—and in some ways it exceeded the Bureau's. Bob had told the FBI he would do anything to speed up the process. "I said, 'put me in Kabul as the father and see who approaches me. I'll just move there. I'll move next to Mullah Zaeef's house,'" he told them.

Bob had spent years urging the government to pay a legal ransom. With Mullen's support, he had lobbied the State and Treasury Departments to use Haqqani money confiscated from foreign banks. He pushed at CENTCOM too, reminding the military that payoffs for hostages had been U.S. policy for centuries. No one seemed to have taken him seriously. But that winter, without his knowledge, an FBI team pursued one of Bob's sources on their own, deemed it legitimate, and teamed up with a SOCOM unit to plan a covert joint ransom-recovery mission. Bob was not informed and later said he would not have supported a rogue plan that could have interfered with the State Department talks.

FBI counterrorism agents, trained and geared up as soldiers, had been joining elite military units on raids in Iraq, Afghanistan, and Somalia for years. In February, Special Operations Command, of which JSOC is part, informed their Pentagon counterparts that they had found a legal method to pay for Bergdahl's release. On February 23, as the contest between the vying efforts escalated, the Taliban publicly called off another round of State Department peace talks, citing the "current complex political situation" in Afghanistan. But the same could have been said for Washington.

On February 27, the FBI-JSOC team in Kabul was so confident of its plan that it informed officers at ISAF that Bergdahl would be brought over the border within seven to ten days; JSOC officers had already drawn up a detailed exfiltration plan complete with its own code name. That week, a key meeting that Amerine's team had scheduled with a Quetta Shura representative to discuss the Noorzai trade was abruptly canceled. Days passed in anticipation, then weeks. Before long, the story had spread that yet another Taliban con artist had played the FBI and disappeared with a reported $10 million.

***THE GUARDIAN*'S SEAN SMITH** arrived in Idaho in early March. As an embed with Blackfoot Company at OP Mest in June 2009, he was the last journalist to see Bowe in person. Bob invited him to Croy Creek Canyon that winter to continue telling the story. Smith trailed him on a snowshoe hike through sagebrush and aspen groves to the winter hut that he kept in the woods as a place for his son to come home and recuperate. The five-year anniversary loomed.

"I wake up each morning and my first thought is, 'My son is still a prisoner of war in Afghanistan. And I need to do something about that,'" Bob told Smith.

On March 6, they traveled together to Dubai, where they planned to spend a couple of nights before connecting to Kabul. When Bob had first raised the idea for the trip with Smith a year earlier, he described it as a secret mission, and Smith had leveled with him: "We're not going to track down Bowe," he said. "We are not seeking out Taliban leaders." Instead, he offered himself as a guide on a short orientation trip. They agreed that their most ambitious goal would be to film Bob visiting prisoners at the U.S.-run Parwan Detention Facility at Bagram Airfield.

Bob and Jani didn't tell their military contacts that Bob had left the country, but assumed that he would be monitored. He was let go after extensive questioning by customs agents in Dubai, and Smith took him to a budget hotel in a seedy part of town. In Idaho, Jani's phone rang soon after with a call from CENTCOM.

"Jani, where's Bob?" It was Amber Dach, the lead analyst on the case and one of their most trusted handlers. "You need to tell him to come home now," Dach said. She couldn't explain why but told Jani that his timing was bad and it was vitally important that Bob turn around.

In Dubai, Bob and Sean Smith had met up with a European journalist who dropped hints that Taliban leaders were also en route to the city for a meeting related to the American talks. Bob said he wanted to be included. He was convinced that if he could just sit with them and talk man-to-man, father to father, they could all solve this thing together. But when his phone lit up with a text from Jani relaying Dach's orders, he knew he had to comply.

"I cried half the flight home," he said. "I thought I abandoned Bowe."

ACT V.

CODES OF CONDUCT

EIGHTEEN

WELCOME HOME

With about an hour's notice, the Taliban told the Americans to meet at 4:00 p.m. local time near Batai Pass, a remote border crossing in the mountains above Khost City, about sixty miles northeast of OP Mest and not far from Camp Chapman. The location was accessible by helicopter, but isolated enough for a clandestine operation. The Americans agreed, and a regional, one-day cease-fire was arranged.

Bergdahl's guards shaved his head and gave him a fresh change of clothes, some stale bread, and an orange soda. They blindfolded him with a scarf, pulled a woman's burka over him, put him in a car, and began driving toward the border. In the days leading up to the rendezvous, the Taliban media affairs team prepared for one of its biggest propaganda opportunities of the war: the handover of the American prisoner by a well-armed Taliban security force in Taliban-held territory.

The film opens with several gunmen standing around a beat-up silver Toyota Hilux, the near-indestructible Japanese pickup favored by generations of mujahideen. The red scrawl of a faux-spray-paint decal runs the length of the side panels, and the hood is propped open, as is the hood of an old white Corolla parked nearby—proof the vehicles weren't rigged with explosives.

The gunmen are in high spirits. They pass a white truce flag between them. Three fighters dressed in three different color shalwars pose, wave, and cheer for the camera. Bergdahl sits in the backseat, blinking, dressed head to foot in a white shalwar, his skin pale, his head shaved bald like a pawn's. The camera pans to an American surveillance plane flying overhead. On the ground there are Taliban soldiers in every direction. Sentries armed with sniper rifles and a rocket-propelled grenade (RPG) stand high on a steep hill above the truck. A narrator explains in Pashto: "We told them there are eighteen armed fighters, and the Americans said, 'That's all right.'"

The tallest masked Taliban soldier approaches Bergdahl, who is still blinking, a reaction to the sunlight after hours in a blindfold. By the time he returned to the U.S., rumors had already spread on social media claiming the blinks were coded transmissions to his terrorist brethren. As the tall Taliban soldier points a finger and then pats Bergdahl on the shoulder, his voice can be heard on the video telling him in Pashto: "Don't come back to Afghanistan. If I catch you again myself, you will not get away again. I won't let that happen, even if I get killed."

An English message in black cartoon letters flashes on the screen:

Don'come back
to
Afghanistan

Then they appear: two UH-60 Black Hawk helicopters flying a high lazy circle above them. The sentry on the hill has his RPG shouldered. Bergdahl stands dazed, now wearing a checkered shawl draped over his shoulders, and flanked by guards whom he had never seen or met before that day, all of them watching as one Black Hawk crests the sentry's hill and descends in a cloud of swirling dust.

The Taliban hold the white flag high, and as the chopper touches down they march Bergdahl toward three fast-approaching commandos in civilian clothes and sunglasses. The two teams exchange quick greetings and handshakes. The Americans pat Bergdahl down for explosives, pivot, and take him by the arm toward the helicopter. He is unsteady and loses his balance several times in the thirty paces to the helicopter door, where they frisk him again.

The handoff has the Americans on the ground for less than a minute. As the Black Hawk flies a low pattern out of the valley and recedes into the distance, the cartoon message flashes again:

Don'come back
to
Afghanistan

In the air, Bergdahl was surrounded by the kind of special operators he once believed he was destined to become, in a Black Hawk flown by one of the Army's elite aviation units, returning to base after a highly classified mission. It was a perverse and cruel way to live out his once closely held dream. To help Bowe communicate above the roar of the rotors, the commandos gave him a paper plate and a marker.

"SF?" Bergdahl wrote.

They nodded. "Yes," one soldier shouted, "we've been looking for you for a long time."

Bergdahl broke down in tears, grabbed the man's hand, and for the remainder of the flight to the American base, didn't let it go.

ABOUT NINETY MINUTES after the handoff and more than eight thousand miles to the west, a U.S. security detail escorted five Qatari officials and the five Taliban detainees to one of two C-17 Globemaster cargo planes that had been inexplicably parked at the Guantanamo airfield for the prior four days. The planes had been one of the only visible examples of the secrets the administration had withheld from Congress over the preceding months.

Following the alarming January proof-of-life video, the White

House concluded that it was not going to achieve the reconciliation terms it had sought through the talks with Tayeb Agha. Officials at the National Security Council decided it was time to salvage the only part of the negotiation they could and bring Bergdahl home through the prisoner swap Agha had demanded all along. As the Taliban sensed their advantage, they pressed for more, at one point demanding that Bergdahl would not be released until every Taliban detainee in Cuba was freed. Even after the White House had made its decision, reaching a final agreement took months.

The tortured arbitration was managed by a small cadre of senior officials at the State Department, National Security Council, on Defense Secretary Chuck Hagel's staff at the Pentagon, and in the Qatari government. In Washington, Hagel received direct written approval to execute the trade from Secretary of State Kerry, Chairman of the Joint Chiefs of Staff General Martin Dempsey, Attorney General Eric Holder, Secretary of Homeland Security Jeh Johnson, and Director of National Intelligence James Clapper. (As the former Pentagon lead counsel, Johnson had been traveling to Doha to negotiate the same trade since September 2011.) Hagel would testify before Congress that, even in the final days, it was a touch-and-go operation to the final hours.

On the morning of May 27, 2014, the final stage of the process was set in motion with a series of phone calls that began when President Obama received the personal pledge from Qatari Emir Tamim bin Hamad al-Thani to uphold his end of the deal enforcing security on the five former Taliban leaders. Hours later, Michael Lumpkin, whom Hagel had appointed to oversee the operation at the Pentagon, called John F. Kelly, the Marine general (and future White House chief of staff) in charge at Southern Command (SOUTHCOM), in Doral, Florida. Guantanamo fell under SOUTHCOM's jurisdiction, and Kelly relayed the orders to Michael Butler, a former Top Gun flight instructor and the two-star Navy admiral in command at the detention camp. In the eighteen months since Kelly had arrived at SOUTHCOM, twelve detainees had been transferred out, and the two men had grown familiar with the process, an orderly series of legal, administrative, and medical screenings that in most cases lasted a month or longer. Kelly told Butler to have the Guantanamo Five ready to go in two days.

There would be no time for exit interviews with the FBI or the International Committee of the Red Cross. By the time a Red Cross executive responded to Pentagon emails on the topic, the prisoners were already gone. Butler, who in 2005 had served as a flight operations director at the Al Udeid Air Base in Qatar, also learned that he would be hosting the Qatari delegation that would be escorting the detainees to their new home. Above all, Kelly told him, the entire operation needed to be kept out of public view, a particular challenge given the gaggle of civilian and military attorneys, paralegals, reporters, and Indiana University law school students scheduled to attend legal hearings on the same days the Taliban would be smuggled out.

Butler drew up a compressed schedule. The Qataris arrived on the afternoon of May 29, finishing the last leg of their journey on a short flight from Tampa aboard Kelly's official plane. At the Guantanamo airfield, U.S. personnel stood guard as the Qataris met the five men and presented each with statements written in Pashto explaining the conditions of their imminent release: They would not engage in militant fundraising, recruiting, or incitement, and for at least one year, would not leave Qatar for any reason, including the Hajj. There were no objections. U.S. military personnel would join them on the flight to Doha, a specific security request from the Pentagon.

Together with their Qatari and American handlers, the prisoners waited eight hours at the Guantanamo airfield for news from Khost. When it didn't come, Butler's team improvised: The Qataris were whisked to a nearby military hotel, and the five spent their last nights in U.S. custody in a Department of Homeland Security immigration detention center. Every hour that passed with no word about Bergdahl's location threatened operational security. *The Miami Herald*'s Carol Rosenberg, who was in the press pool for the military commission hearings at Guantanamo that day, saw the C-17s and knew there was only one transfer that could require such large planes. But as she pieced the story together and started asking questions, she received no answers. A leak at this late hour would not only jeopardize the entire deal, but with the special mission unit waiting for orders to fly into the isolated hand-over spot in Khost, it could endanger American lives.

On the morning of May 31 around 10:30 a.m., Lumpkin called the National Military Command Center—the central node of the Pentagon matrix—with orders for the Defense Department to release the five prisoners into Qatari custody. Forty-five minutes later, with the planes still on the runway, President Obama called the Republican chairman of the House Armed Services Committee, Congressman Howard "Buck" McKeon, with the news. McKeon was stunned. His committee had been wrangling with the White House over Guantanamo transfers since Obama's first days in office and had amended the 2011 NDAA with this exact scenario in mind. Yet here was the president informing him that the Taliban Five, as McKeon's committee called them, had already left the prison and within minutes would be gone. The Taliban prisoners, McKeon realized, knew about their release before any member of Congress did. In the weeks and months that followed, McKeon learned that not only had the White House conspired to hide the decision, but to his greater shock, so had officials at the Pentagon. In short, they had likely broken the law, and they had done so knowingly. It was Iran-Contra logic at work in the Obama administration: Yes, we did it, and it worked. So what?

BOB AND JANI BERGDAHL were in Washington, D.C., where they had stayed for a few days following the annual Rolling Thunder rally, when their phone rang with a call from SOCOM in Tampa. It was the kind of phone call that in 2009 would have been a big deal. By the spring of 2014—when, despite the best efforts of Norwegian, German, Saudi, and Qatari mediators, diplomatic failures had become routine—the Bergdahls had reasons to be skeptical.

The SOCOM operator told Jani to hold while the call was patched through to the president. "We got him," Obama said.

By noon, as Bowe heard English spoken by Americans for the first time in five years and the Guantanamo Five tasted freedom for the first time in twelve, the White House made its first attempts to turn the event into a good news story. The press office held a preliminary call with select reporters and producers who agreed not to publish or broadcast the news for thirty minutes—just enough time for the West Wing to rush out a three-paragraph statement from the president.

"Today the American people are pleased," it began. Obama lauded the Bergdahls' courage and sacrifice and offered somber remembrances for the missing and captured soldiers who never made it home from their wars. Bergdahl's homecoming, the White House said, "is a reminder of America's unwavering commitment to leave no man or woman in uniform behind on the battlefield."

Obama singled out the emir of Qatar for "his personal commitment to this effort," calling it a testament to "the partnership between our two countries." Without naming the Weinstein, Rutherford, Coleman, Foley, Tice, Mueller, Kassig, or Sotloff families, Obama reassured them that his thoughts and prayers were "with those other Americans whose release we continue to pursue."

In closing, the White House reiterated the same message from Obama's speeches earlier that week at Bagram and West Point: that even as the United States prepared to leave Afghanistan, it simultaneously "renewed its commitment to the Afghan people." It was a paradox, but in the hue and uplift of Obama's words, anything seemed possible, including "a stable, secure, sovereign, and unified Afghanistan." Bergdahl's recovery was presented as proof that diplomacy works and is the keystone to Afghan reconciliation. Yet nowhere in the statement did the White House mention the deal that had actually freed Bergdahl, or the five men strapped into a C-17 jetting over the Atlantic that day to start new lives in Qatar.

Given that the news was no longer containable, it was an inexplicable omission. Seven minutes before the White House released its statement, a *Washington Post* reporter, tipped off by an anonymous source, posted details of the swap on Twitter. It fell to the Pentagon and Hagel to fill in the gaps.

"Of course I knew there would be a backlash," Hagel said. "And of course I knew it would come from the Republicans, but you do the right thing. And this was the right thing."

Hagel was in Singapore, speaking at the annual Asia Security Summit, when the news broke. His staff stepped in with a short statement that explained the basics and took Pentagon ownership. Hagel vowed that Qatar would live up to its promises and keep the Taliban under close watch: "The national security of the United States will not be compromised." Minutes after his statement went public, General Dempsey posted on Twitter: "It is our ethos that we never leave a fallen comrade. Welcome home SGT Bowe Bergdahl." Kerry followed with a three-paragraph message written in perfect synchronicity with the White House and Pentagon talking points: the government's "sober and solemn duty" to bring every man home, his own "personal gratitude to the Government of Qatar," and the Afghan people's hopeful future "as they build a secure, stable, sovereign, and unified country."

In the media, the Pentagon began telling a story of accomplishment. On CNN, Pentagon correspondent Barbara Starr conveyed the "exquisite security details" and extensive surveillance required to pull off the historic battlefield rendezvous. Hagel said the teams involved that day had done "a masterful job."

By any measure of American politics, the prisoner exchange was not a victory, and the story of the operational success was quickly subsumed. In the two and half years since it had first been floated by the State Department and summarily shot down by Congress, the deal hadn't become any more popular. The White House's inability to reveal the details of the trade in its initial press statement wasn't just clumsiness; it was the visible symptom of deeper dysfunction. For five years, the administration had struggled to organize and maintain a unified war policy. For the families of Americans held captive in multiple countries, the lack of a functional hostage policy had become equally plain. On Capitol Hill, the same congressmen who had spent years demanding that the president bring Bowe home were then the first to reject the only viable option they had been presented to do so. In May, Republican senator Kelly Ayotte had called on the Pentagon to "do all it can" to find him and bring him home. Weeks later, she slammed the deal on grounds that it incentivized future kidnappings. Congressman Richard Nugent had introduced two bills on the House floor specifically demanding his recovery. The government must "do everything possible not to leave any members of the armed forces behind," he had said. But after the swap, he parsed the definition of his earlier words: "Doing 'everything possible' in my mind does not include breaking the law and jeopardizing national security."

When the decision was finally made in the Conflict Resolution Cell at the White House, there was good reason not to alert Congress; every prior time it had, the plans had been leaked to the press. To get anything accomplished amid such division and disunity, the administration, and the NSC in particular, had to hold its information close and commit itself to a precision operation. At the White House, Jeff Eggers, who had been working under Doug Lute as the NSC's senior director for Afghanistan and Pakistan, had taken over Lute's position in 2013. Eggers was also a former Navy SEAL with multiple combat deployments, and as the final tense days unfolded, he spent several nights sleeping on the floor of his White House office.

The Bergdahls had arrived in Washington, D.C., a week earlier, ahead of the Rolling Thunder rally. As they had in the prior two years, they were invited to a West Wing meeting, this time with NSC staffers, including Navy Captain Alexander Krongard, Homeland Security and Counterterrorism adviser Lisa Monaco, and Deputy National Security Adviser Tony Blinken. The officials knew that the gears of the swap were already in motion, but when they updated Bob and Jani on Friday May 30, they couldn't say a word. The next morning, when Sergeant Bergdahl was confirmed safe, Eggers went home to rest for the first time in days.

White House staffers had gone into work that day in jeans and sandals with a plan for a brief, clean statement that would pass the baton to Hagel and the Pentagon. In their heady buzz over the day's events—a disaster averted, a soldier saved, and a family united—the plan began to change, and a faulty assumption began circulating, that the relief and happiness that they felt in the White House would be shared by all Americans. The president told his aides that political fallout was inevitable, so he didn't want to shy away from it; he wanted to own it. When his aides then told him that the Bergdahls were coincidentally already in Washington, it seemed like serendipity. Someone blurted out: "Let's do something in the Rose Garden." Obama liked the idea.

IT WASN'T AS THOUGH Bob Bergdahl had been keeping his opinions to himself. In public appearances, he had openly appealed to the mercy of his son's captors based on his understanding of them as men of faith. His entrepreneurial efforts, including the March flight to Dubai, were known to Mullen, Mattis, and officials at several agencies. A week earlier on Twitter, before he knew that the deal had been made, he had reminded the Taliban, "I am still working to free captives on all sides of this conflict." Earlier in May, he had posted Arabic calligraphy (صبر : "patience") and quoted Supreme Court Justice Robert Jackson: "It is the function of the citizen to keep the government from falling into error." And yet no one at the White House suggested keeping Bob away from the cameras that day.

Inside the Oval Office, he and Jani were ecstatic. Obama apologized for months of chronic leaks, but kept the mood light, chatting with Bob about the Dairy Queen and basketball courts where they had both hung out as kids in Honolulu. Suddenly, aides ushered them into the Rose Garden, where the press was waiting.

"We were just supposed to stand there," Jani recalled. "We weren't supposed to say anything." The president wore a blue shirt and blazer, no tie. Flanking him, Jani wore a sleeveless beige Sunday dress, heels, and a smile. Bob wore a white shirt, blue tie, ponytail, and beard. Things had moved so fast, he hadn't had time to find a jacket. Before the president said a word, it already looked improvised.

"Good afternoon, everybody. This morning, I called Bob and Jani Bergdahl and told them that after nearly five years in captivity, their son, Bowe, is coming home."

Jani looked at the president, then her husband, and bit her lip to fight back tears. Obama reminded the country that while in captivity, Sergeant Bergdahl had missed birthdays, holidays, "and the simple moments with family and friends, which all of us take for granted." Jani closed her eyes and nodded along to Obama's cadence.

In its three-and-a-half-minute entirety, the president's address added no new information to what had already been reported and repeated by Hagel, Kerry, Dempsey, and others. But Obama had wanted to own the story, to spread good news, and without a word of warning, he invited Bob and Jani to address the nation.

After Jani said a brief word of thanks, Bob stepped behind the presidential podium, where he did not appear uncomfortable or unprepared.

"I'd like to say to Bowe right now, who is having trouble speaking English, *bismillah il rahman il rahim, ze aba yem*. I'm your father, Bowe."

President Obama pursed his lips into a tight smile as Bob spoke the Islamic peace blessing, thanked Khalifa al-Thani, emir of Qatar, and the Americans who had saved his son's life earlier that morning.

In closing, he shared his repeated gratitude and hope that the media would respect his family's privacy in the days ahead. Obama hugged them both, kissed Jani on the cheek, and put his hands on their backs as all three walked off stage.

In the years that followed, the Bergdahls both felt that Obama's spur of the moment decision to have them speak came from a place of genuine grace and empathy. But regardless of the president's motivations, Bob had defined the moment. Anger simmered below his joy that day. Why had this gone on for five years? What about the other hostages? In his work as an asset for the FBI and JPRA, he knew the answers, and he didn't like them. Inside the White House, Obama's senior aides knew immediately that the bearded white guy speaking Pashto was going to be a problem.

Mullen was watching from home, incredulous for a different reason. Somebody in the president's inner circle had thought this was a good idea, he surmised: to use real people as stage props to make the president look good. "There was no need for that. To put a very vulnerable couple front and center. Actually, I was appalled by it," Mullen said. "It never should have happened."

NINETEEN

FOX NATION

Anna Fontaine was at home in Hailey when she saw the news. She called Jani to confirm and then rushed to the local restaurant where she and ten more of Bowe's friends popped a bottle of champagne. On the sidewalk's chalkboard sign that listed the night's specials, they wrote the news: "BOWE IS FREE!!"

Four blocks north on Main Street, Jane Drussel was busy spreading the word from her art supply store, which for five years had filled the town's yellow-ribbon needs. Drussel, who was also serving a term as the president of the Hailey Chamber of Commerce, told the young women working that morning to start making yellow posters with Bowe's smiling face and to go hang them around town. On Main Street cars started honking their horns in a spontaneous chorus of glee.

For nearly half a decade, the courteous boy who had ridden his bicycle everywhere was the town's most visible cause. Each year on Memorial Day, local Scout troops tied fresh yellow ribbons donated by the Blaine County Republicans around the big old trees on Main Street. At the annual Hailey Days of the Old West 4th of July Celebration rodeo, one young girl competitor had designed her routine around Bowe, riding a horse she decorated with yellow ribbons and carrying the black POW flag held high, the entire routine set to the Christian rock anthem, "Set Me Free." The yellow stickers framing Bowe's face were everywhere: at the supermarket, at the gas stations, and on the rear windshields of hippie campervans and Ford pickups alike. "Bring Bowe Home" had united the community, and by the time the complicating factors of the day had emerged—that Bowe had not been released for nothing or that his father would address the nation from the White House with the Koran's opening blessing—Hailey had already announced Bowe's welcome-home party.

By Sunday morning, the high emotions in Southern Idaho hit the pages of *The New York Times*, which declared, "Planned Celebration for Sgt. Bowe Bergdahl Just Got a Whole Lot Bigger." National media correspondents started showing up at Zaney's, where they greeted Sue Martin with bear hugs and tears in their eyes. As her gravel parking lot turned into a satellite-truck staging zone, camera crews went crawling along Main Street for feel-good footage of a rare good news story about the war.

Across the county, politicians from both parties rushed to join the drum circle forming on Twitter. "Welcome home, Sgt. Bowe Bergdahl. A grateful America thanks you for your service," wrote Mississippi Republican senator Thad Cochran. Nevada Republican Mark Amodei wrote: "Best news I've heard in a long time! #standwithbowe." Ohio Republican Jim Renacci called him "a true American hero."

The next day, Bob and Jani arrived to their own hero's welcome in Boise. On their flight from Washington, when the airline crew announced the couple was on board, the plane burst into applause. Arriving at Idaho National Guard headquarters flanked by Colonel Brad Poppen and Major Kevin Hickey, the family's indefatigable casualty assistance officer, they were cheered again by a crowd of national guardsmen and dozens of POW-MIA bikers and supporters. Tim Marsano, Bob's original media mediator and now a colonel, welcomed them back. It hadn't always been a smooth ride for Marsano and Bob; the family's decision in the spring of 2012 to take their story public had been a significant stress point. But none of that mattered anymore. Marsano told the audience that his time helping this soldier's family was "one of the great honors" of his career.

Outside the auditorium, the country was still processing what it had seen the day before. Even as Bob and Jani spoke to what would be their last supportive public audience for years, Blackfoot Company veterans were talking among themselves, outraged that Bergdahl's parents had been feted as if their son had been a hero. The veterans of 2nd Platoon had known the truth for five years, and this wasn't it. The problem was the Army; they had all signed the nondisclosure agreements and feared the repercussions of breaking a Defense Department contract. In Texas, Cody Full considered the dilemma, cracked open a case of beer, and logged on to Twitter.

"Fuck what you heard. I was there," Full wrote. He always thought something was just a little off with Bergdahl: "Like mental off, I felt like he thought life was a movie in his head." Full told the story of an oddball who wouldn't drink beer and eat barbecue with him and the others, who stayed inside by himself studying maps and languages, who rarely wore deodorant, and who didn't own a phone or a car.

Full tweeted about the first frantic hours after Bergdahl went missing, and as his memories mingled with recollections of four-year-old gossip, he wrote:

"Villagers said an American did come through the area and was wanting water and someone who spoke English. Wanted to meet with Taliban."

Though other 2nd Platoon veterans would go on to repeat that claim, the interpreter with them at OP Mest, John Mohammed, rejected the story outright. To date, no evidence has been presented that Bergdahl ever sought out the Taliban.

As Full's story lit up online, congressional Republicans wasted no time hiding their own dismay. House Intelligence Committee Chairman Mike Rogers told CNN that he was "extremely troubled . . . that the United States negotiated with terrorists." As the grumbles grew, National Security Adviser Susan Rice booked an appearance on ABC's *This Week with George Stephanopoulos.* The show's dramatic opening teaser laid the groundwork for a rising scandal: "American POW Bowe

Bergdahl finally freed. His dramatic release, and new controversy: Was it an illegal trade for terrorists?"

Sunday morning television had been dangerous territory for Rice before. Following the September 11, 2012, attack on a U.S. government compound in Benghazi, Libya, Rice had falsely claimed on several shows that the well-organized attack had been the work of a spontaneous mob. Her interview with Stephanopoulos seemed no better informed:

> Anybody who has been held in those conditions in captivity for five years has paid an extraordinary price. But that is not the point. The point is that he's back. He's going to be safely reunited with his family. He served the United States with honor and distinction.

One White House official later described it as a case of "imprecise wording." But with it, Rice had reasserted the most far-fetched conceit of the Rose Garden spectacle: that the lopsided prisoner swap was a decisive political victory. To a community of veterans already seething under five years of Army message control, lauding Bergdahl's service looked like inexcusable ignorance at best, and an egregious taunt at worst. Senator Lindsey Graham called for Rice to resign. John McCain advised her to "stay off the Sunday talk shows." Before sunrise the next morning, the story had taken a decisive turn with an essay published on the *Daily Beast* by former U.S. Army Captain Nathan Bradley Bethea, a Blackfoot Company officer who served during the DUSTWUN and, like Cody Full, believed the truth was more important than his legal bills.

"[Bergdahl] is safe, and now it is time to speak the truth," Bethea wrote from Seoul, South Korea, where he was stationed on his last duty assignment before leaving the Army. "The truth is: Bergdahl was a deserter, and soldiers from his own unit died trying to track him down."

Since they had returned home in early 2010, this was the story that the soldiers of Task Force Geronimo could not tell. A few had spoken to *Rolling Stone* in 2012, and a few others had written surreptitious online posts, but they had been the exceptions. The Army's gag orders, including one that had greeted them when they returned from their deployments in early 2010, had done a remarkable job keeping them quiet.

"Our families and friends wanted to understand what we had experienced, but the Army denied us that," Bethea wrote on his way to revealing the greatest outrage of the event: that in one three-week period (August 18, 2009, to September 6, 2009), six men had died searching. Bergdahl "has finally returned," he wrote. "Those men will never have the opportunity."

Some of Bethea's Army friends told him that his story was an oversimplification. But it was well written and emotionally raw, and it had the ring of truth, at least as Bethea understood it. As the story went viral, a Pentagon spokesman promised an investigation. By the time the Army rebutted the claim five days later, it had already taken root as fact. In the years that followed, Bethea learned the extent of information that the Army had withheld: that ISAF had high-confidence reports placing Bergdahl over the border within three days of his disappearance and that CENTCOM had rejected its own internal analysis and that of the intelligence community from July 14, 2009, and for roughly two months thereafter. The truth, Bethea eventually realized, was indeed more complex, and the line he had drawn from Bergdahl's stunt to the six dead soldiers was not as clear or direct as he had once thought.

"Knowing what I know now, I should have shut the fuck up about it," he said.

By Monday morning, it had become clear that the politics of the war, the business of politics, and the seductions of an election-year scandal were converging, and the operatives were already working their own angles. Richard Grenell, a Republican strategist and future Trump administration ambassador to Germany, spearheaded the effort with a midday appearance on Fox News, where he repeated Full's claim that Bergdahl "deserted the military and went to the Taliban." Even in the ruthless world of political operatives, Grenell had a reputation for hard-ball tactics. (Roger Stone, the veteran political strategist and self-avowed "dirty trickster," once said he considered Grenell too shady to work with.) Since 2009, Grenell had been running his own consulting firm, Capitol Media Partners, and, together with his deputy, Brad Chase, began lining up interviews for 2nd Platoon veterans ready to talk to the press.

In one of their first, Full and Cornelison told *The New York Times* that Second Lieutenant Darryn Andrews and Private First Class Matthew Martinek had been searching for Bergdahl when they were ambushed on September 4, 2009. With Grenell and Chase working as liaisons, similar stories followed on CNN, NBC News, *Time* magazine, *The Weekly Standard*, the *New York Post*, and the *Daily Mail*. As the bereaved parents of the men killed were pulled into the mix, the scandal took on the power of moral injustice, and, to White House critics, an outrage bordering on treason.

"It's a big cover-up like Benghazi, just like everything Obama has done," Gold Star father Andy Andrews told the *Daily Mail* on Monday, June 2, 2014. "We want the truth to come out."

THE ACTUAL HISTORY—of a dysfunctional intelligence apparatus, Bergdahl's own delusions, and the highest echelons of the Army chain of command turning the battlefield crisis into an opportunity of war—served no political interests. Five months before the 2014 midterm elections, however, the scandal did meet the needs of the Republican Party; and as the GOP geared up for its best opportunity to regain the Senate since 2006, the timing could not have been better. L'affaire Bergdahl was an offer too good to refuse.

The mood in Hailey quickly turned dark. Harassing emails and phone calls began flooding City Hall, the Chamber of Commerce, and any small business that had been caught on camera celebrating or had ever been listed as sponsors for Bergdahl awareness events over the prior five years. At a bed and breakfast near the airport, the first call came in on Monday at 4:30 a.m. "Someone oughta come in and shoot bleeding-heart liberals like you." Fifty or sixty more calls followed that week, about a quarter of them death threats. At Jane Drussel's store, typically a high-spirited hub selling birthday balloons with messages such as "So many candles, so little cake," high school students hired for their first summer jobs picked up the phone and froze. After one older employee broke down in tears and went home for the day, a thicker-skinned manager began fielding all phone calls, listening patiently to the voices that said, "I hope you burn in hell. I hope you fucking die." To each she replied, "Thank you. Have a nice day," and hung up the phone.

The mayor's office put out its first public statement on Monday afternoon. While acknowledging that all sides of the issue deserved to be heard, Hailey mayor Fritz Haemmerle made the case for Bergdahl's equally vital right to due process. "In the meantime, our celebration will focus on Bowe Bergdahl's release and the relief of his family and those who live here."

Hours later on Fox News, network star Bill O'Reilly told his 2,658,000 viewers that Bob Bergdahl "looks like a Muslim." At the *Drudge Report,* Monday's "HERO DESERTER?" headline gave way to Tuesday's "OBAMA SAVED A RAT?" On Tuesday, O'Reilly opened his show by asking, "Is the father of Sergeant Bowe Bergdahl an Islamist sympathizer?"

The Bergdahls had expected a backlash, which they assumed would cycle through the media's outrage machine within a couple of days. But in the weeks before the prisoner exchange, Bob had gained several Twitter followers who worked at the Heritage Foundation, the Foundation for Defense of Democracies, and other hawkish think tanks. As conservative media filled with synchronized messages about his beard, his activism, and his religion, Bob had little doubt that opposition researchers had studied him for a choreographed campaign.

On Wednesday, June 4, CNN's Jake Tapper reported that the searches for Bergdahl had misdirected so many assets in Afghanistan for so long that the Army had been unable to meet its scheduled date to shut down COP Keating, a remote mountain combat outpost in northeastern Nuristan Province. The battle that raged at Keating on October 3, 2009, took the lives of eight U.S. soldiers, and Tapper's unnamed military sources told him that there was a clear connection between Bergdahl's June 30 walkabout and one of the Army's worst battlefield losses of the war more than three months later.

Major Ron Wilson was shocked by that claim. "I don't know how they can get away with saying that," he said. Tapper had cited no evidence, and Wilson didn't believe any existed. Nevertheless, unnamed Pentagon sources repeated the claim to the *Daily Mail* and Fox News. As the Bergdahl fever burned across the airwaves, Hailey police officer Jeff Gunter received calls from attorneys representing veterans' groups in California and Texas, each of whom told him they were planning to bring a couple thousand protesters to the Hailey celebration later that month. In Boise, the *Idaho Statesman* received calls from the same groups with the same message. "I believed they were actually going to come," Gunter said. As the police department pondered four thousand protesters on Harleys swarming their town of eight thousand people, Haemmerle and Gunter saw a disaster in the making. Thursday afternoon, June 4, the city put out its second and final public statement on the matter. "In the interest of public safety, the event will be canceled," it said.

As Gunter breathed a sigh of relief, the party cancelation triggered yet another media convulsion and fresh fodder for the news crews prowling the town for quotes. For conservative media outlets and the GOP, the signal was clear: Bowe Bergdahl's political value had not yet been fully tapped.

HOURS LATER in New York City, six veterans of 2nd Platoon were navigating Manhattan's skyscraper canyons. Fox News had made the arrangements, flying them all in from Texas, Michigan, California, South Dakota, Washington State, and New Mexico, and putting them up in a budget hotel near Times Square. By the time they arrived at the News Corp. Building at the corner of Sixth Avenue and Forty-seventh Street, the headline about the canceled party in Hailey was already circling the red-lettered news ticker that wraps around the building's first-floor studios. The veterans had an appointment for a prime-time interview with the network's rising star, Megyn Kelly.

"I was kinda overwhelmed," Gerald Sutton said. He had never even watched Fox News, much less had any live in-studio experience. The invitation had been vague. "I had no idea I'd be going out and speaking in front of people on camera."

After returning from a second tour in Afghanistan in 2012, Sutton left the Army with an honorable discharge. He enrolled at the University of Michigan in Ann Arbor, where he majored in history on his way to earning a Fulbright scholarship to study in Seoul, South Korea. Cody Full had invited Sutton as well as Joseph Coe, Bergdahl's closest friends in the unit, to join the group in New York. Coe turned it down; he didn't trust the media and had no desire for the attention. But Sutton felt compelled to set the record straight. Bergdahl had been his friend, but the world needed to know what he had done.

"In a world exclusive, this is the first time these men have been together since they left Afghanistan," Kelly said in her introduction. They sat in a semicircle facing her and the cameras. Some were in church attire, and some had packed only sneakers. Kelly wanted their story, but first she wanted to talk about the scandal's latest sensation: chief Fox News Washington correspondent James Rosen had just published a bombshell: "Bergdahl declared jihad in captivity, secret documents show."

The secret documents were raw, unvetted Eclipse Group reports, which Dewey Clarridge had shared with Fox earlier that week. Some of the Eclipse information was accurate, including the report that Bergdahl had been held "in a metal cage, like an animal." But it was the contradictory claims—that Bergdahl had enjoyed playing soccer with his guards, who had also given him a loaded AK-47 and invited him along for target practice—that the network promoted most. In the hard light and cold electronic hum of the Fox studio, with nearly three million Americans watching at home, Kelly dove right in.

"What do you make of this latest reporting by James Rosen that [Bergdahl] had converted to Islam, that he fraternized openly with his captors, and declared himself a warrior for Islam at least by August of 2012?"

Sergeant Evan Buetow, Bergdahl's team leader, answered first: "Initially after he left, we knew that he had deserted. We knew that he was trying to find the Taliban, or trying to find someone who could speak English so he could talk to the Taliban." It was a point which Buetow had already repeated more than two dozen times that week, on ABC News, NPR, CNN, Fox News radio, and three other Fox News shows prior to the group interview. When Kelly suggested that this anecdote could be interpreted several ways, Buetow agreed that he couldn't know the truth without hearing from Bergdahl himself. "America wants to hear what he has to say," he said. Moments later, pushing back on accusations that he and the others were politically motivated, Buetow repeated his claim: "This is not about politics. This is about the fact that Bergdahl walked away from us, went to try to find the Taliban, and we know that for a fact."

Sutton told Kelly that he had considered Bergdahl a really good friend and had taken it all "a little bit harder than some of the other guys." Now, he had just one question: "Why?"

For several of them, the Taliban propaganda videos had been betrayals that held clues to a deeper untold story, and maybe some answers to Sutton's question. "He doesn't seem like a captive," Cornelison said of the tapes. "He seems like someone who is potentially enjoying himself."

Kelly's interview and Rosen's bombshell capped a tremendous week for Fox ratings. It marked the first time Kelly bested her network rival, O'Reilly, and firmly established her as a cable powerhouse. With its week-ending blockbusters, Fox had also completed the logical and narrative arc of treason, a shocking disgrace that left many in the network's aging audience at their agitated peak. Their anger had no better target than Hailey, Idaho, where the media's social experiments continued. Local business owners who had been harassed told Blaine County commissioner Larry Schoen that they were afraid to be seen with their families in public. At Zaney's, Sue Martin had gone from serving coffee and breakfast burritos to the news crews camping out in her parking lot, to feeling like a fugitive in her own town. The store's voicemail and Facebook page filled with threats, and by the third time she was personally accosted as a "Taliban sympathizer," Martin's family feared for her safety and told her to close shop.

As Martin headed for the hills and the FBI opened an investigation into multiple death threats on Bob and Jani, the vitriol flowed in both directions. When Fox News' Jesse Watters and his camera crew ambushed the bike shop where Bob sometimes worked, he was heckled by several customers. "Turn that fucking camera off!" one man shouted at Watters. "You're the problem with this country! Not us. *You* are the problem!"

That weekend, in an interview with *The Wall Street Journal*, military historian Paul J. Springer said that Bergdahl's place in American history had been determined. "Even if it turns out that he was kidnapped, I don't think you can ever reverse the narrative at this point."

TWENTY

DEBRIEFING

In Germany, Bergdahl's reintegration team was told that it was time to bring him home. Nearly two weeks in the hospital had him talking, walking and on the road to health. Army staff at the Pentagon had its own priorities to manage in Washington; a criminal investigation needed to begin as soon as possible. They loaded him onto a nondescript military transport jet on June 12, 2014, and shortly after midnight, 1,809 days after he had slipped off OP Mest, Sergeant Bowe Bergdahl touched down in San Antonio, Texas.

The satellite trucks had been on-site at Lackland Air Force Base, cameras at the ready for Bergdahl's first moments back on U.S. soil. But Army public affairs had corralled them behind a distant chain-link fence. *The New York Times* ran its story with a photo not of Bergdahl on the tarmac, but of the media gaggle waiting in a dark parking lot.

On the flight home, Bergdahl had been joined by the team of intelligence analysts and Survival Evasion Resistance Escape (SERE) instructors whom he had first met in Germany, including one of the special operators who had recovered him in Khost. The team was a protective bubble, a deliberate design by SERE psychologists to surround him with the first people he could allow himself to trust after years of isolation and brutality. They drove him to Brooke Army Medical Center (BAMC), the first stop for all government and military personnel captured and detained overseas, and his next station on the reintegration track that the JPRA had set for him years earlier.

At a press briefing later that morning, Major General Joseph P. DiSalvo, the commander of Army South at Fort Sam Houston, encouraged the media to focus on Bergdahl's well-being rather than his infamy. He called the recovery operation "the culmination of Herculean efforts" and credited the interagency teams that made it happen. The scandal surrounding his alleged crimes was a Pentagon matter, he said. As far as DiSalvo was concerned, Bergdahl was a wounded warrior returning home, and it was the job of his team in Texas to get him back on his feet.

The program at BAMC had significantly expanded in the years before Bergdahl arrived, from what had been an Army-specific treatment center into the government's premier reintegration facility for returning prisoners and hostages. The FBI had an agreement with the Army to conduct its own hostage debriefings there, and the Defense Department welcomed all returning civilians to participate in its post-isolation support activities, which offered counseling, clergy, and public affairs teams to help victims and their families deal with the inevitable media spotlight.

Bergdahl was not their first high-profile case. In July 2008, after the Pentagon recovered three contractors who had been held for more than five years by Colombian FARC rebels, BAMC had also welcomed them home. According to Terrence Russell, the lead Pentagon debriefer on their case, all three FARC hostages arrived in San Antonio in better condition than Bergdahl did. The reason was straightforward: "They were held together and had each other. They never left each other's company," said Russell, a former SERE instructor who later became the Defense Department's senior expert on isolated hostages and POWs. One of the Northrop Grumman contractors held in Colombia has made the same point in his own interviews.

"I would never wish what happened to me on my worst enemy," Marc Gonsalves said in 2016. "But I'm glad I wasn't alone there."

Russell, a tall, broad-shouldered man with sandy hair, a bushy mustache, and a booming baritone voice, passed his first combat survival course in 1977 at Fairchild Air Force Base in Spokane, Washington. Two years after the fall of Saigon and four years after Operation Homecoming recovered what the Pentagon said (but many doubted) was the last of the POWs, the Air Force was still internalizing the lessons of Vietnam; it lost more men to missing-captured status in Southeast Asia than every other military branch combined. Russell served twenty-two years as an instructor at the Fairchild Survival School, notorious among graduates for its traumatizing curriculum: wilderness survival, prolonged sleep deprivation, (naked) refrigeration, claustrophobic confinement, and an escape from the "dunker," during which pilots are strapped into flight seats and dropped upside down into a pool in the dark.

When he retired from the Air Force in the early nineties, Russell went from teaching survival skills to men who might one day be captured to studying those who already had. In 1993, he joined the newly formed JPRA, an office designed by the Pentagon to manage the entire POW experience, from capture to homecoming. Following 9/11, while some of his former colleagues were reverse engineering SERE tests like waterboarding into government-sanctioned "enhanced interrogation methods," Russell was busy writing classified instruction manuals that would prepare U.S. personnel for long-term isolation in eighty-nine separate countries, each one a potential "low-intensity" American battlefield of the future. At JPRA, Russell also launched the Pentagon's first oral history program devoted to archiving POW stories; it grew into the largest collection of its kind in the U.S. government, and to Russell's knowledge, anywhere in the world. Every high-profile case crossed his desk: Army Private First Class Jessica Lynch (Iraq, 2003), Army helicopter pilot Mike Durant (Mogadishu, 1993), Army pilot Bobby Hall (North Korea, 1994), as well as dozens of other citizens and soldiers, both Americans and foreign nationals who had been held alone by hostile regimes and enemy combatants.

By the time Russell met him, Bergdahl was already a historic case.

Emerging from the FATA as the longest-held American POW since Vietnam, he carried immense intelligence potential from one of the world's most inaccessible terrorist hideouts. Not all foreign hostages return to weeks of formal questioning from a procession of intelligence analysts, FBI agents, Pentagon psychologists, and government lawyers. With Bergdahl it was all a forgone conclusion. Teams from Spokane, Tampa Bay, and Northern Virginia had been meeting in Texas for drills and rehearsals every six months for three years to prepare for his homecoming, an event that CENTCOM analyst Amber Dach and her colleagues had been referring to as "the Super Bowl" during years of anticipation. "The whole operation was planned down to the paperclip," Russell said.

On the flight from Afghanistan to Germany, Bergdahl had asked for paper and a pen and began drawing detailed diagrams of his prison cells. The reintegration team put him in an isolated and secured hospital wing at Landstuhl, where visitors had to be cleared by Army staff at the Pentagon, leading to yet another round of nondisclosure forms for everyone who came into contact with him, including the Army dentist. When the team reintroduced him to concepts like choice and free will, he asked for peanut butter. They gave him a private room with a bed; he chose to sleep on the bathroom floor. Bergdahl had been promoted twice in captivity. On June 15, 2011, Brigadier General Richard Mustion, Army Human Resources Command, had flown to Hailey for a promotion ceremony in Bob and Jani's backyard attended by Idaho governor Butch Otter and his wife, Lori. But in Germany, Bowe was uncomfortable with the title of sergeant, which he did not believe he had earned, and asked people to call him private, the rank he held when he was captured. Mostly, he was fixated on providing his debriefers with intel about his captors.

For Bergdahl's first three days under U.S. supervision, Dach, despite having been CENTCOM's lead intelligence analyst on the case for five years, was not permitted to see him in person. She conducted her initial debrief like a childhood game of telephone, delivering written questions to a male debriefer because SERE psychologists were worried that after his exposure to cruel women captors, Bergdahl might not trust her. (That same Army logic was not applied to the male guards who had beaten and tortured him.) In reality, Bergdahl had always been more trusting of women, and when they did meet, Dach was taken aback by his courtesy. Over days of interviews, he would not sit down until she had. "It shook me," she said. "He was still a gentleman."

When Bergdahl began talking, his voice was like an instrument he had forgotten how to play. Having never met him, the debriefers didn't realize it was an octave above his normal register. He began slowly, straining and squeaking his way through. The rhythms and cadences were all off. When he couldn't remember a word, he made little grunts and then resumed in a jumble of clashing accents, the echoes of his guards' voices still lingering in his mind. "It was like the absence of a cadence," Dach said, "the absence of any language."

He talked a lot about his captors. The men were "prehistoric pricks" who sat around picking at their feet, shouting at the women, and watching videos of IEDs, beheadings, and suicide bombers on their cell phones. The women and children abused the American prisoner gleefully; they spat in his food, tossed cups of urine at him, whipped him with chains, and deliberately scattered his food into the puddles of diarrhea on the floor of his cell.

He told the debriefers that he had made a point of filing away memories that he thought might be worth something to the Army one day—details about his captors' radios, weapons, and the types of locks and shackles he had been chained with. When they asked him to describe these locations, he said that he had been blindfolded so often that his memories were useless. Dach and her team didn't accept that for an answer and pushed him for more.

"Did you hear a call to prayer? From what direction?"

Bergdahl would sit up ramrod straight, a hand on each knee, close his eyes, and stay silent, as if searching for a scene in years of mental video.

"Were there children around? Were the roads gravel or dirt?"

In captivity, time had fused into the unbearable monotony of what he called "an Afghan minute," more anguishing in its duration than the days, months, and years. "An empty mind is a torture chamber," he told them. So he latched onto whatever he could: the sounds of children playing and cars driving, the number of steps to the latrine, the dimensions of the room, his guards' routines, and when he had a window, the movements of shadows and light. "In our best work, it was the things that he didn't realize he remembered," said Dach.

Before enlisting, Bowe was already a bundle of contradictions: the ballet dancer who dreamed of being a Special Forces soldier, an eager-to-please loner who yearned to fight the system as much as he needed to prove himself within it. At twenty-three, that split impulse to both satisfy and reject authority had jolted him into a trap of his own making, and his own ruin. When the Army took him back at Landstuhl, the institution became both his caretaker and taskmaster. And while Dach and the SERE officers were sympathetic to Bergdahl's suffering, they had their own tasks to accomplish. All that ultimately mattered to their chain of command was the quality and precision of Bergdahl's memory.

Skepticism is the first rule of all intelligence work, and Dach prided herself on being a finely tuned cynic. But as Bergdahl spewed information that her team could compare against existing U.S. intelligence, "we knew he was telling us the truth." They started making fast progress, identifying three of his holding locations in succession with high confidence. One was just a mud hut, one of countless like it, a needle in a haystack in a field dotted with haystacks. With each confirmation, they encouraged him to believe in himself and in the power of his memories.

"We could show him, 'Hey, the system works. We are working together. We make a pretty good team,'" said Dach.

When their interviews ended, he said he wanted to keep going. Between sessions, when they thought he was resting or eating, he was drawing intricate sketches of his shackles, his cage, and an arcane symbol he had seen on a wall. His reintegration was managed in three phases in three locations: Afghanistan, Landstuhl, and BAMC. At the end of Phase III, the debriefing totaled about eighty hours of tape-recorded questioning, an influx of raw information that both Dach and Russell independently referred to as "a gold mine." It provided new detail to the U.S. intelligence picture of the Taliban-Haqqani captor network; led to the direct creation of several SERE training products for soldiers, pilots, and spies headed overseas; and supplied the Pentagon with a dozen new intelligence reports. Those reports remain classified. What is known, however, is that eleven days after the prisoner exchange, the Obama administration ended its five-and-half-month drone cease-fire in the skies over Pakistan's FATA, the longest pause of its kind in nine years.

In a June 8 interview with CNN, Mattis defended Bergdahl's family as "salt-of-the-earth people" and "regular old Americans." He told the media to back off its harassment and explained the tactical advantages to be gained following Bergdahl's recovery: the Haqqani and Taliban were now newly vulnerable.

"There's a freedom to operate against them that perhaps we didn't fully enjoy so long as they held Bowe as a prisoner," Mattis said.

Three days after Mattis's comment, the CIA resumed its drone campaign with a series of targeted strikes in villages on the outskirts of Miran Shah, the Haqqani stronghold where Bergdahl was sometimes held and from which David Rohde had escaped. The first attack killed several Uzbek and Pakistani TTP fighters. The second hit a truck loaded with bomb-making materials parked at a house used as an explosives cache, triggering a massive, deafening explosion that shook the entire surrounding area. Among the dead were a Haqqani commander, Haji Gul, and twelve other Taliban fighters. A third strike on a Haqqani compound the following week killed between four and eight more Taliban. Before the end of August 2014, drones over North Waziristan killed roughly four dozen more alleged Taliban and al-Qaeda militants.

EVEN AS THE U.S. government mined and processed his recollections into intelligence reports shared across federal agencies, the Pentagon was faced with managing two versions of the same soldier. The Department of the Army opened a criminal investigation even as it awarded Bergdahl with two Good Conduct Medals for his service in captivity. These were not rote awards conferred simply for showing up; by Army doctrine, the medals were an elective decision by his immediate commanders to recognize "exemplary conduct, efficiency, and fidelity."

In San Antonio, he adapted to the Army's rigid reintegration routine. Every morning and afternoon, he was escorted by a security detail to U.S. Army South Headquarters (USARSO) at Fort Sam Houston for formal debriefing. In the debrief room, he sat across a coffee table from two inquisitors—one asking questions, one taking notes—while down the hall some fifteen additional agents and officers watched on a closed-circuit feed. By the end of their first day together, Russell was struck by two revelations: the totality of Bergdahl's isolation, and the totality of the Pentagon's ignorance about it. Over the course of his 1,797 days as a prisoner, Bergdahl did not see or communicate with a single Westerner. Of his captors and guards, only a few were conversational in English, and he saw them only rarely. Whereas CENTCOM had assessed that the Haqqanis were by and large treating him humanely, the opposite was proving true.

Torture was the only topic that Bergdahl would not or could not address during formal questioning. "I let it go," Russell said, knowing that he would have another chance in a more private setting. When that opportunity arose later that summer, Bergdahl shared details about the three months he had spent with his four limbs chained to the corners of the metal bed frame.

Dach couldn't believe how thoroughly U.S. intelligence methods had been deceived. "We thought that we had sources with placement and access," she said. But as Bergdahl recounted the reality of how few people he had seen and spoken to, her team realized that their sources had been lying. There were many reasons to bias them toward thinking that he was being treated well, Dach said. “If we got that wrong, we got everything else equally as wrong.” More than one hundred sources claiming specific knowledge had fed false reports to the Americans over the years, and they were paid well for their stories. At the higher levels, Taliban propaganda had been more coordinated. The August 2010 story in *The Sunday Times* about Abdullah Bergdahl teaching bomb-making seminars was an early example of a strategy that would prove to be, at times, artfully persuasive.

“This was an organized disinformation campaign,” Russell said. In the weeks leading up to the prisoner swap, the Taliban had a dedicated office pumping out false information, much of which was sent directly to Bergdahl’s parents, a reality Mattis described as “an extremely coercive experience.” To the Taliban, Bob was an easy mark and a tool to leverage their ongoing efforts to free their detainees.

Taliban manipulation didn’t end at the prisoner swap. On June 5, *Time* published exclusive insights from a Taliban commander who had “consistently supplied reliable information about Bergdahl’s captivity.” The Taliban source explained how Bergdahl’s captors had paid a local tailor to customize the white shalwar kameez he wore at the Batai Pass. “You know we are also human beings and have hearts in our bodies,” he said and claimed that they had given it to Bergdahl as a parting gesture of goodwill. “We wanted him to return home with good memories.”

False sentimentality was pervasive. In the May 31 Taliban video of the handoff, the narrator shared his hurt feelings about how rude the Americans had been: “They were in such a hurry, they didn’t even let us shake hands with Bergdahl to say goodbye. It was very strange.” In formal questioning, Bergdahl told Russell that he had never seen any of the men at the handoff until that day. Nevertheless, conservative commentator Glenn Beck replayed and parsed the comment on his national radio and television shows to laughter, and former 2nd Platoon soldier

Matt Vierkant told Megyn Kelly how angry it made him to learn that Bergdahl and his guards had grown so close.

"The Taliban is not doing this in isolation," said Russell. "They are listening to the news and the chatter. They hear what's being reported in the Western press. They reinforce the impression that he was being helpful, that he converted, that they are treating him well. Then the guy comes out, has physical evidence that he was beaten and clubbed and abused, the intel community can verify this, and it starts to run counter to what all the reporting was."

Toying with morale is, of course, the entire objective of wartime propaganda. "This isn't anything new," said Russell. But what surprised him in Bergdahl's case was how easily—or willingly—American information systems had been manipulated to achieve Taliban goals. In the months and years following the prisoner swap, Russell watched in disbelief as a procession of former military officers took to the airwaves to disseminate the very messages that Taliban propagandists had planted years earlier.

By the end of his first week in U.S. Army custody, an alternate history of Bergdahl's persona and motives had already been written. Confusingly, the two versions often existed side by side, sometimes at the same time on the same network. Even as Fox News promoted Rosen's derogatory report as a conclusive coup de grâce to end a week of speculation, his story quoted Mattis bluntly refuting the entire thesis: "We kept an eye on this," Mattis told Rosen. "There was never any evidence of collaboration."

Nevertheless, with Buetow reiterating his claim that Bergdahl had gone "looking for the Taliban," cable news latched onto it as evidence. Fox News commentator Sean Hannity answered the question even as he asked it: "If you hear on a radio transmission that you're monitoring that Bergdahl is looking for the Taliban, that means he's going to collaborate with the enemy, isn't it?"

Speaking to O'Reilly on Friday, Rosen described Bergdahl as a "modern day Lee Harvey Oswald." But even O'Reilly saw the inconsistencies. How could Bergdahl escape twice, spend years caged like an animal, and also be a willing collaborator? "You got two polar opposite reports under the same banner!" O'Reilly shouted. Rosen explained that it wasn't his fault, that he had never reported that Bergdahl "was actively collaborating with the enemy," and then reminded O'Reilly that Bergdahl had declared himself "a warrior for Islam." As the bewildering segment came to an end, O'Reilly settled the discussion around what all of it ultimately meant.

"Right now, the president's whole legacy is riding on this story. That's how important it is. His *whole* administration is riding on it. If it turns out this guy was a collaborator, Rosen, you know what's gonna happen. His administration is done. That's how big this story is."

The message from O'Reilly was clear: The facts were important, but only insofar as they served the greater political purpose. By then, the GOP strategy to leverage Bergdahl and his family against Obama was working as designed. According to polls that month, twice as many Americans were following the scandal than were paying attention to that fall's upcoming elections, a plurality believed that Obama had done "the wrong thing" with the prisoner swap, and the president's approval rating began a three-week slide. On June 22, 2014, Gallup tallied Obama's disapproval ratings at 55 percent, the highest of his presidency.

When Sergeant Bowe Bergdahl landed in San Antonio, *Time* ran his photo on its cover with a question: "Was He Worth It?" By the time he reported to his duty assignment at Fort Sam Houston, the first batch of "FUCK BERGDAHL" T-shirts that had appeared on the internet had already sold out.

TWENTY-ONE
SQUARED AWAY

On June 16, 2014, Bergdahl's third day back on American soil, the Pentagon announced that Major General Kenneth Dahl would lead the Army's criminal investigation, and *Deadline Hollywood* announced that screenwriter Mark Boal and director Kathryn Bigelow would write and direct the film version. As the powerhouse duo behind *Zero Dark Thirty* and *The Hurt Locker*, Boal and Bigelow were not a surprising arrival to the military story. Their timing, however, was a bright signal that the history of the Bergdahl affair had yet to be written. Indeed, General Dahl's inquest hadn't even begun.

Dahl had been in his office in Tacoma, Washington, at Joint Base Lewis-McChord, when he first saw the message from Army staff headquarters looking for candidates to lead the investigation (known as an Army Regulation 15-6). The Pentagon wanted a specific kind of officer to do the job: a two-star general with a recent Afghanistan deployment, available immediately, and for at least two months. To his dismay, Dahl realized he was on the short list. For senior officers, whose every promotion requires congressional confirmation, it is both military code and sound career strategy to avoid even small political controversies. Inheriting the Bergdahl case was just bad luck. After he briefly lobbied his superiors to pick one of the other generals, Dahl accepted his fate. "I pretty much saw it coming," he said.

Dahl flew to Washington to accept his assignment from the director of Army staff, Lieutenant General William Grisoli. His orders were unambiguous. As the lead investigating officer (IO), Dahl was responsible for establishing the official record of the facts and circumstances of Bergdahl's disappearance and capture. "Your responsibilities as an IO take precedence over all other duties," the orders told him. By the end of the day, Dahl's anonymity had been shot, his appointment announced across the media, and his name forever bound to the scandal.

The assumption at the Pentagon was that Dahl would conduct his investigation from Army headquarters—an office had already been reserved for him. But while his orders were nonnegotiable, Dahl had the autonomy to run the investigation his own way. He knew that, under Article 37 of the Uniform Code of Military Justice (Unlawful Command Influence), any political pressure from his own chain of command could invalidate his work before he even started. Savvy to the ways of Washington, he decided to conduct the investigation back in Tacoma, as far away as he could get from what he called "the noise" in Washington, D.C.

The case consumed the next sixty days of Dahl's life. His first call was to an infantry platoon leader to help him understand the group dynamics at OP Mest. He added nine officers, ten enlisted men, an intelligence analyst, a psychologist, and a psychiatrist to the investigative team, which in turn identified fifty-six witnesses for questioning. Dahl wanted to know everything about Bergdahl: his behavior patterns, his relationships and upbringing, and above all, his state of mind when he decided to ditch his platoon and weapon and walk into nearly certain harm. In August 2009, Major General Scaparrotti, commander of the 82nd Airborne, and Lieutenant Colonel Horton, a senior MP in Eastern Afghanistan at the time, had left their own initial 15-6 investigation open, determining that without a statement from Bergdahl, they could reach no firm conclusions. Dahl faced the same reality, but the Army had higher priorities for Bergdahl in June 2014 than his criminal case. In the interests of his health and his value as an intelligence asset, debriefing took precedence, and Dahl was told he would have to wait.

While Dahl turned his attention to calling witnesses, Mark Boal went straight for Bergdahl himself. He contacted Kim Dellacorva, who had been listed as Bergdahl's next of kin on his Army paperwork. Following a divorce, she had changed her name from Harrison to Dellacorva, an approximation of an Italian translation of a Wiccan concept: "of the crows." By 2014, she had left Idaho and moved to the largest cannabis-producing region in the United States, Northern California's Emerald Triangle, with plans to work the land. She and her daughter had been like family when Bowe deployed, and when he landed in Texas, they were some of the first people he spoke to. Three days after touchdown, on Dellacorva's advice, Bergdahl agreed to have Boal tell his story.

Boal had cut his teeth as a military journalist for *Rolling Stone*, *Playboy*, and *Mother Jones*. In 2004, he embedded with an Army bomb squad in Iraq. In 2007, Boal based his first feature film, *In the Valley of Elah,* on his article about Army infantryman Richard Davis, who had been murdered by his own platoonmates near Fort Benning, Georgia, just days after they returned from a heavy combat tour in Iraq. Both the story and film cast a harsh light on how the Army cares for its own. The following year, Boal and Bigelow teamed up for the first time on *The Hurt Locker,* which earned the Academy Award for Best Picture and established them as an industry force.

As Boal's star rose in Hollywood, he walked a creative tightrope, striving to tell the true and difficult stories of U.S. military personnel while cultivating sources for bigger government stories to come. But his relationships with the powerful fared better than those with his subjects. Master Sergeant Jeffrey Sarver, the explosive ordnance removal specialist whose story Boal had adapted for *The Hurt Locker,* sued the screenwriter just before Oscar season, claiming defamation for the film's allegedly inaccurate portrayal of his Army career and life back home after his tour. Boal won the lawsuit on First Amendment grounds, and Sarver was ordered to pay $187,000 to cover the defense costs. Compared to the controversies that lay ahead, it would be a mere speed bump in Boal's career.

In December 2012, *Zero Dark Thirty*, the $40 million blockbuster that depicted the decade-long search for bin Laden and the final lethal raid in Abbottabad, began playing in theaters just seventeen months after the event itself. Along its path to box office success, the film irritated a wide range of political constituencies with its not so subtle suggestions that the CIA's post-9/11 torture program had supplied intelligence critical to the manhunt. A bipartisan letter from the ranking members of the Senate Intelligence Committee, Senators Dianne Feinstein, Carl Levin, and John McCain, sought to clear up any confusion about torture that the film had created. Calling it "grossly inaccurate and misleading," the senators reminded Sony Pictures that their committee had completed an exhaustive study that had arrived at opposite conclusions from what the film depicted. At a time when a narrow majority of Americans believed that torture worked, the filmmakers were "perpetuating the myth," and the senators told them that they had "a social and moral obligation to get the facts right" and correct the record.

The homage to torture was only one part of the *Zero Dark Thirty* legacy. The film had also blurred the lines between entertainment and propaganda. Three months after the Abbottabad raid, the CIA and Pentagon had successfully fed its own favorable versions of the event to specific print journalists, and word got around that Hollywood was next. New York Republican congressman and chairman of the House Committee on Homeland Security, Peter King, wrote a letter to CIA and Pentagon inspectors about what appeared to be a deliberate strategy to publicize (and glorify) classified information. Such collaborations between government spymasters and their chosen Hollywood partners undermined the very idea of government transparency, King wrote, "in favor of a cinematographic view of history."

Reporting by journalist Jason Leopold and CIA historian Tricia

Jenkins would later reveal the extent to which Boal and Bigelow had plied CIA officers for access—and the mutual affection the filmmakers had received in return in the weeks immediately following bin Laden's death. Troves of agency documents detailed the extent of the dalliance as Boal and Bigelow attempted to woo their sources and the agency repaid the filmmakers by making them feel like part of the team. This relationship peaked when Boal and Bigelow flew east from Los Angeles to attend a June 24, 2011, closed-door, classified awards ceremony at the Langley campus honoring agency personnel involved in the bin Laden hunt.

Boal denied that any official government vetting had taken place. But an internal December 2012 CIA report told a different and more nuanced story: the agency's Office of Public Affairs had violated CIA regulations. The audit also revealed that, as part of standard agency procedure, the creative professionals who thought that they were working the CIA for information were in fact being worked. Of the eight entertainment projects audited, one received the bulk of the agency's attention, which included meetings with several CIA officers, "the majority of whom were under cover." Still, the report found "nothing to suggest that the projects' results would be inconsistent with CIA's goal."

By the time Bergdahl arrived at Fort Sam Houston, *Zero Dark Thirty* had grossed more than $100 million for Sony, and Boal and Bigelow had cemented their role as Hollywood's most prolific storytellers of the country's post-9/11 wars. This they did with amazing speed, while shrugging off the ethical charges leveled by Feinstein, McCain, and Levin. "I've been saying from the beginning, 'It's a movie,'" Boal said in his acceptance speech for best director award from the New York Film Critics Circle at a Manhattan nightclub. "That shouldn't be too confusing."

Impressionable and vulnerable even before he joined the Army and spent five years in brutal isolation, Bergdahl was an easy mark for Boal. Before he had even met his own attorneys, the two began speaking regularly by phone with the understanding that the chats were background research for a movie about Bergdahl's ordeal. Boal soon recorded twenty-five hours of conversation.

A SOLDIER COULD do worse than an assignment at Fort Sam Houston. What began as a frontier outpost in Indian country had grown into one of the Army's most serene bases: a bucolic campus of Spanish Colonial–style homes and offices with terra-cotta shingle roofs on manicured green lawns. The parade grounds were dotted with ornamental husks of retired matériel: artillery pieces, decommissioned M-60 tanks, M113 armored personnel carriers, and UH-1 Iroquois helicopters. Each afternoon at 1700 hours, the cannon and bells sounded and the flag was lowered in the Army ritual called "retreat."

A month after he arrived, Bergdahl was assigned to a staff office job at U.S. Army North Headquarters, just off the historic Fort Sam Houston Quadrangle, a picturesque anachronism popular with tourists. Along with the base museum and limestone clock tower, the Quadrangle was also home to an Army menagerie: peacocks (blue and albino), Texas deer, and chickens roamed the grassy lawn. Army lore held that the animals were put there for Geronimo to hunt when the Apache renegade was held on Fort Sam as a prisoner of war in the 1890s. The exotic collection included a rooster of a breed that Bergdahl had been fond of as a kid. Each morning when he arrived for work before flag raising, its crowing triggered a post-traumatic flood. In captivity, his guards had forced him to watch and rewatch a videotaped beheading. Before the execution began, as the doomed man stared at the camera, the only sound was of a rooster crowing somewhere out of the video's frame.

Aside from the flashbacks and martial trappings, it was a typical Army desk job. Sergeant Bergdahl was accepted by his colleagues and superiors, who appreciated his work ethic and consistency. Compared to many young NCOs returning from war, he was steady and never a source of workplace drama. In the evenings, sleep was a challenge. His dreams filled with visions of his former guards standing over him with a knife, or one who enjoyed pantomiming the way he had allegedly slit an American soldier's throat. Bergdahl's doctors at BAMC prescribed sleeping pills, and he developed habits he had never had in his youth: sleeping with a flashlight, compulsively checking his locks, and tying string around the doorknob so it couldn't be manipulated while he slept.

On August 6, 2014, at 8:00 a.m., Sergeant Bergdahl and his new civilian attorney, Eugene Fidell, met Major General Dahl in a nondescript office in Building 268 on Fort Sam Houston. To ease the tension, Dahl noted the irony of their situation: more than five years after Bergdahl had set out with the goal of airing his grievances to a general, the opportunity had finally arrived. Bergdahl spoke for about eight hours over two days, providing Dahl with 370 pages of sworn testimony to supplement his team's extensive information gathering.

Dahl submitted his 15-6 report to the Pentagon in late September, a few days ahead of the deadline. He included Bergdahl's sworn statement along with a two-page summary of his findings, which, in contrast with the scare headlines dominating the media, was remarkably concise, dispassionate, and clear. The consistency of the witnesses' statements had helped. Nearly three dozen people who had known Bergdahl at various points in his life described his character, virtues, and shortcomings in nearly identical terms.

"Overwhelming testimony from those in his unit indicates that, prior to his disappearance, Private First Class Bergdahl was a good soldier. He was disciplined, serious, motivated, and he excelled at his basic warrior tasks and skills," Dahl wrote. Since returning to U.S. custody, he had been cooperative and helpful. Nevertheless, he had done precisely what his former comrades said: He left OP Mest deliberately and knowing that he would miss his morning guard shift. That alone, Dahl wrote, even though Bergdahl had intended to return, was sufficient basis for a desertion charge. Next, Dahl answered the question to which everyone involved—by now including several million Americans, Bergdahl's own parents, his platoon buddies, President Obama, and a sizable audience of international news readers—demanded an answer: Why?

Their interview had filled in the blanks. Bergdahl, reticent for most of his life, talked for the bulk of their time together, speaking in long stream-of-consciousness tangents. Where his mind needed to go, the general followed, listening patiently to Bergdahl's analysis of the history of military strategy, the role of the U.S. Army in American culture, and, most important for Dahl's task, the dire leadership issues that had been so evident to Bergdahl in Lieutenant Colonel Baker's Task Force Geronimo in the spring of 2009.

"The basis for his stated motive was incorrect," Dahl wrote. "Although Private First Class Bergdahl may have perceived it to be so, there was no failure of leadership that created an urgent and dangerous situation." Excessive idealism, coupled with a hyperactive imagination, "caused his anxiety to grow to a level where he believed it was necessary to act immediately to correct the perceived moral wrong and protect members of his platoon from imagined danger."

Dahl considered the possibility that Bergdahl had spun him a wild tale, but like Russell and Dach before him, he ultimately ruled it out. If Bergdahl had been lying, he had done so with miraculous consistency. Bergdahl's truth was far sadder than the version that his country had written for him upon his return. His truth also matched what Coe and his friends in Idaho had believed all along: Bowe was a well-intentioned, remarkably naïve twenty-three-year-old with the impulsiveness and judgment of a kid half his age. It was an odd end to a long mystery, but with the rigor Dahl had applied, it was the closest anyone had come—and likely ever would—to cracking Bergdahl's code.

The Department of the Army accepted Dahl's recommendations. Among them, he advised the Pentagon to better identify behavioral health issues in those ejected from the armed services and improve screening for those trying to get back in. As for Bergdahl's comments to other soldiers that he had planned to walk to Pakistan or China, Dahl characterized them as bravado that could be taken seriously, but not literally. Regardless of whether one believed that he left for the reasons he told General Dahl, or to go "to India to eventually join the

Russian mob," his crime was the same: desertion. Dahl recommended that he be charged with one count of UCMJ Article 85: desertion with intent to avoid hazardous duty or shirk important service.

Desertion charges are common in the Army, particularly in wartime. Between 2006 and 2014, roughly twenty thousand soldiers left as deserters. Since 2001, the Army has pressed charges against fewer than two thousand, of whom about half pled guilty and just seventy-eight were tried and convicted. While Bergdahl's lawyers would later argue that their client had merely gone AWOL and was then captured, Dahl had made a clear case for pressing charges; he had also provided his superiors at the Pentagon with a solution that could be wrapped up quickly. It would be up to the Army to decide how to process his findings.

ON MARCH 25, 2015, six months after Dahl submitted his report, the Army, despite Dahl's recommendation, hit Bergdahl with two crimes: Article 85 (desertion) and a second, rarely used and more serious allegation, Article 99: misbehavior before the enemy. The second charge carried a maximum sentence of death and up to life in prison.

In those six months of deliberation, the Army had managed the case with at least one conspicuously unprecedented legal maneuver. Three days before Christmas, Lieutenant General Grisoli, director of the Army staff at the Pentagon, had referred Dahl's recommendations to General Mark Milley at U.S. Army Forces Command (FORSCOM) for legal processing—at the direction of the secretary of the Army. Since its founding in 1973 by General Creighton Abrams at Fort Bragg, North Carolina, FORSCOM had been designed with a specific function: to oversee the Army's warfighting formations. Unlike Army commands that focus on training, doctrine, or institutional support, FORSCOM is all about combat, and since its founding it had never held a general court-martial. To Bergdahl's attorneys, the decision was at once institutionally inexplicable and politically obvious; as

FORSCOM built a prosecution team from the ground up for its first ever general court-martial, it would do so under the watchful eye of the Army staff. The Bergdahl case was unlike any court-martial before it, and it would be managed with a bespoke legal process tailored for Pentagon control.

Along with its charge sheet on March 25, FORSCOM also enforced a sweeping gag order that denied Bergdahl and his attorneys the right to share with the public or the press any case evidence. This "protective order," as the Army euphemized it, was presented as a method to shield Bergdahl's privacy. But in practice, it was a repeat of the NDAs with which the Army had sought to contain the story for five years. As long as Bergdahl was an Army soldier, the Army would control the facts of his case.

The surprising charges made national headlines, which led in turn to another round of high-octane media analysis.

"There is clear evidence," said former Army intelligence officer and Fox News contributor Tony Shaffer, "that [Bergdahl] was going over to the other side." Shaffer, along with Fox senior intelligence reporter Catherine Herridge, cited government sources with access to a classified 2009 report. Shaffer said that while he had not seen the report personally, he stood by his sources.

As the media debate raged, Mark Boal was growing impatient. It had been ten months since he had announced his film, but the story writ large was no closer to a conclusion that would enable him to roll cameras. Meanwhile in New York, the producers of the podcast *Serial* were searching for their follow-up hit. In 2014, the first season of this investigative spinoff of NPR's *This American Life* had become a sensation and the first ever podcast to reach five million downloads.

Operating with a small, scrappy staff and a line of advertisers knocking at their digital doorstep, *Serial* was under pressure. Producers had promised season two would air in 2015, and millions of listeners were wondering what was taking so long. Some had donated money to support the show's journalistic mission. But as spring turned to summer, and early advertisers Audible, MailChimp, and Squarespace were joined by larger funders, second album syndrome had set in. When Boal and *Serial* made contact that summer, his timing and offer were too good to refuse: exclusive tapes of America's most notorious soldier in an intimate confessional. In return, *Serial* gave Boal editorial control. The alliance would help Boal introduce the subject of his upcoming film to a wider and younger audience, while etching its plotlines into the grooves of public consciousness. The plan in motion, Boal and *Serial* host Sarah Koenig set out to tell Bergdahl's story and report on his legal case in real time.

GENE FIDELL HAD TAKEN on Bergdahl's case pro bono. Fidell was a native New Yorker with a law degree from Harvard who had been introduced to military law during Vietnam. He had served four years in the Coast Guard during the war, and forty years later, in the courtroom, he still wore a miniature Coast Guard Achievement Medal pinned onto his jacket lapel. Fidell was a busy man. While working as a partner in a Washington, D.C., firm specializing in federal cases, he was based in Connecticut, where he had been a lecturer at Yale Law School since the early 1990s. He did all this while also publishing an online journal devoted to the cause that had defined his career: *Global Military Justice Reform*.

Fidell was at once a respected scholar and something of an iconoclast in the small community of military justice experts. Following his introduction to its obscure workings, he commited himself to improving and modernizing what he saw as an archaic system. In 2004, he had defended Army Captain James Yee, the West Point graduate who had worked as a Muslim chaplain at Guantanamo. After a list of detainees was found in Yee's luggage, he was arrested at Naval Air Station Jacksonville and held in solitary confinement for seventy-six days, most of that time in shackles and chains, a punishment that Fidell noted was worse than those of the detainees themselves. After months of obfuscation and claims that Yee had been engaged in espionage, his case was dismissed at an Article 32 preliminary hearing, due to a lack of evidence.

In the spring of 2015, Fidell saw the Pentagon handle Bergdahl's case with familiar overkill. The protective order that had sealed Dahl's findings and Bergdahl's sworn statement was an early sign that the Army was more interested in control than transparency. Bergdahl had not been legally required to sit for questioning with Dahl; he had done so because he wanted to explain himself. What the Army had ordered, Dahl had delivered: an official, confirmed record of the facts. The public and the media wanted to know these things. And yet, even as Fox News regurgitated Taliban rumors, the Army refused to release its own verified findings. So Fidell began pushing back, lobbying news outlets to submit Freedom of Information Act (FOIA) requests and to demand the public's right for a transparent legal process.

That September, the Army held an Article 32 preliminary hearing to decide whether and how the case should proceed to trial. A low-ceilinged, fluorescent-lit basement conference room on Fort Sam Houston was the venue for Sergeant Bergdahl's first public appearance. He sat with his spine perfectly straight, his jaw muscles constantly clenching and unclenching, his face gripped by what looked like constant pain.

During opening statements, Fidell informed Lieutenant Colonel Mark Visger, the case hearing officer, that he had just one sentence to offer: "The government should make Sgt. Bergdahl's statement available to the public and not just to you."

In the two days of hearings that followed, Dahl's report and Bergdahl's statement were accepted as evidence and frequently referred to by JAG prosecutors, who flipped through its pages just feet away from reporters whose own companies were at that moment preparing a formal legal petition to compel its release. That month, Bergdahl's defense team filed its first formal complaint on the issue with the Army Court of Criminal Appeals. Denied, they appealed the matter to the Court of Appeals for the U.S. Armed Forces, where they were denied again. At a press conference in San Antonio, Fidell pleaded, "If anyone in the halls of government is listening to this, ask yourself, 'Why is the Army withholding its own investigation and Sgt. Bergdahl's testimony from the public eye?'"

In early October, a dozen national media companies, led by the local *San Antonio Express-News* and its parent company, Hearst Newspapers, filed their own petition with the Army Court of Criminal Appeals. Joined by the Associated Press, Bloomberg, BuzzFeed, Dow Jones (owner of *The Wall Street Journal*), McClatchy, *The New York Times*, Reuters, and *The Washington Post*, the companies cited the public's First Amendment right to know how this exercise in military justice—"a public act, conducted on the public's behalf, and therefore necessarily open to public scrutiny"—was being handled. There is a reason that civilian courts do not bar access to unsealed documents in such an authoritarian manner, they argued: "Without access to records, the public is left in the dark on the full nature of proceedings." In December, the Army turned the media companies down without explanation. Meanwhile, Mark Boal's production company, Page 1, had already somehow obtained the coveted report and shared it with his partners at *Serial.*

Following the hearing in San Antonio, all eyes were on Lieutenant Colonel Visger, to whom it fell to adjudicate what he had heard over two days of emotionally charged testimony from both sides of the case. The government had called officers Billings and Silvino to describe the chaos of June 30, 2009, and the dangers and miseries of the searches that followed. As her final witness, lead prosecutor Major Margaret Kurz called Lieutenant Colonel Baker. She asked the battalion commander how severely the searches had handicapped his mission, but was caught off guard when Baker replied that the DUSTWUN, while difficult, had also produced some of the greatest disruptions of Taliban networks that he had seen at any point during the war.

On the second day of hearings, every uniformed soldier and officer in the basement hearing room stood at attention as Fidell called Major General Kenneth Dahl to the witness stand to convey in his own words what the Army had refused to release to the public. For his final question, Fidell asked if Dahl had an opinion regarding a possible jail sentence.

"I do not believe that there is a jail sentence at the end of this process," Dahl said. "I do not think it would be appropriate."

Terry Russell was the final defense witness, and his brutal testimony froze the room.

"I don't know about you, sir," Russell said, turning to address Visger directly, "but if I have diarrhea more than a couple or three days, I'm thinking there's something seriously wrong with me, and I want to get some treatment. And you and I have the luxury of using toilet paper. . . . When you are cleaning yourself of diarrhea and your clothing is soiled, your bedding is soiled, you are cleaning yourself with your hands and the only way to clean your hands is to rub your hands in dirt to get the fecal matter off, and the only water that you have available to clean your mud-covered hands is your own urine—that's what Sgt. Bergdahl had to do."

Russell dispelled the popular myths. Bergdahl hadn't helped the Taliban with military strategy, he said, because "the Haqqanis hold the United States soldier in absolute contempt" and they didn't care about or respect what he had to say. Russell recounted the many ways that Bergdahl had tried to escape until he finally succeeded and was captured again. Russell called him "an Army of one" who took command of his own hopeless battle for four years and eleven months.

"Bowe Bergdahl has been accused of many things, but what you cannot accuse him of is his lack of resistance, his willingness to serve his country with honor in captivity, to do what he had to do to maintain his dignity and return." In closing, Russell grew emotional. "I've asked this question of many POWs. 'Did you do your best?' And all you can do is look at yourself in the mirror and say to yourself, 'I did the best job I could do.'" Russell gathered himself and concluded: "I think Sgt. Bergdahl did that. He did the best job that he could do, and I respect him for it."

To the media assembled at Fort Sam that day, Russell and Dahl's testimonies marked what seemed like a turning point. Now that the facts of Bergdahl's suffering were known, surely the national mood toward his case would swing in his favor. But the feeling was short-lived. On October 5, in a strenuously balanced report, Visger delivered his recommendations: Given the lack of evidence that anyone was killed or wounded searching for Bergdahl, the case should proceed to a special court-martial (also known as a "straight special"), a lesser trial for lesser crimes that cannot result in jail time.

This time, the call-and-response cycle between events and the entertainment news business grew more focused and more punitive. Fox News anchors were outraged, or at least they acted that way. That month, audiences of millions were told that Bergdahl had "defected" and given aid and comfort to the enemy, that seven men from his own platoon had died searching for him, that he had told his fellow soldiers that he wanted to "join the Taliban," that he had departed his post "during combat," and that the U.S. government had "intercepted phone calls" from Bergdahl to his platoon telling them that he was gone and not coming back.

There was no evidence for any of this, but it was the perception of reality that mattered most.

ON OCTOBER 12, 2015, Senator John McCain was at a campaign stop in Pelham, New Hampshire, rallying support for his comrade, Senator Lindsey Graham. McCain had been a man of two minds on Bergdahl and the prisoner exchange. In August 2009, he had seemed sympathetic to Bergdahl's family's plight. Over the ensuing years, he had vacillated between supporting and opposing a Taliban prisoner swap, and, in 2014, he lobbied Obama to bring the country's last POW home sooner. But when a *Boston Herald* reporter in New Hampshire asked McCain for his reactions to Visger's recommendations, he was blunt:

"If it comes out that he has no punishment, we're going to have to have a hearing in the Senate Armed Services Committee."

As chairman of said committee, McCain controlled Pentagon budgets and officer assignments and promotions, and he was the gateway through which every officer's career must pass, including those now deciding Bergdahl's fate. Fidell spoke out immediately, accusing McCain of "unlawful congressional influence," a play on the common terminology of unlawful command influence (UCI), codified in Article 37 of the UCMJ. Several military legal experts concurred: McCain was meddling with due process and had all but guaranteed that the Army would take a harder line than if he had said nothing.

Sentiments toward Bergdahl were no better in the House Armed Services Committee (HASC), where Texas Republican Mac Thornberry, who had taken the chairmanship from McKeon the prior January, was overseeing an independent investigation into the Obama administration's quasi-legal prisoner swap. What was done was done. There would be no charges against Obama or Hagel or Kerry or anyone else, but the committee could at least make its case that their NDAA amendment had been broken. While House Republicans assembled the evidence for their report, Mark Boal and Sarah Koenig readied for podcast launch. As Koenig interviewed more and more Blackfoot Company veterans, word of what was coming had spread fast, and by the time the first episode was set to drop onto millions of cell phones worldwide, *Serial*'s audience was primed with a weeklong news crescendo orchestrated by a savvy House committee staffer.

While repeating the official line that the report would be released on Thursday, December 10, the Hill staffer shared it with a select few national security writers in a series of incremental leaks. On Monday, Tuesday, and Wednesday, stories about Obama's alleged lawlessness trickled into the news, and when *Serial*'s first episode dropped that Thursday morning, the streams converged into a flood of headlines about *Serial*'s scoop. Bergdahl had admitted what he had done. He even had an explanation: He had wanted to prove that he was a real-life Jason Bourne. For a soldier accused of serious crimes, this was not a sound legal strategy. Friday's *New York Post* called it, "The Bourne Stupidity."

Before *Serial* went to air, Bergdahl's attorneys had been awaiting an imminent decision on the future of the case from FORSCOM commander, four-star General Robert Abrams, who was not bound to Dahl or Visger's recommendations. On Thursday and Friday, as Bergdahl's confessions surged through the media, General Abrams and his legal team were in their final days of deliberations, and they were listening to the news. Abrams knew the case well; during Bergdahl's captivity he had been Hagel's top military aide. He was also the scion of an Army dynasty—his father and both of his older brothers had been generals.

There were only a select few positions in the uniformed military where Abrams could still climb, all of which ran through McCain's committee. If McCain's comment about the case had shown Abrams the path, then hearing the accused soldier admit his crime to a Hollywood screenwriter on national airwaves was something approaching a dare. On Monday morning, December 14, Abrams announced his decision: Sergeant Bergdahl was going to a general court-martial. If he was found guilty of both charges, he could go back inside a cage for the rest of his life.

TWENTY-TWO

THE NOISE

In July 2015, after the Army had determined Bergdahl's charges but before General Abrams had called for a general court-martial, Bergdahl's commanders in Texas approved his request to take a personal leave to visit Kim Dellacorva in Northern California. He flew in plainclothes on a commercial airliner. Shortly after arriving at what had been planned as an opportunity to unwind in a peaceful remote setting with one of the only people with whom he had ever felt truly at ease, a Mendocino County Sheriff's Office task force arrived at Dellacorva's home with warrants to search the property.

Growing limited amounts of marijuana is legal in California, and while Mendocino had long been known as a place where police and pot growers coexisted with a tacit understanding, the task force arrived that day on what it said was an anonymous tip about a serious criminal operation. (It was later revealed that the series of events began with a call from Bergdahl's Army commanders in Texas, intending to inform local law enforcement about his travels amid innumerable death threats. The exact motives for the sheriff's department's next decision—to raid Dellacorva's home while Bergdahl was there—remain unclear.) Bergdahl presented his military identification, and explained who he was and what he was doing in Northern California. They did not arrest him, and, as far as Bergdahl was concerned, the incident might have ended there. But when the police report appeared in a local Mendocino newspaper, conservative media outlets ran the story with gleeful scorn.

The Washington Times reported that Bergdahl had been "busted," even as the county sheriff explained that the infamous soldier had not, in fact, been arrested. Rather, said Sheriff Tom Allman, Bergdahl had gone "above politeness" while trying to help his deputies handle his delicate legal situation; one sheriff's deputy called him "a perfect gentleman." After his commanders at Fort Sam were alerted, news of Bergdahl's brush with the law reached the Pentagon, where officials requested that the local police drive him south to Santa Rosa to meet an Army officer who would escort him to his appropriate duty station.

Appearing on *Fox & Friends,* retired Special Forces officer (and future 2018 congressional candidate) Lieutenant Colonel Michael Waltz added new, highly questionable embellishments to his original story: "[Bergdahl] is responsible for the death of multiple soldiers that I personally witnessed," Waltz claimed, incredibly. "I'm glad the Army is going to hold him accountable, but this is just another selfish act by a soldier who doesn't have regard for the Army and his country."

Two weeks later, a wounded Navy SEAL veteran stepped forward with a grave new allegation. Retired Senior Chief Petty Officer James "Jimmy" Hatch told his DUSTWUN story to his local newspaper in Norfolk, Virginia, which led in turn to a call from CNN. On September 11, journalist Anderson Cooper sat down with Hatch in an exclusive prime-time interview, part of a special episode commemorating 9/11 and the ever-widening ripples of its impact. Hatch recalled the night of July 9, 2009, in harrowing detail: the SEALs and their service dog, Remco, jumping off a helicopter into a hot landing zone and taking heavy fire from Taliban with AK-47s, a belt-fed machine gun, and RPGs. "It was chaos," Hatch said. But as he understood it, they were there to rescue a U.S. soldier, and no matter what the kid had done or how little they thought of him, they accepted their mission without protest.

"He was an American, and he had a mom, and I didn't want his mom to see him get his head chopped off on YouTube," he told Cooper.

When Hatch saw two Taliban maneuvering a few hundred yards away, he sent Remco out front to intercept them. The Taliban opened fire: two bullets hit Remco, dropping him immediately, and one 7.62-caliber bullet caught Hatch just above the knee, shattering his femur and sending shards of bone out through an exit wound. The force of the impact flipped him, and although he tried to tell himself not to make any noise that could draw the enemy's attention, he hit the ground screaming in pain. As the firefight raged around him, the SEALs gave Hatch a morphine lollipop and loaded him and Remco's limp body onto a medevac helicopter.

A week after he was shot, Hatch lay in Walter Reed Medical Center in Bethesda, Maryland, confronting his new realities. His career as a SEAL was over. Remco was dead. Hatch would undergo eighteen operations on his leg in two years. Depressed and adrift, he began washing down painkillers with vodka and made a suicide plan. When his wife saw him with a gun in his mouth, she called the SEAL friend who had put him on the helicopter the night of the raid, and they checked him into the psychiatric ward on the fifth floor of the Naval Medical Center in Portsmouth, Virginia. As he began the long work of rebuilding his body and mind—what he called "the war after the war"—his SEAL buddies would call to check in anytime Bergdahl appeared in the news.

On the 9/11 broadcast, Hatch said that Bergdahl, as an American, deserved his day in court, but that he should also understand what his fellow soldiers had sacrificed for him. As for the mission that ended his career and killed a beloved dog, Hatch blamed himself for taking the Taliban bullet. "It was a failure," he said, "and I was the cause of it."

Three days before Christmas in 2015, Army judge Colonel Jeffery Nance arraigned Sergeant Bergdahl on Fort Bragg. Bergdahl had flown to North Carolina from Texas alongside soldiers assigned to travel with him for his own protection—the first run of what would become a routine 2,800-mile commute to an eventual twenty-five hearings. While millions of Americans clamored for violent and vengeful justice, Bergdahl was never recognized in public and traveled without incident.

The Fort Bragg Courthouse sits atop a knoll flanked by a grove of Carolina pines and the base dental clinic. A cold December rain fell as Bergdahl arrived in full Army dress. Over his right shoulder, he wore the braided blue cord of the infantry. His chest included the combat infantry badge he had earned following the firefight at Omna, and his upper arms showed the sergeant stripes the Army had issued during his captivity. He was joined in court by his senior military counsel, Lieutenant Colonel Frank Rosenblatt, who had joined Fidell's team in October 2014, while he was stationed in Hawaii as legal staff to a Navy SEAL Special Operations Command. (Fidell did not fly in for the brief arraignment formalities.)

Raised in a military family, Rosenblatt had been commissioned as a second lieutenant in the Army after graduating from James Madison University in Virginia, where he studied religion and philosophy. He served as an infantryman for two years in South Korea before shifting to intelligence. In 2002, he deployed to the Balkans, where he briefed a young, fast-rising brigadier general named David Petraeus on the hunt for high value Bosnian Serbs who had been indicted for war crimes by the International Criminal Court at the Hague. Before 9/11, Rosenblatt hadn't planned on making his career in the Army. But as they had for so many, the attacks altered his trajectory. In 2003, he deployed to Iraq with the 82nd Airborne. His unit had been tasked with jumping into a combat zone to seize Saddam International Airport, but ended up fighting off Iraqi attacks on the supply lines that kept the 3rd Infantry Division's tanks rolling on what would be known as the Thunder Run route to Baghdad. Iraq was also where Rosenblatt first saw how quickly men in combat could spiral out of control and how much damage they could cause. After one company in his battalion killed several unarmed civilians in Fallujah, the backlash turned the city into one of the country's bloodiest.

After Iraq, Rosenblatt earned his law degree at the University of Virginia. In one of his first big cases, he prosecuted a group of infantrymen who had returned from Iraq in 2007 and gone on violent sprees in Colorado Springs. At Fort Carson, he worked under Major General Mark Graham, one of the first Army generals to sound the alarm about the military's mental health crisis. As veteran suicides turned into an urgent epidemic, Rosenblatt's attention turned to the less publicized trend of criminality spreading through the ranks. The cause was clear: Fighting two wars at once, the Army had lowered its standards too fast and issued too many waivers for bad candidates, including men who had criminal rap sheets, suffered from mental illness, or, like Bergdahl, had washed out of other service branches. In 2015, Rosenblatt, by now a lieutenant colonel, had been reassigned from his Special Operations Command in Hawaii to take over as the executive officer for the military's Trial Defense Services at Fort Belvoir, Virginia. Defending Bergdahl was a job that few wanted, but one for which he was uniquely prepared.

Over the 2015 Christmas break, the Pentagon readied its case against its most hated soldier in generations. In 1970, when the Army convicted Lieutenant William Calley as the only guilty party for the My Lai Massacre, he attracted fierce support among the rank and file who, even after he admitted to killing twenty-two Vietnamese civilians (including young children and a Buddhist monk), saw him as a scapegoat for orders that came from men above him. Even Bobby Garwood—the Marine private who disappeared under murky circumstances from his base near Da Nang before collaborating for years with his North Vietnamese captors—had been spared the collective enmity that greeted Bergdahl upon his return.

Bergdahl's prosecutors had public opinion on their side, but with it came expectations of swift justice. The collective outrage over the prisoner swap led to an equally widespread assumption that the Army had not brought its best case to the preliminary hearing the prior September. By this logic, Visger had made lenient recommendations because he had not been presented with Hatch's case, or any of the abundant evidence that would convict Bergdahl beyond a reasonable doubt—and which Army lawyers were deliberately withholding from the defense ahead of trial. Left out of this hypothesis was the possibility that the case was never as simple as those narratives had made it seem.

Army prosecutors were at the bottom of a narrow chain of command that began at the highest levels of government. It extended downward from McCain (the lawmaker with the most power over the military) to Abrams (the legacy-bearing scion to an illustrious Army dynasty) to the military attorneys on the Judge Advocate General (JAG) staff at FORSCOM, which, without ever having staged a general court-martial, was expected to build a crack squad that would prove what everyone who listens to the news already believed: Bergdahl was responsible for numerous deaths and casualties.

After the arraignment, the prosecution team was overhauled. Kurz was removed as the lead JAG, and the government's team more than tripled in size as ten more attorneys were brought on ahead of trial. When the defense responded in May by adding four more JAGs to its team, conservative outlets pounced. "Army Goes All-in on Bowe Bergdahl Defense," *The Washington Times* declared, without mentioning that the Pentagon's legal team was roughly twice as large. As the trial neared, FORSCOM would ultimately assign fifty JAGs to Bergdahl's prosecution, an incredible reallocation of resources that, in a bizarre simulacra of the early days of the DUSTWUN itself, took active-duty attorneys away from assignments at command posts across the country and backlogged case files throughout the military court system. (By comparison, the case of Khalid Sheik Mohammed, the 9/11 mastermind held at Guantanamo, had merited only fourteen JAGs.)

As the Pentagon team swelled, so, too, did the government's trove of classified evidence. At the preliminary hearing, prosecutors had told Visger that they had obtained roughly three hundred thousand pages of classified documents, a number that struck Bergdahl's defense attorneys as inexplicably high. By the following summer, the number had climbed into the millions. The message was clear: The Pentagon had the evidence it needed, but because the government controlled both the documents and the classification procedures, those materials would not be shared through the usual discovery process. Prosecutors also attempted to block the defense from making their own independent reviews of any classified material. To the defense, the classification juggernaut looked like a bureaucratic bypass around due process. Whether it was media-fueled demands for mob justice, or McCain's interference, Bergdahl's legal case was now being guided by a series of extrajudicial circumstances that had left Bergdahl in a legal purgatory, floating somewhere between the Army chain of command and the feedback loops of conservative entertainment news.

To Fidell, the case provided clear incentives for constitutionally guided reforms. The Pentagon was as aware of these issues as it was institutionally disinclined to address them. From the "Don't ask, don't tell" policy on gays in the military to endemic sexual harassment, recent history had shown that few things more easily rankled the Pentagon than congressional interference with internal military affairs. If Fidell thought, as several of his trial motions indicated, that Bergdahl's case illustrated the need for reform, the Army couldn't allow itself to be caught off guard. After Fidell and Rosenblatt flew to Prague in April 2015 to attend an international conference on military law, they discovered that the Army staff had sent a uniformed officer to attend the conference with them so that he could report back to the Pentagon on Fidell's activities. The defense demanded an explanation, which was never provided, and the moment passed as yet another curiosity of uncertain import and a reminder that this was no simple desertion case. From 2010 to 2014, deliberations over how and even whether to bring

Bergdahl home had revealed ideological rifts at the highest levels of government. Bitterness over the prisoner swap and Visger's recommendations had only driven the political wedge deeper into the divide.

In early 2016, the tussling over classified evidence came to a head. Media onlookers speculated that the defense was deliberately delaying things. In truth, Army JAGs' insistence on shielding millions of documents behind classification laws had paralyzed the entire process. When Colonel Nance ruled that prosecutors needed to abide by the norms of discovery, the government appealed the decision to the Army Court of Criminal Appeals (ACCA), and the court-martial was put on hold for four months.

By the time hearings resumed on May 17, 2016—with the ACCA upholding Nance's ruling—the case faced a swarm of political distractions. As Obama attempted to pass his legacy to Hillary Clinton, one of the most polarizing and entrenched figures in the Washington establishment, Donald Trump's campaign of media domination had turned the election into an all-consuming spectacle—and Bergdahl into a punching bag of populist ire. Fidell argued that the rhetoric surrounding the case—what General Dahl had called "the noise"—was so inescapable that it deprived Bergdahl of his constitutional right to due process and a fair trial.

Trump had latched onto the scandal early. In mid-July 2014, as Bergdahl was being escorted to twice-daily intelligence debriefings, Trump called in to Fox News with a stark read on the situation:

> So here we trade five killers that want to destroy us, that are already back in service to try and knock us out, and we trade five killers for one traitor, and now we're going to give the traitor $350,000 and we put him back to work like nothing happened, and they don't investigate.

Fox anchor Martha MacCallum didn't challenge Trump's hysteria. Instead, she speculated that since the Army's promised court-martial hadn't yet begun, the delay was an early sign of a White House cover-up. Trump's analysis may have been warped, but he wasn't the only American baffled and outraged by the entire affair. Bergdahl, as he saw it, was a crucible of every national ill:

> This is just one of many disasters. This is a catastrophe what's going on in the country, just an absolute catastrophe. . . . Everything happening in this country is a calamity. There's nothing good.

One year later, when Trump descended a gilded escalator to the event where he declared his candidacy, he included Bergdahl in his opening rant of patriotic grievances. That summer, Trump made Bergdahl one of his favorite campaign rally gags, calling him a traitor at more than sixty-five separate campaign events while also cycling through a slideshow of punishment fantasies, including dropping him into ISIS territory "before we bomb the hell out of it," or tossing him from an airplane without a parachute. Most frequently, though, Trump called for Bergdahl to be executed.

> In the old days when we were strong and wise, we shoot a guy like that. A traitor! He's a traitor. He's a traitor. . . . No, no, we shoot him! I don't care! In the old days, when we were strong, and wise, traitors were treated very, very harshly.

To the approving shouts and hollers of his supporters, Trump would raise his arms and pantomime pulling the trigger himself.

***SERIAL* WAS MEANT** to be everything Trump wasn't. Where Trump exploited the voiceless soldier for his own gain, *Serial* would give Bergdahl the chance to speak for himself. With the same deft storytelling and investigative chops that had made the first season a hit, Boal and Koenig would bring fairness and humanity to a wartime tragedy that Trump had exploited for bloodlust and laughs.

From their first moments, Boal's taped phone calls were a revelation. Here was something that no one else could provide: an invitation to sit with Bergdahl, lean back, and listen with an open mind as he explained himself. The trauma was still raw as he laid bare the hells he had endured, including torture that he hadn't been able to retell in formal questioning before a gallery of psychologists and government agents. He had been held in one tiny cell in total darkness for so long that he had lost the ability to understand not merely who he was, he told Boal, but *what* he was.

"He's a mystery," Boal told Koenig in the first episode. "Nobody even really knows who he is. . . . Nobody knows why he did it." For Boal, helping a traumatized soldier rebuild the pieces of his identity seemed like a return to his journalistic roots. It also made for a good story. Most compelling was the paradox at the heart of his alleged crimes; Bergdahl had abandoned his buddies in a war zone, he claimed, in order to save them.

"How do you judge somebody like that?" Boal asked. "How do you judge him?"

It was a compelling question—which a military judge had only just begun considering. To the story's central tension, Koenig applied the same detective's skepticism that had made her relationship with convicted murderer Adnan Syed so engrossing in the show's first season. Just as she had questioned the fairness and rigor in Syed's case, she didn't rely on Dahl's findings and instead set out to solve Bergdahl's riddle anew. Koenig asked whether she could even trust Bergdahl, and specifically, "whether his description of what was happening around him is accurate or believable. Because of course this explanation could be a story he invented."

With each new episode, Boal and Koenig rummaged through the

same dubious intelligence and Taliban propaganda that had sensationalized the scandal and aggravated Russell during Bergdahl's reintegration. Months after Russell's testimony in Texas had seemed to provide a definitive dismissal to the rumors, Boal and Koenig wondered aloud whether Bergdahl had converted to Islam, collaborated with the Taliban, or gone rabbit hunting with his guards. "I heard another [rumor] that he played soccer," Boal recalled.

To get to the bottom of these and other questions, Koenig called the Taliban, playing up the surreal comedy of the situation while providing no insight into who the source was or how she came by him. The Taliban spokesman provided her with a detailed itinerary about Bergdahl's first days in captivity, which matched the early Taliban misdirection and baited ambush traps from July 2009—and directly contradicted Dahl's report. Faced with having to rely on Dahl's investigation or her Taliban source, Koenig went with the latter. And while that decision made for entertaining listening, it introduced irreconcilable contradictions that strayed further from the facts and closer to Congressman Peter King's feared "cinematographic view of history."

Though Koenig cited Dahl's report throughout the eleven episodes of *Serial*, and despite the pleas from Fidell and the rounds of First Amendment lawsuits from media companies demanding the Pentagon release it, *Serial* never disclosed that Boal had shared the secret documents with them months earlier. When a *New York Times* reporter asked whether they had indeed obtained them, *Serial* producers declined to comment.

The concern for Bergdahl's lawyers wasn't whether Boal and *Serial* were breaking any laws; the legality of the Army's protective order blocking media access to the report had always been suspect. If anything, Boal's cavalier methods highlighted the absurdity of the Army's rules. As one defense motion in February 2016 pointed out, the documents had been unsealed and openly referred to throughout the Article

32 preliminary hearing, theoretically providing an opportunity for a courtroom filibuster: "Had doing so not been so flagrantly wasteful of all parties' time, these documents could literally have been read into the record for all to hear."

That winter, Koenig, Boal, and executive producer Julie Snyder embarked on an energetic promotional campaign. Koenig asked for patience from her critics. "Everyone wait for us to be done. That's my dream world," she told *New York* magazine. Snyder reassured *The New York Times* that they recognized the ethical minefield into which they had wandered, and that they would not put entertainment value ahead of the public interest. "No, we're not holding back on something that the world needs to know," Snyder said.

But military law experts were skeptical. Beyond the widespread and genuine confusion about *Serial*'s methods, it was unclear what public interest was served by recycling sensational and scurrilous evidence in a case with the potential to determine policy reforms not only on domestic issues like mental health screening for the military, but on the future viability of the detainment camp at Guantanamo Bay—all before the trial had even begun.

Bergdahl's parents had been hopeful when they first heard that Koenig was going to address their son's case. But when it emerged that she had teamed up not just with the entertainment industry, but with the CIA and Pentagon's most reliable Hollywood client, they backed out. Boal flew to Idaho to make his plea in person, and Bob explained why he would not be a cooperative source: "I told him that anyone who promotes torture for profit doesn't have the integrity to tell my son's story." As far as Bob was concerned, *Serial* was engaging in deception. "Every episode should have opened with a warning: 'Warning: This series has been micromanaged by a public relations asset for CIA.'"

Serial interviewed a staggering number of sources covering the full range of perspectives. Koenig gained fresh insights from key players involved in the DUSTWUN, including Mike Flynn, who, without citing any evidence, told her that he had zero doubt that men had died searching for Bergdahl. From Flynn—who had seen the same intelligence that Furlong and Wilson had and who knew that by July 14, 2009, the intelligence community had consensus that Bergdahl was already in North Waziristan—the reply smacked of politics. Koenig didn't buy it, and she was tenacious about getting answers. The challenge was that the facts depended on the perspectives and perceptions of the men involved.

At the end of the show's first episode, Command Sergeant Major Kenneth Wolfe, the battalion's ranking NCO, effectively let Koenig in on the secret that the Army had been covering up from the start. The DUSTWUN had been miserable for Wolfe's young soldiers, and he worked to keep up morale any way he knew how. He told jokes, gave out tobacco, and reminded them that no matter why Bergdahl had walked off, looking for him was the "good and honorable" thing to do. And yet, in the back of his mind, Wolfe told Koenig, he knew it was all pointless, because Bergdahl was already over the border.

Soldiers like Sergeant Johnny Rice had figured out the ruse from the start. Others, like Cornelison, accepted the Army logic of their catch-22; even if Bergdahl was no longer in Afghanistan, they would damn sure do their best to find him there. Koenig refused to believe that the Army would knowingly engage in such deception, because, she said, "that's just wrong." But as the former Blackfoot Company officer explained it, that's exactly what had happened.

Specific terms, like "personnel recovery" and "Bergdahl," were used as cheat codes by mission planners for months. In some cases, the officer said, the scheme reflected the Army's own internal bureaucratic machinations: "Type this code, get the asset, and my boss will be happy." Just as Rice had seen the logic behind the madness, the former officer didn't blame mission planners who found opportunities in the crisis. "It's not lying," he said. "That's just the way it works."

According to one former Pentagon official, the strategic decision had been made early on by upper echelon officers, who then kept the dynamic alive as long as possible. "It was common knowledge that commanders in the field used the search for Bergdahl as a justification for more aggressive tactics to achieve stability in the area," the former official said. "Everyone knew it was going on."

TWENTY-THREE

GUILTY

In May 2016, Donald Trump was invited to deliver the keynote address at the annual Rolling Thunder rally, the same speaking slot that had been reserved for Bob Bergdahl four years earlier. Trump delivered his speech in front of the steps of the Lincoln Memorial, where, each year from 2010 to 2014, hundreds of POW activists calling themselves "Bowe's Army" had gathered in his support. But in 2016, outside of Idaho, where Pocatello bikers never stopped supporting the former prisoner and his family, Bergdahl was something that the vast majority of patriotic bikers decided they would rather forget about.

Trump should have been an awkward fit to address the country's largest POW rally. He himself had deferred military service multiple times, and he had gone after McCain just days after declaring his candidacy. "He is not a war hero," said Trump. "He is a war hero because he was captured. I like people who weren't captured."

Rolling Thunder kept Trump's invitation under wraps until the day of the event, a decision that led to a smaller crowd and a complaint from Trump, who said that he had expected crowds similar to those that had greeted Martin Luther King Jr. when he delivered his "I Have a Dream" speech in the same spot in April 1963. Trump's address was a brief version of his usual routine and a rare instance with no mention of Bergdahl. At one point, when he called Obama "grossly incompetent," a lone voice rang out from the crowd: "Obama's a traitor!"

That summer, Bergdahl's attorneys noted the incredible volume of vitriol directed at their client on the internet, much of it casting him as Obama's treasonous accomplice. Twenty-four hours a day, seven days a week, social media brimmed with #Bergdahl posts and memes from what appeared to be an inexhaustible army of grassroots activists. Trafficking in paranoia, some used the menacing graphics of traditional negative campaign ads while presenting the prisoner swap as proof of Obama's secret plot for Muslim domination, Obama's Muslim subversion of American Christendom, and Obama's Rose Garden activation of Bob Bergdahl as a sleeper agent of Islamic terror.

American politics had always been a sporting arena in which half-truths and spin were common maneuvers for seasoned operatives. But Trump didn't play by the old rules, and as his rise consumed the country's attention, his fixation on Bergdahl provided an early sound check for his campaign's feedback loop of social media amplification: the paid trolls, engineered bots, and other cyber innovations that would define the political moment in the United States and much of Europe. Businesses in Bergdahl's hometown began receiving harassing comments from random Facebook users with no connections to Hailey or to Idaho, and in some cases, with no friends at all. No one could explain it. But in 2016, as Trump's hypnotic fugues carried him to the Republican nomination, inexplicable phenomena were becoming the norm.

Trump told his crowds that thirty years earlier Bergdahl would have been shot. In fact, the Army hadn't sentenced a deserter to death since 1945, and in that case there had been no disputing the charges. In Private Eddie Slovik's own words, he deserted his infantry unit in the midst of battle in the Hürtgen Forest in Germany because he was afraid to die. "I was so scared, nerves and trembling," he wrote in a letter to General Eisenhower pleading clemency. "I couldn't move. I stayed there in my foxhole till it was quiet and I was able to move. I then walked into town."

Slovik hadn't come from much. Before the war, he was a juvenile delinquent in Detroit who saw better chances for himself in the Army. The draft board told him the only reason they took him was that his rap sheet had cleaned up after marriage, and the Army was desperate for soldiers. Slovik's court-martial was held on Armistice Day, November 11, 1944, on the second floor of an occupied Nazi building in Röetgen, Germany, just a few miles from the Hürtgen Forest, where every combat officer in his division was being shot at in a raging battle. After less than two hours of jury deliberations, the Army ordered Slovik "shot to death with musketry." Eisenhower's approval of the sentence surprised many subordinate officers, including even the division commander who had filed charges for it. Eleven privates and one sergeant were selected from each of the three battalions in Slovik's regiment and given their orders: Kill the deserter.

Despite pep talks from officers and a chaplain, some of the soldier executioners had doubts. "I hope I don't have to live the rest of my life thinking it was my bullet that killed him," said one man. "It's bad enough we have to kill these goddam krauts, much less one of our own," mused another. Others were eager. "I got no sympathy for that sonofabitch," another said. "He deserted us, didn't he? He didn't give a damn how many of us got the hell shot out of us; why should we care about him? I'll shoot his goddam heart out. If only one shot hits him, you'll know it's mine."

A few days after Trump was elected president, Gerald Sutton considered how he would feel if Obama pardoned Bergdahl. Along with Chelsea Manning, the former Army intelligence soldier who was then serving thirty-five years for leaking government secrets, Bergdahl's name had been added to an informal list of potentials. Sutton lived near Coe in Michigan, and when they spent time together the conversation inevitably returned to their brief friendships with the Army's most-hated soldier. By the time Trump's rainy inaugural arrived, Sutton felt that the media had turned his legitimate gripe with Army censorship into a political circus. He'd seen enough and figured Bergdahl had too. He was ready to forgive. Coe had been as angry as any of them. But he also believed that Bergdahl had been punished enough.

"I think he was just a dude that made a really, really messed-up decision. He paid for it. He paid for it dearly," Coe said. But ultimately, "You gotta forgive people. I'm a Christian. God forgave all of us. It'd be pretty arrogant of me not to forgive."

SUTTON AND COE were the outliers. As an institution and a community, the Army demanded justice, and as Bergdahl's trial neared, the prosecution built its case around three men who it alleged had been wounded, maimed, and nearly killed as a result of Bergdahl's actions: Chief Petty Officer Jimmy Hatch, Specialist Jonathan Morita, and Master Sergeant Mark Allen, all now medically retired.

Allen was a national guardsman assigned with a small group of Americans as embedded tactical trainers (ETT), living with and leading Afghan soldiers. On July 8, 2009, Allen's ETT team was sent into a remote area of Paktika to track down information on the missing soldier when Allen was shot in the head. He was now brain damaged, wheelchair bound, and barely functional. The prosecution wanted him or his wife, Shannon, on the stand as victims of Bergdahl's decisions. Shannon thought Bergdahl was a traitor, the reason her husband was broken. The prosecution and defense sparred over whether she could testify in his place.

Captain John Marx, who had led Allen's mission that day, said it was messed up from the start; they hadn't been given updated maps or intelligence before they were thrown into the fray. Marx was an Air Force intelligence officer with no combat experience assigned to an Army billet in an Army mission because of personnel shortages. He reported in to FOB Kushamond, south of Mest. There was no intel brief delivered before the team set out toward Dila, a town where American troops had engaged Taliban soldiers every year since at least 2006. There was only a vague order: investigate two towns. Their only intel, that one town was friendly, was out of date. The five other

American soldiers in the unit had infantry training, but only one had combat experience. They lacked basic items: maps, secure comms, enough water for both themselves and the fifty Afghan National Army soldiers they led. By midnight they were critically low on water, radioing Kushamond for resupply before stepping off to the second village, but were denied. They had to call in their location several times because no one kept track of where they were. Kushamond's intelligence officers had no idea they were even in the area. That night, an Army after-action report claimed the soldiers let their guard down, most of them falling asleep. They woke up to orders to go back to the same village they'd visited the day before. This time, the intelligence officers at Kushamond warned them to expect more than one hundred fifty Taliban. It infuriated one of the team members, Staff Sergeant Jason Walters, to hear that threat assessment—it would have been nice to know that yesterday, he thought. The team's long-range radio ran out of batteries and they found themselves in a firefight.

Three Americans were wounded—Allen, Morita, and Specialist Charles Benson. Throughout the firefight, Walters had asked for air support, first requesting close air support (CAS), then demanding it, and finally begging for it, or any other help from higher—a medevac, a quick reaction force, an exfiltration team. Nothing got through to Kushamond; the radio operators inside the wire kept telling them that their water supply would be delivered shortly. An investigation into Allen's injuries faulted the leadership that sent the ETT team out despite their inexperience, lack of communications equipment, and unfamiliarity with the enemy, terrain, and weather.

The defense maintained that the chain of causality between Bergdahl's act and Allen and Morita's injuries was tenuous, composed of countless intervening decisions and events, and therefore impossible to prove beyond a reasonable doubt. The ETT mission, they noted, had already been planned before the DUSTWUN, not as a result of it. And, the emotional outrage that any jury of veterans would feel in the face of such horrific suffering would interfere with the cold logic of the law. After all, the summer of 2009 had been filled with bad decisions, and while prosecutors had cast Bergdahl as the first domino in an unambiguous chain reaction, the defense argued that it was more akin to the butterfly effect of chaos theory, in which a butterfly flapping its wings in California can trigger a typhoon weeks later in Thailand. No one blames the butterfly.

On June 30, 2017, Nance delivered his final ruling on the issue: The relevance of these men's injuries depended on whether or not Bergdahl was guilty of the second charge against him. If he was innocent, then the charges were immaterial. But if was guilty, then regardless of his motives or the intervening factors, he would be held fully responsible.

Nance had an unlikely résumé for a judge. As an artillery officer, he had seen combat in Iraq, joining patrols and kicking down doors before returning home and rising through the JAG Corps. With his arrival to Bergdahl's case, Nance had now presided over two of the most infamous, and dissimilar, criminal cases to come out of Afghanistan. In 2013, he had conducted the trial of Staff Sergeant Robert Bales, who, the previous year, had slipped off his base in Kandahar twice in one night, walking into two nearby villages and murdering sixteen unarmed civilians in their homes, in front of their families. With Nance on the bench, a military jury sentenced Bales to life in prison without parole. Nance had earned a reputation as a no-nonsense jurist with a blistering work ethic who could efficiently process criminal cases with minimum drama. JAGs arguing before him were held to high standards. Those who performed well, he mentored; those who didn't, he let know with blunt dressings down.

But Nance also relished intellectual sparring sessions with young JAGs over legal exactitudes. He had a wry sense of humor and would often remind both sides that the case required teamwork and civility. According to attorneys who knew him best, Nance loved what he did and had an abiding faith in the fairness and process of the law.

Bergdahl had been offered the choice at arraignment of being judged by a military jury or by Nance alone. At Fort Bragg, the jury pool would be drawn from the 82nd Airborne and the 18th Airborne corps, some of the Army's most hardcore combat divisions. On September 27, 2017, Bergdahl decided to take his chances with Nance alone.

As pretrial motions dragged into their second year, FORSCOM called in huge numbers of support staff for public affairs officers (PAO) at Fort Bragg. Units were flown in from Texas, Oklahoma, and Washington State to manage the media, regardless of how little there was to manage. This maximalist approach led to absurd staging scenes; fewer than ten reporters and photographers would meet at 6:00 a.m. to be loaded onto an idling motorcade of school buses and passenger vans capable of carrying more than one hundred people. One officer estimated that over the course of Bergdahl's twenty-five hearings, these PAO teams cost the Army tens of millions of dollars.

By the fall of 2017, with both sides still wrangling over classified evidence, Nance was pushing them to wrap it up and prepare for trial. There would always be more questions that the defense wanted explained but that the Army was either unwilling or unable to answer, such as why Bergdahl had received a mysterious eleven-year extension of his enlistment papers. Then, in mid-October, as the trial date loomed, the defense announced a stunning reversal: Sergeant Bergdahl had decided to plead guilty.

BOWE'S PARENTS AND CLOSEST friends offered to be in North Carolina for his plea. Most had already made trips to see him in Texas since his return. But after his decision to throw himself on the mercy of the court, Bergdahl and his attorneys asked his parents and friends not to come. Their appearance would only trigger another media frenzy. He needed to face his consequences alone.

At the October 16 hearing, Nance asked Bergdahl to explain in his own words why he believed he was guilty of each charge. Sitting up in his characteristic perpendicular posture and speaking in a clear and affectless baritone, Bergdahl said that he had intended to shirk his responsibilities on the morning he left.

"I understand I had a duty to defend OP Mest and Task Force Yukon," he said. "I knew it was against the law."

Nance took him through his plea step by step, a rigid question-and-answer meant to ensure that he understood the gravity of his decision and actually believed that he was guilty per the precise language of the charge: "Desertion with intent to avoid hazardous duty or shirk important service." Only once, when Nance asked whether he had seen his duties at OP Mest as "important," did their conversation crack the barrier of formality. Part of the platoon's mission at Mest had involved manning a traffic checkpoint to look for cars carrying Taliban fighters or explosives, a task which, since the Taliban could simply cross the road a quarter mile away, had struck Bergdahl as "a bit of a joke."

"Did you believe that your plan was more important?" Nance asked.

"Yes, sir," he replied. "That was the choice."

Before his guilty plea, Bergdahl's attorneys had been planning to move forward with a motion to declare him as lacking the mental competency to understand what the Army had required of him. It was a form of an insanity plea. But as Rosenblatt stood to introduce the motion in late September, Bergdahl tugged at his sleeve and spoke softly but urgently in his ear. Nance called for a recess, and when both sides returned, Rosenblatt explained that the defense had decided not to pursue that argument. For the first time in nearly three years, Bergdahl had publicly taken charge of his own legal team. There were many things he was willing to admit about himself, but insanity was not among them.

Dellacorva once said of Bergdahl that the part of his psyche that made him different was also what had kept him intact, alive, and resilient in captivity. His parents agreed with her assessment. What men like Cody Full had seen as Bergdahl's greatest flaws had become his greatest strengths. And yet, over the course of his legal hearings, his attorneys had presented his psychological history as critical mitigating evidence. The Coast Guard had identified his defects, and the Army took him anyway. Soldiers in his own unit had noted them, and in at least one instance, when Sergeant Greg Leatherman tried to air his concerns about Bergdahl's mental status, his superiors turned a deaf ear.

Each time the issue was raised in court, Bergdahl's mind was put on display for public dissection. Reporters transcribed what they heard about his inner torments, his early reading difficulties, his pained relationship with his family, and his private disclosures to a defense psychologist about his innermost thoughts of self-mutilation. It was an inhuman public flaying. But it also helped Bergdahl's case.

At sentencing, the defense called on Dr. Charles Morgan, a Yale University professor, forensic psychologist, former CIA medical officer, and SERE specialist (who had deployed to Afghanistan with the Army in 2011), to explain the nuances of Bergdahl's disordered thinking. By the end of his testimony on November 1, 2017, Morgan would spend more time on the stand than any other defense witness. After nineteen hours of evaluation, Morgan diagnosed Bergdahl with schizotypal personality disorder, the same condition that a board of Army psychologists had independently diagnosed three years earlier. The disorder is rare, afflicting fewer than 5 percent of Americans, and it can present in ways that would strike most people as mere eccentricity—just Bowe being Bowe. Unlike schizophrenics, schizotypals do not suffer from total breaks with reality, but are often preoccupied and lost in their own thoughts. They rarely have intimate relationships, and tend to build rich fantasy lives to compensate; overactive imaginations fuel big ideas about life, the universe, and unseen forces determining outcomes that others cannot see. The disorder is commonly shared by first-degree family members. There is no known treatment.

According to Morgan, the rare disorder was compounded by the stress of Bergdahl's lesser conditions of PTSD and social anxiety. In his youth, his fraught relationship with his father had been a source of disabling anxiety and fear—Bergdahl told Morgan stories of his dad putting his fist through walls and smacking him for disobedience. Bowe began sleepwalking and having stress-induced nightmares, signs of emotional distress in children. In his adolescence, his father's anger, even over little things like forgetting the name of a power tool, could trigger paralyzing anxiety and tunnel vision. Morgan concluded that Bergdahl had suffered from PTSD even before enlisting in the Army.

The tricky thing about the condition, Morgan cautioned, is that he had no way of knowing whether Bowe was recounting a record of facts or a record of feelings. Had his father been abusive, or was Bowe oversensitive? Morgan said that the distinction was beside the point. One's perception defines one's reality. This is particularly true in children, and Morgan cited cases in which two children of the same parents growing up in the same house emerge with entirely different psychological outcomes: "One is fine. One is not."

Morgan explained that Bergdahl tested as highly intelligent, well above average. But with schizotypals, intellectual assets often don't translate to insight or emotional processing. Fishing in Alaska, he confessed to Morgan, had disturbed him because he hadn't expected to kill any fish. Arriving in Paris to enlist in the French Foreign Legion, he was shocked by the realization that people in France spoke French.

Pleading guilty to the second more severe charge of misbehavior, Bergdahl told Nance that he had had no intention of triggering search-and-recovery missions. "I had no thoughts that anyone would actually come look for me. Now it seems obvious."

In many ways, Bergdahl came to the Army the same person he had been as an adolescent: the teenager who had told his mother and roommates that he did not need to sleep on a mattress. In Morgan's testimony, it all added up: Fragmented thinking, amplified by post-traumatic anxiety and charged with impulsiveness, had brought everyone to the courtroom that day.

The question was how any of this was supposed to make the men who had sacrificed their lives looking for him feel about *their* realities. When Mark Allen came home to Tampa in August 2009, he was in a vegetative state. The urgent care he had received in Afghanistan and in Germany had saved his life, but the emergency craniotomy that removed both frontal lobes of his brain had left him with little hope for recovery. Despite numerous strokes and seizures, and 90 percent paralysis, he could still feel pain, which, due to constant muscle spasms that stressed and deformed his joints, was chronic and severe. When he was discharged from the VA hospital in 2011, he had regained consciousness, but his condition was essentially unchanged. He sleeps at night, his doctors said, but when his eyes are open during the day, he "has no awareness of his environment or response to commands."

Shannon Allen's testimony contradicted that of his doctors in this regard. When Mark was with her and their young daughter, he made eye contact, smiled, cried, and even laughed, she said. When they were married in 2006, he had been outgoing, boisterous, and happy-go-lucky. By 2017, he had regained some movement in his right hand and could now make a thumbs-up sign. Not that there was much cause for optimism. After some twenty operations, Allen was wheelchair bound for life. An intrathecal pump delivered painkillers directly into his spine. Shannon and nurses took turns feeding, washing, and dressing him: "Instead of a wife, I am a caregiver," she said on the witness stand.

Bergdahl sat motionless during her testimony. Shannon choked up with tears only once, when prosecutors played a video showing her and Mark's morning routine in their home in Florida, where he sleeps in an ICU-grade hospital bed. Each day, he is rolled into a body sling attached to a pulley system that lifts his one hundred seventy pounds into one of two wheelchairs. A percussion vest prevents fluid from collecting in his lungs. A feeding tube sustains him. Shannon crushes pills for his eighty-odd prescriptions and uses a suction machine to clean his mouth. Before Bergdahl's trial, an emergency tracheotomy had put him in the

ICU for three weeks, but now he was back home, Shannon said, "where he's safe."

WHEN JIMMY HATCH TOOK the stand, a therapy dog sat at his feet, licking his shoes as Hatch shared new details of his final raid, including how, before Remco was shot, the dog had attacked several young Afghan children, whom Hatch then picked up and moved to safety. All of it was done as part of a mission "to rescue an American." That was a stipulation that numerous Pentagon and intelligence officials, including Hagel, Sedney, and Dach refuted; they maintain that there is no credible evidence that a rescue mission was ever approved. But the mission orders were classified, and Hatch only knew what he had been told, and the defense made no objections.

The Army called on Evan Buetow to describe the impacts of the DUSTWUN on his platoon. More than three years after spreading the rumor through the media that Bergdahl had gone looking for the Taliban, Buetow took a deep breath as he sat down and looked at Bergdahl for the first time in eight years. The ten days he spent living in the bunker built in the graveyard were sheer hell, he said. There were bones of dead Afghans sticking out of the ground all around him and dung beetles crawling everywhere. He came down with dysentery and was stricken for days, drained of all energy and worried he might not survive.

"Those living conditions are something I think about everyday," he said. "It makes me appreciate everything I have in my life now."

Despite that misery, Buetow said it was the context that still haunts him, the fact that "my guy was gone." With that, he broke down crying on the witness stand, cradled his head in his hands, and took a few minutes to regain his composure. Later that night in a bar near Fort Bragg, Buetow said he felt lighter after testifying, as if a weight had been lifted off him.

During Bergdahl's sentencing, the topic of collaboration with the enemy never came up, because the Army had no credible evidence for it. Despite the media's narratives, the facts told a starkly different story. The letters that Bergdahl had written from captivity in 2012 and 2013 were prime examples. With help from Hamid Karzai and his brother, Qayum Karzai, the International Committee for the Red Cross arranged a channel through which Bergdahl could send a rare written message home. In a neat hybrid of cursive and print, Bergdahl wrote about the weather, the coming spring, and his faith in God. He told his family that he missed them every day and that he believed everything happens for a reason. The letters contained many of his familiar quirks, but there was more to it than idiosyncratic grammar and peculiar wording. Like James Stockdale and dozens of other American POWs preceding him, Sergeant Bergdahl had devised his own system of coded communications in his letters:

> *"And as I stand, my pack on, the question is, where to go? For the world is fully there." Those are the words of a man who was exploring the South Artic* [sic] *Mountains of Canada.*

There are no South Arctic Mountains of Canada, a fact unlikely to draw attention from Taliban censors. According to Russell, "I stand, my pack" was an intentional word scramble clue. Pack I Stand: Pakistan. I am in Pakistan, near rugged mountains, like the Canadian Rockies. Look there. Find me.

He used the system again in a second, shorter letter in 2013, in which he got to the point more quickly:

> *To: Family and Friends,*
>
> *Taking care and well. Months into 2013, winter over and warm weather here. Letter from dad came today. Missed thanksgiving, wonder who is winning the race now. good hunting to you and our friends, wonder*

how the weather was Southland and how big the herds are now.

Bergdahl was not asking about the size of cattle south of the Wood River Valley; he was talking about the other kinds of hunters he knew from Sun Valley and Mississippi: the JSOC teams he hoped were looking for him.

A JPRA report confirmed that Bergdahl saw the letters as an opportunity to convey hidden messages. Far from collaborating with his captors, he risked his life by inserting these oblique clues. Years later, Bergdahl told Russell that his captors had given him scripts for these letters written in English with the same talking points that he had been told to recite on video: that the U.S. should get out of Afghanistan, that the war was being fought in the interests of American corporations, and that he was expendable to the U.S. government. But in between, he had tried to sneak in any message he could.

FOLLOWING SHANNON ALLEN'S TESTIMONY, Bergdahl himself took the stand. As he chose to deliver an unsworn statement, he was not subject to cross-examination. But he wanted to explain what he had done and what he had lived through. He began by reading an apology from a piece of paper trembling in his hands.

"It was never my intention for anyone to be hurt," he said. "I made a horrible mistake. As my mom used to tell me, 'Saying sorry isn't enough.' My words can't take away the pain that people have been through. Offering condolences isn't enough. People went through things that they never should have. I was trying to help, and the fact that I did not breaks my heart."

In his closing statements, the Army's lead prosecutor, Major Justin Oshana, challenged Bergdahl's choice of words. "It wasn't a mistake," he said. "It was a crime." He challenged Morgan's assessment, too, noting that Bergdahl had made careful, systematic plans. Oshana framed the case as a study in contrasts, between Bergdahl's selfish negligence and the honor of those who worked together to find him. The harm he caused, Oshana said, was greater than the pain he had experienced.

"Sergeant Bergdahl does not have a monopoly on suffering," he said. "All suffering in this case stems from his choices." For punishment, Oshana and the government sought fourteen years of confinement, reduction in rank, and a punitive discharge. One of the Army's final witnesses was a warden at the military prison where Bergdahl would be sent. They were ready for him. This, Oshana said, "is what justice requires."

Captain Nina Banks, the youngest of Bergdahl's attorneys, was a surprise choice to deliver his closing defense. Normally one of the fastest talkers on the team, Banks now spoke slowly and deliberately. She began by echoing Oshana's words. "What justice requires," Banks said, is a sentence "tailored to the facts of the case." She described Bergdahl as a young man who had needed but never received psychological care. Eight years after the incident, the man in court that day was not the twenty-three-year-old private who, oblivious to his own mental condition, but wanting to do the right thing, had committed the wrong actions.

The courage and sacrifice displayed by Hatch, Allen, Morita, and the rest were undeniable, but did not negate the fact that Bergdahl's motive was free of malice. The Army wanted retributive punishment, Banks said, but "an eye for an eye is not appropriate." And even if it were, "Sergeant Bergdahl has been punished enough," said Banks, who then walked Nance through the inhumanity that Bergdahl had lived through: the illness and filth, the neglect that had his bones protruding through his skin, the isolation so complete that even his voice had atrophied.

"How did he keep going?" Banks said, her voice catching with emotion as she quoted what Bergdahl had said on the stand the day before: "Because I didn't want them to win."

Judge Nance leaned back in his chair as he listened. Unlike General Dahl, Nance had not been subjected to orders from above to take on this case. He had been on the verge of retirement. If it weren't for Bergdahl, he would have been there already, in a house he owned on a golf course in Georgia. But his son had persuaded him to delay his retirement, telling him that if he didn't take on this challenge he would always regret it. As a combat veteran, Nance understood the men's anger, the value of their sacrifice, and their demands for justice in ways most senior military judges could not. As Oshana and Banks delivered their final arguments, Nance scanned the faces in the courtroom one by one, holding eye contact with members of the public in the gallery, as if storing his memories for a later time.

Among the written statements that Nance reviewed prior to sentencing were two letters from Bergdahl's parents. Neither claimed their son was innocent. In fact, Bob wrote, when he first saw his son in person after six years, he told Bowe that whatever legal consequences were headed his way, they "expected him to stand at attention and take it." They understood what he had done and why with a mixture of pride and remorse for their own idealism. "We raised up our children in the way they should go and when they are old they will not depart from it," Jani wrote, citing the Book of Proverbs. They even named him after a fictional character, she said, "a Texas Ranger known for his ethics, courage, and kindness." Bob had educated his son to be a missionary, a calling irreconcilable with the realities of a soldier at war. "The U.S. Army was not in my view of vocations for him. . . . He signed his enlistment papers without my consent," Bob informed Nance. "I accept the blame and carry a great burden, having raised Bowdrie the way we did."

In the more than three years since their son was freed, his parents had received so many death threats in the mail that they stopped reading the letters. The envelopes sat unopened and yellowing in a Southern Idaho storage unit. And while they accepted their share of responsibility, they also believed that they had all been used as instruments of political theater. At their moment of greatest joy at his recovery, "at the miracle of his being set free, our own political party sabotaged him," Jani wrote.

Bob told Nance that in his time working as an asset with JPRA and the FBI, "I witnessed powerful, unlawful, political obstruction to attempts by several U.S. agencies to recover a U.S. soldier from enemy hands." The gears of the machine, he implied, had propelled the case from the start. By calling Amber Dach as a witness, Bergdahl's defense had made a brief, subtle, but powerful argument about the mitigating factors of the Army's decisions during the DUSTWUN. Dach's unaccepted assessment—not to mention the intelligence reports that Mike Furlong had kept quiet—cast doubt over the entire established narrative of the DUSTWUN and Bergdahl's role in it. At the top of his letter to Nance, Bob repeated the odd and telling quote from Colonel Mike Howard during their first intercontinental video teleconferences in July 2009: "Thank you, Mr. and Mrs. Bergdahl. For the first time in my career, I have the resources I need to do my job."

Two days after closing statements, on November 3, Nance convened the court to deliver his sentence. The bailiff instructed all parties to rise, and Nance shot out of his chambers like a bullet, his black robe billowing and his face set into a grimace as he mumbled, "Be seated." Fidell and Rosenblatt leaned forward in their chairs. Only Bergdahl needed to stand, which he did slowly, his legs shaking. He was flanked by the two female attorneys on his team, Captain Banks and Captain Jennifer Norvell, each with a hand on his quaking back as Nance read his verdict:

> Reduction in rank to E-1 (Private).
>
> Forfeiture of his Army paycheck at $1,000 per months for ten months.
>
> Dishonorable Discharge.

Bergdahl began sobbing. He was not going back behind bars. Oshana and the prosecution stared into space as they processed the magnitude of their loss. Nance adjourned the room. Bergdahl gathered himself and was hurried out first. Twenty reporters poured down the courthouse steps to their cell phones and news vans as a Black Hawk helicopter flew low and loud over the scene.

Reactions from the veterans who had attended Bergdahl's trial contrasted starkly with the anger and outrage in the press. Even before the verdict, Hatch told the Associated Press that he had gone from "I'd like to kill him" to "he should go to jail forever" to a final, more peaceful acceptance that the process was just and fair. Another Special Forces soldier who said that he had searched for Bergdahl for years left the courthouse feeling the same way. "I was very angry with him. And then I came here, and I found out the truth," he said.

The social media mob went into a predictable rage. But Nance's ruling also broke the silence of veterans who had lived the case, but never said what they had known all along.

"The battalion and brigade staff know, and knew then, that it was a chain of command failure. He shouldn't have deployed and when he started exhibiting signs of behavioral health issues, he should have been on the next plane home," one Geronimo veteran wrote under a pseudonym. More problematic, he continued, was the uneven application of the UCMJ. As a specialist in Logar Province in January 2012, he had seen one of his own men sentenced to just seven months in prison and an other than honorable discharge for murdering a fellow soldier with an antitank weapon.

Gerald Sutton keeps a framed photo of Matthew Martinek on his mantel, next to his own Purple Heart (which the Army erroneously inscribed with the name "Gary Sutton"). Six days after Bergdahl's release, Martinek's mother, Cheryl Brandes, was invited onto Fox News to share her response to the prisoner exchange. Her son was twenty years old when he died from wounds suffered during the September 4, 2009, ambush that also killed Second Lieutenant Darryn Andrews. Their comrades had told both families what they knew about their patrol that day: They had been searching for Bergdahl.

"There needs to be an investigation," Brandes told Fox News. "Why is this such a cover-up? What is the issue here? Why can they not just tell us, 'Yes, your son was looking for another soldier?' What's so bad about that? There's nothing bad about that. We just want the truth."

The soldiers who searched for Bowe Bergdahl did so without question. A decade later, the full story of the war they were sent to fight remains untold.

EPILOGUE

The scene would linger for a lifetime in the memories of the witnesses of the Army's degradation ceremony. The parade ground was filled with an audience of the state: soldiers, press, and civil servants all performing their solemn duty to observe the spectacle. Thousands more gathered outside the walled courtyard, where a carnival atmosphere took hold as civilians strained on step stools to see the accused and shout their refrain: "Death to the traitor!"

The young artillery officer stood tall as the adjutant tore his rank insignia from his uniform, drew the young officer's sword from its scabbard, and broke it in two over his knee. His fellow soldiers then ripped away the buttons, gold lace, stripes, and epaulets, all rigged by a military tailor in preparation for the day's theatrics. Stripped of his symbolic trappings, Army Captain Alfred Dreyfus was marched solemnly past the official witnesses to begin his life sentence.

Dreyfus's legal case was more complicated than the accepted narratives that had led him to the courtyard of the École Militaire on January 5, 1895. It would be more than a decade—and five years of exile in the notorious Devil's Island penal colony, thousands of miles from home—before the facts of the case would be revealed and exonerate him. By the time the Army took him back, promoted him to major, and reassigned him to command another unit, the Dreyfus scandal had divided French society, testing the values of the very institutions of government that Dreyfus had been falsely accused of betraying. Those who had conspired against him had known that though their young Republic was founded on Enlightenment concepts of liberty and equality, the machine of state held hidden levers of power, if one knew how to use them.

On November 3, 2017, in Fort Bragg, North Carolina, an analagous scene played out in its own way. Outside the courthouse, a warm, autumn sun shone on the cameramen and reporters waiting to catch a glimpse of the infamous soldier walking free down the courthouse steps. An hour after Judge Nance announced his verdict, President Trump, en route to Hawaii aboard Air Force One, tweeted his own: "The decision on Sergeant Bergdahl is a complete and total disgrace to our Country and to our Military." In the courthouse parking lot, cable news producers paced in nervous circles clutching their cell phones to their ears to discuss the latest presidential bulletin.

It had come as no surprise. More than anyone, Trump had exploited Bergdahl and spread the lie of his alleged treason for his own benefit. Moments after his tweet, military law experts noted the irony: Now that he was president, Trump's Twitter feed was a factor in the chain of command and with his airborne decree, he had veered into the territory of unlawful command influence and done Bergdahl a legal favor. In his ignorance of U.S. military law, Trump was likely unaware that the end of Bergdahl's trial was not the end of his court-martial in sum. General Robert Abrams still needed to approve Nance's verdict (which he would in May 2018), and then, as in all dishonorable discharge rulings, Bergdahl's bad paper would be automatically appealed. In having what he thought was the final word—and with Bergdahl's back pay and lifetime health benefits hanging in the balance—Trump had blundered into helping Bergdahl more than anyone else could have done on purpose.

There would be no ceremony to banish Bergdahl from the military. Instead, in a spare room in the courthouse, he simply took off the uniform with the sergeant's stripes that he had been deemed no longer fit to wear and changed into civilian clothes. He slipped out a side door, still flanked by his security detail, and into an unmarked government car idling by the curb.

ON JANUARY 14, 2015—following months of intelligence reports generated from Bergdahl's debriefings—a CIA drone fired a missile at a target in Pakistan in a signature strike with unintended consequences. The Hellfire hit its mark, killing two American al-Qaeda members, Ahmed Farouq and Adam Gadahn. It also killed two hostages: Warren Weinstein, a seventy-three-year-old American contractor, and Giovanni Lo Porto, a thirty-seven-year-old Italian aid worker. It had been two years since Jason Amerine added Warren Weinstein to his list of prisoners to recover along with Bergdahl. Now, he never would: After 1,250 days as a hostage, Weinstein was fatally freed from all forms of earthly captivity by a mistake. CIA characterized it as a routine oversight: The agency had no idea he was even there when the strike was approved.

On that same day, Amerine was abruptly escorted out of the Pentagon, his pay temporary halted, his retirement put on hold. Trigged by a formal FBI complaint, the Army had opened a criminal investigation into the lieutenant colonel's collaboration with Congressman Duncan Hunter during Amerine's hostage recovery efforts. In early 2014, when every other official he met was happy to send Amerine running in circles, Hunter had written several letters to Defense Secretary Hagel, urging him to break up the gridlock and promote Pentagon solutions. Amerine had planned for the FBI coming for him, but never thought the Army—his home since he was a fourteen-year-old ROTC cadet—would so enthusiastically cooperate, and the Army Criminal Investigative Division Agents on his case were stunned that they even had to investigate him.

Five months later, Amerine was at the Capitol to testify for a hearing called Blowing the Whistle on Retaliation: Accounts of Current and Former Federal Agency Whistleblowers. It took a total of ten months before the Army dropped the charges. Amerine left the Army on Halloween 2015, his retirement, full rank, and military pension intact. The Army even gave him an award, draping the Legion of Merit medal around his neck. The Obama administration, roundly criticized for its inability to recover American hostages abroad, had taken a serious look at Amerine's complaints. In June 2015, the White House announced reforms that included a Hostage Recovery Fusion Cell, to be led by the FBI, and a presidential envoy for hostage affairs at the State Department. This progress carried into the Trump administration, leading to successful recoveries of hostages and prisoners from Pakistan, Egypt, North Korea, and China. On October 13, 2017, three days before Bergdahl pled guilty, Caitlan Coleman, Joshua Boyle, and their three children were released from their five-year ordeal in the FATA. Diane Foley, the mother of James Foley, told David Rohde that she considered the Trump administration more willing to negotiate than previous administrations: "I think they see the return of Americans detained abroad as a win."

IN THE DAYS BEFORE Nance's verdict, Terrence Russell explained that Bergdahl still had a valuable role to play in the U.S. Armed Forces, in the SERE community. The records from their debriefings totaled twelve hundred pages, from which Russell had produced four classified JPRA reports, which he said combatant commanders had requested from him "immediately." SERE instructors with the Air Force and Navy told him they wanted more information from the only American servicemember with a record of survival and escape in the FATA. But as long as Bergdahl was in legal hearings, Russell could not arrange more sessions. "We have forces at risk," Russell said, citing ongoing operations in Afghanistan and Syria. "We need this information," he told Nance, his voice rising. "The fact that I can't get that information is wrong." In December 2017, even as twenty-one congressmen cosponsored H.R. 4413, the "No Back Pay for Bergdahl Act," the former prisoner had decided to accept Russell's invitations, sit for more interviews, and speak to military and government audiences at the SERE School at Fairchild Air Force Base in Spokane, Washington. The multimillion-dollar facility trains pilots and aircrew in survival tactics behind enemy lines with one goal: "to ensure America's warfighters 'Return with Honor.'" Two months later, in early February, Bergdahl visited for several days. He recorded interviews and delivered two talks—one at the JPRA Academy and another to forty active-duty Air Force SERE school instructors at Fairchild. Bergdahl took questions, and several people approached him afterward with words of gratitude and support. If anyone was offended by Bowe Bergdahl's appearance, Russell said, he hadn't heard it.

For their part, his family is trying to move on. Bob shaved his beard soon after the Rose Garden episode. Jani stopped watching the news, which she suspects is mostly scripted political drama. Bob thinks that if the Army had just appointed Fox News anchors as prosecutors, the legal process would have been a lot more efficient. As Christians, they believe that forgiveness is their obligation. Watching the young men spread lies about Bowe on television tested their faith, but Bob saw that they too had been exploited. "I don't blame them," he said. "I blame the Army. They were being lied to by their commanders." The death threats never fully stopped, and the FBI had to be called back to monitor the situation from time to time. Jani sees Bowe's survival as a miracle, where the Almighty put countless capable individuals in the places and roles where they needed to be.

In the Wood River Valley, there's a park close to where the Bergdahls first lived when they moved to Idaho. During the ordeal, supporters planted a tree in the park for each year Bowe was gone, five in a row. In July 2014, the town took down its yellow ribbons and posters, and the mayor told local businesses to remove their stickers of support.

"The city of Hailey is not Bowe-Bergdahl-ville," Mayor Haemmerle said. Five years after Bergdahl was freed and more than seventeen after the war began, those trees bear no signs explaining why they were planted, and Americans are still serving and dying in Afghanistan for reasons most people can't explain.

ACKNOWLEDGMENTS

MATT FARWELL:

I would like to acknowledge the following people for their role in making this project happen—first, my coauthor, Michael Ames. This book would not exist without you.

Writing a book, it turns out, is quite hard, and I have to thank the following for their support, friendship, and advice. These people made it easier along the way.

To Emily Cunningham, the editor and shaping force of the *American Cipher* project, thank you for your tireless work on this book—you made everything about this process better; I appreciate your faith, patience, and judgment.

To Farley Chase, my agent and dear friend, who long ago took a gamble on a down-on-his-luck guy just out of the service—none of this would have happened without you. You changed my life, for the better. Thank you for being a trusted friend, advisor, and always helpful ear. . . . Now, I've got this idea . . .

To Ann Godoff and Scott Moyers at Penguin Press, thank you for providing us the chance to tell this story the way it deserved to be told; I could not have dreamed of a better team at the top.

To my family: my parents, Dr. Gary and Louise Farwell; my siblings, Gary Marc Farwell, Tawnya Farwell, Robert and Jeni Farwell, Marrianne Tullis and Dr. Jason Tullis; my nieces and nephews, Jakob,

Emma, Ashlyn, Ethan, Isabella, Henry, Charlie, Louisa, and Dr. Toni Jensen, Eva, and Miss Marie Claire and everyone in the extended Farwell, Funk families—thank you for making me who I am today and giving me something to live for.

Lieutenant Colonel Jason Amerine, Bowe Bergdahl, Robert and Jani Bergdahl, Sky Albrecht and Michael Albrecht. Dr. Carl Jenkins, thank you for your time and your trust.

To everyone who helped my development along the way—including quite a few who cannot be named, but should be acknowledged here with at least a single [REDACTED], thank you for allowing me to learn from you. I cannot single out all the people who've helped me along the way by name—there are that many—but thank you again.

To Command Sergeant Major David M. Bruner & Nam Bruner, Lieutenant General David P. Valcourt and Diane Valcourt, Command Sergeant Major John Sparks and Karen Sparks, General William Wallace and Mrs. Wallace, General Martin Dempsey and Deanie Dempsey, General John Nicholson, Miss Cynthia in the DCG's office, Maxie McFarland, The TRADOC JAG Staff, Colonel Chris Toner, Colonel Robert Helvey Major General Robert "Pat" White, Lieutenant Colonel John Machesney, Sergeant Major Michael Adams, Sergeant Major Dewayne Blackmon, First Sergeant Kevin Smith, First Sergeant Ty Shillito, Major Gerard Torres, Lieutenant Colonel Frank Rosenblatt, Sergeant Mike Laroche, Sergeant Carlie L. Lee, Sergeant Anthony Bautista, Staff Sergeant Sony Suprinvil, Staff Sergeant Edward Oros, Lieutenant General Karl Eikenberry, Brigadier General Marty Schweitzer, Drill Sergeant (DSOY) Herbert Thompson, Drill Sergeant (DSOY) Delfin Romani, Staff Sergeant John Stanton, Colonel Clint Baker, Major General Michael Howard, Colonel Scott Howard, Chief Warrant Officer Four Michael Tobin, Lieutenant Colonel Chris Nunn, Lieutenant Colonel Tim Lynch, Colonel Michael Furlong, Dr. Frank Ochberg, Dr. Eugene Lipov, Suanne Massey, Julie Pearson, the staff of the VAMC of the Ozarks & the Menlo Park Psychiatric Campus, Walter Kirn, Amanda Fortini, Elise Jordan, David Fisher, Bob

Kotlowitz, The United World College of the American West, Shelby and Gale Davis, Dr. Phil and Amy Geier, Justin Hulog, Susan Keppelman, Elian Maritz, Writer's Block Bookstore, Scott and Drew Plympton, Jennifer Lee, Black Mountain Institute, The University of Arkansas, The University of Virginia, Echols Scholar Program Dean Nicole Eramo, Professor Sidney Blair, Professor Stephen Knott, Michael Lemaster, Grey Huffman, Dr. Jenni Allen, Blake Briddell, Maia Smith, Dwayne Swanson, Dr. Victoria Greenfield, Ambassador Marc Grossman, Tommy Vietor, Ned Price, Thomas Nelson Community College, Jeff Hastings, Caitlin Hayden, Congressman Duncan Hunter, Joe Kaspar, Senator Orrin Hatch, General James C. McConville, Robert Baer, Doug Laux, Tony K., Ned Price, Mohammad Tanin, Mohammad Khan, Sakhi Khan, Nabi Khan, Greg Vogle, Gary Berntsen, Jose Rodriguez, Jeff Wassmer, Colonel Nathen Noyes, The Salvador Dali Museum, The Wizards in the J-33.

Thank you for all the help along the way.

Elsa Givan and Megan Parry merit special mention for their invaluable contributions to the research for this book. You are both brilliant.

MICHAEL AMES:

This book began with a story that never belonged to me, but that through the trust, generosity, and goodness of others has been shared with us by those who lived through it.

As an Idaho resident from 2002 to 2011, and as a Wood River Valley local during the first years of Bowe's captivity, his family's ordeal was a daily reminder of the sacrifices made by so many American families who send their children across the world to serve their country. As a civilian, I had little comprehension of their lives, and this project has brought me an invaluable education. I would like to thank Matthew Farwell for asking me to join him on this journey and encouraging me to learn about the vital, and too often hidden, realities of my own country.

This book would not exist without Chris Parris-Lamb, who had a vision before we ever began. Chris, in times good and less than good, your support and insight was indispensable. Thanks as well to Farley Chase for your thoughtfulness and skill bringing this to life. I will never be able to express my gratitude to Emily Cunningham at Penguin Press. Thank you, Emily, for sticking with us, your tirelessness, and your persistent optimism, which has carried the day.

This book came at a hard time, and I am indebted to each of you who refused to let me give up. My everlasting gratitude and love to Danielle Travers, for understanding all of it, and all of me; to Dean Sluyter, for setting me on this path before I was old enough to drive, your stubborn belief in me, and your effortless and graceful kindness. You are a Sherpa of the soul and a damn-good proofreader too. To my father, Roger Ames, who took the first flight to New Jersey in March 2017, and my sister, Jennifer Ames Yarznbowicz, for your undying support every day since. And to Jennifer Tuohy, for believing in me even when I worked in the basement, for your friendship and wisdom, and for always making time to read.

Research and reporting took me back to Idaho so many times, and those trips would not have been possible without the generosity and warmth of Deborrah Bohrer. Thank you, Deb, for understanding the time and energy of creative work. Equal thanks are owed to Bill Fowler and the Silver Creek Writers' Residency, and Sabina Dana Plasse, for introducing me to such kind and smart readers and fellow writers.

Sometimes in Idaho, office space was scarce, food forgotten, and work a form of madness. Thank you Nina Jonas and Andreas Heaphy for the office space and the spicy sustenance; to Shaun, Casey, Cru, Rome, and Bender Mills Kelly, for taking me in, always making me feel at home, and for your hearts full of love, and trees full of chickens; to Evelyn and Jim Phillips, for feeding me food from your garden and history about the community that shaped this story (and for the VW loaner when times were tight); to Dana Dugan and Ken Ferris, for your extended hospitality; to Phoebe and the entire Pilaro family; and to Matt Furber, for your support and your magical Saab.

ACKNOWLEDGMENTS

Like all writers, I share any and all credit with my editors, mentors, and colleagues. I am indebted to Robert Young Pelton, who has been both a source and an inspiration; and to Sean Langan for your trust, compassion, and unreasonable good cheer. I am also grateful to Bob Roe, without whom this story would not have been told; to Chris Beha for giving me a shot and showing me the way; to Jeremy Keehn for seeing the longer tale within; and to Andrew Cockburn and Anand Gopal for inspiration and encouragement. And a second thank you to Evelyn Phillips for contributing your tireless creativity and energy in our maps; and to Jason Nadler for reading; Aaron Pearson for IT and various other emergencies; and Tad Tuleja for the writing boot camp back in Waterville, Maine.

When overwhelmed, which was not uncommon, I was beyond fortunate to work with brilliant researchers: Anudari Amartuvshin, I can never thank you enough for being a part of this. Thanks also to Ben Rashkovich for taking the meandering detour before law school, and to Elsa Given, who was a critical part of our team in our reporting phase.

This book is the product of hundreds of interviews with dozens of sources, more than we can ever thank in full. But a few stand out for your trust, patience, and time: At Fort Bragg, Monica Cash for the education on the POW-MIA movement; in Idaho, Bob and Jani Bergdahl; and on countless interviews, phone calls, text messages, and emails: Barney Rubin, Gerald Sutton, Joseph Coe, Frank Rosenblatt, Jason Amerine, Amber Dach, Terry Russell, "Ron Wilson," Nate Bethea, Admiral Michael Mullen, Defense Secretary Chuck Hagel, David Sedney, Joe Kasper, Johnny Rice, Rachel VanLandingham, John Mohammed, Qayum Karzai, Michael Furlong, Joshua Cornelison, Greg Leatherman, and Dr. Frank Ochberg. In Idaho: Mark Farris, "Anna Fontaine," Sue Martin, Jane Drussel and the crew at Jane's Artifacts, Noah Bowen, Matt Larson, Jeff Gunter, John Shaw, Chip Deffé, Hailey Tucker, Willy Cook, and so many others in the valley who took time out of their days to help.

Beyond the work, I am grateful for my friends and my tribe who helped propel me across the finish line: Cameron Alice Packer, for the cartography and dog booties; Dr. Michael Schlatter, for the feels and the tunes; Peter Boice, Greg Hedin, and Jay DiPietro for the brotherhood; and the entire Purple House Society. In Brooklyn, perpetual props to David Schoetz, Nick MacInnis, and Amdé Mengistu for the abundant texts, bountiful sticky flags, moral support, and emergency pluots. To the Nielsons, for our garden and your friendship; to Cyrus Garrett for keeping me honest and laughing, and Wafa Ghnaim for your expertise and translations; Michael Rollins for fixing my body; and to Julie and Michael Corwin, Jane Brick, Ken and Karen Englander, and Mary Ore for checking in on me.

Finally . . . Chris Pilaro, you are a brother to me always, and your spirit lives on in everything and everyone you touched. Peace, love, and healing. And Elyse Ames, the only thing in this world greater than the void you have left is the love that you brought. You will carry me for the rest of my days.

IMAGE CREDITS

Pp. 1 and 2: Courtesy of Bob and Jani Bergdahl; p. 3: Sean Smith/Copyright Guardian News & Media Ltd 2009; p. 4, top left: Keith Maupin, General Data Company, Inc./Courtesy Monica Cash; top right: Al-Emara; p. 4, top right: Al-Emara; p. 4, bottom: Unknown Taliban photographer; p. 5: Al-Emara; p. 6, top: AP Photo/Charles Dharapak; p. 6, middle: Roland Lane/*The Idaho Mountain Express*; p. 6, bottom: Courtesy of Patrick J. Hughes; p. 7, top: Courtesy of Jason Amerine; p. 7, bottom: John Harrington/Pool via CNP Photo; p. 8: Andrew Craft/*The Fayetteville Observer.*

NOTES

PROLOGUE

1 Major General Kenneth Dahl: Bowe Bergdahl sworn statement, U.S. Army 15-6 Investigation, August 6, 2014, p. 3, https://bergdahldocket.files.wordpress.com/2016/03/stmt20of20accused202014_redacted.pdf.

2 The prisoner swap that freed: Kendall Breitman et al., "Polls: Plurality against Bergdahl Deal," *Politico,* June 10, 2014, http://politico.com/story/2014/06/bergdahl-poll-swap-wrong-usatoday-pew-107640.

2 The night of Bergdahl's release: Donald J. Trump (@realDonaldTrump), "At some point Sgt. Bergdahl will have to explain his capture. In 2009 he simply wandered off his base without a weapon. Many questions!," Twitter, May 31, 2014, 9:31 p.m. http://twitter.com/realDonaldTrump/status/472913311596441601.

2 When the city hall: Hailey City Hall press release, "Bring Bowe Back/Bowe Is Back Event Canceled," Hailey, Idaho, June 4, 2014.

3 Bowe wasn't the only target: Ashley Ross, "Serial Bowe Bergdahl Story: What to Know While You Listen," *Time*, December 10, 2015, http://time.com/4144493/serial-new-season-bowe-bergdahl.

3 The Army was his life: Michael Winerip, "After 30 Years in the Army, Cocktail Hour Counts," *New York Times*, March 15, 2013, http://nytimes.com/2013/03/17/booming/after-30-years-in-the-army-cocktail-hour-counts.html.

4 Or he wanted to walk: Bowe Bergdahl sworn statement, U.S. Army 15-6 Investigation, August 6, 2014, p. 259.

4 One soldier couldn't recall: Lt. Gen. Kenneth Dahl, "Investigation into Private First Class (PFC) Bowe Robert Bergdahl's Disappearance from Afghanistan and Related Matters," September 28, 2014, p. 02450. (Notated hereafter as "Dahl Report.")

CHAPTER ONE: LITTLE AMERICA

9 Bob's sister was: Interviews with Bob and Jani Bergdahl, 2012, 2018.

9 After qualifying for: Author interview, July–August 2018.

10 Moscow, Carter said: "Jimmy Carter: Address to the Nation on the Soviet Invasion of Afghanistan—January 4, 1980," *American Presidency Project*, http://presidency.ucsb.edu/ws/?pid=32911.

10 Protests, many organized: "Soviet Invasion of Afghanistan Draws Protests," UPI, January 1, 1970, http://upi.com/Archives/1979/12/31/Soviet-invasion-of-Afghanistan-draws-protests/6310753428720.

11 In notes Brzezinski: "Interview with Zbigniew Brzezinski," National Security Archive, June 13, 1997, http://nsarchive.gwu.edu/coldwar/interviews/episode-17/brzezinski1.html; David N. Gibbs, "Brzezinski Interview," http://dgibbs.faculty.arizona.edu/brzezinski_interview.

12 Operation Cyclone, as: Tim Weiner, *Legacy of Ashes: The History of the CIA* (New York: Penguin, 2011), p. 308.

12 The American initiative: David Rohde, *A Rope and a Prayer* (New York: Viking, 2010), p. 15.

12 Southern Idaho, like: U.S. Agency for International Development, *A.I.D. Evaluation Special Study No. 18: The Helmand Valley Project in Afghanistan* (USAID: December 1983), p. 1, http://www.dtic.mil/dtic/tr/fulltext/u2/a518306.pdf.

13 Before the Soviet withdrawl: Andrew J. Bacevich, *America's War for the Greater Middle East*, (New York: Random House, 2016), p. 54.

13 About six million: Rüdiger Schöch, "Afghan Refugees in Pakistan During the 1980s: Cold War Politics and Registration Practice," UNHCR, Geneva, Switzerland, p. 5.

13 Moscow learned the hard way: "Background Report: Paktika Province, United Nations High Commission on Human Rights," September 1, 1989, http://afghandata.org:8080/xmlui/bitstream/handle/azu/3338/azu_acku_pamphlet_ds374_p35_p36_1989_w.pdf?sequence=1&isAllowed=y, p. 4.

14 A 1989 Army report: Bacevich, *America's War for the Greater Middle East*, p. 56.

14 The seed Brzezinski planted: Barnett R. Rubin, *Afghanistan from the Cold War through the War on Terror* (Oxford: Oxford University Press, 2015), p. 25.

14 With a job building: Author interviews with Bob and Jani Bergdahl, July–August 2018.

15 Tourists were a good thing: Wendolyn Holland, *Sun Valley: An Extraordinary History*, (Ketchum, Idaho: The Idaho Press, 1998), p. 223.

15 Bob and Jani decided: John Accola, "To Most Idahoans, A Plague of Locusts Is Californians," *Washington Post*, December 22, 1979.

15 He tuned skis and bikes: Interviews with Bob and Jani Bergdahl, July–August 2018.

16 In twenty-eight years: Interview with Bob and Jani Bergdahl, April 2012.

16 Ten feet of snow: Author interviews with Bob and Jani Bergdahl, July–August 2018.

17 "We don't have safe deposit": Interview with Bob and Jani Bergdahl, April 2012.

18 Gunter watched Bowe: Interview with Jeff Gunter, October 2016.

18 ninety Nez Perce lay dead: "Nez Perce NHP: Nez Perce Summer, 1877 (Appendix B)," National Parks Service, U.S. Department of the Interior, http://nps.gov/parkhistory/online_books/nepe/greene/appb.htm.

20 "only one going to heaven": Author interview, April 2016.

CHAPTER TWO: BLOWBACK

22 "The United States is now at war": *Idaho Mountain Express*, September 12, 2001.

22 a set of nonnegotiable demands: George W. Bush, "President Bush Addresses the Nation," *Washington Post*, September 20, 2001, http://washingtonpost.com/wp-srv/nation/specials/attacked/transcripts/bushaddress_092001.html.

22 For the first time since: Suzanne Daley, "For First Time, NATO Invokes Joint Defense Pact with U.S.," *New York Times*, September 13. 2001, http://nytimes.com/2001/09/13/us/after-attacks-alliance-for-first-time-nato-invokes-joint-defense-pact-with-us.html.

23 "When I said no negotiations": Elisabeth Bumiller, "President Rejects Offer by Taliban for Negotiations," *New York Times*, October 15, 2001, http://nytimes.com/2001/10/15/world/nation-challenged-president-president-rejects-offer-taliban-for-negotiations.html.

23 American greenbacks shrink-wrapped: Gary Berntsen, *Jawbreaker: The Attack on Bin Laden and al-Qaeda: A Personal Account by the CIA's Key Field Commander* (New York: Crown, 2005).

24 Take away that safe space: Eric Blehm, *The Only Thing Worth Dying for: How Eleven Green Berets Fought for a New Afghanistan* (New York: HarperCollins, 2010).

24 It took little more: Norimitsu Onishi, "Taliban Leader Is Hiding in Mountain Province Near Kandahar, Afghan Official Says," *New York Times*, 18 December 18, 2001.

24 "Don't the Americans": Kate Clark, "2001 Ten Years on (3): The fall of Loya Paktia and why the US preferred warlords," Afghanistan Analysts Network, November 24, 2011, https://afghanistan-analysts.org/2001-ten-years-on-3-the-fall-of-loya-paktia-and-why-the-us-preferred-warlords.

24 In the south, Omar's exodus: Interview with Barnett R. Rubin, September 2016.

25 They gave Karzai: Anand Gopal, *No Good Men Among the Living: America, the Taliban and the War through Afghan Eyes* (New York: Henry Holt and Company, 2014), p. 47.

25 On December 7, 2001: "The United States and the Global Coalition against Terrorism, September 2001–December 2003," U.S. Department of State Archives, 2001–2009, https://2001-2009.state.gov/r/pa/ho/pubs/fs/5889.htm.

25 "When we're through with them": *CBS News*, "Hank Crumpton: Life as a Spy," CBS Interactive, http://cbsnews.com/news/hank-crumpton-life-as-a-spy.

26 They had "captured": The President's State of the Union Address 2002, National Archives and Records Administration, http://georgewbush-whitehouse.archives.gov/news/releases/2002/01/20020129-11.html.

26 Dostum was ready: Dexter Filkins and Carlotta Gall, "A Nation Challenged: The Standoff; Foreign Militants Seek Safe Passage from Afghan City," *New York Times*, November 22, 2001.

26 Fazl even vowed: Carlotta Gall, *The Wrong Enemy* (New York: Houghton Mifflin Harcourt, 2014), p. 10.

26 It would be more than: "Shackled Detainees Arrive in Guantanamo," CNN, January 11, 2002, http://edition.cnn.com/2002/WORLD/asiapcf/central/01/11/ret.detainee.transfer/index.html.

26 budget slashed to a scant: Amy Belasco, *The Cost of Operations in Iraq, Afghanistan, and Enhanced Security*, Congressional Information Service, Library of Congress, 2005, p. 14.

27 The official mission statement: *Operation Enduring Freedom: March 2002–April 2005*, U.S. Army Center of Military History, 2005, https://history.army.mil/html/books/070/70-122-1/CMH_Pub_70-122-1.pdf, p. 16.

27 Jalaluddin Haqqani had been: Mapping Militant Organizations, Stanford University, 2017.

28 In the mid-nineties: Mapping Militant Organizations, Stanford University, 2017.

29 Kahn was a truck driver, criminal: Mark M. Bryant, *Afghan Militia Forces: ODA 361 2nd Battalion 3rd Special Forces Group March–October 2002*, in *Long Hard Road: NCO Experiences in Afghanistan and Iraq* (Fort Bliss, TX: U.S. Army Sergeants Major Academy, 2007), p. 21–25.

29 According to one CIA: Interview with CIA Operations Officer A, June 2016.

30 president's hour-long weekly briefings: The White House Office of the Press Secretary, "Fact Sheet: President Bush Receives Briefing From Military Commanders," February 17, 2006, National Archives and Records Administration, http://georgewbush-whitehouse.archives.gov/news/releases/2006/02/text/20060217-2.html.

30 Chairman Mao described guerrillas: "Mao Tse-Tung on Guerrilla Warfare: Fleet Marine Reference Publication 12–18," United States Marine Corps, April 5, 1989, https://www.marines.mil/Portals/59/Publications/FMFRP%2012–18%20%20Mao%20Tse-tung%20on%20Guerrilla%20Warfare.pdf.

31 "have the patience to persevere": *U.S. Government Counterinsurgency Guide,* Department of State, January 2009, https://state.gov/documents/organization/119629.pdf.

CHAPTER THREE: ADJUSTMENT DISORDER

33 At fencing, Bowe: Author interviews, December 2016.

34 the teacher, Anna Fontaine: Interview with "Anna Fontaine," December 2016. The source's name has been changed.

34 The bully had it coming: Interviews with Bob and Jani Bergdahl, July–August 2018.

36 She talked about her Hollywood: Interview with Kyle Koski, September 2016.
36 They had an extra room: Interview with Kyle Koski, May 2018.
36 Mark was an industrial designer: Interview with Mark Farris, November 2017.
37 "'Great, you do that'": Interview with Kyle Koski, August 2016.
38 Along with Bear Grylls: Interviews with Bob and Jani Bergdahl, July–August 2018.
38 experiments with self-surgery: Interview with source with firsthand knowledge.
38 On open mic nights: Interview with Kyle Koski, August 2016.
38 "Seeing the UPS truck": Interview with John Shaw, October 2016.
39 When Shaw met him: Jeff Cordes, "Naval Academy Is First Class for Michael Albrecht," *Idaho Mountain Express*, January 12, 2000.
41 The lone bright spot: Kim Dellacorva sworn statement, August 13, 2014, p. 2.
41 "He was too good a kid": Interview with Bob and Jani Bergdahl, April 2012.
42 Still, he bought: Testimony of Dr. Charles Morgan, Fort Bragg, North Carolina, November 1, 2017.
42 It was his eyesight: Interview with Bob and Jani Bergdahl, April 2012.
42 He told his mom: Interviews with Bob and Jani Bergdahl, July–August 2018.
44 Bowe told him to go away: Interview with John Raffa April 2016.
44 "I am responsible": Bowe Bergdahl sworn statement, U.S. Army 15-6 Investigation, August 6, 2014, p. 15.
44 Should former Seaman Recruit: Dahl Report, p. 02456.
44 get out of the Coast Guard: Kim Dellacorva sworn statement, August 13, 2014, p. 2.
45 "You don't just 'get out'": Ibid.
45 "I never met anybody": Interview with Matt Larson, October 2016.
46 "Hey, this is a truck!": Interview with Walt Femling, April 2016.
47 "He would just be": Interview with Mark Farris, December 2016.
47 He made it as far: Interviews with Bob and Jani Bergdahl, July–August 2018.

CHAPTER FOUR: AN ARMY OF ONE

48 He never told his parents: Interviews with Bob and Jani Bergdahl, July–August 2018.
48 But Bowe never complained: Author interview with a former Bergdahl employer, June 2016.
49 Bowe told his parents: Interview with Bob and Jani Bergdahl, April 2012.
49 As Iraq burned: Fred Kaplan, "The U.S. Army Lowers Recruitment Standards . . . Again," *Slate*, January 24, 2008, http://www.slate.com/articles/news_and_politics/war_stories/2008/01/dumb_and_dumber.html.
50 Her parting words: Author interview, December 2016.
51 On graduation day: Interview with Joseph Coe, September 2016.
52 "Bowe was good to go": Interview with Bob and Jani Bergdahl, April 2012.
52 "There is nothing": Gabriel Trollinger email to Matt Farwell, 2007.
53 The Army considered it: Solomon Moore, "G.I. Gets 10-Year Sentence in Killing of Unarmed Iraqi," *New York Times*, February 11, 2008, https://nytimes.com/2008/02/11/world/middleeast/11sniper.html.
53 Stangely, Hensley escaped: Tom Junod, "The Six-Letter Word that Changes Everything," *Esquire*, June 2008, https://esquire.com/news-politics/a4753/michael-hensley-0708.
53 He was crammed into: Interview with Joseph Coe and Gerald Sutton, September 2016.
53 "I will learn Russian": Stephanie McCrummen, "Bergdahl's Writings Reveal a Fragile Young Man," *Washington Post*, June 11, 2014.
53 sat in motionless meditation: Interview with Joseph Coe and Gerald Sutton, September 2016.
53 "He wasn't well accepted": Interview with Joseph Coe, February 2015.
54 When Bergdahl closed his eyes: Interview with Joseph Coe and Gerald Sutton, September 2016.

54 the Army ran for $25 million each: "Preparing to Succeed at the National Training Center," United States Army, www.army.mil/article/128699/preparing_to_succeed_at_the_national_training_center.

54 But he carried on: Interview with Jason Fry.

55 Wolfe emphasized that: "5 O'Clock Shadow," *Serial Podcast*, https://serialpodcast.org/season-two/6/5-oclock-shadow/transcript.

56 with his arm red and swollen: Interviews with Bob and Jani Bergdahl, July–August 2018.

56 "The closer I get": McCrummen, *Washington Post*, June 11, 2014.

57 expected to top one hundred thousand: Amy Belasco, *The Cost of Iraq, Afghanistan, and Other Global War on Terror Operations Since 9/11*, Congressional Research Service, September 2010.

57 "Don't take cross-border lightly": Afghanistan ROE in-theater briefing notes, 2006.

57 it grew sevenfold: Nicholas O. Melin, *Expanding Forward Operating Bases in Afghanistan*, United States Army, March 2007, http://www.dtic.mil/dtic/tr/fulltext/u2/a596611.pdf.

58 "'Are you serious?'": Bowe Bergdahl sworn statement, U.S. Army 15-6 Investigation, August 6, 2014, p. 62.

60 Bergdahl heard gunfire: Bowe Bergdahl sworn statement, U.S. Army 15-6 Investigation, August 6, 2014, p. 97.

CHAPTER FIVE: OP MEST

62 Task Force Yukon was commanded: James Russell, "Innovation in War: Military Operations in Afghanistan and Iraq," CENTCOM briefing, April 2010.

62 Howard seemed to see all: Interview with Nate Bethea, 2012.

64 shit between the graves: Interview with Joseph Coe and Gerald Sutton, September 2016.

65 no different from the child rapists: Bowe Bergdahl sworn statement, U.S. Army 15–6 Investigation, August 6, 2014, p. 55.

66 "This is a graveyard!": Interview with Gerald Sutton and Joseph Coe, September 2016.

66 "Actions may become . . .": McCrummen, "Bergdahl's Writings Reveal a Fragile Young Man," *Washington Post*, June 11, 2014.

67 "I plan better than that": Dahl Report, p. 02470.

67 email to Kayla: Ibid.

67 a Kindle to Kim: Ibid.

67 His parents were immediately worried: Michael Hastings, "The Last American Prisoner of War," *Rolling Stone*, June 21, 2012.

68 Conceited soldiers from: Dahl Report, p. 02472.

68 "'Whatever, you're full of shit'": Interview with Joseph Coe, February 2015.

69 leave Cross's 9mm: Dahl interview, p.183.

69 Bonding with them could prevent: Dahl interview, p. 189.

70 known as the Q Course: Dahl Report, p. 0229.

70 "mark of a man": Nat White, illustrator, Army recruiting poster, June 29, 1951.

72 afghanis and U.S. dollars: Dahl interview with Bergdahl, p. E0110.

72 he knew from books and movies: Ibid., p. E0177.

72 village and the Taliban fighters: Lt. Col. Clint Baker Article 32 testimony.

72 asked his sergeant what DUSTWUN meant: Dahl interview with Bergdahl, p. E0172.

73 "until I see a general": Ibid., p. E0123.

73 Deserters run away: Ibid., pp. E0129, E0125.

74 "I am done compromising": "Bergdahl in Email 3 Days Before Walking Off Base: 'I Am Done Compromising,'" CBS DC, June 12, 2014, https://washington.cbslocal.com/2014/06/12/bergdahl-in-email-3-days-before-walking-off-base-i-am-done-compromising.

CHAPTER SIX: DUSTWUN

78 **The men were always within:** Interview with Joseph Coe and Gerald Sutton, September 2016.

78 **There were Full and Gerleve:** Interviews with soldiers in the platoon; Bowe Bergdahl sworn statement, U.S. Army 15-6 Investigation, August 6, 2014, p. 36.

78 **It was a basic function:** Author experience with perstat reports as company RTO for D Co 2–87 Infantry.

79 **Tools: knives and his compass:** Bowe Bergdahl sworn statement, U.S. Army 15-6 Investigation, August 6, 2014, p. 154.

80 **He sent a team:** "Record of Preliminary Hearing Under Article 32 for Sergeant Robert Bowdrie Bergdahl," Joint Base San Antonio, Texas, September 17–18, 2015, p. 64.

80 **Six months earlier:** Text message to author from Joseph Coe, August 2018.

81 **He was quiet:** "Record of Preliminary Hearing Under Article 32 for Sergeant Robert Bowdrie Bergdahl," Joint Base San Antonio, Texas, September 17–18, 2015, pp. 56, 107.

81 **"Go ahead and send it":** Ibid., p. 66.

81 **The Eclipse Group:** Separate interviews with Dewey Clarridge and Michael Furlong, both 2016.

81 **The first official Taliban:** *Mail Foreign Service*, "Taliban Captures 'Drunk' U.S. Soldier in Afghanistan and Sells Him to Militant Clan," *Daily Mail,* July 2, 2009.

81 **He walked over:** Dahl Report, p. 02476.

82 **He saw their flashlight:** Bowe Bergdahl sworn statement, U.S. Army 15-6 Investigation, August 6, 2014, pp. 155-156, 160.

82 **He started down:** Ibid., pp. 160, 348.

82 **He thought about other soldiers:** Ibid., p. 129.

83 **"Stupid actions. Stupid":** Ibid., p. 130.

84 **It was close to noon:** Ibid., pp. 152, 163-64, 349.

84 **Captain Silvino Silvino was:** "Record of Preliminary Hearing Under Article 32 for Sergeant Robert Bowdrie Bergdahl," Joint Base San Antonio, Texas, September 17–18, 2015, p. 137.

84 **He took the job:** Interview with Joseph Coe and Gerald Sutton, September 2016.

85 **Baker decided to accompany:** "Record of Preliminary Hearing Under Article 32 for Sergeant Robert Bowdrie Bergdahl," Joint Base San Antonio, Texas, September 17–18, 2015, p. 204.

85 **"Sir, it is. Unfortunately":** Ibid., p. 147.

85 **It wouldn't be much:** This account of the hasty patrol is drawn from Billings's Article 32 testimony and interviews with Joseph Coe, John Mohammad (interpreter), Josh Cornelison, and Gerald Sutton.

86 **"A soldier went out for milk":** Interview with John Mohammad.

86 **the exact time: 0602:** Billings recalled an approximate time of 8:06 in his Article 32 testimony, but the U.S. Army Criminal Investigation Command Memorandum 2015/05/06, Subject: Law Enforcement report, SIR (Category 1)/1ST Final Supplemental—00152–2009-CID369–065293–5K2, page 10, says 0602 was compiled based on interviews and reports from Army Criminal Investigation Division (CID) agents who interviewed the platoon directly after the DUSTWUN.

87 **Command's eyes were:** Times derived from the timestamps on WikiLeaks Afghan War Logs KIDNAPPING REPORT B Co 1–501 PIR 30 June 2009 Ref # AFG20090630n1790. Those times are reported as Zulu time (Greenwich Mean Time) in the WikiLeaks reports, but have been converted to the local time, which is +4 hours and 30 minutes.

87 **M drones were:** "Hellfire Family of Missiles," United States Army Acquisition Support Center, http://asc.army.mil/web/portfolio-item/hellfire-family-of-missiles.

87 **The man was a pathfinder:** "Record of Preliminary Hearing Under Article 32 for Sergeant Robert Bowdrie Bergdahl," Joint Base San Antonio, Texas, September 17–18, 2015, p. 72.

88 **The pathfinders were:** *U.S. v. Robert Bowdrie Bergdahl*, Third Defense Motion to Compel (UCI), June 30, 2016, p. 24.

88 If he knew about: "New U.S. Commander Aims to Turn Afghan Tide," NBCNews.com, June 15, 2009, https://nbcnews.com/id/31363630/ns/world_news-south_and_central_asia/t/new-us-commander-aims-turn-afghan-tide.

CHAPTER SEVEN: THE LOST PUPPY

89 "I spend 80 percent": Michael Hastings, *The Operators* (New York: Blue Rider Press, 2012), p. 281.

89 President Obama had tapped McChrystal: Elisabeth Bumiller and Thom Shanker, "Commander's Ouster Is Tied to Shift in Afghan War," *New York Times*, May 11, 2009.

90 Flynn, who'd been: Michael T. Flynn and Michael Arthur Ledeen, *The Field of Fight: How We Can Win the Global War Against Radical Islam and Its Allies* (New York: St. Martin's Press, 2017), pp. 23–26.

90 Flynn was a good officer: Interview with Mario Caraballo, who was an 82nd Airborne NCO in Flynn's unit at the time.

91 The role that McChrystal: Elizabeth Bumiller and Mark Mazzetti, "A General Steps From the Shadows," *New York Times*, May 12, 2009, https://nytimes.com/2009/05/13/world/asia/13commander.html.

91 McChrystal had a reputation: Interview with Jeff Hayes, June 2016.

91 It was the same CIA: William J Broad, David E Sanger, and Raymond Bonner, "A Tale of Nuclear Proliferation: How Pakistani Built His Network," *New York Times*, February 12, 2004, https://www.nytimes.com/2004/02/12/world/a-tale-of-nuclear-proliferation-how-pakistani-built-his-network.html.

92 Furlong had ideas: Interview with Michael Furlong, May 2016.

92 It was one of the Alaska: Ibid.

92 Where Flynn was all confidence: Hastings, *The Operators*, p. 27.

92 McKiernan had called him: Mark Mazzetti, *The Way of the Knife: The CIA, a Secret Army, and a War at the Ends of the Earth* (New York: Penguin Books, 2014), p. 194

93 named part of Fort Irwin: Ibid., p. 177.

93 From there, he helped: Jeff Gerth, "Pentagon Linking Secret Army Unit to Contra Money," *New York Times*, April 22, 1987, https://www.nytimes.com/1987/04/22/world/pentagon-linking-secret-army-unit-to-contra-money.html.

93 He then worked: William Arkin, "Phreaking Hacktivists," *Washington Post*, January 18, 1999, https://washingtonpost.com/wp-srv/national/dotmil/arkin011899.htm.

93 He returned to the regular Army: "6th PSYOP Battalion Commanding Officers," USAPOVA, https://usapova.com/commanders-of-the-6th-psychological-operations-battalion.

94 An information security: "Student Guide, Personnel Security: Diplomatic Security Service," United States Department of State, http://dss.mil/multimedia/shorts/jpas-4-6/includes/JPAS_Levels_4-6_SG.pdf.

95 He told Furlong: Interview with Michael Furlong, May 2016.

95 While he was a CIA officer: Clarridge gives an entertaining account of his career in the CIA in his memoir. Duane R. Clarridge and Digby Diehl, *A Spy for All Seasons: My Life in the CIA* (New York: Scribner, 1997).

95 Clarridge was the first: *United States of America, Appellant v. Fawaz Yunis*, 867 F.2d617 (D.C. Cir. 1989).

95 He was investigated: George Lardner Jr., "Iran-Contra Prosecutors to Drop 2 Charges Against Ex-CIA Official," *Washington Post*, December 11, 1992.

96 payments to arms-dealing middlemen: Lawrence E. Walsh, *Firewall: The Iran-Contra Conspiracy and Cover-Up* (New York: Norton, 1998).

96 Bush, a former CIA man: George Bush, "Proclamation 6518—Grant of Executive Clemency," December 24, 1992, The American Presidency Project, University of California, Santa Barbara, http://presidency.ucsb.edu/ws/?pid=20265.

96 There was a plastic surgeon: Aram Roston, "The Trump Administration Is Mulling A Pitch For A Private 'Rendition' And Spy Network," BuzzFeed, November 30, 2017, https://buzzfeednews.com/article/aramroston/trump-administration-mulls-private-rendition.

96 Eclipse also used: Interviews with Michael Furlong, Tim Lynch, and Dewey Clarridge, December 2015–May 2016.

97 Furlong recalled how easy: Interview with Michael Furlong, May 2016.

97 There were five motorcycles: Bowe Bergdahl sworn statement, U.S. Army 15-6 Investigation, August 6, 2014, p. 233.

98 Through the cracks: Ibid., p. 236.

98 One struck him: Ibid., p. 238.

98 they used a cell phone: Ibid., p. 242.

98 first proof-of-life video: Linda Robinson, *One Hundred Victories: Special Ops and the Future of American Warfare* (New York: Public Affairs, 2013), p. 18.

99 "If you move": Bowe Bergdahl sworn statement, U.S. Army 15-6 Investigation, August 6, 2014, p. 239.

99 The American operations officer: The operations officer is identified throughout by the pseudonym Ron Wilson. This passage is taken from multiple interviews with the officer between March 2015 and September 2017.

100 goat fat and hashish: Interview with Ron Wilson, September 2016.

100 "If an American was kidnapped": Interview with Ron Wilson, March 2015.

101 According to one U.S. officer: Interview with U.S. military official, March 2015.

102 MICE was the mnemonic: Randy Burkett, "An Alternative Framework to Agent Recruitment," *Studies in Intelligence,* Vol. 57, No. 1 (Extracts, March 2013).

103 "We figured it would be": Interview with Ron Wilson, March 2015.

CHAPTER EIGHT: RIVER CITY

104 Colonel Mike Howard punched: WikiLeaks, "(CRIMINAL EVENT) KIDNAPPING RPT B CO 1-501 PIR: 0 INJ/DAM," Afghan War Diary.

104 The troops were accustomed: "'River City' and the Importance of the Military Death Notification Process," *The Funeral Law Blog*, https://funerallaw.typepad.com/blog/2014/04/river-city-and-the-importance-of-the-military-death-notification-process.html.

104–105 the USS *Dwight D. Eisenhower*: CVN-69 Locations, www.gonavy.jp/CVLocation69.html.

105 UIM INDICATES THAT: WikiLeaks Afghan War Diary.

105 At 8:13 p.m., the Americans: Ibid.

106 The Taliban told the ANP: Interviews with John Mohammad, December 2015; Joseph Coe and Gerald Sutton, September 2016.

106 One CIA case officer: Interview with CIA Case Officer "John Smith," June 2016.

106 interpreter "body shops": L3 company profile, https://www.l3t.com/about-l3/company-profile; Mission Essential Personnel, http://www.missionessential.com/about-us/locations/.

107 "I didn't go to spread democracy": Author interview with former interpreter, May 2016.

107 Afghan Special Immigrant Visa: Based on multiple interviews with Special Immigrant Visa applicants; one example is interpreter Nabi Mohammad, who was assigned to Farwell's platoon in 2006 and went to Fort Worth on a Special Immigrant Visa after three years in the queue. Farwell spent many hours on the phone with the women employees in New Hampshire.

108 If he were ever caught: Interviews with John Mohammad, December 2015.

109 "HE CAN GO [LOL]": The military's transcripts express audible laughter using the abbreviation LOL.

110 The Taliban who held Bergdahl: WikiLeaks Afghan War Diary.

110 Crapo's superiors told him: "Record of Preliminary Hearing Under Article 32 for Sergeant Robert Bowdrie Bergdahl," Joint Base San Antonio, Texas, September 17–18, 2015.

111 "It doesn't sound like much": Interview with former senior Pentagon official, October 2015.

112 living on orange soda: Interviews with Gerald Sutton.
112 "We're looking for Bergdahl": Interview with Joseph Coe and Gerald Sutton, September 2016.
113 In reality, Coe figured: Interview with Joseph Coe, February 2015.
114 For the ninety minutes back: Interview with former Army soldier, November 2017.
114 design and print single-page leaflets: Interview with former Blackfoot Company officer, March 2016.
115 they only found old men: Interviews with Gerald Sutton.
115 When they didn't comply: Ben Evans, *Serial* podcast, Season 2, Episode 2 "The Golden Chicken," December 2015.
115 wanted to re-create his identity: Interview with Sgt. Johnny Rice, March 2015.
115 "*Hopefully he's dead*": Ibid.

CHAPTER NINE: DIVERSIONS AND DECEPTIONS

116 forces had "fanned out": Richard A. Oppel Jr., "U.S. Soldier May Be Held by Taliban, Military Fears," *New York Times*, July 2, 2009, https://www.nytimes.com/2009/07/03/world/asia/03soldier.html.
116–117 Sangeen was a known quantity: Bill Roggio, "Mullah Sangeen Zadran," *FDD's Long War Journal*, July 17, 2009, https://longwarjournal.org/archives/2009/07/mullah_sangeen_zadran.php.
117 the early hours of July 3: Bowe Bergdahl sworn statement, U.S. Army 15-6 Investigation, August 6, 2014, p. 171.
117 Furlong was privy: Interview with Michael Furlong, May 2016.
117 On the afternoon of July 4: WikiLeaks Afghan War Diary.
117 Five years later in Texas: Bowe Bergdahl sworn statement, U.S. Army 15-6 Investigation, August 6, 2014, pp. 236, 243, 343.
118 In reality, it was the kidnappers: Robert Young Pelton, "Finding Private Bowe Bergdahl," *Vice*, July 21, 2014, https://www.vice.com/en_us/article/4w7q3d/finding-bergdahl-081.
118 Bergdahl was blindfolded: Bowe Bergdahl sworn statement, U.S. Army 15-6 Investigation, August 6, 2014, pp. 236.
119 doled out money: Multiple Geronimo soldiers and officers reported that money was paid for intelligence.
119 front-page *New York Times* story: Jane Perlez and Pir Zubair Shah, "Porous Pakistani Border Could Hinder U.S.," *New York Times*, May 4, 2009, https://www.nytimes.com/2009/05/05/world/asia/05fighter.html.
119 her superiors told her: Interview with Amber Dach, December 2017.
120 search for Bergdahl was over: Interview with Ron Wilson, March 2015.
121 Furlong spoke at Pentagon: Mazzetti, *The Way of the Knife*, p. 177.
121 Furlong knew he needed: Ibid., p. 196.
122 "Keep doing what": Interviews with Robert Young Pelton, 2015–2018.
122 invited an ISAF colonel: Interview with ISAF staff officer.
122 this "intel ring": It wasn't spying, Furlong explained, but "atmospherics," language he used to avoid running afoul of the law.
122 criteria for extrajudicial killing: Interview with Michael Furlong, May 2016. Criteria drafted by State Department legal adviser Harold Koh.
122 "brown people talking to brown people": Ibid.
123 he worked against them: Interview with ISAF staff officer, May 2016.
123 series of apparent leaks: Mazzetti and Filkins, "Contractors Tied to Effort to Track and Kill Militants," *New York Times*, March 14, 2010, https://nytimes.com/2010/03/15/world/asia/15contractors.html?pagewanted=all.
123 eliminate shadowy figures: David Ignatius, "When the CIA's Intelligence-Gathering Isn't Enough," *Washington Post*, March 18, 2010
123 assume it was authorized: Interview with Michael Furlong, May 2016.

123 Under the cover of: Ibid.

124 an alphabet soup: "Defendant in Procurement Fraud Case Involving Services in Afghanistan Sentenced to 42 Months in Federal Prison," United States Department of Justice, March 17, 2015, https://www.justice.gov/usao-ut/pr/defendant-procurement-fraud-case-involving-services-afghanistan-sentenced-42-months.

124 the best thing to do: By December 2015, Furlong was working as an informal adviser to the Trump presidential campaign.

124 On July 13, Bergdahl's captors: VillageDigital, "Taliban Video Shows Captive US Soldier Bowe Bergdahl," YouTube video, 2:22, July 18, 2009, www.youtube.com/watch?v=Q0snkYYCcb4.

124 ABC News cited military sources: Matthew Cole, "Exclusive: Missing U.S. Soldier May Be in Pakistan," ABC News, July 20, 2009, https://abcnews.go.com/Blotter/pfc-bowe-bergdahl-pakistan/story?id=8127636.

125 "You pay us": Interview with Amber Dach, December 2017.

126 the ruse went on: The "language tactic" strategy described by the former officer has been corroborated by multiple Army and Pentagon sources with direct knowledge of the case.

CHAPTER TEN: NOT THE WORST NEWS

130 "the endless acronyms": Interview with Bob and Jani Bergdahl, April 2012.

130 "greatest concern about Bowe": Interview with Glenn Ferrell, September 2016.

131 a Ketchum firefighter: "Zaney's River Street Coffee House," *Sun Valley Magazine*, http://sunvalleymag.com/business/zaneys-river-street-coffee-house.

131 phone calls from Oprah Winfrey: Interview with Nicki Chopski, April 2015.

132 included two retired Navy admirals: Author interview with Bob and Jani Bergdahl, April 2012.

133 Director Jim Spinelli: Plum TV, Hailey, Idaho, July 2009.

133 another smaller vigil: Susan Page, "Comfort for Our Only POW's Kin," *MidWeek*, August 12, 2009, http://archives.midweek.com/content/columns/susanspage_article/comfort_for_our_only_pows_kin.

134 the Taliban can save us: PoliticsNewsPolitics, "Fox News Military Pundit Calls Bowe Bergdahl 'A Liar,'" YouTube, July 19, 2009, www.youtube.com/watch?v=AL9P6W9vt6E.

134 "Perhaps Mr. Peters": Leo Shane, "Vets in Congress Disgusted by Analyst's Comments on Missing Soldier," *Stars and Stripes*, July 22, 2009, https://stripes.com/blogs/stripes-central/stripes-central-1.8040/vets-in-congress-disgusted-by-analyst-s-comments-on-missing-soldier-1.8257.

135 Peters found himself: Ralph Peters email, April 2012.

135 intelligence gatherers bearing cash: Interview with senior Pentagon official, September 2015.

135 commentator Michelle Malkin: Michelle Malkin, "Exclusive: The Story You Haven't Yet Heard about Bowe Bergdahl's Desertion," MichelleMalkin.com, June 3, 2014, http://michellemalkin.com/2014/06/03/exclusive-the-story-you-havent-yet-heard-about-bowe-bergdahls-desertion.

135 "It rejected Bowe Bergdahl": Interview with David Sedney, January 2018.

136 was "a jihadi": Interview with journalist who spoke to Gen. Flynn.

136 "One wonders, if he had been": Interview with Ahmed Rashid, March 2015.

137 JSOC was a bigger: Dana Priest and William M. Arkin, "'Top Secret America': A Look at the Military's Joint Special Operations Command," *Washington Post*, September 2, 2011.

137 To go into Pakistan: Ibid.

137 the "10–50 dance": Robert Chesney, "Military-Intelligence Convergence and the Law of the Title 10/Title 50 Debate," University of Texas Law, Public Law Research Paper No. 212, October 17, 2011.

138 Objective Cat Stevens: Interview with former Army officer, July 2015.

138 "never the primary purpose": This statement from Sedney—"It was never the primary purpose or one of the top two or three purposes of any operation that took place"—has been corroborated by multiple U.S. intelligence and defense officials, including Amber Dach.

CHAPTER ELEVEN: THE PAKISTAN PARADOX

139 "America needs Pakistan": Husain Haqqani, *Magnificent Delusions: Pakistan, The United States, and an Epic History of Misunderstanding* (New York: PublicAffairs, 2013), p. 8.

140 three thousand Pakistanis descended: Ibid.

141 the terminology changed: Waleed Ziad, "How the Holy Warriors Learned to Hate," *New York Times*, June 18, 2004, http://nytimes.com/2004/06/18/opinion/how-the-holy-warriors-learned-to-hate.html?_r=0.

141 By the early 1950s: Haqqani, *Magnificent Delusions*, p. 70.

141 American jazz trumpeter Dizzy Gillespie: "Jazz Strategy: Dizzy, Foreign Policy, and Government in 1956," *Americana: The Journal of American Popular Culture* 4, no. 1 (Spring 2005), http://americanpopularculture.com/journal/articles/spring_2005/gac.htm.

141 Gillespie was appalled: Penny M. Von Eschen, *Satchmo Blows Up the World: Jazz Ambassadors Play the Cold War* (Cambridge, MA: Harvard University Press, 2006), p. 33.

141 "an unruly horse by the tail": Haqqani, *Magnificent Delusions*, p. 87.

142 When Iran's Ayatollah: John Kifner, "Khomeini Accuses U.S. and Israel of Attempt to Take Over Mosques," *New York Times*, November 25, 1979, https://www.nytimes.com/1979/11/25/archives/khomeini-accuses-us-and-israel-of-attempt-to-take-over-mosques.html.

142 burned the American Embassy: ABC News, "For Diplomats, Pakistan Post Is No Party," *Nightline*, May 24, 2018, http://abcnews.go.com/Nightline/story?id=128457&page=1.

142 Muslim world's first atomic bomb: Rashid, *Pakistan on the Brink*, p. 169.

142 *New York Times* reporter: David Rohde, "U.S. Will Celebrate Pakistan as a 'Major Non-NATO Ally,'" *New York Times*, March 19, 2004, http://nytimes.com/2004/03/19/world/us-will-celebrate-pakistan-as-a-major-non-nato-ally.html?rref=collection%2525252Fbyline%2525252Fdavid-rohde.

142 Assistance from Germany, the U.K.: Rashid, *Pakistan on the Brink*, p. 32.

142 Pakistani military was not content: "How Much Did the U.S. Give Pakistan?" Fox Business, March 26, 2015, http://foxbusiness.com/markets/2011/05/11/did-pakistan.html.

143 Daniel Pearl was abducted: "Reporter Daniel Pearl Is Dead, Killed by His Captors in Pakistan," *Wall Street Journal*, February 24, 2002, http://wsj.com/articles/SB1014311357552611480.

143 they had two ultimatums: Frank Pellegrini, "Daniel Pearl: 1963–2002," *Time*, February 21, 2002, http://content.time.com/time/nation/article/0,8599,212284,00.html.

143 complicit in the Pearl atrocity: Jere Van Dyk, *Captive: My Time as a Prisoner of the Taliban* (New York: St. Martin's Griffin, 2011), p. 165.

143 "become America's slave": Steve Coll, *Directorate S: The C.I.A. and America's Secret Wars in Afghanistan and Pakistan* (New York: Penguin Press, 2018), p. 289.

143 Negroponte spoke frankly: "Pakistan's FATA Challenge," U.S. Department of State, 2001–2009, https://2001-2009.state.gov/s/d/2008/105041.htmm.

144 militias, terror groups, and Taliban: Rashid, *Pakistan on the Brink*, p. 161.

144 Fifty-eight people were killed: Coll, *Directorate S*, p. 312.

144 "We're going to stop playing": Bob Woodward, *Obama's Wars* (New York: Simon & Schuster, 2010), p. 5.

145 Pakistani court acquitted him: Mehreen Zahra-Malik, "Militant Leader Hafiz Saeed Is Released by Pakistani Court," *New York Times*, November 23, 2017, http://nytimes.com/2017/11/23/world/asia/hafiz-saeed-pakistan-militant.html.

145 "Make no mistake": "Obama's Remarks on Iraq and Afghanistan," *New York Times*, July 15, 2008, http://nytimes.com/2008/07/15/us/politics/15text-obama.html.

145 Obama read intelligence reports: Coll, *Directorate S*, p. 293.

145 "No administration in my entire career": Robert Michael Gates, *Duty: Memoirs of a Secretary at War* (New York: Vintage Books, 2015), p. 476.

145 Mullen led the diplomatic charge: Coll, *Directorate S*, p. 326.

145 sooner go to war with India: Rashid, *Pakistan on the Brink,* p. 64.

146 earned his master's degree: Karin Brulliard and Karen De Young, "U.S. Courts Pakistan's Top General, with Little Result," *Washington Post,* January 1, 2011, http://washingtonpost.com/wp-dyn/content/article/2010/12/31/AR2010123103993.html.

146 Pasha even vowed: Mark Mazzetti and Helene Cooper, "C.I.A. Pakistan Campaign Is Working, Director Says," *New York Times,* February 26, 2009, http://nytimes.com/2009/02/26/washington/26intel.html.

146 Obama ramped up: Rashid, *Pakistan on the Brink*, p. 54.

146 launch its drones from Shamsi Airfield: Ibid.

146 temporary nuclear winter: TheRealNews, "73 Years After Atomic Bombing of Japan: Nuclear Threat More Immediate Than Ever," YouTube, August 6, 2018. Analysis by Peter Kuznick, professor of history and director of the Nuclear Studies Institute at American University, https://www.youtube.com/watch?v=8NsRD60W92c.

147 only Muslim nuclear arsenal: White House, "White Paper of the Interagency Policy Group's Report on U.S. Policy toward Afghanistan and Pakistan," Homeland Security Digital Library, Library of Congress, Congressional Research Service, March 27, 2009, http://hsdl.org/?abstract&did=38004.

147 Taliban gunmen stopped a bus: Blaine Harden, "South Koreans Held by Taliban Arrive in Seoul, Offer Apologies," *Washington Post*, September 2, 2007, http://www.washingtonpost.com/wp-dyn/content/article/2007/09/01/AR2007090101376.html.

147 the Korean government in Seoul: Massoud Ansari, "Taliban Use Hostage Cash to Fund UK Blitz," *Telegraph*, October 14, 2007, http://telegraph.co.uk/news/worldnews/1566163/Taliban-use-hostage-cash-to-fund-UK-blitz.html.

148 Jere Van Dyk, a CBS: Jere Van Dyk, *The Trade* (New York: Hachette, 2017).

148 "felt like Icarus": "Kidnapped by the Taliban, Sean Langan Kept Sane by Dreaming of Kissing His Sons Goodnight," *Evening Standard,* April 13, 2012, http://standard.co.uk/news/kidnapped-by-the-taliban-sean-langan-kept-sane-by-dreaming-of-kissing-his-sons-goodnight-6869415.html.

148 he ignored his gut: Jeff Baker, "How 'Captive' Author Jere Van Dyk Discovered Himself While at the Taliban's Mercy," OregonLive.com, July 9, 2010, http://oregonlive.com/books/index.ssf/2010/07/how_captive_author_jere_van_dy.html.

149 Tory politicians and: Anand Gopal, "The Most Deadly US Foe in Afghanistan," *Christian Science Monitor*, June 1, 2009, http://m.csmonitor.com/World/Asia-South-Central/2009/0601/p10s01-wosc.html.

149 had paid £150,000 each: Jerome Starkey and Dipesh Gadher, "C4 pays £150,000 to Free Kidnapped Film Maker from Terror Camp," *The Times*, June 29, 2008.

149 final dose of irony: "Taliban Commander: Afghan Officials Are Helping Kill Americans," Axis of Logic, July 31, 2008, http://axisoflogic.com/artman/publish/Article_27831.shtml.

150 "a New York–based": David Rohde and Kristen Mulvihill, *A Rope and a Prayer: The Story of a Kidnapping* (New York: Penguin Books, 2011), p. 3.

150 bandits on the road: Ibid., p. 2.

150 body language visibly relax: Interview with David Rohde, December 2017.

151 "Don't get captured again": Ibid., p. 101.

151 That was $5 million more: Harden, *Washington Post.*

152 On June 19: David Rohde, "A Rope and a Prayer," *New York Times*, October 21, 2009, https://nytimes.com/2009/10/22/world/asia/22hostage.html.

152 the once-isolated infection: Rashid, *Pakistan on the Brink*, pp. 53, 140.

153 assassination of Benazir Bhutto: Joby Warrick, "CIA Places Blame for Bhutto Assassination," *Washington Post*, January 18, 2008, http://washingtonpost.com/wp-dyn/content/article/2008/01/17/AR2008011703252.html.

153 a ski-lift operator: Rashid, p. 141.

154 Musharraf had been lavished: Rashid, p. 138.

154 largest internal displacement of refugees: Declan Walsh, "Pakistani Civilians Flee Swat Valley as Major Ground Offensive Draws Closer," *Guardian*, May 10, 2009, http://theguardian.com/world/2009/may/10/pakistan-taliban-swat-valley.

154 "The military was ruthless": Ghulam Qadir Khan Daur, *Cheegha: The Call from Waziristan, the Last Outpost* (Sweden: Wisehouse Imprint, 2014) p. 38.

155 vague and evasive: Rashid, *Pakistan on the Brink*, p. 151.

CHAPTER TWELVE: FIXING INTEL

156 Bergdahl's second public: *U.S. v. SGT Robert B. Bergdahl*, Defense Motion to Suppress Alleged Statements from Captivity, July 17, 2017, p. 3.

Throughout his captivity, Bergdahl's captors filmed at least eighteen propaganda videos, nine of which were sent to U.S. military and government entities. Others were used for internal Haqqani and Taliban propaganda. In July and August 2014, Bergdahl told government debriefers how his captors scripted the videos: They removed his restraints, ordered him to wash up, change into fresh clothes, and read from scripts or repeat messages told to him by a man with a British accent who arrived at his holding locations with recording equipment. The man ordered him to appear natural and unrehearsed. When Bergdahl refused or his performance was insufficient, guards beat him and threatened him with firearms.

Further data and information on propaganda videos can be found in the unclassified report: "US Army Soldier Hostage Detention in Afghanistan and Pakistan; 30 June 2009–31 May 2014; Survival, Evasion, Resistance and Escape (SERE) Debriefing Analysis Product; Executive Summary," October 23, 2014, Joint Personnel Recovery Agency, Fort Belvoir, Virginia.

159 Blizter asked Hoh: *The Situation Room*, "Interview with Matthew Hoh," Real Clear Politics, November 10, 2009, https://www.realclearpolitics.com/articles/2009/11/10/interview_with_matthew_hoh_99115.html.

161 "not mind a prisoner exchange": "Taliban Seize U.S. Soldier in Afghanistan," CBS News, July 2, 2009.

161 Haqqani delivered their first: Edward M. Reeder, Jr., Five Star Global Security, https://www.fivestarglobalsecurity.com/edward-m-reeder-jr/.

162 Reeder passed the messages: Robinson, *One Hundred Victories*, p. 19; interview with Linda Robinson, March 2015.

162 he sent a short video clip: Karen DeYoung, "Letter Gives Glimpse of Al-Qaeda's Leadership," *Washington Post*, October 2, 2006, http://washingtonpost.com/wp-dyn/content/article/2006/10/01/AR2006100101083.html?nav=rss_world/mideast/iraq.

163 Langley issued orders: Robert Baer, "A Dagger to the CIA," *GQ*, February 26, 2010, http://gq.com/story/dagger-to-the-cia.

163 baked him a cake: A fuller description of the Camp Chapman attack and al-Balawi's life can be found in Joby Warrick, *The Triple Agent: The al-Qaeda Mole Who Infiltrated the CIA* (New York: Vintage Books, 2012).

163 Balawi stepped out: Theodore Weaver, "Camp Chapman Anniversary," Inglorious Amateurs, http://ingloriousamateurs.com/blogs/cables/camp-chapman-anniversary.

163 by Al Jazeera and on YouTube: Bill Roggio, "CIA Suicide Bomber Appears on Tape with Leader of Pakistani Taliban," *FDD's Long War Journal*, January 9, 2010, http://longwarjournal.org/archives/2010/01/cia_suicide_bomber_a.php.

163 The wise men: Stephen Farrell, "Video Links Taliban in Pakistan to C.I.A. Attack," *New York Times*, January 9, 2010, http://nytimes.com/2010/01/10/world/middleeast/10balawi.html?pagewanted=all.

163 In early February a secret report: "Foreign Intelligence Service and Haqqani Network Involvement in the December 30, 2009 Suicide Attack on FOB Chapman," Defense Intelligence Agency Information Report 20100114, https://nsarchive.files.wordpress.com/2016/04/hqn9.pdf.

164 heavily redacted portion: Chidanand Rajghatta, "Pakistan's ISI Funded Deadly Attack on CIA Camp in Afghanistan: US National Security Archive," *Times of India*, April 14, 2016, http://timesofindia.indiatimes.com/world/us/Pakistans-ISI-funded-deadly-attack-on-CIA-camp-in-Afghanistan-US-National-Security-Archive/articleshow/51819428.cms.

164 Pakistani intelligence was represented: "Pakistani Agents 'Funding and Training Afghan Taliban,'" BBC News, June 13, 2010, https://bbc.com/news/10302946.

164 General Flynn's staff updated: Noah Shachtman, "'Afghan Insurgency Can Sustain Itself Indefinitely': Top U.S. Intel Officer," *Wired*, January 1, 2010, http://wired.com/2010/01/afghan-insurgency-can-sustain-itself-indefinitely-top-us-intel-officer.

165 David Petraeus's 1987 Princeton: Rachel Dry, "Petraeus on Vietnam's Legacy," *Washington Post*, January 14, 2007, http://washingtonpost.com/wp-dyn/content/article/2007/01/12/AR2007011201955.html.

165 H. R. McMaster's 1997 book: H. R. McMaster, *Dereliction of Duty: Johnson, McNamara, the Joint Chiefs of Staff, and the Lies That Led to Vietnam* (New York: HarperCollins, 1997).

165 largest man-made nonnuclear: Senior Airman Emily Kenney, "Beirut Bombing: Reflections from Lebanon," Holloman Air Force Base, New Mexico, October 21, 2016, https://www.holloman.af.mil/Article-Display/Article/982634/beirut-bombing-reflections-from-lebanon/.

165 Sixty-three people were killed: Jane Mayer, "Ronald Reagan's Benghazi," TheNewYorker.com, May 5, 2014.

166 Flynn sent it to: Major General Michael T. Flynn, USA; Captain Matt Pottinger, USMC; Paul D. Bachelor, DIA; *Fixing Intel: A Blueprint for Making Intelligence Relevant in Afghanistan*, Center for a New American Security, January 2010.

167 President Obama had vowed: "Transcript of Obama Speech on Afghanistan," CNN, December 2, 2009, http://cnn.com/2009/POLITICS/12/01/obama.afghanistan.speech.transcript/index.html.

167 "Flynn was a guy": Interview with CIA Operations Officer B.

169 "the insurgency fights": Matthew P. Hoh, resignation letter to Ambassador Nancy J. Powell, director general of the Foreign Service, September 10, 2009, https://www.washingtonpost.com/wp-srv/hp/ssi/wpc/ResignationLetter.pdf.

169 on the path to quagmire: Woodward, *Obama's Wars*, p. 248.

169 This sorry state of affairs: Ibid.

169 didn't have enough troops: Ibid.

170 A CENTCOM investigation: Adverse Information Summary, CENTCOM AR 15–6 Investigation into Major General Michael T. Flynn, Investigations of Senior Official Directorate, Department of Defense Inspector General (DoDIG), http://apps.washingtonpost.com/g/documents/national/read-the-military-investigation-into-michael-flynn-trumps-national-security-adviser/2246.

170 Flynn had disclosed sensitive information: Craig Whitlock and Greg Miller, "Trump's National Security Adviser Shared Secrets without Permission, Files Show," *Washington Post*, Deccember 14, 2016, http://washingtonpost.com/world/national-security/trumps-national-security-adviser-shared-secrets-without-permission-files-show/2016/12/13/72669740-c146-11e6-9578-0054287507db_story.html?utm_term=.b4c9bdf59543.

170 McChrystal was fired: Michael Hastings, "The Runaway General," *Rolling Stone*, June 2010, https://rollingstone.com/politics/politics-news/the-runaway-general-the-profile-that-brought-down-mcchrystal-192609. Also see: Helene Cooper and David E. Sanger, "Obama Says Afghan Policy Won't Change After Dismissal," *New York Times*, June 23, 2010, https://nytimes.com/2010/06/24/us/politics/24mcchrystal.html.

170 Mike Flynn remained: Dana Priest and Greg Miller, "He Was One of the Most Respected Intel Officers of His Generation. Now He's Leading 'Lock Her Up' Chants," *Washington Post*, August 15, 2016, https://www.washingtonpost.com/world/national-security/nearly-the-entire-national-security-establishment-has-rejected-trumpexcept-for-this-man/2016/08/15/d5072d96-5e4b-11e6-8e45-477372e89d78_story.html?utm_term=.3c8017a8fab2.

NOTES

CHAPTER THIRTEEN: MEANS OF ESCAPE

172 He had done it twice: Dahl 15-6 interview, August 6, 2014.
173 free for less than fifteen: Bergdahl courtroom statement, Fort Bragg, North Carolina, October 30, 2017.
173 the next three months: Bowe Bergdahl personal statement, March 25, 2015.
173 Is Obama gay?: *Serial* podcast, Season 2, Episode 3, "Escaping."
173 the man twirled the hose: Terrence Russell testimony, Article 32 preliminary hearing, Fort Sam Houston, September 18, 2015.
173 kneeled on Bergdahl's chest: Interview with Terrence Russell, January 2018.
174 fed him elbow noodles: Bowe Bergdahl interview conducted by Sean Langan, December 2016.
174 cut away the dead flesh: Bergdahl statement, Fort Bragg Courthouse, October 30, 2017.
174 Bergdahl would spend: Bergdahl personal statement, March 25, 2015.
174 at least nine locations: JPRA report, October 23, 2014, p. 3.
174 The women would spit: Ibid., p. 4.
174 One school-age boy: Bowe Bergdahl interview conducted by Sean Langan, December 2016.
175 "It was usually about a week": Ibid.
175 The perpetual light was worse: Ibid.
175 when Bergdahl motioned: Ibid.
175 Into his cell walls: JPRA report, October 23, 2014, p. 6.
175 His illnesses had become: Bergdahl statement, Fort Bragg Courthouse, October 30, 2017.
175 he would die there: Bergdahl personal statement, March 25, 2015.
175 he had dug four or five feet: Bergdahl statement, Fort Bragg Courthouse, October 30, 2017.
176 "You can't go insane": JPRA report, p. 5.
176 "In so many ways": Bowe Bergdahl interview conducted by Sean Langan, December 2016.
176 He hid the key: Bergdahl statement, Fort Bragg Courthouse, October 30, 2017.
177 "I said to myself": Bowe Bergdahl interview conducted by Sean Langan, December 2016.
177 He began preparing: Bergdahl statement, Fort Bragg Courthouse, October 30, 2017.
178 Bergdahl walked through a night: *Serial* podcast, Season 2, Episode 3, "Escaping."
178 For the next eight nights: JPRA report, p. 7.
178 he heard the drones: *Serial* podcast, ibid.
178 a lone Taliban emerge: Bergdahl statement, Fort Bragg Courthouse, October 30, 2017.
179 "specifically built for me": Ibid.

CHAPTER FOURTEEN: PAWNS

183 the practice of negotiating, paying: Tom Eisinger, "Pirates: An Early Test for the New Country," National Archives and Records Administration, https://prologue.blogs.archives.gov/2015/07/12/pirates-an-early-test-for-the-new-country; Jack Kenny, "Bane of the Barbary Pirates," *New American*, https://thenewamerican.com/culture/history/item/4709-bane-of-the-barbary-pirates.
183 thousands of skeletons were found: Ebenezer Fox, *The Adventures of Ebenezer Fox, in the Revolutionary War* (Boston: Charles Fox, 1838), p. 139; Benedict Cosgrove, "The Grisly History of Brooklyn's Revolutionary War Martyrs," Smithsonian.com, March 13, 2017, https://smithsonianmag.com/history/grisly-history-brooklyns-revolutionary-war-martyrs-180962508/.
184 These young noblemen: David Hume, *The History of England from the Invasion of Julius Caesar to the Revolution in 1688* (London: Jones & Co., 1825), p. 384.
184 Prisoners, hostages, and detainees: Sibylle Scheipers, ed. *Prisoners in War* (Oxford: Oxford University Press, 2011), p. 3.
184 4,714 were held as POWs: Records of American Prisoners of War During the Korean War, created 1950–1953, documenting the period 1950–1953—Record Group 319 National Archives, https://aad.archives.gov/aad/fielded-search.jsp?dt=240&tf=F.

184 More than a third died: "North Korea and the Korean War 1951–1953 Peace and POWs," *Wide Angle,* PBS, August 5, 2004, https://pbs.org/wnet/wideangle/uncategorized/north-korea-and-the-korean-war-1951–1953-peace-and-pows/1365.

185 moved en masse to Pyongyang: "Treatment of US Prisoners of War," Central Intelligence Agency Report October 19, 1950 CREST Document Number CIA-RDP82–00457R0061001 50010–1, https://cia.gov/library/readingroom/document/cia-rdp82-00457r006100150010-1.

185 about Communist brainwashing: "Suggested Guidance for Public Aspects of U.S. Position on Korean Prisoner of War Talks," Psychological Strategy Board, Washington 25, D, C.PSB D.41 April3,1953April3,1953CRESTDOCUMENTNumberCIA-RDP80R01731R003200100001–9, https://cia.gov/library/readingroom/document/cia-rdp80r01731r003200100001-9.

185 fuses lit by masters in Pyongyang: "North Korea and the Korean Wars," *Wide Angle.*

185 the code of conduct itself: Lawrence E. Hinkle, "Notes on The Physical State of the Prisoner of War as It May Affect Brain Function," Bureau of Social Science Research Inc., January 1963.

186 "We were bombing": John Wilkens, "Defiant Vietnam POWs, Defiant Wives at Home," *San Diego Union Tribune*, August 25, 2016, www.sandiegouniontribune.com/military/sdut-vietnam-war-pows-2015jan10-story.html.

187 been "brainwashed" by American generals: Bart Barnes, "George Romney Dies at 88," *Washington Post*, July 27, 1995.

188 threatened American retaliation: Michael J. Allen, *Until the Last Man Comes Home: POWs, MIAs, and the Unending Vietnam War* (Chapel Hill: University of North Carolina Press, 2009), p. 16.

188 "a day for an appeal": Congressional Record, Senate, January 2, 1971, Volume 116, Part 33, p. 44541 (Washington, D.C.: Government Printing Office).

189 "Americans in South Vietnam": "Richard Nixon: The President's News Conference—February 17, 1971," the American Presidency Project, http://presidency.ucsb.edu/ws/index.php?pid=3309.

189 "I hope you can survive": Joseph Lelyveld, "Dear President Nixon, The Last 24 Hours Has Again Been Another Day of Pure Hell for Americans in Prison Camps, Cells, Cages in Southeast Asia," *New York Times*, October 3, 1971, https://nytimes.com/1971/10/03/archives/dear-president-nixon-the-last-24-hours-has-again-been-another-day-o.html.

189 five million remembrance bracelets: Ken Burns and Lynn Novick, *The Vietnam War*, Florentine Films and WETA, Washington, D.C., September 2017.

190 "I don't believe the Vietcong": Ibid.

190 "We have to hope": Sky Albrecht email.

191 "If nothing else": Interview with Roy Breshears, March 2016.

192 Bowe's maternal grandfather: Interview with Bob and Jani Bergdahl, April 2012.

193 Bob suspected that his son: Ibid.

193 how little had changed: Ibid.

194 Obama replied, coolly: Ibid.

194 Bob didn't need a classified briefing: Ibid.

195 "My son is a Marine": Interview with Susan Page, April 2018.

195 In February, the Dutch: Reed Stevenson and Aaron Gray-Block, "Dutch Government Falls over Afghan Troop Mission," Reuters, February 20, 2010, https://independent.co.uk/news/world/europe/dutch-government-falls-over-afghan-troop-mission-1905407.html.

195 first major NATO ally: Nicholas Kulish, "Dutch Government Collapses Over Its Stance on Troops for Afghanistan," *New York Times*, February 21, 2010, https://nytimes.com/2010/02/21/world/europe/21dutch.html.

195 botched February 12 night mission: Jerome Starkey et al., "U.S.-Led Forces in Afghanistan Are Committing Atrocities, Lying, and Getting Away with It," Nieman Watchdog, March 22, 2010, www.niemanwatchdog.org/index.cfm?backgroundid=440&fuseaction=background.view.

195 killing them all: Richard A. Oppel Jr., "U.S. Admits Role in February Killing of Afghan Women," *New York Times*, April 5, 2010, https://nytimes.com/2010/04/05/world/asia/05afghan.html?ref=world.

195 an American atrocity: Scott Horton, "The Trouble with Embeds," *Harper's Magazine*, "No Comment," March 24, 2010, https://harpers.org/blog/2010/03/the-trouble-with-embeds.

195 Obama's surge had sent: UN News, "World Must Act Now to Reverse Worsening Situation in Afghanistan—Ban," UN News, January 4, 2010, https://news.un.org/en/story/2010/01/325772-world-must-act-now-reverse-worsening-situation-afghanistan-ban.

195 "lose this fucking war": General Stanley McChrystal, *My Share of the Task* (New York: Portfolio/Penguin, 2013), p. 310.

196 Bob and Mullen had graduated: Interview with Bob and Jani Bergdahl, April 2012.

196 "There were many times": Interview with Michael Mullen, February 2018.

196 For Mattis, it was growing up: Dexter Filkins, "James Mattis, A Warrior in Washington," *New Yorker*, May 29, 2017.

196 Mattis hung it: Interviews with Bob and Jani Bergdahl, July–August 2018.

197 "until we hear from Bowe": Interview with Bob and Jani Bergdahl, April 2012.

197 first proof-of-life video: Associated Press, "Taliban Release Video of Captured US Soldier," YouTube, 1:14, April 7, 2010, www.youtube.com/watch?v=vHfSHVwJVFA.

197 Karzai made a bold call: Julian Borger and Ian Black, "UN-Taliban Peace Talks Spur Karzai to Action," *Guardian*, January 28, 2010, https://theguardian.com/world/2010/jan/28/afghanistan-un-peace-talks-taliban.

198 "Just as the infidels are one": Bill Roggio, "An Interview with Mullah Sangeen," *FDD's Long War Journal*, September 17, 2009, https://longwarjournal.org/archives/2009/09/an_interview_with_mullah_sange.php.

198 (The White House was not aware): Interview with senior White House official, June 2018.

198 "Greetings and peace": Images of both letters were provided to author.

199 the party was using him: Interviews with Bob and Jani Bergdahl, July–August 2018.

199 ISAF airstrikes had killed: Bill Roggio, "Senior Taliban Commander Killed in Kandahar," *FDD's Long War Journal*, May 31, 2010, https://longwarjournal.org/archives/2010/05/senior_taliban_comma_1.php.

199 Security ahead of the June 2 event: Jonathon Burch, "Kabul Readies Security Ahead of Peace Jirga," Reuters, May 31, 2010, https://in.reuters.com/article/idINIndia-48929820100531.

200 rocket attack issued: Kristen Chick, "Afghanistan Taliban Attack Hamid Karzai's 'Peace Jirga,'" *Christian Science Monitor*, June 2, 2010, https://csmonitor.com/World/terrorism-security/2010/0602/Afghanistan-Taliban-attack-Hamid-Karzai-s-peace-jirga.

200 "They are the sons": Ernesto Londoño, "Suicide Bombers Try to Disrupt Start of Afghan Peace Meeting," *Washington Post*, June 2, 2010, https://washingtonpost.com/wp-dyn/content/article/2010/06/02/AR2010060200263.html?sid=ST2010060103567.

200 Karzai accepted resignations: Alissa J. Rubin, "Afghan Leader Forces Out Top 2 Security Officials," *New York Times*, June 6, 2010, https://nytimes.com/2010/06/07/world/asia/07afghan.html.

200 "Mayor of Kabul": Woodward, *Obama's Wars*, p. 68.

200 These were the people: Interviews with Bob and Jani Bergdahl, July–August 2018.

201 "So we pray": Author notes from June 2010 event.

CHAPTER FIFTEEN: THE NO-NEGOTIATIONS NEGOTIATIONS

204 They gave Pelton: Interviews with Robert Young Pelton, 2015–2018.

204 fully integrated Taliban collaborator: Interview with Miles Amoore, August 2015.

205 "CAPTURED U.S. SOLDIER HAS JOINED": Miles Amoore, "Captured U.S. Soldiers Has Joined Our Cause, Say Taliban," *Sunday Times*, August 22, 2010.

205 no coherent diplomatic policy: Peter Baker, "How Obama Came to Plan for 'Surge' in Afghanistan," *New York Times*, Deccember 5, 2009.

205 peace talks were never: Coll, *Directorate S*, p. 427.

205 would be granted amnesty: Kate Clark, "Releasing the Guantanamo Five? 1: Biographies of the Prisoners," Afghanistan Analysts Network, https://afghanistan-analysts.org/releasing-the-guantanamo-five-1-biographies-of-the-prisoners-first-posted-09-03-2012.

206 aboard the USS *Peleliu*: Ben Fenton, "Taliban Chiefs Held on US Warship," *Telegraph*, December 21, 2001, https://telegraph.co.uk/news/worldnews/asia/afghanistan/1366019/Taliban-chiefs-held-on-US-warship.html.

206 carried the first Marines: Katharine Q. Seelye, "A Nation Challenged: The Detention Camp: U.S. to Hold Taliban Detainees in 'the Least Worst Place,'" *New York Times*, December 28, 2001, http://nytimes.com/2001/12/28/us/nation-challenged-detention-camp-us-hold-taliban-detainees-least-worst-place.html.

206 sedated with rectal suppositories: The practice of anal sedation was common for extraordinary rendition cases in the War on Terror. A full description can be found in James E. Pfander, *Constitutional Torts and the War on Terror* (New York: Oxford University Press, 2017).

206 None had been charged: "Taliban to Surrender Kunduz," Associated Press, November 22, 2001.

206 open-air U.S. detention camp: Seelye, "A Nation Challenged."

206 Støre waited until December: Norwegian Ministry of Foreign Affairs and Ministry of Defense, "A Good Ally: Norway in Afghanistan 2001–2014," Official Norwegian Reports NOU 2016: 8, June 6, 2016; English Edition February 2018.

207 Norwegians soon accepted: Ibid.

208 had met with former ISI directors: Memo from Barnett R. Rubin to Richard Holbrooke, "Schedule and Activities," December 27, 2008.

209 flew to Kabul to meet with: Interview with Barnett R. Rubin, September 2017.

209 wrote a memoir: Nick Meo, "My Life with the Taliban by Abdul Salam Zaeef: Review," *Telegraph*, January 24, 2010, https://www.telegraph.co.uk/culture/books/7053973/My-Life-with-the-Taliban-by-Abdul-Salam-Zaeef-review.html.

209 kind of moderate Taliban: The Guantanamo Docket, *New York Times*, https://nytimes.com/interactive/projects/guantanamo/detainees/306-abdul-salam-zaeef.

209 fighting the war forever: Coll, *Directorate S*, p. 445.

210 "Talk to them or arrest them?": Interview with Barnett R. Rubin, September 2017.

210 death of Mullah Awal Gul: Autopsy Report: Awal Gul, Guantanamo Bay (Natural) (Death Certificate Included), the Torture Database, www.thetorturedatabase.org/document/autopsy-report-awal-gul-guantanamo-bay-natural-death-certificate-included. The Pentagon said that Gul died of a heart attack following a workout on an elliptical machine, but Rubin wasn't so sure. "Being in Guantanamo is not good for your health," he said.

210 fly to Dubai to meet: Interview with Barnett R. Rubin, September 2017.

210 Mullah Omar wanted to talk: Coll, *Directorate S*, p. 420.

210 in 1998, the young man had served: Rubin email, September 2018.

211 Rubin told Holbrooke: Ibid.

211 an Iranian double agent: Interview with Barnett R. Rubin, September 2017.

211 Lieutenant General Douglas Lute: Helene Cooper, "War Czar for Bush to Keep His Job," *New York Times*, January 13, 2009, thecaucus.blogs.nytimes.com/2009/01/13/war-czar-for-bush-to-keep-his-job.

211 appointed by President Bush: Peter Baker and Robin Wright, "Bush Taps Skeptic of Buildup as 'War Czar,'" *Washington Post*, May 16, 2007, http://washingtonpost.com/wp-dyn/content/article/2007/05/15/AR2007051501612.html.

212 "The Taliban want to talk": Interview with Barnett R. Rubin, September 2017.

212 "We're gonna need you full time": Ibid.

213 Obama agreed that Agha could travel: Coll, *Directorate S*, p. 243.

213 "most important objective": Hillary Rodham Clinton, *Hard Choices: A Memoir* (New York: Simon & Schuster, 2014).

214 German and Qatari diplomats: Interview with Barnett R. Rubin, September 2017.

214 meeting began with each side reading: Coll, *Directorate S*, p. 512.

214 the Haqqanis and the Taliban: Interview with Jeff Hayes, June 2016.

215 the prisoner exchange: In his opening bid, Agha called for twelve Taliban detainees to be released from Guantanamo and Bagram in exchange for Bergdahl.

215 In the ambulance: Ronan Farrow, *War on Peace: The End of Diplomacy and the Decline of American Influence* (New York: Norton, 2018), p. 121.

215 National Defense Authorization Act: Josh Gerstein, "Obama Signs Defense Bill that Could Cripple His Guantanamo Policy," *Politico,* January 7, 2011, http://politico.com/blogs/under-the-radar/2011/01/obama-signs-defense-bill-that-could-cripple-his-guantanamo-policy-031996.

215 direct aim at Obama's pledge: Barack Obama, "Statement by the President on H.R. 6523," National Archives and Records Administration, January 7, 2011, http://obamawhitehouse.archives.gov/the-press-office/2011/01/07/statement-president-hr-6523.

215 Washington hard-liners had: Interview with White House official.

215 on his first day in office: Exec. Order. No. 13492, 74 Fed. Reg. 4669 (January 22, 2009), https://www.archives.gov/federal-register/executive-orders/2009-obama.html.

CHAPTER SIXTEEN: BOB'S WAR

216 The stickers had been sent: Interview with Keith Maupin, May 2016.

217 "My theory was": Bob Bergdahl email, July 2017.

217 "Former Spy with Agenda": Mark Mazzetti, "Former Spy with Agenda Operates a Private C.I.A.," *New York Times*, January 22, 2011, http://nytimes.com/2011/01/23/world/23clarridge.html.

217 Such blood-money payoffs: M. Ilyas Khan, "CIA Contractor Ray Davis Freed over Pakistan Killings," BBC News, March 16, 2011, http://bbc.com/news/world-south-asia-12757244.

218 "If you're a CIA Blackwater": Interview with Bob and Jani Bergdahl, April 2012.

218 A tall, kind-eyed man: Interview with Marc Grossman, April 2016.

218 Clinton asked him: Mark Landler, "Richard Holbrooke to Be Replaced by Marc Grossman," *New York Times*, February 14, 2011, http://nytimes.com/2011/02/15/world/asia/15envoy.html.

218 negotiating with Omar's direct blessing: Coll, *Directorate S*, p. 527.

218 The Fake Mullah: Carlotta Gall and Dexter Filkins, "Taliban Leader in Secret Talks Was an Impostor," *New York Times*, November 22, 2010, https://nytimes.com/2010/11/23/world/asia/23kabul.html?ref=asia.

219 "dealing with the real guy": Interview with Jeff Hayes, June 2016.

219 If he followed through: Coll, *Directorate S*, p. 528.

219 the Bergdahls feared: Interview with Bob and Jani Bergdahl, April 2012.

220 "I am the father": Robert Bergdahl, "Captured American Soldier in Pakistan," YouTube, 3:09, May 6, 2011, https://www.youtube.com/watch?v=yJmmZQ3byKQ.

221 The Rutherford video: Blazing Catfur, "Taliban Video of Colin Mackenzie Rutherford," YouTube, 3:09, May 8, 2011, https://www.youtube.com/watch?v=dapJEDKFXjo.

221 returned to the Munich safe house: Coll, *Directorate S*, p. 567.

222 letter for President Obama: The letter was typewritten, and the Americans considered it an unverifiable claim. Earlier that year, the *Washington Post* had reported that Omar had been rushed to a hospital in Karachi by his ISI minders and had suffered mild brain damage as a result. (The story cited Clarridge's Eclipse Group as its source.) The Taliban leader had not been seen in public in years, and for all the Americans knew, the letter could have been written by any Taliban imposter, including the ISI.

222 presssing for the prisoner exchange: Coll, *Directorate S*, p.568.

222 when Grossman reiterated: Ibid., p. 581.

223 getting the plan through: Ibid., p. 583.

223 "It was incomprehensible": Interview with Barnett R. Rubin, September 2016.

223 "peaceniks sitting around": Interview with Jeff Hayes, June 2016.
224 "If I added up": Notes taken by Jani Bergdahl, November 2011.
224 "If you don't know": Bob Bergdahl email, August 2018.
224 the alias used by: Rod Nordland, "One Voice or Many for the Taliban, but Pegged to a Single Name," *New York Times*, June 14, 2011.
225 Sergeant Bergdahl's weeklong escape: Bergdahl had been promoted in absentia on June 15, 2011. Brig. Gen. Richard Mustion, Human Resources Command, flew to Hailey for the promotion ceremony in Bob and Jani's backyard, where they were joined by Idaho governor Butch Otter and his wife, Lori. Email from Brig. Gen. Mustion to Bob Bergdahl, June 15, 2011; CNN Wire Staff and Larry Shaughnessy, "Captured U.S. Soldier Receives Second Promotion in Two Years," CNN, June 17, 2011, https://cnn.com/2011/US/06/17/afghanistan.captured.soldier/index.html.
225 "They just blew a gasket": Interview with Jeff Hayes, June 2016.
225 one Republican staffer: Michael Hastings, "The Last American Prisoner of War," *Rolling Stone*, June 21, 2012.
225 his "Willie Horton moment": In September 1988, George H. W. Bush's presidential campaign ran an infamous but effective television ad about Horton, who, as a convicted murderer in Massachusetts, was out of jail on a weekend a furlough program approved by Governor Michael Dukakis when he went on a violent spree of rape and robbery. The ad put the blame squarely on Dukakis and shifted the race decisively in Bush's favor.
225 the Taliban officially withdrew: "Afghanistan's Taliban Suspend Peace Talks with US," BBC News, March 15, 2012, http://bbc.com/news/world-asia-17379163.
225 "Leave this to me": Bob Bergdahl email, August 2018.
226 "How deep is the water": Bob Bergdahl email to Matt Farwell, April 29, 2012.
227 Instead, McDonough pledged: Interviews with Bob and Jani Bergdahl, July–August 2018.
228 highly polished granite: The Korean War Veterans Memorial, http://www.koreanwarvetsmemorial.org/the-memorial/.
229 "Do you understand Pashto?": Ibid.
230 "We love you": Hastings, Ibid.

CHAPTER SEVENTEEN: THE FIVE-SIDED WIND TUNNEL

231 In casual off-the-record: Interviews with journalists, December 2017, June 2018.
231 Linda Norgrove, a thirty-six-year-old: Julian Borger, "Linda Norgrove: US Navy Seal Faces Disciplinary Action over Grenade Death," *Guardian*, October 13, 2010, https://www.theguardian.com/world/2010/oct/13/linda-norgrove-us-commando-disciplinary.
232 Amerine carefully maintains: Interview with Jason Amerine, May 2016.
232 that dull-sounding job: The portrait of Amerine's organization is drawn from interviews with Army officials who requested anonymity to discuss the organization. Further references can be found in "Report on the Inquiry into the Department of Defense's May 2014 Transfer to Qatar of Five Law-of-War Detainees in Connection with the Recovery of a Captive U.S. Soldier," December 9, 2015, Committee on Armed Services, U.S. House of of Representatives, (see below as "HASC report"), https://armedservices.house.gov/sites/republicans.armedservices.house.gov/files/wysiwyg_uploaded/Report%20on%20the%20Inquiry%20into%20the%20Taliban%20Five%20Transfer_0.pdf.
232 When President Truman abolished: Exec. Order. No. 9621, 10 Fed. Reg. 12033 (September 20, 1945), https://www.archives.gov/federal-register/executive-orders/1945-truman.html.
232 Identifying itself by the number: House Armed Services Committee Report, December 9, 2015, p. 80.
233 no single official in charge: Interview with Jason Amerine, May 2016.
233 "How can nobody know": Ibid.
234 septuagenarian Warren Weinstein: Daniel Bergner, "The Killing of Warren Weinstein," *The New York Times Magazine*, February 11, 2016, https://www.nytimes.com/2016/02/14/magazine/the-killing-of-warren-weinstein.html.

235 a missionary couple: John McWethy, "Ransom Arranged to Rebel Group," ABC News, April 11, 2003, https://abcnews.go.com/WNT/story?id=130394&page=1

236 Mattis and a plainclothes bodyguard arrived: Bob Bergdahl emails; interviews with Bob and Jani Bergdahl, July–August 2018.

237 "If it were my son": Interviews with Bob and Jani Bergdahl, July–August 2018; interview with Amber Dach, September 2018.

237 "U.S. to Launch Peace Talks": Karen DeYoung, "U.S. to Launch Peace Talks with Taliban," *Washington Post,* June 18, 2013.

238 Rubin, already in Doha: *Serial* podcast, Season 2, Episode 9, "Trade Secrets."

238 "The flag remains": Dawood Azami, "Afghan Taliban Open Doha Office," BBC News, June 20, 2013.

238 But it was too late: Dan Roberts and Emma Graham-Harrison, "US-Taliban Afghanistan peace talks in Qatar canceled," *Guardian,* June 20, 2013.

241 a successful opium trader: Interview with Barnett R. Rubin, September 2016.

241 one of Mullah Omar's: Matthieu Aikins, "The Master of Spin Boldak," *Harper's,* December 2009, p. 55, https://harpers.org/archive/2009/12/the-master-of-spin-boldak/4.

241 Noorzai feared he was next: Gopal, p. 113.

241 a historic catch: James Risen, *Pay Any Price* (New York, Houghton Mifflin Harcourt, 2014), p. 116.

241 they arrested him: Interview with Alan Seidler, Noorzai's defense attorney, September 2016.

242 found widespread support: HASC Report, p. 80.

242 "This is a DoD issue": Interview with Jason Amerine, May 2016.

243 when Obama traveled to Kabul: Coll, *Directorate S*, p. 638.

243 included Bob Bergdahl himself: Letter from Bob Bergdahl, September 2017.

244 With Mullen's support: Interviews with Bob and Jani Bergdahl, July–August 2018.

244 an FBI team pursued: Corroborating versions of these events have been described in interviews with several Pentagon officials. Further documentation can be found in the December 2015 House Armed Services Committee report, pp. 82–83.

244 FBI counterrorism agents, trained: Adam Goldman and Julie Tate, "Inside the FBI's Secret Relationship with the Military's Special Operations," *Washington Post,* April 10, 2014.

244 On February 23: Taliban: Calls Off Talks over Sgt. Bowe Bergdahl," Associated Press, February 23, 2014.

244 detailed exfiltration plan: HASC Report, pg. 83.

244 reported $10 million: Aram Roston, "Exclusive: Inside the Other Bergdahl Negotiations," BuzzFeed News, June 26, 2014.

245 On March 6, they traveled together: Sean Smith email, December 2017.

CHAPTER EIGHTEEN: WELCOME HOME

249 With about an hour's notice: Chuck Hagel testimony to House Armed Services Committee: "U.S.-Taliban Prisoner Exchange," C-SPAN video, 4:46:57, June 11, 2014, https://c-span.org/video/?319849-1/secretary-hagel-bergdahl-prisoner-exchange.

249 The Americans agreed: Translation of Taliban video by former ISAF interpreters.

249 a regional, one-day cease-fire: Chelsea J. Carter and Barbara Starr, "Army Sgt. Bowe Bergdahl: Flight to Freedom," CNN, June 1, 2014, https://cnn.com/2014/05/31/world/meast/afghanistan-bergdahl-aboard-helicopter/index.html.

249 They blindfolded him: JPRA Report.

249 The film opens with several gunmen: Storyful, "Taliban Releases Video of Bowe Bergdahl Exchange," YouTube, 17:03, June 3, 2014, https://www.youtube.com/watch?v=eQKd7pYFx5Y.

250 "We told them there are": Emma Graham-Harrison, "Bowe Bergdahl: Taliban Release Dramatic Video of Handover to US," *Guardian,* June 4, 2014, https://theguardian.com/world/2014/jun/04/taliban-releases-video-bowe-bergdahl-handed-over-us.

250 Bergdahl, who is still blinking: Interview with Terrence Russell, December 2016.

250 guards whom he had never seen: Ibid.

251 "we've been looking for you": "Bowe Bergdahl, a Taliban Captive since 2009, Has Been Freed," *CBS News*, May 31, 2014, https://cbsnews.com/news/bowe-bergdahl-a-taliban-captive-since-2009-has-been-freed.

251 Bergdahl broke down in tears: Sam Frizell and Zeke J. Miller, "Sgt. Bowe Bergdahl Returned from Taliban Custody in Afghanistan," *Time*, May 31, 2014, https://time.com/2803616/bowe-bergdahl-american-afghanistan-returned.

252 it was time to salvage: Interview with White House official, June 2018.

252 As the Taliban sensed: House Armed Services Committee Report, December 2015, p. 12.

252 direct written approval: Hagel testimony to House Armed Services Committee: "U.S.-Taliban Prisoner Exchange," C-SPAN video, 4:46:57, June 11, 2014, https://c-span.org/video/?319849-1/secretary-hagel-bergdahl-prisoner-exchange.

252 former Pentagon lead counsel: HASC Report, December 2015, p. 11.

253 Butler, who in 2005: "United States Navy Biography: Rear Admiral Richard W. Butler," Department of the Navy, http://navy.mil/navydata/bios/navybio_ret.asp?bioID=643.

253 Indiana University law school students: Whitney Coffin, "Washington Trip 5/29/14," Gitmo Observer, http://gitmoobserver.com/2014/05.

253 conditions of their imminent release: Anne Gearan, "Sources Outline Conditions on Taliban Leaders' Release in Exchange for Bergdahl," *Washington Post*, June 5, 2014, http://washingtonpost.com/world/national-security/sources-outline-conditions-on-taliban-leaders-release-in-exchange-for-bergdahl/2014/06/05/4ed9d8a0-eceb-11e3-93d2-edd4be1f5d9e_story.html?utm_term=.957dbdcefe50.

253–254 there was only one transfer: *Serial* podcast, Season 2, Episode 9, "Trade Secrets."

254 On the morning of May 31: House Armed Services Committee Report, December 2015, p. 31.

254 first days in office: Barack Obama, Executive Order 13492—Review and Disposition of Individuals Detained at the Guantánamo Bay Naval Base and Closure of Detention Facilities, January 22, 2009, American Presidency Project, http://presidency.ucsb.edu/ws/index.php?pid=85670.

254 likely broken the law: The legality of the exchange has never been conclusively settled. The congressional Government Accountability Office ruled it illegal, but the Departments of Justice and Defense said Obama had acted within his presidential powers. Constitutional scholars remain divided on the issue. GAO memorandum from August 21, 2014, Government Accountability Office, https://www.gao.gov/assets/670/665390.pdf.

255 told Jani to hold: Interviews with Bob and Jani Bergdahl, July–August 2018.

255 press office held a preliminary: House Armed Services Committee Report, December 2015.

255 Obama lauded the Bergdahls': Barack Obama, "Statement by the President on Sergeant Bowe Bergdahl," May 31, 2014, National Archives and Records Administration, http://obamawhitehouse.archives.gov/the-press-office/2014/05/31/statement-president-sergeant-bowe-bergdahl.

256 a *Washington Post* reporter: Rajiv Chandrasekaran, "US Army Sgt. Bowe Bergdahl Released Today after 5 Yrs in Taliban Captivity, in Exchange for 5 Afghan Prisoners at Gitmo," Twitter, May 31, 2014, https://twitter.com/rajivscribe/status/472774927737970688.

256 "there would be a backlash": Interview with Chuck Hagel, January 18, 2018.

256 Hagel was in Singapore: "Chuck Hagel: Beijing 'Destabilising' South China Sea," BBC News, May 31, 2014, http://bbc.com/news/world-asia-27646223.

256 General Dempsey posted: GEN(R) Marty Dempsey. "It Is Our Ethos That We Never Leave a Fallen Comrade. Welcome Home SGT Bowe Bergdahl," Twitter, May 31, 2014, http://twitter.com/martin_dempsey/status/472779295086379008.

256 Kerry followed with: John Kerry, "Sergeant Bowe Bergdahl," U.S. Department of State, May 31, 2014, http://2009-2017.state.gov/secretary/remarks/2014/05/227013.htm.

256 Pentagon correspondent Barbara Starr: Chelsea J. Carter and Barbara Starr, "Army Sgt. Bowe Bergdahl: Flight to Freedom," CNN, June 1, 2014, https://www.cnn.com/2014/05/31/world/meast/afghanistan-bergdahl-aboard-helicopter/index.html.

256 Hagel said the teams involved: Interview with Chuck Hagel, January 18, 2018.
257 Ayotte had called on: Boc Cesca, "Republicans on Sgt. Bergdahl: Then & Now," Daily Banter, June 4, 2014, https://thedailybanter.com/issues/2014/06/04/republicans-sgt-bergdahl-now.
257 Nugent had introduced: David Fahrenthold and Jaime Fuller, "The Bergdahl Boomerang: Some Lawmakers Who Long Urged a Rescue Now Sour on the Idea," *Washington Post*, June 5, 2014, https://washingtonpost.com/politics/the-bergdahl-boomerang-gop-lawmakers-who-long-urged-a-rescue-now-sour-on-the-idea/2014/06/06/a538698a-ece3-11e3-93d2-edd4be1f5d9e_story.html?utm_term=.78e892a527a7.
257 gears of the swap: Interview with White House official, June 2018.
258 "something in the Rose Garden": Interview with White House official, February 2018.
259 Jani looked at the president: Interviews with Bob and Jani Bergdahl, July–August 2018.
260 "no need for that": Interview with Michael Mullen, February 2018.

CHAPTER NINETEEN: FOX NATION

261 Anna Fontaine was: Interview with "Anna Fontaine," December 2016.
261 Each year on Memorial Day: Interview with Tanya Olson, December 2016.
261 Hailey Days of the Old West: Interview with Sue Martin, July 2014.
262 Bowe's welcome-home party: City of Hailey, Office of the Mayor, "City of Hailey Statement re: Bowe Bergdahl Release," June 2, 2014.
262 "Planned Celebration for": Matt Furber, "Planned Celebration for Sgt. Bowe Bergdahl Just Got a Whole Lot Bigger," *New York Times*, June 1, 2014.
262 greeted Sue Martin: Interview with Martin, July 2014.
262 "a true American hero": Brian Ries, "Politicians Scramble to Delete Pro-Bergdahl Tweets as Backlash Grows," Mashable, June 5, 2014, http://mashable.com/2014/06/04/politicians-delete-bowe-bergdahl-tweets/#0nBdSAKiSZqT.
262 airline crew announced the couple: Interviews with Bob and Jani Bergdahl, July–August 2018.
262 Marsano told the audience: *Idaho Statesman*, "Bob and Jani Bergdahl Press Conference," YouTube, 19:42, June 1, 2014, www.youtube.com/watch?v=GozpHyxHhEI.
263 "Fuck what you heard": "Soopermexican," "American Soldier Who Served with Freed POW Casts Doubt on Official Story; Fears Reprisal from Obama Administration," *Independent Journal Review*, June 1, 2014, http://ijr.com/2014/06/143437-american-soldier-served-bowe-bergdahl-casts-doubt-official-story-fears-reprisal-obama-administration.
263 repeat that claim: "This is fucking bullshit," said John Mohammad about the claim. Authors' interview, December 2015.
263 was "extremely troubled": CNN Staff, "Political Divide: 'Don't Negotiate with Terrorists' vs. 'Leave No Man behind,'" CNN, May 31, 2014, http://politicalticker.blogs.cnn.com/2014/05/31/political-divide-dont-negotiate-with-terrorists-vs-leave-no-man-behind.
264 case of "imprecise wording": Interview with White House staffer, February 2018.
264 McCain advised her: Mark Landler, "Obama Aide Defends Remarks on Bergdahl's 'Honor,'" *New York Times*, June 6, 2014, http://nytimes.com/2014/06/07/world/susan-rice-defends-remarks-on-bowe-bergdahl.html.
264 "time to speak the truth": Interview with Nate Bethea, January 2018.
264 "The truth is": Nathan Bradley Bethea, "We Lost Soldiers in the Hunt for Bergdahl, a Guy Who Walked Off in the Dead of Night," *Daily Beast*, June 2, 2014, http://thedailybeast.com/we-lost-soldiers-in-the-hunt-for-bergdahl-a-guy-who-walked-off-in-the-dead-of-night.
265 Pentagon spokesman promised: Fox News Politics, "Pentagon to Review Claims US Soldiers Killed during Search for Bergdahl," Fox News, June 2, 2014, http://foxnews.com/politics/2014/06/02/pentagon-to-look-into-allegations-soldiers-killed-effort-to-recover-bergdahl.html.
265 Bethea learned the extent: See notes 4, 6, 11, and 12 in chapter 9.

265 "Knowing what I know now": Interview with Nate Bethea, January 2018.

265 Richard Grenell, a Republican strategist: LSUDVM, "Former State Dept. Spox Rich Grenell: Soldier Who Served with Bowe Says He Deserted," YouTube video, 1:33, June 1, 2014, www.youtube.com/watch?v=puG3pVSZBVw.

266 (Roger Stone, the veteran): Text messages from Roger Stone.

266 Full and Cornelison told: Eric Schmitt, Helene Cooper, and Charlie Savage, "Bowe Bergdahl's Vanishing Before Capture Angered His Unit," *New York Times*, June 2, 2014.

266 With Grenell and Chase working: NBC News, "Not Everyone's Hero: Soldiers Question Bowe Bergdahl's Bravery," NBCNews.com, June 2, 2014, https://www.nbcnews.com/storyline/bowe-bergdahl-released/not-everyones-hero-soldiers-question-bowe-bergdahls-bravery-n120051; Mark Thompson, "The 6 Soldiers Who Died Searching for Bowe Bergdahl," *Time*, June 2, 2014, http://time.com/2809352/bowe-bergdahl-deserter-army-taliban/; Daniel Bates, "Parents of Officer Who Died Hunting for Bowe Bergdahl Accuse Obama of 'Cover-up,'" *MailOnline*, June 3, 2014, http://dailymail.co.uk/news/article-2646345/EXCLUSIVE-Outraged-parents-officer-died-searching-deserter-Bergdahl-hit-Obama-cover-just-like-Benghazi-claiming-told-LIES-hero-son-died.html; David K. Li, "6 Soldiers Killed Searching for 'Deserter' POW, Fueling Backlash," *New York Post*, June 2, 2014, https://nypost.com/2014/06/02/six-soldiers-died-searching-for-deserter-pow-fueling-backlash/; Michael Warren, "Meet the Six Men Who Died Searching for Bergdahl," *Weekly Standard*, June 2, 2014, https://www.weeklystandard.com/michael-warren/meet-the-six-men-who-died-searching-for-bergdahl.

266 Gold Star father Andy Andrews: Ibid., *MailOnline*.

267 "I hope you fucking die": Interview with Hailey resident, December 2015.

267 The mayor's office: City of Hailey press release, June 2, 2014.

267 the *Drudge Report*: "Hero Deserter?" Drudge Report, http://drudgereportarchives.com/data/2014/06/02/20140602_170544.htm.

267 O'Reilly opened his show: mediamatters4america, "Fox's Feelings on Beards: It Depends," YouTube video, 1:05, June 3, 2014, www.youtube.com/watch?v=f0jpImbkR5c.

268 Bob had little doubt: Interview with Bob Bergdahl, July 2018.

268 CNN's Jake Tapper reported: Jake Tapper, "Fellow Soldiers Call Bowe Bergdahl a Deserter, Not a Hero," CNN, June 5, 2014, https://cnn.com/2014/06/01/us/bergdahl-deserter-or-hero/index.html.

268 Gunter received calls: Interview with Jeff Gunter, October 2016.

268 "interest of public safety": Hailey City Hall press release, "Bring Bowe Back/Bowe Is Back Event Cancelled," Hailey, Idaho, June 4, 2014.

269 "Bergdahl declared jihad": James Rosen, "Bergdahl Declared Jihad in Captivity, Secret Documents Show," Fox News Politics, June 6, 2014, http://www.foxnews.com/politics/2014/06/06/exclusive-bergdahl-declared-jihad-secret-documents-show.html.

270 Kelly dove right in: Michael O'Connell, "Megyn Kelly Scores Rare Ratings Victory Over Bill O'Reilly During Bergdahl Coverage," *Hollywood Reporter*, July 5, 2018, http://hollywoodreporter.com/live-feed/megyn-kelly-scores-rare-ratings-710470.

271 first time Kelly bested: Dominic Patten, "Fox News' Megyn Kelly Tops Cable Kingpin Bill O'Reilly for First Time for Entire Week," Deadline, June 9, 2014, http://deadline.com/2014/06/megyn-kelly-beats-bill-oreilly-ratings-fox-news-channel-786809.

271 "You're the problem": The altercation with Fox News's Jesse Watters was independently corroborated by Chip Deffé in November 2016 and Bob Bergdahl in July 2018. While the men present at the store had told Watters that Bob was not present, he was in fact hiding behind a wall and heard the conversation clearly.

271 "reverse the narrative": Julian E. Barnes, Jennifer Levitz, and Dion Nissenbaum, "U.S. Official: Sgt. Bowe Bergdahl Has Declined to Speak to His Family," *Wall Street Journal*, June 8, 2014, https://wsj.com/articles/u-s-official-sgt-bowe-bergdahl-has-declined-to-speak-to-his-family-1402242356.

CHAPTER TWENTY: DEBRIEFING

272 the media gaggle: Manny Fernandez and Eric Schmidt, "No Ceremony for Bowe Bergdahl upon Return to U.S. Soil," *New York Times*, June 13, 2014, http://nytimes.com/2014/06/14/us/bergdahl-returns-to-us-for-more-treatment.html.

272 On the flight home: Interviews with Amber Dach, December 2017–June 2018.

273 program at BAMC: Interview with Terrence Russell, December 2017.

273 "I would never wish": Patricia Zengerle, "Former U.S. Hostages Move Closer to Restitution for Colombia Ordeal," Reuters, April 27, 2016, http://reuters.com/article/us-usa-colombia-hostages/former-u-s-hostages-move-closer-to-restitution-for-colombia-ordeal-idUSKCN0XO2TO.

274 some of his former colleagues: Shawn Vestal, "Fairchild's Torture Ties Extend Their Reach," *Spokesman-Review*, November 18, 2012, http://spokesman.com/stories/2012/nov/18/fairchilds-torture-ties-extend-their-reach.

275 for three years to prepare: Interview with Terrence Russell, December 2017.

275 Dach and her colleagues: Interviews with Amber Dach, December 2017–June 2018.

275 visitors had to be cleared: Ibid.

275 private room with a bed: Ibid.

275 Brigadier General Richard Mustion: See page 364 note, "Sergeant Bergdahl's weeklong escape."

276 more trusting of women: Bowe's high regard for women, and trust in them, was described by multiple sources who knew him prior to his Army enlistment and after his return.

276 echoes of his guards' voices: During court-martial sentencing hearings, an audio recording from Bergdahl's interviews at Landstuhl was submitted as defense evidence and played in the courtroom.

277 "an Afghan minute": Interviews with Amber Dach, December 2017–June 2018.

277–78 an arcane symbol: Interview with Terrence Russell, December 2017.

278 dozen new intelligence reports: Ibid.

278 "freedom to operate": CNN, *State of the Union with Candy Crowley*, June 8, 2014, http://cnnpressroom.blogs.cnn.com/2014/06/08/gen-mattis-we-no-longer-have-that-concern-that-they-have-this-pawn-that-they-can-then-play-against-us-on-cnns-state-of-the-union.

278 CIA resumed its drone campaign: NBC News, "10 More Killed in Second Suspected U.S. Drone Attack in Pakistan," NBCNews.com, http://nbcnews.com/news/world/10-more-killed-second-suspected-u-s-drone-attack-pakistan-n129181.

278 first attack killed several Uzbek and Pakistani: Mehreen Zahra-Malik and Haji Mujtaba, "Drones Hit Taliban Hideouts in 'Joint Pakistan-U.S.' Raid, Say Officials," Reuters, June 12, 2014, http://reuters.com/article/us-pakistan-drones/drones-hit-taliban-hideouts-in-joint-pakistan-u-s-raid-say-officials-idUSKBN0EN0TP20140612.

278 killed roughly four dozen more: "Pakistan: Reported US Strikes 2014," Bureau of Investigative Journalism, http://thebureauinvestigates.com/drone-war/data/obama-2014-pakistan-drone-strikes.

279 "exemplary conduct, efficiency, and fidelity": Code of Federal Regulations: Title 32 § 578.37(a), www.gpo.gov/fdsys/pkg/CFR-2007-title32-vol3/xml/CFR-2007-title32-vol3-sec578-37.xml.

279 In San Antonio, he adapted: The interviewers and witnesses included the team of intel analysts and SERE psychologists who had started the reintegration process in Germany; intelligence officers; two or three FBI agents; multiple intelligence analysts; two noncommissioned officer investigators from U.S. Army South; and two Pentagon lawyers.

280 "organized disinformation campaign": Interview with Terrence Russell, December 2017; for Mattis quote, see page 369 note, "freedom to operate."

280 Bob was an easy mark: On May 28, 2014, three days before the exchange that he did not know was coming, Bob tweeted, "I am still working to free all Guantanamo prisoners. God will repay for the death of every Afghan child, ameen!"

280 *Time* published exclusive: Aryn Baker, "Behind the Scenes of Bowe Bergdahl's Release," *Time*, June 5, 2014, http://time.com/2826534/bowe-bergdahl-taliban-captors.

280 Glenn Beck replayed: Alcohollica2000, "Marcus Luttrell on Bowe Bergdahl," YouTube, 15:26, June 4, 2014, https://www.youtube.com/watch?v=5HuJP2MnnTs.

281 Sean Hannity answered: Fox News, "Bergdahl's Former Platoon Leader Sets the Record Straight," *Hannity*, June 4, 2014, http://video.foxnews.com/v/3606109856001/#sp=show-clips.

282 Rosen explained that: Michele Richinick, "What Republicans Have Said about Bergdahl," MSNBC, June 10, 2014, http://msnbc.com/msnbc/what-republicans-have-said-about-bowe-bergdahl.

282 According to polls: Gregory Korte, "USA Today Poll: Obama Mishandled Bergdahl Exchange," *USA Today*, June 9, 2014. http://usatoday.com/story/news/politics/2014/06/09/obama-bergdahl-opinion-poll/10234425.

282 twice as many Americans: Meredith Dost, "Public Has Doubts about Bergdahl Prisoner Exchange," Pew Research Center, June 9, 2014, http://people-press.org/2014/06/09/public-has-doubts-about-bergdahl-prisoner-exchange.

282 Gallup tallied Obama's disapproval: "Presidential Approval Ratings—Barack Obama," Gallup, http://news.gallup.com/poll/116479/barack-obama-presidential-job-approval.aspx.

282 "Was He Worth It?" *Time* cover,"Was He Worth It?: The Cost of Bringing Sgt. Bergdahl Home," *Time*, June 16, 2014, http://time.com/3758604/bergdahl-sentence-2014-cover-story/.; David von Drehle, "No Soldier Left Behind," *Time*, June 5, 2014.

282 "FUCK BERGDAHL" T-shirts: "F***K BERGDAHL BIKER SHIRT," Teespring, http://teespring.com/shop/Burgd#pid=2&cid=2397&sid=back.

CHAPTER TWENTY-ONE: SQUARED AWAY

283 Mark Boal and director Kathryn Bigelow: Mike Fleming, "UPDATE: Todd Field, Searchlight Jump into Bowe Bergdahl Fray After 'Zero Dark Thirty' Filmmakers Stake Out Pic," *Deadline*, June 17, 2015, https://deadline.com/2014/06/bowe-bergdahl-movie-kathryn-bigelow-mark-boal-zero-dark-thirty-791048.

283 General Dahl's inquest: Department of Defense News Release, "Statement by U.S. Army on Sgt. Bowe Bergdahl Investigation," United States Army, June 16, 2014, www.army.mil/article/128101.

283 "I pretty much saw": "Record of Preliminary Hearing Under Article 32 for Sergeant Robert Bowdrie Bergdahl," Joint Base San Antonio, Texas, September 17–18, 2015, p. 264.

284 He added nine officers: Dahl Report Executive Summary, p. 02447.

284 In August 2009, Major General Scaparrotti: Dahl Report, p. 02451.

286 Sarver was ordered to pay: Matthew Belloni, "Iraq War Vet Ordered to Pay $187,000 in Failed Lawsuit Against 'Hurt Locker' Producers," *Hollywood Reporter*, December 8, 2011, https://www.hollywoodreporter.com/thr-esq/hurt-locker-lawsuit-jeremy-renner-jeffrey-sarver-271605.

286 "perpetuating the myth": Senators Feinstein, Levin, McCain to Sony Pictures CEO Michael Lynton, December 19, 2012.

286 Peter King, wrote a letter: Rep. Peter King to Inspectors General Heddel and Buckley, August 10, 2011, https://homeland.house.gov/document/king-letter-dodcia-bin-laden-mission-film/.

287 weeks immediately following bin Laden's death: Jason Leopold and Ky Henderson, "Tequila, Painted Pearls, and Prada—How the CIA Helped Produce 'Zero Dark Thirty,'" *Vice News*, September 9, 2015, http://news.vice.com/article/tequila-painted-pearls-and-prada-how-the-cia-helped-produce-zero-dark-thirty.

287 Troves of agency documents: At one point in his research, Boal offered a CIA officer a Prada handbag and tickets to the designer's fashion show (she declined). After the movie's premiere, Bigelow and Boal gave the same officer a set of black Tahitian pearl earrings, which a CIA-contracted appraiser later determined were fake.

287 Boal and Bigelow flew east: Leopold and Henderson, *Vice News,* September 2015.

287 Boal denied that: THR Staff, "THR's Writers Roundtable: Mark Boal Breaks Silence on CIA's Role in 'Zero Dark Thirty,'" *Hollywood Reporter,* video, November 14, 2012, https://hollywoodreporter.com/news/zero-dark-thirty-mark-boal-390327.

287 "nothing to suggest": Central Intelligence Agency Office of Inspector General, "Report of Audit: CIA Processes for Engaging with the Entertainment Industry," p. 5.

287 "shouldn't be too confusing": Ben Child, "Kathryn Bigelow and Mark Boal Respond to Zero Dark Thirty Torture Row," *Guardian,* January 8, 2013, https:/theguardian.com/film/2013/jan/08/bigelow-zero-dark-thirty-torture.

288 historic Fort Sam Houston: 502nd Air Base Wing Public Affairs, "Quadrangle at JBSA-Fort Sam Houston a Popular Destination," May 25, 2018, http://www.jbsa.mil/News/News/Article/1532187/quadrangle-at-jbsa-fort-sam-houston-a-popular-destination/.

288 Before the execution: Bowe Bergdahl statement, Fort Bragg Courthouse, October 3, 2017.

288 he was steady: Audry Ellingson courtroom testimony, Fort Bragg, October 31, 2017.

288 His dreams filled: Bowe Bergdahl interview conducted by Sean Langan, December 2016.

289 string around the doorknob: Courtroom testimony, Fort Bragg, October 30, 2017.

289 spoke for about eight hours: Interview with Bergdahl defense team source.

289 intended to return: Dahl Report, p. 02483

289 sufficient basis for a desertion charge: Ibid., p. 2447.

290 he advised the Pentagon: Ibid., p. 2482.

291 Desertion charges are common: Lolita C. Baldor, "Army Data Shows Rarity of Desertion Prosecutions," Associated Press, December 24, 2014, www.military.com/daily-news/2014/12/26/army-data-shows-rarity-of-desertion-prosecutions.html.

292 Shaffer, along with Fox: Fox News Insider," O'Reilly Slams Admin's '5 Years of Calculated Deception' on Bergdahl," Fox News, April 8, 2015, http://insider.foxnews.com/2015/04/07/oreilly-5-years-calculated-deception-obama-admin-bergdahl.

293 Audible, MailChimp, and Squarespace: Carl Swanson, "Inside the Making of *Serial* Season Two," *Vulture,* December 23, 2015, www.vulture.com/2015/12/inside-serial-season-two.html.

293 *Serial* gave Boal editorial control: Interviews with Bob and Jani Bergdahl, July–August 2018.

293 native New Yorker: "Eugene R. Fidell," Feldesman Tucker Leifer Fidell LLP, http://feldesmantucker.com/attorneys/eugene-r-fidell.

293 lecturer at Yale Law School: "Eugene R. Fidell," Yale Law School, Florence Rogatz Visiting Lecturer in Law and Senior Research Scholar in Law, http://law.yale.edu/eugene-r-fidell#biography.

293 as an archaic system: April Siese, "Who Is Bowe Bergdahl's Lawyer, Eugene Fidell?" *Bustle,* March 25, 2015, http://bustle.com/articles/72156-who-is-bowe-bergdahls-lawyer-eugene-fidell-he-has-a-history-in-military-law-high.

293 a punishment that Fidell noted: Neil A. Lewis and Thom Shanker, "As Chaplain's Spy Case Nears, Some Ask Why It Went So Far," *New York Times,* January 4, 2004, http://nytimes.com/2004/01/04/us/as-chaplain-s-spy-case-nears-some-ask-why-it-went-so-far.html.

294 Yee had been engaged in espionage: James Polk and Bob Franken, "Muslim Chaplain Proposes to Resign," CNN, May 5, 2004, https://cnn.com/2004/LAW/03/11/muslim.chaplain.resigns/index.html.

294 "The government should": "Record of Preliminary Hearing Under Article 32 for Sergeant Robert Bowdrie Bergdahl," Joint Base San Antonio, Texas, September 17–18, 2015, p. 17.

295 "If anyone in the halls of government": Reporter notes, San Antonio, Texas, September 18, 2015.

295 "a public act": *Hearst Newspapers, et al. v. Robert B. Abrams, General, U.S. Army, et. al.*, p. 2, https://ccrjustice.org/sites/default/files/attach/2015/10/Hearst%20Petition.pdf.

295 Army turned the media companies down: Army reply to media: https://ccrjustice.org/sites/default/files/attach/2015/12/Writ%20Appeal%20Disposition%20Order.pdf.

295 his partners at *Serial*: *Serial* staffers errantly left several dozen pages of the confidential Army documents on top of a soda vending machine in a Brooklyn, New York, copy and print shop.

295 Baker replied that the DUSTWUN: "Record of Preliminary Hearing Under Article 32 for Sergeant Robert Bowdrie Bergdahl," Joint Base San Antonio, Texas, September 17–18, 2015, p. 214.

297 special court-martial: Army Memorandum—Subject: Article 32 Preliminary Hearing Report, United States vs. Sgt. Robert Bowe Bergdahl, October 5, 2015, https://bergdahldocket.files.wordpress.com/2016/03/article203220preliminary20hearing20report.pdf.

297 Fox News anchors were outraged: Questioned on Fox News's methods on the case, one Fox producer replied, "Don't you get it? No one takes Fox News seriously."

297 aid and comfort: *Fox & Friends*, October 11, 2015.

297 died searching for him: *O'Reilly Factor*, September 14, 2015.

297 gone and not coming back: *Justice with Judge Jeanine*, October 11, 2015.

297 he lobbied Obama: Doug Mataconis, "John McCain Was for Trading Taliban Prisoners For Sgt. Bergdahl Before He Was Against It," Outside the Beltway, June 3, 2014, http://outsidethebeltway.com/john-mccain-was-for-trading-taliban-prisoners-for-sgt-bergdahl-before-he-was-against-it.

297 "going to have to have a hearing": Laurel J. Sweet, "McCain Wants Answers If Bergdahl Avoids Prison," *Boston Herald*, October 13, 2015; archived at RealClearDefense, http://realcleardefense.com/2015/10/13/mccain_wants_answers_if_bergdahl_avoids_prison_274999.html.

298 Hill staffer shared it: Author emails.

299 Abrams and his legal team: Interview with former JAG Corps officer, November 2017.

299 Abrams knew the case: Michelle Tan, "Bergdahl's Lawyers: General Torched Key Evidence," *Army Times*, August 12, 2016, www.armytimes.com/news/your-army/2016/08/12/bergdahl-s-lawyers-general-torched-key-evidence.

299 scion of an Army dynasty: Gen. Creighton Abrams, his father, was famous enough that in 1980 the Army named the M1 Abrams tank after him.

CHAPTER TWENTY-TWO: THE NOISE

300 the series of events: Interview with source with direct knowledge, July 2018.

301 *The Washington Times*: Douglas Ernst, "Bowe Bergdahl Busted in California Marijuana Raid," *Washington Times*, July 24, 2015, https://washingtontimes.com/news/2015/jul/24/bowe-bergdahl-busted-marijuana-raid.

301 one sheriff's deputy: "Mendocino County Today," *Anderson Valley Advertiser*, July 23, 2015, http://theava.com/archives/45742#0.

301 drive him south to Santa Rosa: "Alicia Silverstone's Brother Arrested for Drug Possession During Raid," *Inside Edition*, July 27, 2015, https://insideedition.com/headlines/11185-alicia-silverstones-brother-arrested-for-drug-possession-during-raid.

301 (future 2018 congressional candidate): In his 2018 congressional campaign, Waltz further claimed that he "led the search for Bowe [Bergdahl]," https://michaelwaltz.com/about.

301 "I'm glad the Army": "Bowe Bergdahl found during California pot raid, released by officials," *Fox and Friends*, July 24, 2015, http://foxnews.com/politics/2015/07/24/bowe-bergdahl-found-during-california-pot-raid-released-by-officials.html. When it was revealed that several illicit plants had been recovered from the property, which was owned not by Dellacorva, but by David Silverstone, older brother of Hollywood actress Alicia Silverstone, the Bergdahl scandal bled for several days into the pages of Hollywood gossip tabloids; Glenda Anderson, "Brother of Alicia Silverstone arrested in Mendocino County pot raid," *Press Democrat*, July 28, 2015, https://pressdemocrat.com/news/4267002-181/brother-of-alicia-silverstone-arrested.

302 bullet caught Hatch: *Anderson Cooper 360*, "Former Navy SEAL Describes Mission to Save Sgt. Bowe Bergdahl," *Anderson Cooper 360* video, 6:16, September 12, 2015, https://cnn.com/videos/us/2015/09/11/navy-seal-speaks-bergdahl-mission-part-1-ac.cnn.

302 Remco was dead: Remco was posthumously awarded a Silver Star. The citation noted the gallantry the trained dog had displayed by drawing enemy fire.

302 Naval Medical Center in Portsmouth, Virginia: Mike Hixenbaugh, "Hoping to Repay a Debt, Retired SEAL Makes It His Mission to Help Working Dogs," *Virginian-Pilot*, August 9, 2015, https://pilotonline.com/news/military/article_c8135677–6409–574a-a8bf-7113c2421853.html.

302 "It was a failure": "Man Sent to Save Bergdahl: He Needs to Know How Much Was Risked," CNN, September 12, 2015, https://cnn.com/videos/us/2015/09/11/navy-seal-speaks-bergdahl-mission-part-2-ac.cnn.

303 Bergdahl was never recognized in public: Author interview with source with direct knowledge, July 2018.

304 Major General Mark Graham: In rapid succession, General Graham had lost two sons, one an ROTC cadet with untreated depression who committed suicide, and the other a lieutenant killed by a roadside bomb in Iraq.

305 Pentagon's legal team: Rowan Scarborough, "Army Goes All-in on Bowe Bergdahl's Defense, Assigns Four Military Lawyers," *Washington Times*, May 17, 2016, http://washingtontimes.com/news/2016/may/17/army-goes-all-bowe-bergdahls-defense-assigns-four-.

305 As the trial neared: Interview with JAG Corps officer, July 2018.

305 assign fifty JAGs: Defense Motion to Dismiss (Unreasonable Multiplication of Charges for Findings), August 25, 2017, https://bergdahldocket.files.wordpress.com/2016/03/defense-motion-to-dismiss-unreasonable-multiplication-of-charg.pdf.

306 three hundred thousand pages: Reporter's notes, Article 32 hearing, September 2015.

307 Trump called in to Fox News: Evan McMurry, "Donald Trump Now a Fox News Bowe Bergdahl Expert," Mediaite, July 15, 2014, http://mediaite.com/tv/donald-trump-now-a-fox-news-bowe-bergdahl-expert.

308 rant of patriotic grievances: *Time* Staff, "Here's Donald Trump's Presidential Announcement Speech," *Time*, June 16, 2015, https://time.com/3923128/donald-trump-announcement-speech.

309 convicted murderer Adnan Syed: Syed's 2000 conviction was overturned in 2016 by a Maryland Circuit Court of Appeals. In late 2018, Maryland's Court of Appeals was scheduled to hear the government's case to reinstate Syed's conviction (see https://www.rollingstone.com/culture/culture-news/adnan-syed-case-stalled-for-at-least-another-year-699265 and https://mdcourts.gov/coappeals/petitions/201807petitions).

310 *New York Times* reporter: Richard A. Oppel Jr. and John Koblin, "Bowe Bergdahl Case at Center of 'Serial' Season 2," *New York Times*, December 10, 2015, http://nytimes.com/2015/12/11/business/media/serial-season-2-bowe-bergdahl-recalls-his-afghan-odyssey.html?_r=2.

311 "these documents could literally": Defense Motion, February 4, 2016.

311 Koenig asked for patience: Swanson, "Inside the Making of *Serial*."

CHAPTER TWENTY-THREE: GUILTY

314 "not a war hero": "Trump on McCain: 'He Is a War Hero Because He Was Captured . . . I Like People Who Weren't Captured,'" RealClearPolitics video, 3:22, July 19, 2015, https://realclearpolitics.com/video/2015/07/19/trump_on_mccain_he_is_a_war_hero_because_he_was_captured_i_like_people_who_werent_captured.html.

315 an early sound check: Darren L. Linvill and Patrick L. Warren, "Troll Factories: The Internet Research Agency and State-Sponsored Agenda Building," Clemson University Researchers, Working Paper, June 2018.

315 "scared, nerves and trembling": William Bradford Huie, *The Execution of Private Slovik* (New York: Delacorte Press, 1970), p. 131.

316 after Trump was elected: Interviews with Gerald Sutton.

317 Their only intel: Sworn Statement from Staff Sergeant Walters in the AR 15–6 Investigation.

319 Nance delivered his final ruling: Nance Ruling, June 30, 2017.
319 an unlikely résumé: Interview with retired JAG Corps officer, November 2017.
319 Nance had now presided: Jack Healy, "Soldier Sentenced to Life Without Parole for Killing 16 Afghans," *New York Times*, August 23, 2013, https://nytimes.com/2013/08/24/us/soldier-gets-life-without-parole-in-deaths-of-afghan-civilians.html.
319 Those who performed well: Interview with a retired JAG Corps officer.
320 On September 27: Courtroom notes, Fort Bragg, North Carolina, September 2017.
320 As pretrial motions dragged: Interviews with PAO units at Fort Bragg, September 2017.
320 Bergdahl's twenty-five hearings: Interview with Army officer, July 2017.
322 After nineteen hours of evaluation: Department of the Army memorandum, "RCM 706 Sanity Board Evaluation (Conclusions Only) ICO Bowe Bergdahl, SGT," https://bergdahldocket.files.wordpress.com/2016/03/rcm2070620board20conclusions.pdf.
324 "has no awareness of his environment": Testimony of Allen's doctor, Dr. Rafael Mascarinas.
327 A JPRA report confirmed: JPRA Report, paragraph 9.
327 "never my intention:" Courtroom notes, Fort Bragg, North Carolina, October 30, 2017.
328 "monopoly on suffering": Courtroom notes, Fort Bragg, North Carolina, November 1, 2017.
329 son had persuaded him: Interview with Army JAG officer, November 2017.
331 Hatch told the Associated Press: Jonathan Drew, "AP Interview: SEAL Wants Bergdahl Dishonorably Discharged," Associated Press/*Fayetteville Observer*, October 27, 2017, www.fayobserver.com/news/20171027/ap-interview-seal-wants-bergdahl-dishonorably-discharged.
331 specialist in Logar: Jared Richardson, "Army Specialist gets 15 Months for Killing Fellow Soldier," Q13 Fox, May 1, 2013, https://q13fox.com/2013/05/01/soldier-who-killed-tacoma-private-with-rocket-launcher-gets-15-month-sentence/.

EPILOGUE

333 Dreyfus's legal case: Adam Gopnik, "Trial of the Century: Revisiting the Dreyfus Affair," *New Yorker*, September 28, 2009, https://www.newyorker.com/magazine/2009/09/28/trial-of-the-century.
334 after Judge Nance: Daniella Diaz, "Trump Sslams Bergdahl Decision: 'Complete and Total Disgrace,'" CNN Politics, https://www.cnn.com/2017/11/03/politics/donald-trump-bowe-bergdahl-twitter/index.htmlNovember 3, 2017.
335 hit its mark: AFP Network Writers, "American Warren Weinstein and Italian Giovanni Lo Porto Killed after US Operation Against al Qaeda on Pakistan, Afghanistan Border," *AFP*, April 24, 2015, https://www.news.com.au/world/north-america/american-warren-weinstein-and-italian-giovanni-lo-porto-killed-after-us-operation-against-al-qaeda-on-pakistan-afghanistan-border/news-story/fd4bb584defcee8cdf9ee572d39fac2a.
335 abruptly escorted out: Michael Ames, "Fragging, D.C.-Style," *Newsweek*, September 11, 2015.
335 fourteen-year-old ROTC cadet: Jason Amerine speech, Purdue University, October 2016.
336 Legion of Merit: Jeff Stein, "Controversial Green Beret Retires Quietly with High Award," *Newsweek*, October 31, 2015, https://www.newsweek.com/controversial-green-beret-retires-quietly-high-award-389282.
336 Hostage Recovery Fusion Cell: The White House, Office of the Press Secretary, "FACT SHEET: U.S. Government Hostage Policy," June 24, 2015, https://obamawhitehouse.archives.gov/the-press-office/2015/06/24/fact-sheet-us-government-hostage-policy.
336 This progress carried: Christopher P. Costa, Jen Easterly, and Joshua A. Geltzer, "Trump and Obama Have Something in Common When It Comes to U.S. Hostages Held Overseas," *Washington Post*, June 22, 2018, https://www.washingtonpost.com/news/global-opinions/wp/2018/06/22/trump-and-obama-have-something-in-common-when-it-comes-to-u-s-hostages-held-overseas/?utm_term=.9ee98a733aaf.
336 On October 13, 2017: Shaiq Hussain and Greg Jaffe, "American Woman, Canadian Husband and Children Freed in Pakistan after 5-Year Hostage Ordeal," *Washington Post*, Octo-

ber 13, 2017, https://www.washingtonpost.com/world/amerian-woman-canadian-husband-and-children-freed-in-pakistan-after-5-year-hostage-ordeal/2017/10/12/5f69e964-af4b-11e7-a908-a3470754bbb9_story.html?utm_term=.2d155100467c.

336 "return of Americans detained abroad": David Rohde, "Why Did Donald Trump Welcome American Prisoners Home on Live TV?" *The New Yorker*, May 18, 2018, https://www.newyorker.com/news/daily-comment/why-did-donald-trump-welcome-american-prisoners-home-on-live-tv.

336 totaled twelve hundred pages: Terrence Russell testimony, Fort Bragg Courthouse, October 31, 2017.

337 as twenty-one congressmen cosponsored: H.R. 4413, "No Back Pay for Bergdahl Act," November 15, 2017, https://www.congress.gov/bill/115th-congress/house-bill/4413.

337 The multimillion-dollar: United States Air Force Fact Sheet, *SERE Specialist Volunteer* 66 TRS SRLO, 6 April 2017.

337 mayor told local businesses: Interview with Hailey resident, December 2016.

INDEX

INDEX

INDEX

INDEX

INDEX

INDEX

INDEX

INDEX